W9-DFW-866

INTERPERSONAL COMMUNICATION

Interpersonal Communication

COMPETENCY THROUGH CRITICAL THINKING

JOHN S. CAPUTO

Gonzaga University

HARRY C. HAZEL

Gonzaga University

COLLEEN McMAHON

Gonzaga University

ALLYN AND BACON

Boston London Toronto Sydney Tokyo Singapore

Copyright © 1994 by Allyn and Bacon
A Division of Simon & Schuster
160 Gould Street
Needham Heights, MA 02194

Senior Editor: Steve Hull
Editorial Assistant: Brenda Conaway
Production Administrator: Elaine Ober
Production Coordinator: Leslie Olney
Editorial-Production Service: Thomas E. Dorsaneo
Text Designer: Seventeenth Street Studios
Cover Administrator: Linda Dickinson
Cover Designer: Susan Paradise
Manufacturing Buyer: Louise Richardson
Signing Representative: Jerry Bauman

Library of Congress Cataloging-in-Publication Data

Caputo, John S.,
    Interpersonal communication : competence through critical thinking/John S. Caputo, Harry C. Hazel, Colleen McMahon.
      p.   cm.
    Includes bibliographical references and index.
    ISBN 0-205-13765-2
    1. Interpersonal communicaton. I. Hazel, Harry. II. McMahon, Colleen. III. Title.
BF637.C45C35 1994
302.2--dc20
        93-27231
        CIP

Printed in the United States of America

10 9 8 7 6 5 4 3 2 1   98 97 96 95 94 93

DEDICATION

To our parents and teachers who planted the ideas, wet-nursed our hunger, nurtured our exploration, encouraged our thinking, and gave freedom to "our" ideas. We also dedicate this effort to Joann Caputo and Michael McMahon, whose patience, love, and support helped to make it possible. Thank you.

Photo Credits

Page 2, John Eastcott, Yva Momatiui/Woodfin Camp & Associates; p. 5, Dick Durrance/Woodfin Camp & Associates; p. 6, Michael L. Abramson/Woodfin Camp & Associates; p. 7, 91 Mug Shots, The Stock Market; p. 9, Robert Huntzinger/The Stock Market; p. 12, Jeff Greenberg/Photo Researchers Inc.; p. 26, John Curtis/OffShoot Stock; pp. 30, 31, Richard Hutchings/Photo Researchers Inc.; p. 37, John Chiasson/LIAISON; p. 44, Christopher Brown/Stock, Boston; p. 45, John F. Kennedy Library; p. 54, Robert Fried/OffShoot Stock; p. 57, George Haling/Photo Researchers Inc.; p. 62, Nicholas DeVore/Tony Stone Worldwide; p. 65, Rhoda Sidney/Photo Edit; p. 68, Jerry Cooke/Photo Researchers Inc.; p. 74, Nathan Benn/Woodfin Camp & Associates; p. 77, Bob Daemmrich/Stock, Boston; p. 78, Howard Sochurek/The Stock Market; p. 79, Ronnie Kaufman/The Stock Market; p. 83, John Cleare/Mountain Camera; p. 88, Tim Davis/Photo Researchers Inc.; p. 94, John Curtis/OffShoot Stock; p. 97, David Leifer/OffShoot Stock; p. 99, Stacy Pick/Stock, Boston; p. 108, Charles Cole/The Picture Group; 113, Michael Newman/Photo Edit; p. 120, Richard Shock/LIAISON; p. 123, Michael Heron/Woodfin Camp & Associates; p. 125, Spencer Grant/LIAISON; p. 129, Jim Goodwin/Photo Researchers; p. 133, Randy G. Taylor/LIAISON; p. 146, Phil Borges/Tony Stone Worldwide; pp. 151, 259, 262, Richard Pasley/Stock, Boston; p. 153, Jonathan Kirn/The Picture Group; pp. 159, 162, Tony Freeman/Photo Edit ; p. 160, Leslye Borden/Photo Edit; p. 161, Pedro Coll/The Stock Market; p. 165, Brad Bower/Picture Group; p. 180, Dan Nelken/LIAISON; p. 183, Ed Bock/The Stock Market; p. 184, Bruce Ayres/Tony Stone Worldwide; p. 199, Matthew McVay/Tony Stone Worldwide; p. 204, Dale Durfee/Tony Stone Worldwide; p. 208, David Lawrence/The Stock Market; p. 226, Jacques Chenet/Woodfin Camp & Associates; p. 219, David E. Dempster/OffShoot Stock; p. 232, Nick Vedros/Tony Stone Worldwide; p. 235, Stephanie Maze/Woodfin Camp & Associates; p. 238, John Welzenbach/The Stock Market; p. 242, Twentieth Century Fox/Shooting Star; p. 244, Gabe Palmer/The Stock Market; pp. 256, 262, 274, 286, Lou Jones; p. 265, Bob Daemmrich/Tony Stone Worldwide; p. 278, Frank Fisher/LIAISON; p. 296, Jose Azel/Woodfin Camp & Associates; p. 300, W. Bertsch/Fotoconcepts; p. 310, J. M. Turpin/LIAISON; pp. 318, 322, Culver Pictures, Inc.; p. 326, Bernard Gotfryd/Woodfin Camp & Associates; p. 337, Randy Duchaine/The Stock Market.

Brief Contents

Contents

PART II: THE INTRAPERSONAL MONOLOGUE

CHAPTER 3
PERSON PERCEPTION AND COMMUNICATION 55

PART III: THE INTERPERSONAL DIALOGUE

CHAPTER 6

LANGUAGE: NEGOTIATING REALITY   121

CHAPTER 7

NONVERBAL BEHAVIOR IN

INTERPERSONAL RELATIONSHIPS   147

CHAPTER 8

LISTENING   181

CHAPTER 10

FAMILY INTERPERSONAL COMMUNICATION 233

CHAPTER 11

PROFESSIONAL RELATIONSHIPS 257

CHAPTER 12

INTERPERSONALLY SPEAKING IN THE GLOBAL VILLAGE: ISSUES OF CULTURE AND GENDER 287

CHAPTER 13

INTERPERSONALLY COMMUNICATING IN A MEDIATED WORLD: THE TECHNOLOGICAL EMBRACE   319

PREFACE

This book is about the process of building and maintaining relationships through communication. Although it is primarily designed for students enrolled in college classes, it should prove useful for anyone interested in the connection between communication and relational development. This book is both historical and contemporary. That is, it presents current, cutting edge scholarship from both the semiotic and process schools of communication theory, yet asks you to look at these ideas critically and with a broad view of their usefulness. Our perspective is that of the liberal arts, which means the ideas should help you to think critically about what constitutes sound, ethical interpersonal communication and what skills and strategies are important for us to be interpersonally competent communicators. As we examine relational development, we present practical concepts and skills that will guide you in making good choices for communicating more effectively with intimates, close friends, family members, and professional colleagues. Additionally, we will explore implications of cultural differences and mass media for their impact on relationships in modern society.

Themes of the Book

This book is built upon several premises:

- Communication is a learned process. We learn to communicate through observation and experience. Most of this learning is done informally. Through this book, we present a systematic examination of communication that will guide you through the following steps: gaining self-knowledge; discovering commonality with others; identifying the processes of communication; applying communication principles; recognizing the basic elements of communication common to many different settings; developing ethical guidelines in your interpersonal relationships; and striving for quality in communication.

- Critical thinking can help us make intelligent choices and thereby improve the quality of our relationships.

- Interpersonal relationships develop over time and are less dependent upon the setting or context than on the qualitative differences that occur as people get to know one another, negotiate their realities, and become more accurately able to predict each other's behaviors.

- The quality of communication is a critical ingredient in satisfactory interpersonal relationships. Communication is worth working on because it can be improved. Recognition of the process and experience are the foundation of improvement. Quality can be achieved through conscious and consistent effort at improvement.

• Cultural knowledge plays a significant role in both our knowledge and our interpersonal style. Communication is both generated by, and a reflection of, culture.

• A liberal arts perspective helps us 1) to see that we are each responsible for our own learning; and 2) to seek truth in the theory and practice of communication. Quick fixes and cookbooks are not going to help us make informed choices in our relational communication.

• Because interpersonal communication is about relationships and we are in a position to positively and negatively influence others, we must be ethically responsible in our communication.

Plan of the Book

Interpersonal Communication: Competency Through Cricial Thinking is divided into four main parts. Part I, **Foundations,** chapters 1 and 2, focuses on the foundations of interpersonal communication. The chapters comprising this part address the developmental nature of interpersonal communication, set forth various definitions and perspectives, present the value of examining interpersonal communication from a liberal arts perspective, and explore the role of critical thinking in communication skill and strategy development.

In Part II, **The Intrapersonal Monologue,** chapters 3 and 4, you will explore the impact of perception on the development of our self and our understanding of others.

Part III, **The Interpersonal Dialogue**, chapters 5 through 8, looks at the use of symbols, both verbal and nonverbal, as tools of communication that make up our semiotic potential for communication with others. Additionally, you will examine the roles of disclosure and rhetorical sensitivity for their usefulness in developing quality communication. The last chapter in this part, chapter 8, examines the importance of listening.

Chapters 9 through 13 constitute Part IV: **Socio-Cultural Dynamics in Relationships.** We look at our interpersonal communication in specific relational contexts such as families, work, etc., and discusses the impact of gender and culture on interpersonal relationships. The last chapter, chapter 13 Interpersonally Communicating in a Mediated World, is new to a college text on interpersonal communication. The chapter focuses on two dimensions of media and interpersonal relationships. The first part of the chapter looks at how media can enhance interpersonal communication by connecting us with others over great distances of time and space. The second part examines media portrayals of relationships as models, both positive and negative, of actual relationships we form. The concept of media literacy is presented as an approach to help us more carefully and critically examine media reality and interpersonal communication.

Features and Pedagogy

Included in this book are several helpful features and pedagogical tools to enhance understanding and allow you opportunities to directly apply concepts that will further develop your interpersonal skills.

At the beginning of each chapter the **Cognitive Map** provides a synthesis of the outline of the chapter. This graphic maps out the relationships that exist among the major ideas you will study in the chapter.

CHAPTER OBJECTIVES

At the chapter beginning, there are a series of objectives for each chapter. We have identified specific goals which should be mastered upon completion of the readings, discussions, and activities.

CONSIDERING CRITICAL THINKING

Throughout the chapters you will find numerous critical thinking exercises designed to help you focus on the importance of critical thinking in relationships. You will gain experience in distinguishing between logical thinking and subjective thinking. For example, the critical thinking exercise in Chapter 11 asks for your suggestion in working out a problem which involves a professional relationship.

CONSIDERING CULTURE

Many communication guidelines change when we engage with culturally different people. These boxes provide you with opportunities to directly apply concepts from the specific chapters to an intercultural or culturally diverse situation. For example, in Chapter 7 you are asked to come up with examples of ethnic, national, or cultural group differences in nonverbal behavior.

CONSIDERING ETHICS

To reinforce the importance of ethics in interpersonal communication, we provide exercises and discussion boxes in which we ask you to explore the ethical ramifications and your own behaviors in particular communication situations. Chapter 8, Listening, provides an opportunity for you to look at the ethics of your own interpersonal behavior when you are asked to listen to "confidential" information.

COMMUNICATING SKILLFULLY

In addition to the boxes which focus on culture, ethics, and critical thinking, we include activities and exercises designed to focus on key aspects of interpersonal communication presented in the particular chapter.

PUTTING THEORY INTO PRACTICE

To provide further discussion questions and skill building exercises, we include a final section of practical applications, which directly reflects key concepts from each chapter. These are designed for group or individual use as students continue to develop and enhance their interpersonal skills.

REVIEW OF KEY TERMS AND CONCEPTS

This section comes at the end of each chapter as reminders of the concepts and their connections that were first introduced in the cognitive map at the beginning of each chapter.

FOR EXTENDED STUDY

This list of related readings allows you to explore a particular topic in greater depth. In addition to the list, we provide a brief description of the contents.

A culmination of all the key terms is found in the **Glossary,** at the end of the text. The terms, found in alphabetical order, provide definitions and a resource guide for study.

ACKNOWLEDGEMENTS

Numerous people have contributed to the completion of *Interpersonal Communication: Competency Through Critical Thinking*. In particular, we are especially grateful to Stephen Hull; his assistant, Brenda Conaway; Editorial-Production Supervisor, Elaine Ober; Production Coordinator, Leslie Olney; and Thomas Dorsaneo and his staff. All of these people provided invaluable assistance and suggestions through all important phases of this effort. We also give special thanks to several individuals at Gonzaga University, including our colleague Patrick J. Ford, S.J. for his support, Marti Abrahamson, Julia Bjordahl, Sandra Hank, Jennifer Griffith, Virginia DeLeon, Kathleen Morig,and Laura Reinhardt for their typing, proof reading, and graphic assistance, and Deanna Dannels for her invaluable research, input, and organizational help. Finally, we extend our gratitude to our colleagues across the country whose reviews and feedback were most instrumental in completing this book: Judith Bowker, Oregon State University; Dawn Braithwaite, Arizona State University; Dennis Brown, El Paso Community College; Stephanie Coffman, Eastern Montana College; Katherine Dindia, University of Wisconsin–Milwaukee; Claudia Hale, Ohio University; Jennifer Hanlon, Brazosport College; Colan Hanson, Morehead State University; Patrick Hebert, Northeast Louisiana University; Sherry Holman, Albuquerque Technical–Vocational Institute; Kipp Preble, Chaffey College; Melinda Womack, Rancho Santiago Community College; John Stewart, University of Washington; Dick Stine, Johnson County Community College; Art VanLear, University of Connecticut; Shirley Whitfield, Northeast Louisiana University.

INTERPERSONAL COMMUNICATION

You can—and perhaps must—drink deeply from the past, if only to know the shoreline of tomorrow.

JOHN BRADY

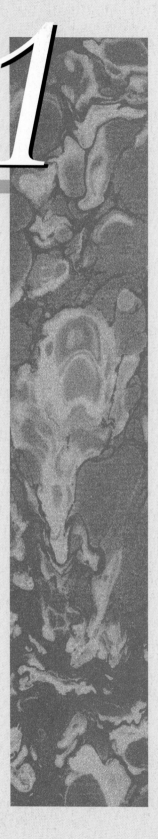

Interpersonal Communication: A Liberal Art

OBJECTIVES

After reading this chapter and taking part in class activities, you should be able to

- Explain why interpersonal communication is important in your personal and professional life.

- Define the concept of interpersonal style and how it develops.

- Explain the difference between the situational and developmental viewpoints of interpersonal communication.

- Describe how a liberal arts, humanistic perspective can help make you a more effective communicator.

- Distinguish between ethical and unethical interpersonal communication.

Interpersonal
communication

What is interpersonal
communication?

Why do we
communicate?

Dyadic and
interpersonal communication
1. Situational view
2. Developmental view

Why study
interpersonal
communication
as a liberal art?

Motivational theory
1. Maslow
2. Schutz

Definition

Truth, knowledge, skills

Models

Learner orientation

Perspective

Goals

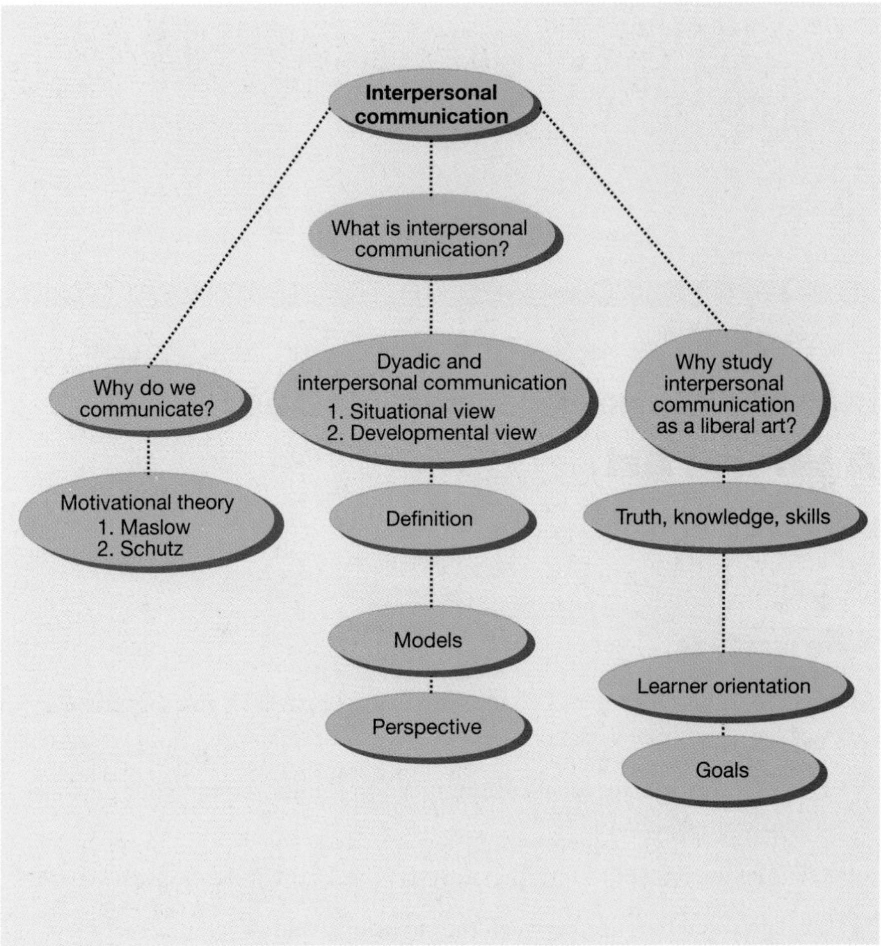

NOT LONG AGO, I stood on the ridge near my home and looked out to the west as the sun set over the tree-covered hills and mountains. As I watched the radiant orange sunset filtering through the thick, luminous clouds, I was aware of the beauty I was witnessing, but I also felt incomplete. I wanted to share this beauty with someone and in the sharing become even clearer with myself about what I was sensing. I wanted the experience validated by a close friend and grow closer to that person. I quickly jogged home and asked my wife to join me out front to catch the sunset before it sank behind the mountains. As we two watched the last few minutes of the sunset, we just looked at it and didn't speak until it was gone. We shared the experience in silence, and afterward talked about what we'd seen—beauty, joy, and creation.

This **interpersonal** experience—this sharing of perceptions, this sharing of

Being able to share our experience and perceptions—negotiating our realities with others—is the essence of interpersonal communication.

meanings—is what interpersonal communication and this book are all about. Humans have a unique capacity to connect with others and communication is that linking mechanism. They can experience joy, fun, excitement, caring, warmth, and personal fulfillment in relationships. Because people are social animals, much of their happiness comes from effectively relating to other humans. The ability to cooperate with others and coordinate actions is important to both survival and professional success. The ability to form strong, healthy relationships helps people develop strong competent selves that can take care of themselves and others. Interpersonal skills are so important that there is no way we could overemphasize their importance.

Communication is all around you—every day, in everything we do and say, in being with others. From the moment you leap (or crawl) from bed in the morning to your final goodnight, you *communicate* to others. From the first TV cartoon in the morning to a goodnight kiss from a friend, you are also *communicated to*. You experience communication, and you observe it from a distance. You understand it, and are confused by it. You accept communication, and reject it.

The uniqueness of man—the superiority of man in the world of animals—lies not in his ability to perceive ideas, but to perceive that he perceives, and to transfer his perceptions to othermen's minds through words.

ALBERT EINSTEIN

DEVELOPING YOUR COMMUNICATION POTENTIAL

In looking at the role of communication in daily life, it's important to look at how human beings have developed their abilities to communicate, and

Communication is multi-modal—that is, it takes many forms as we experience it throughout our day.

thus reach what linguist M. A. K. Halliday called their "semiotic potential"— the unique ability to create and understand meaning.

Build Your Interpersonal Style

Your communication style has developed through experience and observation. This development continues throughout your lifetime. You learned to communicate with people around you as an infant. At birth (and, some even suggest, in the womb), you began the journey of life with the capacity for communication. Soon after birth, you opened your eyes, cried when you were hungry or uncomfortable, smiled when you were content.

For a couple of years, you relied on nonverbal messages— pointing, stamping your feet, making sounds, hugging, hitting, and crying. During this same time, you were practicing language skills and learning the symbolic system and meanings. By age 3, you had developed a good acquaintance with both verbal and nonverbal forms of communication. Linguists point out that the language skills you developed during this period are among the most difficult learning skills you will master in your lifetime.

Much of your time in growing up has been spent in building an effective **personal style** of communication. You have learned to sort out and communicate emotional states (anger from disgust, sadness from hurt). You have learned additional symbols (slang phrases, second languages, occupational jargon). You have learned alternatives in responding to others' verbal and nonverbal communication. You've learned communication values—"How do I get what I want, when do I hurt others' feelings, when do I lie?" An example can help put this process in perspective: If you've ever been around infants, you know they cry when they want to be changed or want some attention. When children get a little older, they may have temper tantrums (usually in a grocery store or some other public place) to get their way. However, if at 18 you cry or have temper tantrums to get attention, you are seen as socially immature. So you have learned more subtle and socially appropriate ways to communicate needs.

At the same time you learned communication values, you were integrating your personality with ethnic and cultural background into personal style. And lastly, you have learned communication skills and strategies that you will use throughout your life.

For the most part, this learning has all been done informally, without the aid of a professional teacher. You evaluate what you learn, choose alternatives that work for you, and let others go. As you acquire new information and have new experiences, you modify what you've learned. Each new relationship teaches you a little more about your ability to communicate. Each group of friends builds expectations about you as a communicator. Each new setting requires a slightly different combination of your communication skills. You modify your communication styles to accommodate your individual needs and wants as well as societal norms for appropriate interaction.

The learning process helps you grow in ability to select the right communication skills, both in sending and receiving messages. Once you build your basic communication style, you grow only through this process of evaluation

> *Any definition is controversial and already embodies a philosophical attitude.*
>
> BERTRAND RUSSELL

Our first course in interpersonal communication.

and modification. This book represents our effort as authors to encourage your continued self-evaluation and modification. We believe this book will help you to become the communicator you want to be by helping you reach your communication potential.

What Is Interpersonal Communication?

To develop your interpersonal style, it's important to clearly understand what we mean by *interpersonal communication*. Communication has been studied in Western cultures for more than 2,400 years. Many people trace the humanistic study of communication as an art back to Aristotle's *Rhetoric* and *Poetics* (about 384 B.C.E.) in Greece. The study of communication continued with Roman rhetorical theory, on the European continent and in Great Britain, and more than two centuries in the United States. Interpersonal communication as a separate study grew out of scholars looking at communication as a social science—that is, looking at the pressures, forces, or probabilities of what happens when humans communicate with each other. This perspective on interpersonal processes began to emerge just after World War II. Three key books that led to a greater understanding of interpersonal processes are David Berlo's (1960) *The Process of Communication*, Sam Keltner's (1970) *Interpersonal Speech-Communication: Elements and Structures*, and C. David Mortensen's (1972) *Communication: The Study of Human Interaction*.

The word *communication* comes from the Latin verb *communicare*, "to share." The word *interpersonal* also has a Latin root and means "between persons." Using these derivations as a base, we define **interpersonal communication** as an ever-changing transactional sharing that develops between people who are finding meaning with each other and come to know one another better as their relationship tends to move from impersonal to personal.

If you look at the definition closely, you'll notice that we don't use the words *intend* or *intentionally*. This is because we believe communication can be both unintentional and intentional. We don't believe that two people who communicate find the same meaning; instead, we believe that meanings are in the receiver (the receiver decides on the interpretation) and are negotiated between speakers and listeners. This process of negotiating meanings is discussed in detail in Chapter 6, "Language: Negotiating Reality."

Man is the model-making organism par excellence.

EDWARD T. HALL

What Makes Communication Interpersonal?

Research on what distinguishes interpersonal communication from other forms comes from two major perspectives: the situational and the developmental views. We take the developmental perspective in this book; let's look at these two views more closely and explain why.

One way to look at interpersonal communication is to observe the factors in the communication situation itself. Communication factors such as the number of communicators and their physical nearness to one another are part

Our interpersonal skills allow us to join with others in collaboration at work and play.

of the **situational view** of interpersonal communication. Another way to distinguish interpersonal communication from other forms of communication is to consider the depth and quality of communication between communicators. This is called the **developmental view**.

THE SITUATIONAL VIEW

People often think interpersonal communication means communication between two people: **dyadic communication**. The technical term dyad was first used by nineteenth-century German sociologist Georg Simmel, who coined it to mean two people in a system of repeated social interactions. In the situational view of interpersonal communication, a small number of communicators is important, and hence the terms *interpersonal* and *dyadic* are often used as synonyms. Miller and Steinberg (1975) suggest that the situational view has four major sets of characteristics: (1) number of communicators, (2) degree of physical proximity, (3) number of sensory channels potentially available for the communicators' use, and (4) immediacy of feedback. According to the situational view, if two strangers on the college campus say hello as they pass by, they're communicating interpersonally. The situational view is static and does not account for the various stages of relational development we discuss later in this book. Book and others (1980) suggest that the situational view does not take account of degrees of interpersonalness. Instead, a communicative transaction either *is* or *is not* interpersonal. From this point of view, your communicating with a stranger and with a long-time friend are the same. Thus, the situational view ignores what we see as a crucial ingredient—**quality**.

Let's take a look at the following two dialogues:

FIRST SITUATION

You are walking across campus and you see someone walking toward you from your English class. You make eye contact with this person when she is about ten feet away from you, and you both say at about the same time,

"How's it going?"

You both smile and say, "Fine."

She says, "I'll see you later when we take our English exam" and keeps walking.

SECOND SITUATION

As you continue to walk, you see your friend Alicia coming toward you. You both say hello to each other.

Alicia proceeds to ask you, "Do you feel any better today?"

You answer, "Not really, but I can't afford to miss my English class today. I have to pass that exam to keep up my scholarship."

Alicia says, "I'm sure you'll do fine, you always do so well! If I can help you in some way, let me know. Maybe right after you take the test you should go back to bed."

The first situation is shorter and has less verbal interaction than the second. How else do they differ? What characteristics makes these two dialogues so different? Do you see any qualitative difference between the two? If so, what? Which dialogue would you label "interpersonal communication"? Why?

Perhaps a more useful way to talk about communication is to say that dyadic communication is communication between two people who are sharing meaning and that such interaction can be represented by the simple model shown in Figure 1.1.

FIGURE 1.1

Interactional Dyadic Model of Communication

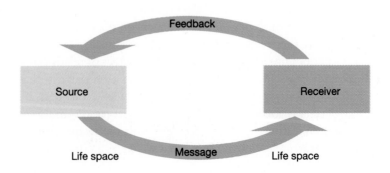

As authors of this text, we take the position that interpersonal communication uses the basic elements of the dyadic model shown in Figure 1.1, but adds depth, shading, details, and quality. In interpersonal communication, to use the term of Kurt Lewin (1935), the "life-space" of each communicant is added. Also, rather than communication flowing from sender to receiver and flowing back to the sender, the communication is flowing at all times, in all directions. For Lewin, "life space" is that totality or sum of learnings and experiences that makes you unique. "Life space" contains all your knowledge, values, and beliefs.

The communication in the **transactional** model moves from the interactional perspective and becomes transactional in nature (see Figure 1.2). Each member of the process influences the other person and is being influenced simultaneously. The more you share your life space with another person, the greater the degree of interpersonalness and the greater degree of understanding you will share with another. To an extent, you share some life space overlap with every other human being. If we have a small degree of overlap, the primary way to increase understanding is through a process of sharing or self-disclosure.

Now, let's look at the developmental view.

THE DEVELOPMENTAL VIEW

The developmental view of communication encompasses the situational view and assumes you share some overlap life space with every other person. Also, in this perspective interpersonal communication is not limited to two people, nor is face-to-face communication necessary. From the developmental perspective, all your initial communications with another person are by necessity impersonal or nonpersonal. That is, you relate to others by their social role,

COMMUNICATING SKILLFULLY

n small groups or with a partner, discuss the following questions:

• What do we have in common with every other human being?

• Have you ever spoken with a person who didn't speak your language? What strategies did you use? What assumptions did you make about the other person? Were your assumptions right? To what degree was your communication effective?

• How do our assumptions about strangers affect the way we communicate with them?

FIGURE 1.2

The Transactional Model of Communication.

When we are communicating interpersonally, we share cultural, sociological, and psychological knowledge of each other.

rather than as persons. In initial contacts with others, you **predict** how they might respond to you given your first perceptions or impressions of them. Berger and Calbrese (1975) suggest that unfamiliarity with another person breeds uncertainty. As a result, you settle for very cautious communication strategies. You may be too polite or make small talk about the weather and engage in what John Powell calls "**phatic communion.**" The words are somewhat irrelevant, but the social behavior is correct. By exchanging this small talk, you reduce unfamiliarity about the other person. Communication theorist Gerald Miller (1975) says that in initial encounters you base your predictions about each other's message responses on cultural and sociological

CONSIDERING CULTURE

William Gudykunst (1989) has done extensive comparisons of cultural differences during a phase he calls "uncertainty reduction" in communication with strangers. He has found that all cultures try to reduce uncertainty during the initial stages of a relationship but do so in different ways. Some cultures rely on the total context of the communication and rely more on nonverbal signals and information about a person's background to reduce uncertainty. Other cultures rely more on verbal communication and ask specific questions about the person's experience, attitudes, and beliefs. Which of these two methods of reducing uncertainty do you think would be considered appropriate for the Japanese? What about the French or Swedish? How about an Italian or African American? Why do you think as you do for each?

---

information rather than on psychological information. **Cultural information** consists of language, values, beliefs, habits, and practices shared by a group. **Sociological information** relates to the individual's roles in various groups. And **psychological information** includes a person's idiosyncratic, learned experiences and behaviors. For Miller, initial encounters are, given the lack of information people have about each other, impersonal by nature. Therefore people base communication on cultural norms and social roles.

If you choose to continue talking and are motivated to get to know a person better, and your interpersonal skills are developed enough to let the relationship develop, the initial relationship may undergo certain **qualitative changes**. As the relationship changes qualitatively, it becomes more interpersonal. As you get to know a person better, you change your prediction to include the person's psychological makeup. This tells you how to interact.

An example should help clarify this developmental view. Let's say you walk into the first meeting of your communication class with a new professor. As you enter the room, she says hello to you and introduces herself as Dr. Herrara. You say hello and introduce yourself as Terry. Your behavior in this interaction was guided by cultural rules of greetings and politeness, and sociological rules about the social roles of student and teacher. After three or four weeks in Professor Herrara's class, you've come to see how she interacts and relates to her students. She told a little about herself and where she came from before coming to your campus. You've noticed some elements of her personality, such as her concern for promptness and her sense of humor. Also, Dr. Herrara has learned many things about you through various activities in the class and talking to you in line at a basketball game.

You find it necessary to go see Dr. Herrara during an office hour. As you knock on her door and enter her office, you say, "Good morning, Dr. Herrera. Do you have a minute to talk?"

CONSIDERING CRITICAL THINKING

Trace two relationships in your life: one that continued to develop over a period of time and one that remained interactional. Why did one develop and not the other? In the relationship that developed, can you remember when your ability to predict the other person's behavior moved from cultural and social information to psychological information and you truly got to know the other person more interpersonally?

She says, "Sure, Terry. Come on in and sit down. Why don't you just call me Maria? That's my first name." You nod, although because of sociological rules you feel just a bit uncomfortable. Then she says, "Did you enjoy the game the other night?" After a few minutes of talking about the game together, she says, "Well, I'm sure you didn't come to talk about the game. What's up?"

You reply, "Well, it's good to know that someone else is at least as big a basketball fan as I am, and maybe we'll see each other at the next game. Anyway, basketball is more fun to talk about than what I'm here to see you about. I came to talk about my score on the exam."

What has happened here is that over a period of a few weeks, several hours of mutual observation and several conversations, Terry and Dr. Hererra's relationship has been developing. As they grow to know more about each other, their predictions about each other move away from cultural norms and sociological rules and become more closely based on the idiosyncratic psychological knowledge they have of each other. Terry and Maria are becoming more interpersonal: they're developing their intrinsic rules for guiding their transactions. They may no longer treat each other as stereotyps of teacher and student, but rather as the individuals each are. Of course, this change still depends on whether they *want* the relationship to develop any further.

As you continue to communicate with another person over time, your opportunities for gathering psychological information grow. Even over time, however, you will only actively gather psychological information if you *choose* to.

In comparing the developmental and situational views, then, we as authors believe the situational view is too limited in scope because it ignores the qualitative changes that occur in relationships. Over time, communication is dynamic and ongoing rather than static. The developmental view implies there are degrees of interpersonalness. Although early encounters with others are normally impersonal, as people communicate over time, they learn more information about each other. They're then able to predict and even explain the behavior of their partners because the relationship has become increasingly interpersonal. DeVito (1992) claims that as relationships grow more interpersonal the effectiveness of communication is characterized by the inclusion of the following qualitative elements (POSEE):

Positiveness A high regard for yourself and the other person, in which both state positive attitudes

Openness A high degree of trust and honesty where self-disclosure can take place freely

Supportiveness Communication that is characterized by descriptive rather than evaluative comments and by receptivity to each other's ideas

Equality Not treating the other person, or letting the other person treat you, as superior or inferior, but rather as a respected equal

Empathy The ability to put yourself in the place of the other person, to try to understand the world through his or her eyes

DeVito believes that these five POSEE elements are interrelated and of equal importance. When they're not present in a communication encounter, the interaction is seen as noninterpersonal.

WHY WE COMMUNICATE? MOTIVATIONAL THEORY

We've been discussing how communication develops, and we've looked at some elements of interpersonal communication. But why do people communicate with others, and what purpose does communication serve? Simply put, people communicate out of the motivation to satisfy needs. Although there are many motivational theorists, we will discuss just two, Abraham Maslow and William Shutz, because of the implications of their theories for understanding motivation in communication.

Abraham Maslow

Perhaps the best-known theory of motivation comes from Abraham Maslow. His humanistic theory is widely cited in books about communication and business because it's considered parsimonious—that is, it is logical and simple and makes only a few core assumptions that lead to a variety of claims about why people do what they do. Maslow was very interested in why some people transcended what might have limited their psychological growth and hence reached their full potential through self-actualization. He identified what he saw as the necessary psychological traits of healthy, well-adjusted individuals. Maslow thought these traits represented the fulfillment of psychological needs all people strive to meet. If people meet these needs, they are fulfilled; if the needs are not met, or not met satisfactorily, people can become mentally ill. The traits are

1. A clear, efficient perception of reality
2. Openness to experiences
3. Increased integration, wholeness, and unity of person
4. Increased spontaneity, expressiveness, full functioning, aliveness
5. A real self, a firm identity, autonomy, uniqueness
6. Increased objectivity, detachment, transcendence of self
7. Ability to maintain creativeness
8. Ability to fuse concreteness and abstractness
9. Democratic character structure
10. Ability to love

For Maslow, all people seek to fill these needs. If someone is blocked from filling them, that person will be motivated to achieve them.

THE NEEDS HIERARCHY

Maslow's theory is unique because he placed needs in a **needs hierarchy**, with basic physiological needs as the base and topped by psychological needs. The ultimate top was self-actualization, the experience of being fully human. Figure 1.3 shows the complete hierarchy. Maslow believes that lower-order needs must be met first or take priority over higher-order needs. Thus physiological needs for water, food, and shelter must be satisfied before needs for safety, esteem, and so on. He calls these **prepotent needs**.

FIGURE 1.3

Maslow's Hierarchy of Needs (Adapted from Globe, The Third Force, *p. 50)*

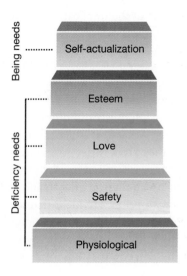

MASLOW'S THEORY AND COMMUNICATION

Figure 1.3 shows that to meet needs, people need to communicate with others. Most, if not all, needs are met in interdependence with others. If Maslow's theory is correct, we should be able to use his hierarchy to explain what motivates people to communicate with others—which needs they are attempting to satisfy. For example, let's say two college roommates must work many hours to earn money for groceries and college. Using Maslow's theory, we would say that food is a basic need that must be met before one earns money for going to college. Going to college represents higher-level needs of self-esteem and perhaps self-actualization. But some people might see going to college as meeting the need for safety and security, because they equate going to college with earning an adequate income.

Drawing by Lorenz;
© 1992 The New Yorker
Magazine, Inc.

William Schutz

Although we discuss Schutz's theory of needs (1966) fully in Chapter 9, it is important to briefly discuss the needs aspect of it here. Schutz explains three types of social needs satisfied through communication. He called these needs the "fundamental interpersonal relations orientation" (**FIRO**—it rhymes with *Cairo*). These needs are for inclusion, control and affection. **Inclusion** is feeling a sense of belonging. This need can be met by being in both formal and informal relationships such as clubs, church groups, neighbors, or marriage.

The second need Schutz describes is the social need for **control** in people's lives and in their ability to influence others. Needs for control can be seen in the positions of authority people take, but also in disagreements with others, or choosing what to see at the movies with a partner. We explain this need for control more fully in Chapter 9 on relationships.

The last of Schutz's social needs is affection. **Affection** can be defined as caring and respect for others. Through this caring and respect *for* others, you receive the caring and respect *of* others. Knowing that you matter to others builds your self-esteem. This affection also lets you enjoy inclusion. Figure 1.4 summarizes Schutz's model of interpersonal needs. Schutz believes the six inner needs are the desires of a well-balanced person.

SELF-ACTUALIZER

	Inclusion	Control	Affection
Wants from others	Acceptance	Guidance	Closeness
Expresses to others	Interest	Leadership	Liking

FIGURE 1.4

(FIRO) Fundamental Interpersonal Relations Orientation

SCHUTZ'S THEORY AND COMMUNICATION

In Schutz's theory of motivation, then, communication is the way people relate socially with others. To the degree they can communicate interpersonally, they can meet their social needs.

Knowing what constitutes interpersonal communication, and why people do it, we would now like to turn our attention to what we think constitutes the best approach to learning about interpersonal communication: a **liberal arts perspective**.

WHY TAKE A LIBERAL ARTS PERSPECTIVE?

What does "liberal arts" mean? Historically, the goal of a liberal arts education has been to prepare a person to search for truth and thereby gain wisdom and character. In ancient Greece, a liberal education meant "the education of a free man through knowledge." The acquisition of knowledge would distinguish a free or liberated man from a woman or a slave. Of course, in the contemporary United States slavery is illegal, women can pursue knowledge, and we would use the more inclusive term person instead of man. However, if you consider the term slave metaphorically and consider how the lack of knowledge can enslave or limit people, you can see the freedom, or liberation, that knowledge brings. In essence, then, truth represents the freedom that makes people free to pursue satisfactory relationships and/or advance in a profession.

Let's turn now to what constitutes a liberal art. In the classic sense, liberal arts didn't deal with subject matter (such as English, math, languages, or rhetoric), but rather was a way to seek truth through the unity of knowledge (that is, not discipline centered). Eventually in the eighteenth century, a liberal education was intended to teach the proper method of discourse (talk, speech) such as grammar, rhetoric, and logic (the part of the curriculum that used to be called the *trivium*), along with geometry, arithmetic, astronomy, and music (the *quadrivium*).

And ye shall know the truth, and the truth shall make you free.

JOHN 8:32

Liberal arts education also includes the principle that learning can only be an act of the learner—the learner is *free* to learn or not. Learning might be helped by a teacher, but learning is never the necessary result of the teacher. Put another way, learning does not involve a passive student sitting before a teacher who informs him or her, but an activity of the student *with* a teacher who may be able to help him or her in a true interpersonal sense. Learning can only take place by your *own* act, out of your *own* desire, and for *yourself*.

So, knowing that learning rests with the student, what should a teacher teach? All teachers face the practical problem that the number of things to know is infinite and the time available to teach students is very short. However, as teachers also know, many alleged "facts" are not true at all and may shortly and usually without acknowledgment be replaced by other facts. For example, we now know the earth is not flat and that the earth revolves around the sun. So from the liberal arts perspective, our role as teachers is to help students master the skills and strategies for seeking the truth—not to pound in "the facts."

In teaching about interpersonal communication through this book, we can't give you a recipe for how you should communicate in all your relationships. Instead, our goal is to help you make wise, informed choices about communication. In that sense, this book and your class is not prescriptive—we won't tell you what to do. Rather, we'll be presenting you with information (theory) and practice that will help you make choices that are right for you. We want you, as the student, to be active, prepared to wrestle with ideas that sometimes might go against your nature. We'll suggest new patterns of behavior to test alternate communication skills. Your involvement will be crucial to your growth and will sometimes have ethical consequences. Let's take a look at some ethical dimensions to see how they're part of the liberal arts tradition stressed in this text.

ETHICAL COMMUNICATION

Because interpersonal communication engages us with other people, you can influence others in positive and negative ways. For this reason, ethics becomes an important facet of interpersonal communication. Johannesen (1990, p.1) writes,

> Ethical issues arise in human behavior whenever that behavior could have significant impact on other persons, when the behavior involves conscious choice of means and ends, and when the behavior can be judged by standards of right and wrong.

Ethical communication concerns itself with the well-being of others, by demonstrating your sensitivity for their feelings and beliefs. Ethical communication expresses the truth and avoids deception or manipulation in relationships. Let's look at the following communication situation and examine some of its ethical considerations.

Throughout this book, we'll be stressing ethical guidelines in interpersonal communication encounters through use of such examples. These examples can help you forge your own sense of ethical communication.

In this chapter, we've defined interpersonal communication, and discussed the importance of interpersonal communication in life and why we think looking at interpersonal communication from a liberal arts perspective is beneficial from both a teaching and a learning standpoint. Now we'll be discussing some goals for you in your class and in reading this book. Also, we

CONSIDERING ETHICS

Gerry and Marcie have been going out with each other since their first year in college, nearly two years now. Gerry tells Marcie that he is going skiing next weekend with a group of his buddies. That weekend comes, and Gerry goes on the ski trip. Marcie's roommates convince her to come along to a party because Gerry is having a good time skiing with his friends.

Gerry comes to see Marcie Sunday evening and asks, "Where were you last night? I tried to call you from the ski resort and there was no answer." Marcie replies there must have been something wrong with the phone because she was home all night. Marcie lied: she and Gerry had been seeing each other exclusively and never did things without the other person knowing it. Gerry told Marcie what he was

doing, but Marcie didn't feel she could be honest. Marcie was afraid she'd lose her relationship with Gerry if she told the truth. Because she told a lie, their relationship is in as much or more jeopardy than if she had told the truth. What could Marcie have done to avoid the unethical communication and still have been able to keep a good, strong relationship with Gerry?

want you to create some personal goals, because as the learner your goals are most important. Learning is personal, and we can only guide you.

GOALS OF THIS BOOK

This book has been written with a number of general goals. These goals can be realized only with your active participation. Although as pointed out earlier you have been communicating since birth, and perhaps many times quite well, there may still be times when your communication seems to fall apart. Probably both your highest and lowest emotional moments in life center around communication and relationships. We want to help you find tools for looking at your communicative self and examining what is going on. We're not just suggesting new words for ideas you already have, or making a simple activity appear complex. We're talking about learning the fundamental concepts of communication.

Gaining Self-Knowledge

Our first goal is to help you sensitize yourself to your personal communication strengths and weaknesses in your quest for truth.

Probe yourself. What kind of person are you? What do you want? What do you need? How did you get to be the way you are? How does the person you are affect your communication behaviors? Are you receptive to feedback? Are you willing to change? These questions and many more like them will help you to understand your **intrapersonal self**.

Discovering Commonality with Others

A second goal is to help you develop skills for recognizing your commonality with others. Psychologist Carl Rogers (1970) suggests that what one thinks is most personal, is also often the most common. Rogers emphasizes that as humans, we often experience the same joys and pains in life but we don't necessarily see others around us experiencing these emotions because we don't share our personal concerns with them.

Identifying the Processes of Communication

Another goal is to identify and understand the essential elements of communication such as speaking, listening, feedback, messages and meanings, and perceptions. You already have your own notions of just what constitutes communication. You certainly recognize when someone seems to be communicating effectively or ineffectively. But could you say what the person is doing right or wrong in any particular communication encounter? We would like to take many of the "foggy" notions about communication behavior, clarify them, and bring them back into a broader whole. By reviewing the major conclusions drawn from communication research and examined in the light of your particular experiences, you can develop your own educated hunches or theories about communication.

Applying Communication Principles

Once you have understood the theories discussed and have even created some of your own, the next goal is for you to apply this wisdom to your own communication encounters, to evaluate your use of these principles or theories. Then you can make them more than "something you know for class." These theories may reinforce what you already think or perhaps they might cause you to make some changes in your communication style.

Recognizing Basic Elements of Communication

The goal of recognizing basic communication elements is to clarify the similarities and differences among communication situations and relationships so you can see the basic elements of each. The key is to be able to apply your knowledge of communication concepts in whatever situation you're confronted with—comforting a grieving friend, demonstrating a process at work, meeting with a dorm group about a complaint you would like to take to the dean of students.

COMMUNICATING SKILLFULLY

GOAL SETTING

Write down three goals you hope to accomplish by taking this course. Your goals can relate to theory, to skills you would like to achieve, or communication behaviors of yours that you would like to change. Bring your goals to class and share in small groups.

Developing Clear Interpersonal Ethics

It is important to communicate with integrity. We will be discussing what constitutes honest, ethical communication and what is manipulative and dishonest. Ethics deals with what people may see as the gray areas of life. For example, is verbal deception ever appropriate? Is a falsehood ever fair or just? Can a lie end up doing something positive such as preventing harm? Is telling the truth always a virtue? Is it fair to hurt other people with actions and words? Is it alright to use people for gain? As we explore ethical concerns in interpersonal relationships throughout the book, we suggest you keep a journal and create your guidelines for ethical communication.

Striving for Quality

Our last goal is to help you strive for quality in your communication experiences. Quality can be a product of all the goals we've listed. Quality can be achieved through conscious and consistent effort at improvement. A basic assumption we share is that communication is worth working on because it can be improved and that recognizing the process and experience is the foundation for that improvement.

LOOKING BACK - LOOKING FORWARD

In this first chapter, we have been describing the components of interpersonal communication, beginning with a definition of interpersonal communication. We then discussed both the situational and developmental views of interpersonal communication. From our perspective, the developmental view is most helpful. In the second half of the chapter, we looked at motivations for communication and explained why a liberal arts perspective is useful to you as a learner and is the philosophy that underlies our work as author and teachers. Lastly, we set out certain goals for you to aim at throughout your reading of this book.

In Chapter Two, "Critical Thinking and Interpersonal Communication," we'll provide a model for applying principles of critical thinking to your interpersonal relationships and begin to explore ethical and cultural considerations in interpersonal relationships.

The remainder of this book is divided into three sections.

"The Intrapersonal Monologue" explores how your sense of self influences what you expect and how you treat others. "The Interpersonal Dialogue" looks at self-disclosure, verbal and nonverbal communication, and listening. In the last section, "Sociocultural Dynamics in Relationships," we examine types of relationships, how they develop, and the impact of cultural differences and media on everyone's interpersonal life.

The underlying assumption of this book is that understanding and developing interpersonal communication skills is fundamental to the quality of life.

REVIEW TERMS AND CONCEPTS

interpersonalness
4

personal style
6

interpersonal
communication
8

situational view
9

developmental view
9

dyadic
communication
9

quality
9

transactional
11

predict
12

phatic communion
12

cultural information
13

sociological
information
13

psychological
information
13

qualitative changes
13

needs hierarchy
16

prepotent needs
16

FIRO
17

inclusion
17

control
17

affection
17

liberal arts perspective
18

ethical
communication
19

intrapersonal self
21

PUTTING THEORY INTO PRACTICE

FOR DISCUSSION:

1. Write your own definition of *interpersonal communication*, and bring it to class for discussion. According to your definition, does interpersonal communication take two people? Can communication take place without intention? Does the communication have to be understood? Why or why not? Is there a difference between communication and effective communication? If so, what?

2. Form small groups, and share the goals you have set for yourself in this class. Why are these goals important to you?

SKILL BUILDERS:

1. In a group of three to five people, create your own communication model and present it to the class. Decide which elements are crucial.

The model can either be a drawing you can put on the board or a three-dimensional object you think can be used to symbolize the communication process.

2. What types of situations make you feel least competent as a communicator? What types of situations make you feel most competent as a communicator? List examples of each type and for each explain why you feel that way. Share your responses in small groups.

FOR EXTENDED STUDY

Duck, Steve, & Gilmour, Robin, (eds.). (1981). *Personal relationships.* New York: Academic Press.

This work looks at relationship development from a research perspective.

Jaska, J. A. & Pritchard, M. A. (1988). *Communication ethics: Methods of analysis.* Belmont, CA: Wadsworth.

Jaska and Pritchard present an excellent survey of ethical concerns in communication. The book also has many good ethical activities and bibliography.

Knapp, Mark L., & Vangelisti, Anita L. (1992). *Interpersonal communication and human relationships.* Boston: Allyn & Bacon.

Knapp's work on relational development has been important for many years. In this work, he and Vangelisti explicate in a clear fashion the latest research on voluntary relational development.

Miller, Gerald R., & Steinberg, M. (1975). *Between people: A new analysis of interpersonal communication.* Palo Alto, CA: Science Research Associates.

In this classic text, Miller and Steinberg introduce the developmental approach to interpersonal communication.

Powell, John, S.J. (1969). *Why am I afraid to tell you who I am?* Chicago: Argus Communications.

Powell's book is an easy read that takes a humanistic look at self-disclosure in our relationships.

*Come now,
and let us
reason together.*

ISAIAH 1:18

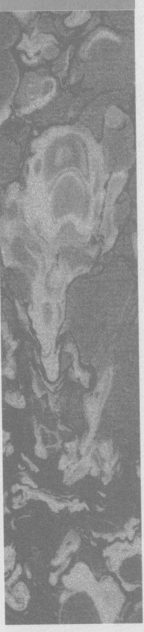

Critical Thinking and Interpersonal Communication

OBJECTIVES

After reading this chapter and taking part in class activities, you should be able to

- Define and describe the elements of critical reasoning.

- Explain how to apply critical thinking skills to interpersonal relationships.

- Identify some fallacies that can undermine a relationship.

- Use your critical reasoning skills to identify a good relationship.

- Apply those same skills to spot some of the obstacles inherent in almost all interpersonal unions.

Critical Thinking

- Ways of using critical reasoning
  - Dialectic
  - Reasoned criticism
    - Avoiding conditions that foster illogical reasoning
      - Groupthink
      - Prejudice
    - Promoting conditions that foster critical reasoning
      - Reflective thinking
      - Open-mindedness

- Definition
- Elements
- Valid reasoning
- Cogency
- Evidence
- Detecting fallacies

- Benefits of applying interpersonal communication
- Reflective rather than reactive behavior
- Matching behavior to models of effective communication
- Better decisions in relationships

N HER BEST-SELLING BOOK, *The Dance of Intimacy* (1990, p. 100) noted psychologist Harriet Goldhor-Lerner remarks, "We all do better in life when we can stay reasonably connected to important others; when we can listen to them without trying to change, convince, or fix; and when we can make calm statements about how we see things, based on thinking, rather than reacting." In relationships, people often engage in **reactive thinking** rather than critical thinking (or reflective reasoning). Reactive thinking means you make quick decisions without considering the consequences. With reflective reasoning, you consider how your behavior will affect the other person. For example, say a roommate snaps at you. Instead of stopping to think that he's going through a rough time and requires some patience, you may snap back with a negative comment of your own. When people react instead of reflect, their interpersonal communication is often not as satisfying and rich as it might be. The application of critical reasoning skills will not solve all commnication prob-lems. But such skills can help people make better decisions about relationships with others. In this chapter, we define critical thinking, discuss advantages of using it in interpersonal relationships, and then explain some elements of criti-cal reasoning you can apply with friends, potential marriage partners, col-leagues, or family members.

WHAT IS CRITICAL THINKING?

Critical thinking, is **intelligent reasoning** with supporting evi-dence to help make wise decisions. The word "critical" comes from the Greek *kritein,* which means to distinguish or sort out. We're not using the word "crit-icize" in a negative sense, as in "He criticized him because he failed to do his work." Internationally known for his work in this field, Richard Paul (1992, p. 1) describes critical thinking as

> an understanding of the relationship of language to logic, leading to the ability to analyze, criticize and advocate ideas, to reason inductively and deductively and to reach factual or judgment conclusions based on sound inferences drawn from unambiguous statements of knowledge or belief.

You already use critical thinking skills every day—at work, in classes and in decision making. Most of the time your critical thinking skills serve you well. You look for evidence to support claims people make. For example, if some-one tries to persuade you to study abroad for a year, you search out data to confirm—or deny—whether that decision would be good for you. If you've been in a relationship with another person for awhile, you normally want some proof that the union is going to last and be satisfying to both of you.

ADVANTAGES OF CRITICAL THINKING

There are at least two advantages of knowing how to apply critical thinking skills to your interpersonal relationships. First, you can use the skills to see if the way you communicate matches what scholars in the field have dis-covered are effective ways of relating to others. If experts have offered many methods for communicating effectively, you can learn those methods and apply them to your own life. Second, you can help yourself make decisions based more on critical thinking than on reactive behavior. As Goldhor-Lerner has emphasized, people do better on a day-to-day basis when they operate more on reason than unthinking reaction. Let's look at each of these benefits in more detail before moving on to describe the elements of critical thinking.

Many comments made during communication are reactive rather than reflective.

SCHOLARSHIP IN INTERPERSONAL COMMUNICATION

Scholars in the field of interpersonal communication have studied why some relationships work well and others fail. People can usually recognize good communication when they observe it, but don't always know *why* it's different from ineffective communication. One reason you're taking a course in this subject is to improve your communication skills. Such improvement comes from recognizing what *is* effective and what *isn't*. For example, experts know that defensive communication (a verbal attack on the other person) often fails, while supportive listening and talking together about problems usually leads to constructive solutions. You also probably realize that to disclose too much about yourself too soon in a relationship can harm that relationship rather than help it. For example, if you tell a potential romantic partner about some character flaws on your first date, you run the risk of turning the person off. If you wait until the relationship is on solid ground, the other person will problably be much more accepting of what you say about your less positive aspects. As another example, you know that most words are abstract and have multiple meanings. Therefore misunderstanding occurs easily unless you check to make sure that what you heard was what the other person really said. People normally acknowledge that more listening and less talking will make them better communicators. In this book, we'll be discussing a number of theories and principles that help contribute to effective communication.

The tools of critical thinking can help you assess whether you're practicing these principles.

REFLECTING INSTEAD OF REACTING

Harriet Goldhor-Lerner underscores the need all people have to establish and maintain satisfying intimate relationships with others. She says (1990, p. 202), "Laying the groundwork for intimacy is such a difficult challenge because what we do 'naturally' will naturally take us in the wrong direction." In matters of the heart, people often react more with emotions rather than with reason. And, frequently, the more intense the emotion, the less they tend to look rationally at their own behavior and how it helps or hinders important unions with others.

In the *Phaedrus* (about 340 B.C.), Plato uses an analogy to make a point about the power of emotions. The famous Greek philosopher describes a chariot with two horses and a driver. One of the horses (passion) constantly tries to veer off the road, while the other (reason) stays on course. The driver (volition—or willpower) must keep the unruly horse in check. Otherwise, driver, chariot, and horses will crash. We're not condemning emotions; some are healthy and others are not, depending on the circumstance. For example, expressing anger is not always wrong, but it can often harm a relationship. Romantic attraction is healthy, but it can sometimes create blinders to the flaws in another person. As Richard Paul (1992, p. 282) writes, "What we should want to free ourselves from is not emotion, feelings, or passion per se,

Angry reactions often block communication between people.

but irrational emotions, irrational feelings, and irrational passions." We want to emphasize that relationships usually work better and are more satisfying when people apply intelligent analysis rather than unthinking reaction.

THE TOOLS OF CRITICAL THINKING

Let's look now at some reflective reasoning tools and demonstrate with examples how they might be applied in interpersonal communication.

Reasoning

When you *reason* well, you make sure that conclusions logically follow from premises. If you've taken a course in logic, you're familiar with the term **syllogism**. A syllogism is a three-part statement containing a major premise, a minor premise, and a conclusion that either follows or doesn't follow from the first two premises. Here is an example:

> *Major premise*: All people who listen well are good communicators.
>
> *Minor premise:* Steve listens well.
>
> *Conclusion:* Therefore Steve is a good communicator.

It's important to emphasize that reasoning and truth are different. The preceding statement is logically valid but is almost certainly not true. Even though most people who listen well are good communicators, there are exceptions. Someone may be an excellent listener, but may not be able to express ideas effectively. But at least the major and minor premises connect to a valid conclusion based on the two premises. Let's say the syllogism read thus:

> *Major premise:* Many people who listen carefully are also effective in communicating their ideas.
>
> *Minor premise:* Lisa listens carefully.
>
> *Conclusion:* Therefore, she also communicates her ideas well.

This syllogism is invalid because Lisa may not fit into the category of "many." She may be an exception to the rule that many people who listen well can express themselves well.

Why is valid reasoning important for interpersonal communication? At the very least, the statements you make and hear from others should be logically valid. Otherwise, you may make decisions based on faulty reasoning. Faulty reasoning, in turn, can lead to mistakes you could have otherwise avoided. Such mistakes may not ruin your life, but people are usually better off following a reasonable path than an unreasonable one. For example, suppose a friend said to you, "Some people I have met from a wealthy suburb of Minneapolis are materialistic. Sandy is from that same section of town, and therefore she has to be materialistic." The previous statement is neither necessarily true nor is it logically valid. It's not true because a number of people from wealthy sections of town are not materialistic and it's invalid because the opening sentence contains the word *some*. If your friend made that comment, you have to decide how you want to react to it, but at least you can recognize it's untruthful and invalid.

Syllogisms are useful because they can help you recognize whether your thinking or the thinking of others is based on reason or on opinions with no logical backing. But most people don't talk in syllogisms—they talk in **enthymemes.** Enthymemes are syllogisms with one premise missing. Also their conclusions are usually probable, not certain. Here's an example: "Most people respond positively to John because he's so friendly." If you wanted to test the logical validity of that statement, you could expand it to a syllogism:

Major premise: Most people who are very friendly receive a positive response from others.

Minor premise: John is very friendly.

"Morrison, you know, has always had extremely sound judgment, but he has never had occasion to exercise it."

A passionate drive for clarity, accuracy and fair-mindedness, a fervor for getting to the bottom of things, to the deepest root issues, to listening sympathetically to opposite points of view, a compelling drive to seek out evidence, an intensive aversion to contradiction, sloppy thinking, inconsistent application of standards, a devotion to truth as against self interest—these are essential commitments of the rational person.

RICHARD PAUL
(1992, P. 282)

Drawing by Stan Hunt;
© *1987 The New Yorker Magazine, Inc.*

Conclusion: Therefore, John probably gets a positive response from others.

Enthymemes can help you sort out the invalid from the valid. People make invalid statements all the time. Such statements are often taken at face value without considering whether they're valid or true. Here are two examples:

1. A professor tells his class, "Only half of you in this room will graduate from college because the national average shows that one of two students who begin college never finish."

2. A bumper sticker reads, "When guns are outlawed, only outlaws will have guns."

The professor may have a statistic that shows less than half of all college students who begin a baccalaureate program finish. But that doesn't mean that members of the class he's addressing will fit into that pattern. It's possible they'll all graduate. Or few may finish.

The bumper sticker is based on a false premise. It assumes that a program of gun control will take away guns from law-abiding citizens—something that has never been proposed.

Deductive and Inductive Reasoning

Two forms of reasoning that can help distinguish the reasonable from the unreasonable are deduction and induction. In *deduction,* specific conclusions are drawn from general premises. For example, consider the following series of statements: "All football players enjoy competition. Sam is a football player. Therefore, Sam enjoys competition." Another example: "Men always interrupt women during a conversation more than women interrupt men. Mario is a man. Therefore, he interrupts women more than they interrupt him." Notice that neither statement is necesssarily true, but both are logically valid. They also follow the format of going from the general to the particular. In a deductive statement, you can tell whether the conclusion logically follows from the premises. This is not necessarily true with induction.

With **induction**, someone presents individual pieces of evidence and then draws a general conclusion from those pieces. In other words, a speaker presents some evidence and then asks the listener to **infer** or draw a conclusion from that evidence. For example, let's say Charlene is trying to convince an instructor that she couldn't take the final exam because she was unavoidably delayed on her way back from a city 200 miles away. Using an inductive argument, she might ask her teacher to check with the three other people who were in her car, to read the newspaper about the major pileup that occurred on the mountain pass on her way home, and to consider the fact that she has taken every exam up to the final. She would be providing three pieces of

elissa says to her friend Janet,
"Every man I have known is afraid of commitment. I'm not just talking about marriage but almost anything that requires them to commit for more than one day. Take my boyfriend,

Vern, for example. We've been going together for over two years and while he might hint on a certain day about marriage, it's really hard to pin him down. The next day he will say that he is afraid of marriage and that he really doesn't know. Then three weeks later he'll propose. The day

after that he'll tell me that he proposed because he had three beers. I'm trying to decide whether to break off the relationship because I don't need this in my life."

Is Melissa using cogent reasoning? If you think she is, why? If you don't think she is, why not?

specific evidence in an inductive way to lead to the conclusion or inference that she is an honorable person. A further inference is that she deserves some type of concession.

Cogency

Syllogisms, enthymemes, deduction, and induction help you examine the validity of arguments. But as you've seen before, validity by itself does not guarantee truth. Cogency helps you go one step beyond validity and discover whether statements are also true. Howard Kahane (1988) says reasoning is **cogent** if it contains three elements: justified premises, relevant information, and valid reasoning. As an example, let's say Janet and her mother, Irene, have had a strong relationship over the years, but Janet is bothered by her mother's need to control her. Since she was a little girl, Irene has decided on the clothes Janet wears, the kind of boys she could go out with, and the activities she could enjoy. Irene lavished attention on her daughter but also expected conformity in return. During her first year of college, Janet confronted her mother on her possessiveness. After much urging, the two of them went to a counselor to get help. Irene resisted at first, but finally accepted the counselor's suggestion that the mother loosen her hold on her daughter's life. The mother kept her promise for about two weeks. Then she started the same possessive pattern by calling and making suggestions about what Janet should wear, where she should go, and how she should deal with her new boyfriend. Janet counters by saying that Irene's action completely contravenes the therapist's suggestions and that she is feeling very uncomfortable. The mother says she would like to try again. Over the next three months, for the most part she keeps her promise except for an occasional call or two or sending an unsolicited gift. If Janet were using cogent reasoning as a basis for deciding whether the mother had really changed, she might start off with the premises that (1) people are capable of change; (2) according to Janet's observation over four months—Irene is making strong efforts to change despite an occasional slip; and (3) Janet might reasonably conclude that her mother really is taking the steps she needs to let her go. In this instance, Janet would fulfill all three requirements of cogent reasoning: a justified premise, as much relevant information as she can get, and a correct conclusion based on the information and the premises. The cogent reasoning formula might help Janet conclude one way or another whether her mother really is freeing her.

Evidence

Evidence is one important feature of cogency. You're familiar with the term *evidence* because you've heard it often in connection with legal cases. Ziegelmueller, Kay, and Dause (1990, p. 57), describe **evidence** as "source materials that are external to us and that are used to lend support or proof to a conclusion." To help understand this definition better, think of a typical prosecutor conducting a criminal trial. The prosecutor must first produce some initial evidence—usually known as "probable cause"—in order to have a suspect arrested. The state can't simply arrest someone because of a hunch that the person may have committed a burglary. But if a few witnesses saw him run out of the convenience store with a gun in his hand, and they are willing to testify, the prosecutor can make an arrest. Initial probability exists to carry the case forward. To build their case before trial, the state would seek additional pieces of evidence to get a conviction. For example, does the accused have a prior record of arrests for robbery? Did he brag to friends that he was going to knock off the store? Did police find the gun he used, with his fingerprints on the weapon?

　　Let's apply the evidence principle to a hypothetical interpersonal communi-

CONSIDERING ETHICS

Herbert Simons (1976), a scholar in the field of persuasion, has drawn a profile of people who are the easiest to persuade and those who are most difficult to persuade. One feature that distinguishes a difficult-to-persuade person from someone who is easy to persuade is that the former often insists on logical argument and is very wary of emotional appeal. For example, attorneys and accountants normally demand logical argument and support to be convinced. In contrast, Simons maintains that someone with a limited education tends to be far more influenced by predominantly emotional appeal.

Let's say you knew someone who was very susceptible to emotional appeal. Do we have any kind of obligation to use reasoned arguments with this person, or can we ignore such arguments and appeal to the emotions, knowing that the emotional appeal will probably work best?

In the political arena, looking at all the evidence is important.

cation example. Suppose Jason and Milo have been assigned to be roommates. For the first month, they get along quite well. Then Milo notices that small items are missing from the bathroom they share. First a monogramed nail-clipper is gone. Then Milo can't find his expensive after-shave lotion. Three days later, he's sure $5 has disappeared from his wallet, which he left on his dresser. He mentions these losses to Jason and gets a "Gee, that's too bad" response. Two days later, he finds the after-shave and nail-clipper hidden under some socks in the bottom drawer of Jason's dresser. He can't trace the missing $5, but he has some initial solid evidence that his new roommate has been helping himself to some of Milo's possessions. Milo now has some choices about what he wants to do, but the evidence looks compelling that he has an untrustworthy roommate.

Kinds of Evidence

There are at least three major kinds of evidence: facts, expert testimony, and statistics. Let's look at each one and then make an application to interpersonal communication.

FACTS

A fact is something obvious to an observer. It's a fact that this textbook is made out of paper and not metal. A fact is different from an opinion. Someone could say, "Italian men make the best lovers." That would be an opinion. Problems arise when people confuse facts with opinions.

When we earlier discussed "relevant information" under the category of cogency, we were referring to facts. A reasonable argument is cogent if it begins with justifiable premises, contains evidence—often factual—and such evidence leads to a reasonable conclusion. The principle of sufficient evidence could be applied to an interpersonal problem. Let's say Natalie has been going with Jim for seven months. For Natalie, honesty in a relationship is very important. Jim has told her that he always speaks the truth and yet she has caught him, on at least seven occasions, telling a lie. Each time he admits that he deceived her, but again insists that he almost always tells the truth. If she believes that truth is a crucial part of a relationship and she has hard evidence that he often does not tell the truth while insisting he does, these instances could be danger signals to her as she decides whether to continue.

TESTIMONIAL EVIDENCE

In addition to factual evidence, testimonial evidence can help you make better decisions. Testimonial evidence is given by reliable witnesses or experts who can verify the validity of a claim. Let's go back to a court case as a familiar example and then provide an interpersonal application. Someone has been injured in an accident. The injured is filing a lawsuit. The plaintiff is claiming that the accident prevents him from working for at least three years and he wants damages to compensate for his injuries. If the defendant disputes his ability to work, the plaintiff can bring a medical expert to verify that indeed the person cannot hold a job for at least three years. Note that the expert is not showing beyond any doubt the truth of the claim, but she is giving credibility to a claim and makes it appear more probable.

To apply this to interpersonal communication, let's say that after going together for seven months Stan and Mary Jane are having problems. Stan wants to be with Mary Jane every single day. Mary Jane loves Stan but is feeling smothered. The couple could approach this problem at least two ways with the use of expert testimony. They could jointly see a counselor. Or they can read books or listen to tapes by an expert on how to solve the problem of maintaining their identity as a couple while at the same time enjoying their separateness.

You, like most people, rely on experts every day to help you gain better insights and to help solve problems. You trust these people because they have been trained in a particular area and they have experience in dealing with problems.

STATISTICAL EVIDENCE

Besides factual and expert testimonial, people also occasionally use statistical evidence to help them make better decisions. Suppose a smoker would like to quit because his fiancee has urged him to do so before their wedding. He knows that what started as a pleasant pastime has turned into an addiction. How does he change? One way is to convince himself that there are great benefits in quitting. If he examines the statistical evidence on smoking, he knows that approximately 450,000 people die every year in the United States as an indirect or direct result of smoking. That is the equivalent of two 747 jets going down per day for an entire year. Although there is no certainty that he will be one of those statistics, the likelihood of such a death is far greater if he continues the habit. We're not maintaining that simply by looking at one statistic someone will change. But most people will modify a habit only because they have given themselves good reasons and really believe those reasons.

WAYS TO USE CRITICAL THINKING

In addition to the elements of critical reasoning we've just discussed, certain methods can help people think more logically. Two are especially useful: the dialectic and reasoned criticism versus disagreement. Let's look at each one.

The Dialectic

Samuel Stumpf (1966, p. 50), a philosophy scholar, describes the dialectic as a "method of dialogue in which a premise or hypothesis is continuously subjected to counter-argument." Socrates is credited with using the dialectic as his chief teaching method. Instead of a lecture, Socrates might begin by making a provocative statement (*thesis*) for example, "One cannot find justice in Athens given the current government." Then he would urge his students to argue with that idea (*antithesis*). Through a clash of ideas, students and teachers would come to better insights (*synthesis*) about the ideas being considered than they would have if Socrates had simply lectured.

COMMUNICATING SKILLFULLY

Divide the class into two separate groups: Each of the two halves then breaks into triads. The pairs in group 1 have a debate about any of the following topics. The two debaters try to convince the observer, but not each other. The pairs in group 2 conduct a dialectic. Their purpose is to build ideas together through an idea clash. The observer's role is to watch and see if a true dialectic give-and-take is occuring. After about ten minutes, have the class discuss the differences between the two approaches. Which produced the most learning and the best rapport between the participants?

SUGGESTED TOPICS (add others of your choice)

1. Capital punishment should be mandatory for first-degree murder.

2. Abortion up to the third month should be legal in the United States.

3. The United States should cut back further on its military budget and funnel the money into programs for the poor and needy.

4. Women are more intuitive than men.

**COMMUNICATING
SKILLFULLY**

igure 2.1 shows a schema that illustrates some of the advantages of applying critical reasoning to almost any issue. If you are or have been dealing with a particular issue with a friend or dating partner, how might you apply the schema? Examples of stated issues are

1. Should I confront my friend or partner about some fault I see that would impair our relationship?

2. If my partner wants to intensify the relationship, but I don't, how will I deal with that?

3. If we have different religions and we don't see either of us converting to the other's, how are we going to address this situation?

FIGURE 2.1

Schema [From: Paul, R. (1992). Critical Thinking: What Every Person Needs to Survive in a Rapidly Changing World, *p. 369.]*

Using a dialectic approach is different from a debate. In a debate, two sides try to win points by presenting their views. They are not building on each other's ideas. The clash of ideas, on the other hand, helps produce new insights that each person could not get on his or her own. In a **dialectic**, each communicator is open to the other's point of view and is willing to change his or her mind for the sake of learning.

Many college teachers use this technique today. Although the dialectic was designed primarily to help people gain knowledge through a clash of ideas, it can also be used in interpersonal relationships. As an example, let's say two partners in a company are trying to decide on the best way to equip their sev-

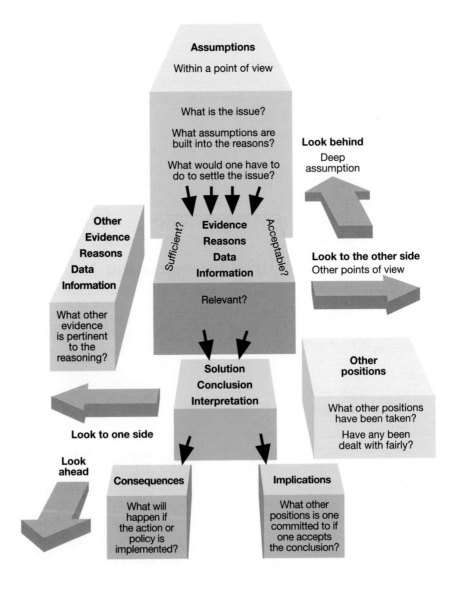

CONSIDERING CULTURE

Do people in some cultures feel more comfortable with reasoned criticism than people in other cultures? For example, do Germans feel more at ease with critical analysis than do Italians? Do Saudi Arabians logically solve problems differently from Koreans? Even within the United States, are people from some areas more comfortable with arguing than others? For example, do New York cab drivers like a good argument far more than two clergymen from Topeka, Kansas? If your answer is yes, explain why. Do you believe there are differences within a particular culture? (For example, one of our colleagues from New Jersey went west to teach at a major university. After about a month of teaching, he remarked that students from the East seemed far more at home with verbal arguments than their counterparts from the Pacific Northwest.)

enty-person office with computers. One partner might suggest that each worker needs a computer. The other partner might counter that very few people should have computers because they're so expensive. The two may go back and forth and modify their positions as they listen to each other. One makes a thesis statement such as "Everyone needs a computer." The other reacts by saying, "Very few people should have computers." Through the clash of ideas, they may come to realize that the office needs as many computers as necessary for each person to do a job well. Neither has held to the original position but by following a dialectic approach the two have produced a solution that is logical and agreeable to both.

Although not every interpersonal relationship would benefit from a constant exercise of the dialectic, sometimes the clash of ideas can be very helpful for two reasons: The dialectic can clarify issues. What was fuzzy in the minds of each can become clearer through listening and analysis. The method can also produce some of the best thinking by each party. Both can gain insights they couldn't get on their own.

DISAGREEMENT VERSUS REASONED CRITICISM

Closely related to the dialectic is reasoned criticism. When two people simply disagree, without any building of ideas, nothing much gets accomplished other than the two digging in their heels and stating their positions more emphatically. A disagreement is much like two adversaries raising the volume during a heated argument in a bar. One says "I can" and the other says, "I can't." In critical thinking, in contrast, each side examines the reasons why the other holds a particular view and then evaluates those reasons based on logical guidelines.

CONSIDERING CRITICAL THINKING

Think back on the best relationships you've ever experienced. Although you felt plenty of emotion in such a union, did you find that in the long run the relationship was well thought out? In other words, did you reflect on how it was developing and why it contained the ingredients that make for a quality union? On the other hand, consider a relationship you now regret. Were you carried along mostly on your emotion, or did you use reason and good sense?

FALLACIES

We've looked at some of the logical devices you can use to make sure you're following a reasoned approach, both in communication with yourself and others. Another way to check the validity of statements is to be aware of logical fallacies. **Fallacies** are errors in reasoning. The ability to recognize them can help you make better decisions. Fallacious reasoning is the opposite of cogent thinking. When you engage in cogent thinking or reasoning, you use justified premises, sufficient evidence, and valid conclusions drawn from your initial premises. With fallacies, the process of cogency breaks down. If the basic premises of an argument are false and everything that flows from the major premises is valid, you have not gained very much because your reasoning is founded on a house of cards. For example, consider the premise "All parents care about their children." If someone develops a series of perfectly valid arguments built on that premise, such arguments don't carry weight logically, because they're based on false or unsubstantiated premises. Obviously, some parents *don't* care about their children. The argument may be persuasive to some people, but it isn't cogent. Let's examine some common fallacies that might apply to interpersonal relationships.

Hasty Generalization

One of the most common fallacies is the hasty generalization. In this type of fallacy, someone draws a conclusion based on very flimsy evidence. Let's say that a university has an enrollment of 10,000 students. Someone takes a survey to find out if students are satisfied with their current academic advisors. The random survey is conducted with fifty people. But the number 50 is much too small a sample to get an accurate reading.

Another example: two people in love have gone out together for two weeks and have focused, as most couples do, on all the positive characteristics they have in common. After two weeks, one or both conclude that they're ready for marriage. But time is one crucible needed to test a strong relationship; they would be far better off to wait until each has had a chance to assess not only common traits, but also differences. They may later discover that they're quite compatible, but they need some time to come to that conclusion.

Begging the Question

People who commit the fallacy of "begging the question" assume the very point that needs to be proved. Let's say Ron states that "College teachers are more interested in research than in teaching because they've always been that way." Here he assumes the very point he needs to prove. One form of begging the question is arguing in a circle. For example, Don is talking with his fiancee, Margaret, who wants to continue working after they get married. He

See if you can identify the fallacies contained in the following conversation between father and son as the son approaches graduation.

FATHER: "So you're not going to follow in the footsteps of five generations of our family. All of us have been lawyers, and you're going to be an artist. Is this why I have worked for so many years—to pay the tuition so you can go out and make no money?"

SON: "Dad, I will make a decent living through my commercial art, but I also want to do some creative painting."

FATHER: "Artists starve and lawyers make a lot of money. Don't you want to make a lot of money?"

SON: "I wouldn't mind making a lot of money, but I want to do so in a profession I really enjoy—not one I feel I'm forced into."

FATHER: "Who is forcing you? I'm only telling you what your mother and I think is best for you and that in the long run will make you happy because you won't be poor."

SON: "I don't intend to be poor and I'm going to enjoy my work. I wouldn't make a good lawyer because my heart wouldn't be in it."

FATHER: "Fine, go ahead and break your mother's heart and mine too."

says, "Women should not work outside the home when they don't have to. And they don't have to because their place is really in the home raising children." Don's statement is both chauvinistic and invalid. It runs in a circle since he hasn't proven to his wife-to-be the very point he wants to make. (This presumes she still wants to marry him after he's made this statement!)

Complex Question

Another form of begging the question is the *complex question*. A familiar example is "Have you stopped beating your wife?" The answer yes implies that you've beaten your wife. The answer no is even worse because you've not only beaten your wife, but you're still doing it. As another example, imagine that Steve has been a classmate of Marcy's for five weeks. During that time, Marcy has made comments in class that are critical of Bill Clinton and Al Gore. Before class one day, Steve confronts Marcy and says, "Do you still have your anti-male attitude?" If Marcy replies, "No, I don't," by implication she could be saying that she carried an antimale attitude before but that she's changed. A few statements in class, about only two males, don't warrant the conclusion that she doesn't like males.

Ad Hominem Fallacy

The Latin phrase *ad hominem* literally means "to the man." Someone committing the fallacy of *ad hominem* attacks a particular person rather than the issue under consideration. For example, John says, "There's no way you should trust Steve's judgment about controlling handguns, because he was once a member of the National Rifle Association." In this statement, John attacked Steve as an unreliable source because he happened to be a member of an organization that advocated a position different from John's. Another example: "Simone should not be on the university antidrug committee because she used to smoke pot." Neither of these statements directly relate to the issue, but rather are attacks on the two persons.

False Analogy

A false analogy is an invalid comparison between two items. Someone using a false analogy assumes that if two people are alike in some ways they must be alike in others. For example, Justin might say, "Those two brothers, Jeremy and Joel, are two peas in a pod. They love violence. They both played football in high school. They have both entered ROTC. I know for a fact that Jeremy is violent, so his brother has to be the same way." Another example might be a statement such as "I know Melody will succeed in the alcohol treatment program because her sister was exactly the same way and she made it." The fallacy assumes that just because one person did something, the other will also do the same.

Slippery Slope

Anyone who commits the fallacy of the slippery slope assumes that if someone undertakes an initial action, all the rest of the actions that follow will lead to

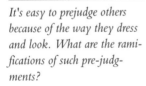

It's easy to prejudge others because of the way they dress and look. What are the ramifications of such pre-judgments?

disaster. To illustrate this concept, imagine yourself standing on the edge of a very slippery hill in the middle of winter. If you take just one step forward, you'll slip all the way to the bottom of the hill. Consider the following two examples. Joe says to Peter, "If we let just one woman into our all-male club, lots of others will want to follow and that will destroy the nature of what we have. We've got to keep this an all-guys group." Or Marianne says to Joe, someone she has met a week before, "If I let you call once, you'll want to call every single night." This may or may not be true, but Marianne doesn't have any evidence to confirm or disprove her prediction. Both these examples show fallacies, because the first steps often don't lead to the dire consequences predicted. At the very least, the speaker is not providing any proof that once you take a first step, other steps will inevitably follow.

Like other elements of critical thinking, a knowledge and application of fallacies can help you make better choices in interpersonal relationships. If you're used to thinking critically and the new person you've been dating for a month constantly engages in fallacious reasoning, you might consider carefully whether you want to continue the relationship over the long-term. Would you be happy with someone who makes errors of judgment on a regular basis? Over time, you're probably better off to watch carefully and then make decisions based on reason rather than on strong infatuation. Critical thinking tools can bring greater long-term satisfaction in interpersonal unions.

> *No mastery is greater than mastering yourself and your own passions: it is a triumph of the will.*
>
> BALTASAR GRACIAN
> (1658)

CONDITIONS THAT BLOCK CRITICAL REASONING

Besides fallacies, certain conditions can diminish your capacity to make effective decisions about interpersonal relationships. Let's look at two of these—prejudice and "groupthink."

Prejudice

Few people can avoid holding onto some preconceived notions that impair their critical thinking or reasoning. One such preconception is **prejudice**. In its mildest form, prejudice is forming judgments before facts are known. In its worst form, prejudice involves a negative, irrational opinion someone holds about a group or an object. For example, Mel could be prejudiced about houses built after 1950. With no effort to check the facts, he concludes that every house built after 1950 is inferior to those built before that date. In the more extreme form, Margaret believes that no male can really be trusted. Such a prejudice could be a result of three bad experiences she's had with males.

Someone who is prejudiced believes that every member of a group has the same characteristics. Although most national groups differ from each other, not every member of a national group exhibits the same traits as others in the group. You may conclude that Italians, for example, are usually more effusive than Germans. It would be prejudicial, however, to conclude that *all* Germans are reserved and that *all* Italians are effusive when you know there are obviously exceptions in both of these cultures. Prejudices can fracture interpersonal relationships. Suppose a father held a prejudice about another race and his daughter was dating someone of that race. The father's bias will probably affect both his daughter and the young man she is dating.

Groupthink

A second condition that can foster invalid thinking is groupthink. Yale psychologist Irving Janis (1982) first coined the term **groupthink** in his now classic book by the same title. Janis describes the phenomenon as the drive for consensus at any cost that suppresses disagreement and prevents the examination of alternative solutions in cohesive decision-making groups. In doing research on decision-making groups, Janis became intrigued by the blunders that U. S. committees made in dealing with such crises as Pearl Harbor, the Korean stalemate, and the war in Vietnam. Particularly perplexing to Janis was the fact that people who were bright and independent by themselves often made bad decisions when they formed groups. As individuals, these same people would have gone through a rigorous process of decision making. But once they joined a group, they found strong pressure to conform to the majority opinion. For example, during a discussion held the day before the attack on Pearl Harbor in 1941, Admiral Husband Kimmel and his advisors kept reassuring themselves that the Japanese would never attack Hawaii. If anyone disagreed with the majority, the other members quickly persuaded the dissenter to go along with the wishes of the group.

Without any intention of doing so, groups can put pressure on an individual to conform to the group's collective ideas.

The same phenomenon occurred with President Kennedy and his advisors during deliberations about the Bay of Pigs invasion in 1961. Early in the first year of his presidency, Kennedy called his cabinet together to consider ways to overthrow Cuban leader Fidel Castro. Because the group was in the process of forming, many of the individual members felt reluctant to express any doubts they had about the plan, which ultimately turned out to be a disaster. Fearing possible rejection from others in the cabinet, some kept silent even when they had serious reservations about the United States sponsoring an invasion by Cuban dissidents.

If you've joined any kind of group—fraternity, class or club—you know that it's hard to go against the ideas of the group. Anyone who disagrees often goes through a process called "wolf-packing." In wolf-packing, the decision-making process shuts down while members of the group try to bring the dissenter back into the fold. Let's say Jeremy, a fraternity member, loves Maureen and calls her every night. Five of his fraternity brothers tell him that he's "spoiling" her and should call only twice a week. Pressure to conform to group ideas can be strong. Ideally, each member of a group critically analyzes all ideas for their validity and proof.

CONDITIONS THAT FOSTER CRITICAL THINKING

Two conditions that promote critical thinking or reasoning are reflective thinking and open-mindedness. Let's look at each of these and show how they can help you make better decisions in interpersonal relationships.

Reflective Thinking

Early in this century, John Dewey devised a process that has come to be called the "**reflective thinking agenda**." Dewey believed that humans solve problems more efficiently by following logical steps in a certain order. Various versions of the reflective thinking process have been proposed over the years; the basic steps are listed here:

1. Clearly describe the problem.

2. Analyze what is causing the problem.

3. Establish criteria for solving the problem.

4. Brainstorm solutions that fit the criteria.

5. Pick the solution or solutions that best fit the criteria.

To illustrate how this process might apply to interpesonal communication, let's say Kyle and Arlene married during their junior year of college. Kyle is

---

CONSIDERING CULTURE

You've decided to spend an academic year in Europe. As you're flying from London to Rome, you sit on the plane with someone from Britain. You start a conversation, and after a while you talk about differences between Americans and Brits. Your companion says, "My experience with all Americans is that they are materialistic and have very little sense of history. We Brits, on the other hand, have a profound appreciation of our roots." How would you respond to this bias? Would you let it go by, would you try to refute it, or would you continue the dialogue, hoping you can change your traveling companion's perceptions?

finishing his degree while Arlene works as a secretary, planning to complete her undergraduate program after Kyle finishes with his. Kyle is so absorbed in his studies that he often ignores his wife. She finds this irksome because she knows she is sacrificing while he finishes his degree program. After a hard day in the office, Arlene wants to do something fun and relaxing—take a walk, go to a movie or visit friends. When she asks Kyle to go along, most of the time he says, "I've got to study. We can do that on Sunday." Her resentment grows by the day until finally she confronts him. Kyle can't understand her frustration because "after all, I'm getting my degree for us, and I need to do well in my studies."

Although the two of them would problably not follow the reflective thinking agenda in the exact sequence described, some adherence to the steps would help them solve their conflict. Their first step would be to clearly describe the symptoms of the problem in some detail. Such symptoms could include Arlene's increasing anger over Kyle's withdrawal or his surprise that she's upset. They could then go on and try to discover the real causes of their diasagreement. In probing causes, each may discover that the real cause is not what seems to be apparent on the surface but something more deeply seated. They both may discover that Kyle stays home not because he wants to succeed at his studies, but because he's a loner who would far prefer to be by himself and his wife than mix with a lot of people. Or they both might find out that Arlene feels resentment because he gets to finish his degree first. Discovering causes is important because most problems have to be dealt with at the cause level to get solved.

During the criteria stage, each party might agree on some standards that will govern whatever solution they decide on. A criterion is a guideline you can use to help make sound judgments. For example, if you're thinking about buying a car, your criteria might include (1) dependability, (2) good gas mileage, and (3) modest price. Criteria for Arlene and Kyle might be (1) "whatever solution we decide on should give us time to cultivate our relationship more than we're doing now," and (2) "our solution should help us get our problems expressed quickly before they start to fester and end in a blowup."

Armed with the criteria, the two could brainstorm solutions. During brainstorming, each participant suggests ideas without stopping to consider if the suggestions will solve the problem. Such solutions might include the following:

1. We'll go out with friends two nights a week.

2. We'll see friends when we *both* decide it's appropriate

3. We'll do something fun by ourselves without friends.

4. Kyle can study every week night and feel comfortable with Arlene doing something with her best friend Peg.

CONSIDERING CRITICAL THINKING

The Cuban missile crisis of 1962 might help illustrate how the reflective thinking process can work to solve problems.

President Kennedy and his advisors may have been victims of groupthink during their handling of the Bay of Pigs crisis in 1961, but they learned from their mistakes. In October 1962, Kennedy's military advisors told him that the Cubans and the Soviets were building long-range missile installations in Cuba. Completion of the missile sites would be a direct threat to the United States because the missiles could strike major U. S. cities.

Kennedy assembled his staff and urged them not to repeat the errors they had made during the Bay of Pigs disaster. One way the group avoided such errors and decided on solutions that proved to be effective was through reflective thinking. Members of the cabinet began by getting a clear idea of the problem. Through reconnaissance photos, they knew the Soviets and Cubans were building the sites around the clock. But they weren't sure why. After some probing, they decided that the Soviets had two reasons for the buildup. First, they wanted to have their missiles installed 90 miles off the U. S. coast to compensate for U. S. missiles in Turkey pointing at the Soviet Union. Second, the Soviet President Nikita Khrushchev needed to re-establish himself as a strong leader. Apparently some of his generals in the Kremlin were disturbed by Khrushchev's seeming appeasement of the Americans. These twin causes left the committee in a quandary. If they focused solely on the first cause and decided on a military response, they would risk backing Khrushchev into a corner. If they tried to appease the Soviet president, the missiles might well remain and the problem would not be solved. So the committee established two criteria: (1) "We need to get rid of the missiles sites," but (2) "We should do so in such a way that would allow Khrushchev to save face with his military advisors in the Kremlin."

Using those criteria, the committee started brainstorming solutions. Some of the key suggestions were

1. Do nothing.

2. Launch a massive air strike, followed by an invasion of troops from Florida and Georgia.

3. Undertake a surgical air strike designed to destroy the missiles with minimal loss of human life.

4. Establish communication lines between Kennedy and Khrushchev.

5. Set up a military blockade 500 miles off the coast of Cuba and announce to the world that supply ships coming from Communist countries would not be allowed to cross the blockade line.

Kennedy and his cabinet rejected the first three suggestions because the solutions failed to fit the criteria. They chose the last two precisely because the solutions had the best chance of stopping the Soviets in a way that would let Khrushchev save face.

How might you apply the reflective thinking approach to an interpersonal relationship you're now experiencing? Do you think you need to get agreement from your partner that this approach might be useful in solving the inevitable problems that can come up during the development of a serious union?

5. They can think and talk about solutions for a week without coming to an agreement before then.

The final step involves each party examining the solutions to see if they fit the criteria they both agreed on. Arlene and Kyle may conclude that they need to think about and discuss this issue for a week and then make a decision. This last solution fits the criteria they established and gives them more time to find a way to satisfy them both.

Open-mindedness

The opposite of prejudice is **open-mindedness**. Someone who is open-minded listens to any idea and then considers it carefully before deciding whether to accept or reject it. If you're open-minded, you try to put aside any preconceived notion you have. Open-mindedness is sometimes difficult to practice. Few people can listen to every idea without bringing in some previous attitude learned over the years. The more intense the attitude, the harder it is to be open-minded. For example, suppose Amy has been brought up to believe that alcohol in any form is unhealthy and sinful. One night, her friend Maury tries to convince that a single glass of wine at dinner can be relaxing and even healthy. Maury presents medical evidence showing that wine in moderation can help people reduce stress and ward off heart disease. If Amy has heard the opposite message for a long time, she finds it hard to block out such an attitude and look at the merits of the argument her friend is trying to make. If she is open-minded, she might reject the idea in the long run, but at least she will consider it carefully before deciding to accept, reject, or think about it in greater detail.

A prejudiced person is one who won't even consider a viewpoint different from his or her own. Someone who is open-minded hears another out before making a decision. In the long run, after examining the evidence, the open-minded individual may be more convinced than ever that his or her position is correct. Such a person has the advantage of being able to look at any issue squarely before making up his or her mind about which side to take.

LOOKING BACK - LOOKING FORWARD

This chapter introduced the concept of critical thinking. Critical thinking is intelligent reasoning with supporting evidence to help make wise decisions. It can help improve a relationship. Some critical thinking tools you can apply to make your own relationships more satisfying are the use of evidence, reflection, and open-mindedness. Critical reasoning won't solve all communication problems. But the ability to reason well is one of the greatest human abilities, and some of the same skills you use in solving problems can also be applied to interpersonal unions. Specifically, critical reasoning can help you make better decisions about relationships. Using validity, cogency, sufficient evidence, and avoiding fallacies, can help in that effort.

In the early part of this chapter, we suggested you could use critical thinking methods to see if the theories and suggestions scholars have developed can be applied to improving your own relationships with other people. Throughout the rest of the book, we invite you to study these theories, see if they make sense, and then carefully consider whether you can apply them in your own life.

In the next chapter, we discuss perceptions and show how perceptions can help color the way people view the world and others. Perceptions can affect any interpersonal communication positively or negatively. If partners tend to see the world in pretty much the same way, their union is usually more harmonious than those who have different perceptions. But, if they perceive themselves and outside events very differently, they're probably in for some difficult times.

REVIEW TERMS AND CONCEPTS

reactive thinking
  28
critical thinking
  29
intelligent reasoning
  29
syllogism
  32
enthymemes
  33
induction
  34

infer
  34
cogent reasoning
  35
evidence
  36
dialectic
  40
fallacies
  42
prejudice
  45

groupthink
  46
reflective thinking
  agenda
  47
open-mindedness
  50

UTTING THEORY INTO PRACTICE

FOR DISCUSSION:

1. Professor Herbert Simons (1976, p. 96) has described the ideally critical listener as "one who has genuinely high self-esteem, is intelligent and well educated, is tolerant of ambiguity, is a cognitive clarifier, has highly differentiated and logically integrated attitude structures, and copes with problems rather than avoids them." Would you agree with this description? Would you add any other traits you believe are important for someone who listens with a critical mind?

2. Richard Paul (1992, p. 105) provides a list of intellectual standards that distinguish strong critical thinking from weak. Please look at Paul's list (following) and rank what you consider the top five standards for anyone involved in interpersonal communication. Then justify why you believe the standards you chose are the most important.

THINKING THAT IS:	THINKING THAT IS:
Clear	Unclear
Precise	Imprecise
Specific	Vague
Accurate	Inaccurate
Relevant	Irrelevant
Plausible	Implausible
Consistent	Inconsistent
Logical	Illogical
Deep	Superficial
Broad	Narrow
Complete	Incomplete
Significant	Trivial
Adequate *(for purpose)*	Inadequate
Fair	Biased or One-Sided

3. Besides theories of interpersonal communication, we make a number of statements in this book. We invite you to challenge them all to see if they're reasonable. The last thing we want you to do is to take at face value anything we maintain. Think about each concept and see if you believe it is supported with solid reasoning and suporting evidence.

SKILL BUILDERS:

1. *The case of George.* George has a problem with his residence hall director (RD). The resident hall policy requires that noise be kept to a minimum after midnight. As fate would have it, George has been afflicted with a noisy roommate who has held four parties on school nights. Since George was in the room with the others—trying to study—the RD blamed him also. How would George present a case to convince his RD that he is innocent and should not be penalized for the misdeeds of his roommate?

2. *Can reason win out over emotion?* Often, the more intense the relationship, the greater the emotion involved. The greater the emotion, the less tendency there is to use critical reasoning. Recall the most intense emotional relationship you have ever had—romantic, family, or friendship. Then break into groups of three or four and discuss how much value critical thinking skills might have been in dealing with these strong emotions. Don't feel you have to justify the use of critical thinking. You may conclude that critical thinking is not helpful in the case you discuss.

FOR EXTENDED STUDY

Janis, I. (1982). *Groupthink* (2nd ed.).Boston: Houghton Mifflin.

This is one of the best books available on how a lack of effective critical thinking can lead groups to make disastrous decisions. Janis also offer some very specific suggestions about how to apply critical thinking skills to solving problems.

Kahane, H. (1988). *Logic and contemporary rhetoric: The use of reason in everyday life.* Belmont, CA: Wadsworth.

Professor Kahane provides numerous examples of how much illogical thinking exists in society. His writing is clear, entertaining, and practical.

Paul, R. (1992). *Critical thinking: What every person needs to survive in a rapidly changing world* (2nd ed.). Rohnert Park, CA: Sonoma State University Press.

Richard Paul is known worldwide as a leader in the critical thinking movement. The book is a series of essays by Paul and other experts. This is not light reading, but the rewards are well worth the effort for anyone who wants to probe in depth the connection between critical thinking and everyday living.

*Many people do
not seem to realize
that very much
of our thinking
proceeds from
assumptions often
experienced as fact.*

VIRGINIA SATIR

Person Perception and Communication

OBJECTIVES

After reading this chapter and taking part in class activities, you should be able to

• Describe perception as a process.

• Explain the role perception plays in interpersonal relationships.

• Identify some perceptual errors.

• Explain how guarding against perceptual errors can increase chances for more effective interpersonal relationships.

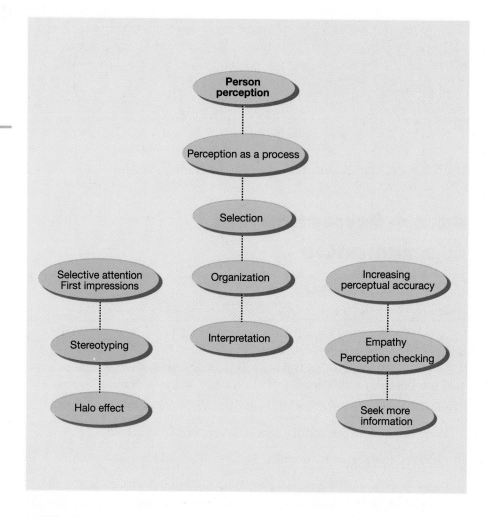

REMEMBER IN GRADE SCHOOL when you memorized all the interesting "facts" about Christopher Columbus? Now history books question whether or not he actually *discovered* America, but it is known that Columbus saw the world as flat. Yet you and I know that the world is round. Using the information available to him at the time, Columbus perceived his view as reality.

In daily life, people are constantly faced with situations where two observers may be viewing the exact same event or participating in the same conversation but walk away with two very different versions of what just took place. A college campus is a likely stage for such happenings. Think about the various interpretations of couples meeting and talking on campus the Monday after a big campus social function or dance that consumed much of the previous weekend's activity. Is it a coincidence that the young man and woman you see huddled closely on a courtyard bench ran into each other that day, or was this a planned rendezvous so they could pick up where they left off on Saturday night? You may think this is a coincidence, but a friend of yours passing by may argue that this was a scheduled meeting. Whether or not you really care why they are there is not the point. The point is that people tend to consider what they perceive or view in a given situation as reality.

This chapter discusses the role perception plays in interpersonal relationships. Chapter 6 discusses how misunderstandings occur through language. Similar problems arise from the meanings people attach and the actions they take that are based on their perceptions. This chapter examines theories about the ways meanings are created. It shows ways to recognize and guard against perceptual errors and increase chances for more effective interpersonal relationships.

THE PERCEPTION PROCESS

Perception is an active process by which people assign meaning to experiences. Psychologists traditionally divide experience into two classes: sensation and perception. Seeing a red octagon on a pole on a street is a sensation, but seeing that red octagon as a "stop sign" is a perception. The process of perception involves the selection, organization, and interpretation of sensory data that helps people make sense of the world.

Perception

It would be impossible to process everything that touches your senses. While you may think you are quite capable when it comes to taking in as much as you can, far more comes your way than you could ever hope to absorb. Geldard (1953) estimates that people are physiologically capable of distinguishing among 7,500,000 different colors. Gordon (1971) adds that normal human ears are capable of sensing 20 to 20,000 vibration cycles per second, and people are capable of differentiating among 5,000 different smells. If you don't smoke, the possibilities for taste can allow you to distinguish among 10,000 different sensations (no statistics tell what the smoker is or isn't capable of tasting). Even your abilities to distinguish among sensations of touch might be surprising. Your fingers have the capability of feeling the separations between objects as little as 3 to 8 mm apart.

Although these statistics may seem impressive, your senses do have limitations. Let's look closely at the three parts of the sense-making process and discuss their capabilities and limitations.

Selection

Many sensory experiences bombard you at any given moment, but you select only a few. You therefore become forced to choose or identify among the stimuli that come your way and decide which you will pay attention to. You call this **selection,** or **selective attention**—that is, you can process only a certain amount of what is going on about you at a given moment. Think— right now as you are reading this, what else is going on around you? Is music playing? Were you aware of the tune? Is the room hot or cold? Did you notice the constant hum of the overhead light? Chances are you were not thinking about all these competing factors (especially because you are reading intensely so you can dazzle your teacher with evidence that you read this chapter), but maybe you were vaguely aware of one or two sensations.

     These selections are not necessarily conscious, either, because people are

Often we choose to pay attention to issues that are of immediate concern to us— just as we "browse" through the newspaper to find an article of interest.

limited by both psychological and physiological factors. For example, people with vision or hearing problems may not notice events happening around them, not because they choose to ignore them, but rather because of their physical limitations.

But people do exercise some control over what they perceive. For instance, you will tend to pay attention to those stimuli that are of interest to you or you are familiar with due to past experiences. For example, if you are seriously shopping for a new car and have a particular color, model, or shape in mind, you will probably pay much greater attention to these characteristics of passing cars than you would have six months ago when you weren't even thinking about this purchase. What may motivate you today in your perceptual selections may not matter to you tomorrow.

Experience will play a major role in what you perceive or choose to perceive at any given moment. Take a classic example: a woman is sitting on the couch in front of the television set with the remote control in hand. As she flips through the channels, she decides to continue looking for something familiar or desirable. Based on her experience with programs on the channels she has chosen to bypass, she knows she would not be interested in watching them at that moment (or maybe ever).

Organization

The perceptual process does not end with selection. Once stimuli have come your way, you need to do something with them. You must arrange them or **organize** them in some form that has meaning for you, some way that will help make sense of the information. Gestalt theorists have provided examples to visually show this principle. The principle of "figure–ground" organization is illustrated in Figure 3.1. Depending on whether you focus on the black or the white areas, you will see the picture as either a vase or two faces. You are making sense of the stimuli by noticing either the ground or the figure. Psychologists use the terms figure and ground to label an object and its background, respectively. Even without three-dimensional cues, people tend to organize what they see in terms of figure and ground. Neither is considered correct or incorrect; it just depends on how you will organize the stimuli at a given moment.

Many factors influence the organizational phase of the perceptual process; in particular the degree of ambiguity (of the information) and our emotional state. As information becomes more ambiguous, the chances for perceptual errors increase. Think about a time when you needed to look at a situation two or three times only to realize that what you thought you saw was not what was actually there. The fact that messages have more than one possible way of being organized, along with individual variation in experiences with the particular stimuli, only leads to further confusion and the possibility of interpersonal misunderstanding.

FIGURE 3.1

Faces or Vases? As we are bombarded with many stimuli, what we focus on at that moment becomes the figure and the rest of what we view is the ground.

How you feel at a particular time may also influence the way you organize sensory stimuli and leave you open to perceptual errors. Think of a time when you were extremely tired and you caught yourself thinking or saying that "you wouldn't trust what you see" or "wouldn't want someone to take your word for what you thought you'd seen" because of your emotional state. "I'm so tired I can hardly see straight" may be a very accurate phrase.

Interpretation

The third step in the process of perception, **interpretation**, plays a major part in every interpersonal transaction. Once you have selected and organized sensory data, you then must give them meaning. Interpretation, simply put, is giving meaning. How often have you wondered how you should respond to another person's message because you could interpret it so many different ways? Several factors cause you to interpret communication events in one way or another.

As with the selection phase, past experience plays a key role in interpreting situations. For example, you may find it difficult to trust someone who has lied to you in the past or betrayed you in some way. You probably would interpret this behavior as something typical of that person, and assume it could happen again in a similar situation. Parents who have left a teenager at home alone while they were out of town can easily relate to this concept. If they came home to damage or evidence that led them to conclude a party took place in their absence, they may hesitate to let such an opportunity arise again. In evaluating information, people bring to bear all of their experiences and knowledge.

Just as feelings can affect how you organize perceptual stimuli, the interpretation step can also be influenced by your emotional state. For example, think about how your mood can affect your analysis of a given situation. Consider the following scenario: Imagine your teacher just returned a paper to you, marked with a poor grade. You were disappointed because you really thought you'd done a better job than your teacher was giving you credit for. You return to your dorm or apartment to find a statement from your bank informing you that you are overdrawn. What else can go wrong? Just then the phone rings—it's your boss from work. There's been a change in the work schedule and they need you to come in right away. Why did they call you? Why couldn't they have called someone else? Perhaps your first thoughts are that they are taking advantage of you or think that you have nothing better to do. But your boss may have called you because you were their first choice. You are their most efficient worker, and they know they could count on you to pull them out of their bind. In your boss's mind, you were being complimented, but you interpreted the request as an assumption that you had nothing better to do. Perhaps if you'd received the *A* you thought you deserved and your bank statement had cleared, you might never have thought twice about your boss's request.

Of course, good moods and positive emotional states can influence (and even distort) interpretation of events as well.

PERCEPTUAL PROBLEMS

In this next section, we explore additional factors that can inhibit the accuracy of perceptions. People tend to make assumptions about people and situations and use barriers that can distort perceptual interpretations. Simple awareness of these problems may help increase the chance for improving interpersonal effectiveness, but understanding the *consequences* of such behavior may motivate people even more.

Cultural Variations

If you have ever traveled out of the country or hosted a foreign visitor, you may have experienced some amusing, or perhaps embarrassing, situations that were caused by differences in cultural perspectives. (Chapter 12 discusses intercultural communication in depth.) Intercultural communication problems arise from varying perceptual interpretations of both language usage (written and oral) and nonverbal behaviors.

A student studying at a university in London was exposed to all sorts of linguistic translations that could lead to potential problems. The student was shocked when the host family parent remarked "I'll knock you up at six in the morning!" This meant that the parent would knock on the door and wake the student up at six. The student learned even more about cultural differences when she heard the host mother telling her 9-year-old son not to leave for school without his "rubber." The American student thought maybe this meant boots, but the reference was to an eraser. At least they were both speaking English. If translations were being made from one language to another, the potential for misunderstanding and misinterpretation would be even greater.

Culturally specific gestures can also lead to communication problems. The Italian gesture for "goodbye" is much like the American motion to "come here." This difference could cause confusion. One innocent gesture could be mistaken for an insulting or lewd message from one culture to another. In some countries, the "victory" or "peace" and the "OK" signs that are typically used in America in a harmless way can be interpreted to mean what the middle-finger gesture means to Americans. This is not a mistake you would want to make.

As with gestures, eye contact (or lack of it) is also culturally specific. In some countries, it is not considered appropriate or respectful to look someone straight in the eye when being addressed. In America you might think a person who is not looking at you straight in the eye or who is avoiding eye contact is lying or being deceitful.

It doesn't necessarily take a trip out of the country or a visit from a foreigner to encounter cultural differences that influence perceptions. There are co-cultures within most cultures that cause members of that particular group to view communication situations in different ways. Whether these behaviors

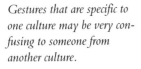

Gestures that are specific to one culture may be very confusing to someone from another culture.

are taught or learned through experience doesn't really matter—the fact remains that the differences can lead to misunderstandings within what may seem to be the same culture. Later in this chapter, we'll explore ways to avoid or at least lessen the chances for these kinds of misinterpretations and misunderstandings to arise.

First Impressions

When you are viewing people and situations, it is only natural to base your impressions on your perceptual interpretations. You make sense of things depending on what you already know or think you know about a particular person or situation. This can be good in one sense, because you are able to use these impressions to guide your future behavior.

You form **first impressions** of others based on physical characteristics and personal attributes: "She's a beautiful redhead," "He's a blue-eyed, blond muscle builder," and so on. Sometimes you have only these superficial things to go by when making a judgment about another. If you are given the chance to speak with the individual, you can enhance your impression by evaluating particular personality traits, and you may even pick up on some of the other person's beliefs and attitudes. When you begin to make guesses about what motivates this person and actually start building a personality for him or her, you have gone beyond simply interpreting what you see and hear. At this point you've begun to speculate that you know things about the person that you can't actually see. As Ross, Greene, and House (1977) suggest, you form attributional biases when you attribute the behavior of another to possible causes.

However, your first impressions aren't always accurate; but once you form an opinion about someone, you tend to hold to it and base your future encounters on that initial perception. Recall an earlier section of this chapter where we discussed some of the psychological influences on the perceptual process. If you meet someone for the first time who has just gone through some kind of emotional crisis, you may get the impression that this person is a real wimp and can't handle his or her emotions. Is this really a fair judgment to make?

Obviously, some people are better than others at making accurate perceptual judgments and interpretations of others. To improve interpretive abilities, people need to be more conscious of *how* they draw conclusions about first impressions.

A television commercial for a dandruff shampoo sums up the power of first impressions. In the commercial, the actress suggests to her dandruff-stricken friend that "You never get a second chance to make a first impression." But that doesn't mean that you can't (or shouldn't) take a second or even a third look when sizing up a person or a situation.

Two topics that are closely related to that of impression formation are *stereotyping* and the *halo effect*.

Stereotyping

Stereotyping is a common perceptual error that results from overgeneralizing or making weak generalizations about people, places, or events. The term was first coined in the early 1920s to describe opinions made about others based on their ethnic group membership. Most people have either been guilty of, or encountered hurt or misunderstanding because of the use of a cultural stereotype. Cultural stereotypes are the tendency to see all members of a particular group of people as having the same characteristics. Often these cultural stereotypes are unfavorable and put people at an unfair disadvantage.

Some stereotypes go beyond simply categorizing people according to cultural background, and respond to people's occupations or roles they portray. Most students are familiar with stereotyping in a college environment about students' major fields of study. People even make judgments about personalities or how to behave in the presence of a person who has chosen to pursue a particular professional field.

Stereotyping can help you determine how to behave in a particular environment. For example, you might be conscious of the need to behave well in a doctor or lawyer's office because you expect that person to behave a certain way, and you assume that he or she has behavioral expectations of you as well.

In general, though, stereotyping can be far more harmful than helpful. At one time or another most people have held fixed impressions (whether consciously or unconsciously) of others according to a specific ethnic or cultural background, occupation, or perhaps even income level.

To improve perceptual capabilities, concentrate on becoming aware of the differences as well as the similarities among people. As communicologist Irving J. Lee suggests, "the more we are able to discriminate *among* individuals, the less we will actively discriminate *against* individuals" (Gamble & Gamble, 1987, p. 62).

Halo Effect

The **halo effect** is the result of a need to simplify the judgment process. It doesn't matter whether an initial impression is positive or negative for the halo effect to be present. It simply means that the first impression becomes the only impression to prevail. This perceptual error occurs when a particular characteristic or individual trait profoundly influences all other impressions of the person. For example, think of a man who is blindly in love with the "wrong" woman. At first the new love gave the impression that she was a most generous, caring, and giving person. As the relationship progressed, it became obvious to all (except the love-struck victim) that the party in question was using the other to recover from a previous relationship (otherwise known as "on the rebound"). She simply wanted it to appear that she had gotten over her old love and could be seen out and about in the social arena. "Love-struck" suf-

CONSIDERING CRITICAL THINKING

Think of a time when you later learned of being judged inaccurately (a false impression).

Also, think of examples where you found yourself being guilty of clinging to a first impression only to later learn that you were way off base.

fered from the halo effect because his initial impression overshadowed any other clues that may have been present.

According to Swann (1984), people are generally poor at making predictions about others' personality traits. Findings conclude that people tend to assume that others are consistent in their behavior from situation to situation, they overlook or misperceive evidence that contradicts their own first impressions, and they overlook the effects that situations have on people's behavior.

Everyone makes observations of people's behavior (both of other people and him- or herself) and draws conclusions about other people's personality traits. People use their knowledge of these traits, and of the effects of various situations, to predict how others will behave. The process by which people make such predictions is called **person perception**.

Identity Cues

In addition to assessing others' personality traits, people often seek to project particular images of their own personalities. One way to do this is by displaying identity cues. **Identity cues** include particular styles of clothing or other nonverbal factors (decoration of office, use of jewelry or hairstyle, and so on) that give others a way to judge identity. If others appear to be perceiving you in a way that contradicts your own view of yourself, for example, you will tend to show cues designed to change the perception.

Think back to the beginning of this chapter, to the discussion of selection and selective attention. These concepts can also be linked to perceptual selec-

CONSIDERING THINKING CRITICALLY

How could "Love-struck" use what you've learned in this book so far to avoid making a bad decision again? At what point in the relationship could he have saved himself from potential grief?

Nonverbal identity cues provide a means for others to make judgements about one's personality. Here one might perceive the occupant of this room to be disorganized or distracted.

COMMUNICATING SKILLFULLY

THE DETECTIVE EXERCISE

Read the following story. Assume that the information contained in it is accurate and true. Answer in order the questions that follow the story. Do not go back and change any of your answers. After you read a statement, simply indicate whether you think the statement is definitely true by writing T, definitely false by writing F, or questionable by writing a question mark. (A question mark means that you think the statement could be true or false, but on the basis of information contained in the story, you cannot be certain.)

A tired executive had just turned off the lights in the store when an individual approached and demanded money. The owner opened the safe. The contents of the safe were emptied, and the owner ran away. The alarm was triggered, notifying the police of the occurrence.

1. An individual appeared after the owner had turned off the store's lights.

2. The robber was a man.

3. The person who appeared did not demand money.

4. The man who opened the safe was the owner.

5. The owner emptied the safe and ran away.

6. Someone opened the safe.

7. After the person who demanded the money emptied the safe, he sped away.

8. Although the safe contained money, the story does not reveal how much.

9. The robber opened the safe.

10. The robber did not take the money.

11. In this story, only three people are mentioned.

How well did you do? You can check your answers in the key at the end of the chapter. The point of this exercise is simply to demonstrate how easy it is to make an inference and accept it as fact.

SOURCE: GAMBLE & GAMBLE (1987) P. 66

tivity in intimate relationships. It may be difficult for people to see their own faults, but they can easily magnify the faults of others. For example, if someone makes a judgment about you that is not consistent with what you believe about yourself, you may tend to screen out that information, creating and reinforcing an illusory self-concept. On the flip side, you may respond to another person given your perception of that person, rather than what the person is really like.

Misperceptions result from the nature of perception itself because perceptions are tentative, learned, and selective. Fortunately, people can take steps to improve perceptual accuracy, which, in turn, makes them better communicators. These steps are discussed later. Before making these suggestions, let's look at three more culprits in the perceptual error department.

OTHER BARRIERS TO PERCEPTION

So far we have discussed a number of barriers that limit and impede our perceptual accuracy. Three additional forces that function as perceptual filters are allness, blindering, and fact-inference confusion.

Allness

The term **allness** refers to the erroneous belief that someone could possibly know all there is to know about something. Obviously it is virtually impossible to know *all* there is to know about a particular topic. This perceptual error occurs because people think they have seen or heard all the facts, all the information, and have put all the pieces together in a given situation. They have no need for further information. Perhaps you've experienced this kind of frustrating situation when you felt that someone wasn't giving you a fair chance to explain your side of a story. The person simply cut you off with the explanation that he or she's heard all that he or she needs to hear. End of conversation.

People fall victim to allness when they close themselves to new or different information. Obviously this kind of allness attitude is not very productive toward developing effective interpersonal relationships.

Blindering

If you have ever watched a horse race, you may have seen a horse wearing blinders. These are used to limit the horse's visual range and eliminate unnecessary distractions. Similarly, sometimes people wear imaginary "blinders" that minimize the perceptual arena. They see only parts of the picture or situation or view things only in certain ways.

People can limit or impede interpersonal understanding by **blindering**—failing to remove blinders and look open-mindedly at the entire view. Recall a time when you had a misunderstanding with someone because one of you had your "blinders" on and couldn't see all the factors the other saw in a given situation. Often people see only what they want or expect to see.

Fact-Inference Confusion

A failure to distinguish between what one infers from a given situation and what is actually observed or known is called **fact–inference confusion** and can inhibit interpersonal relationships. A fact is something known to be true and is based on observation. You look out the window and see the big yellow-orange disk in the sky known as the sun. "The sun is shining" is a factual statement. "It is hot outside" is a statement of inference, because you cannot verify its truth simply by making an observation. While people tend to think of the

"Blinders" tend to limit our view of a situation.

sun as warm, they also realize that the sun can shine on very crisp, cold, or windy days, depending on the particular climate.

People fall prey to perceptual errors when they fail to distinguish between what they deduce from a given situation and what is factual. When this happens, they are likely to jump to conclusions. Table 3.1 summarizes the essential differences between facts and inferences.

As mentioned, a number of factors can inhibit or impede the accuracy of perceptions. Although an awareness of the many facets of perception is important for interpersonal understanding, you need to go beyond this fundamental level of understanding to become more effective communicators. You need to work at improving the validity of your perceptions to increase interpersonal understanding. By becoming aware of your role in perception and recognizing that you have biases, you can increase the likelihood that your perceptions will provide you with accurate information about people and situations.

SHARPENING YOUR PERCEPTIONS

t's quite easy to point fingers and make judgments about other people or to jump to hasty conclusions. Preventing this is another story. Recognizing where the perception process goes wrong is a step in the right direction, but consciously doing something about it is an even better step toward improving interpersonal communication skills/In this next section, we will address several ways in which people can work to increase the accuracy of their perceptions and decrease the chances for misinterpretation and misunderstanding. Mostly, we suggest that you simply take more time and ask more questions before coming to conclusions. The idea of taking more time may not be appealing initially, but these processes actually save time in the long run because less time must be spent clearing up problems that were the result of misperception.

Seek More Information

All too often people base perceptions on very little information. Perhaps they trust their instincts, or simply trust someone else's word. Could they increase their chances for forming a more accurate perception if they had a few more pieces of information? One way for seeking more information is known as **perception checking**. People need to recognize that there is room for error:

TABLE 3-1

THE MAIN DIFFERENCES BETWEEN FACTS AND INFERENCES

Facts	Inferences
1. May be made only after observation or experience	1. May be made at any time
2. Are limited to what has been observed	2. Extend beyond observation
3. Can be offered by the observer only	3. Can be offered by anyone
4. May refer to the past or to the present	4. May refer to any time—past, present, or future
5. Approach certainty	5. Represent varying degrees of probability

SOURCE: GAMBLE & GAMBLE (1987), P. 67

CONSIDERING ETHICS

Think of a situation in your own life in which you purposefully failed to check your perceptions. Perhaps you knew that if you sought more, or more accurate information, you would not get the answer that you wanted, so you avoided seeking further information. Would you have increased your chances for achieving interpersonal understanding had you taken the suggested steps? Test your understanding by sharing your example with a partner.

"I could be wrong in my impression of a person or a situation." Recall the notion of fact–inference confusion, discussed earlier. How well did you answer the questions in the detective exercise? If you could have asked questions as you took the quiz, you probably would have done much better and cleared up any potential confusion. Seeking further verification can save time in the long run instead of leading to conflict.

You may think it takes extra time to check perceptions, but have you ever wasted hours, perhaps even days with a situation that turned out to be the result of inaccurate perceptions or misinterpretation? Asking two or three questions now, versus no conversation for hours or days with someone that you care about—which makes more sense? Life is too short, time is too precious. Who cares which cliché you choose? Why waste time on unnecessary misunderstandings?

Perception checking can be summed up in some simple steps: describe the behavior you observe, look for possible interpretations, and if necessary, seek clarification. Let's take a look at each of these and apply them to a couple of sample situations:

- "When I try to talk to you about going away for the weekend, you change the subject" (behavior description). "I'm wondering if you just don't want to go at all" (first interpretation), "or have you already made plans and you were hoping to surprise me?" (second interpretation). "Can you give me a hint?" (request for clarification).

- "You've been awfully quiet since I told you the news about your father" (behavior description). "Do you want to be left alone" (first interpretation), "or are you waiting for me to offer some advice?" (second interpretation). "How can I be your friend and help you?" (request for clarification)

Another suggestion for seeking more information is to talk with the people about whom you are forming impressions. Check with the actual person(s) you are perceiving. If possible, hold your interpretation until you get a chance to talk. Have you ever had more information surface that changed your impression of a situation? Perhaps you had a misunderstanding with a boyfriend or girlfriend, a spat with your parents, or a disagreement with a teacher. After a simple clarifying chat with the other party, you may have been able to form a more accurate perception of the situation and thus avoid further unnecessary misinterpretations. By talking with another person, you get to know him or her. Even though your perception of that person may still be inaccurate, your chances of increasing the accuracy of your view are greater.

Interpretations are generally tentative and subject to change. People, too, should be allowed to change; allow your perceptions of people to change over time. Allowing people and perceptions to change can move you a step closer to increasing the accuracy of your perceptions.

Empathize With Others

"Walk a mile in my shoes," "Try wearing someone else's hat," "If the shoe was on the other foot," "Put yourself in my place"—all these phrases have to do with the notion of empathy.

Although *empathy* and *sympathy* may sound alike, the two words are very different. If I **sympathize** with you, I may feel *sorry for you* or your situation; but when I **empathize** with you, I try to feel *what* or *how* you feel. Think of a time when someone was confiding his or her feelings about a situation with you, and you responded, "I can relate," or "I've been there before," or "I know exactly how you're feeling." This doesn't necessarily mean that you agree with the other person's position or perspective, but shows that you are communicating that you understand his or her situation by feeling what her or she may be feeling.

Empathy takes place on a cognitive level (understanding) and an emotional level (feeling). By trying to experience the other person's perception, you are increasing your chances for improved interpersonal understanding. The concept of empathy is explored in greater detail in Chapter 8, on listening.

LOOKING BACK - LOOKING FORWARD

The previous two chapters have explored the historical foundations of the field of interpersonal communication and discussed how much critical thinking influences relationships. This chapter took a more specific look at how people relate to others on a one-to-one basis. The process of perception plays a key role in relationships with others. By understanding the perceptual process and making a concentrated effort toward increasing perceptual accuracy, people can increase their chances for more effective interpersonal relationships.

Next we examine why such topics as self-concept and self-talk play an important part in increasing interpersonal understanding. There is a strong connection between your perception of self and your perceptions of others.

REVIEW TERMS AND CONCEPTS

perception	interpretation	person perception
57	60	65
selection	first impressions	identity cues
58	62	65
selective attention	stereotyping	allness
58	64	67
organize	halo effect	blindering
59	64	67

fact-inference   sympathize
  confusion   71
    67   empathize
perception checking   71
  69

PUTTING THEORY INTO PRACTICE

FOR DISCUSSION:

1. Have you ever made an important decision when you were in an exceptionally good mood? What kind of decision was it? How might you have decided differently if you were in a bad mood as you made the decision? What advice could you give to a friend who is faced with a difficult decision if you know that his (or her) current mood might be so extreme that it could negatively influence his interpretation of a situation?

2. *Small-group discussion*: Do you personally hold any racial and/or ethnic stereotypes? What are they? Where did they come from? Have you ever seen any evidence to contradict them? How did such evidence make you feel? Can you look back in your life to an earlier age when you may have held a stereotype that you no longer hold?

SKILL BUILDERS:

1. *Role-play or discussion on impression formation*: In small groups or pairs, role-play a scenario where you might easily make a false first impression. Then replay the scene using what you have learned about perception and turn what might be a negative situation into a positive one.

2. *Role-play*: In pairs, role-play a situation in which one could both empathize and sympathize with another. Distinguish between the two by acting out each scene separately.

Answer Key: The Detective

1. ?	7. ?
2. ?	8. ?
3. F	9. ?
4. ?	10. ?
5. ?	11. ?
6. T	

FOR EXTENDED STUDY

Goldstein, E. Bruce. (1984). *Sensation and perception*, (2nd ed.). Belmont, CA: Wadsworth.

Goldstein discusses human perception in detail.

Kelly, George. (1963). *A theory of personality: The psychology of personal constructs.* New York: Norton.

Kelly expands on the notion of selective perception and how people base perceptions of particular situations on past encounters.

Harvey, J. H., & Weary, G. (1981). *Perspectives on attribution processes.* Dubuque, IA: Brown.

The authors explore important sources of misperception, among other related topics.

*No one can make
you feel inferior
without your
consent.*

ELEANOR ROOSEVELT

Self-Concept and Interpersonal Communication

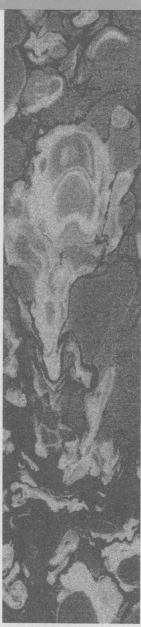

OBJECTIVES

After reading this chapter and taking part in class activities, you should be able to

- Describe the self-concept in detail.

- Explain how the self-concept develops over time.

- Explain how the self-concept affects all interpersonal communication.

- List and describe some methods for strengthening the self-concept.

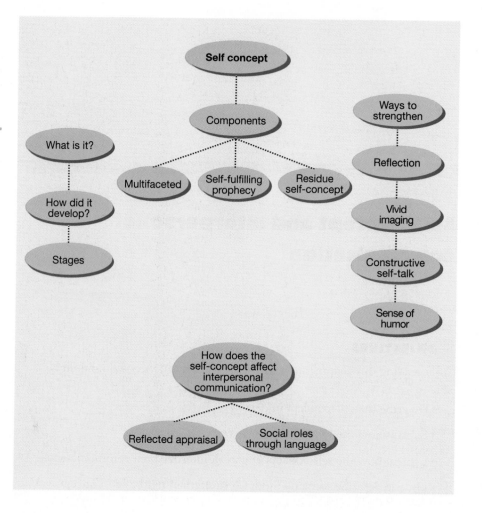

IN ONE SENSE, the longest and most important relationship you'll ever have is the one you have with yourself. At first glance, this statement may seem strange for a book about interpersonal communication. But if you chart all the conversations you've had with other people and all the ones you've had with yourself, you'll probably agree that you do more talking to yourself than anyone else. You've become adept at hiding these conversations by not moving your lips lest anyone think you need some serious counseling. Most people talk out loud when they're alone.

Consider also that the relationship you have with yourself is the only truly permanent one you have. People move away, get divorced, or decide to stop seeing each other. You can't do that with yourself. You can't say, "This is not working out. Why don't you move to another city for awhile and I'll stay here to see if we can get some space from each other." You're stuck with yourself for better or for worse.

So why is a healthy self-concept important both in communicating with yourself and other people? Someone with a strong self-concept is normally better equipped to deal with life's difficulties and challenges than someone with a low or negative self-image. Also, two people usually fare better with each other when both feel good about themselves.

In the last chapter, we discussed people's perceptions of the outside world. Now we look at the way people perceive themselves. In this chapter, we discuss how the self-concept develops and how it affects the relationships you have with yourself and others. We conclude by suggesting some ways to strengthen it.

Victory can be as much a product of confidence as it can of skill. Most winners strongly believe in themselves.

WHAT IS THE SELF-CONCEPT?

Your self-concept is a subjective collection of your attitudes and beliefs about yourself built up over all the years of your life. The word *subjective* is important because someone may be very gifted and highly intelligent, but may not think so. Such a perception can color how you perform in any number of activities. I (one of the authors) vividly recall an ex-airline stewardess named Sandi who approached me on the day she was supposed to give her first speech. She explained that she couldn't give the talk because she had a nervous stomach and had a hard time sleeping the night before. I asked when she wanted to give her speech, and she said, "I don't ever want to give a speech in this class. I hate giving speeches."

I said, "But you were a stewardess. You had to get up in front of plane loads of people and give talks about oxygen masks and safety procedures."

The central nervous system is far more complex than the most sophisticated computer.

She said, "No, I never did that. I used to hide behind the green curtain that separates first class from tourists and I would _read_ the instructions."

When I asked why, the student responded, "Because I think I'm dumb and ugly." Surprised, I probed further and found that she had accumulated this image over the years because she had a mother who put her down and a junior high school math teacher who suggested that she wasn't very bright in mathematics and needed remedial help. In reality, she was quite attractive and had a higher-than-average I.Q. but no one could convince her of that. Her self-concept was affecting her self-esteem.

The **self-concept** is a subjective collection of your attitudes and beliefs built up over the years; **self-esteem** is how well you like what you see. For example, Carlos may realize he's a very artistic person, but he would rather be a gifted athlete. He doesn't care for his superior ability to draw because his father and his older brother have told him often that "real men" don't do such things. The case of Carlos is different from that of the stewardess: she was mistaken about how attractive and smart she was. Carlos, in contrast, had an accurate impression of his talent, but wishes he were better at sports than drawing. Both didn't like what they perceived about themselves.

STAGES IN SELF-IMAGE DEVELOPEMENT

Carlos and Sandi formed their self-concepts over the years through feedback they received from others. In his classic book _The Human Use of Human Beings_, Norbert Wiener (1950) showed that the human central nervous system in some ways resembles a computer. Like a computer, the human mind absorbs information from outside itself and stores the information in the memory section of the brain. A computer contains only thousands of electrical circuits; but the brain houses billions of human circuits called _neurons_ with their dendrites, synapses, and cell bodies. This, in turn, makes you much more complicated than the most sophisticated word processor.

The feedback you receive from others is vital in shaping your self-concept. An infant in a crib picks up sound waves in the middle ear. From the middle ear, the messages speed along neuropathways to the brain and are then recorded in the memory section of the mind. Most babies receive positive messages of love, hugs, touching, and soothing sounds. But if infants get negative or mixed messages, they start developing a poor self-image.

A positive or negative self-image is not something you're born with. It starts forming from the messages others send you over a long time. Unlike a computer, such messages can't be erased by pushing a "delete" button in the brain.

The self-concept is sculpted by the relationships and messages you receive from significant others even before birth. A mother who loves her child in the womb transmits the beginnings of a positive self-image. One pioneer in early childhood development, Harry Stack Sullivan (1953), pointed out that at birth a child sees him- or herself only as an extension of the mother (or mother substitute). If the mother figure fulfills all the child's needs, the baby has what Sullivan describes as "a good experience." The child can also have "a wrong experience" and a "bad experience." In a wrong experience, the child has a need to be fed and the need is not met. This produces tension. In the "bad experience," the child has the need satisfied but still detects from the mother a feeling of tension. Sullivan believes that continued bad experiences can produce anxiety about one's personal sense of identity. In later years, people who have gone through a number of "bad" or "wrong" experiences may question who they really are or how they fit into the world.

Small children model the behavior of those they admire.

Dennis Smith and Keith Williamson (1977) expanded Sullivan's research and suggested that an infant goes through a four-stage process in developing personal identity and shaping the self-image. The four stages are personification, imitation, role-playing, and symbolic role-playing.

At around seven months, a child (let's say she's a girl) makes the distinction between herself and the mother figure. Up until that time she really doesn't know that the big toe she's chewing is her own. Sullivan emphasizes that the separation of self from the mother—**personification**—is a crucial stage in the development of a human being's self-identity.

In the **imitation** stage, a child mimics the actions of others, but without knowing why. A 2-year-old might put foam all over his face as he watches his

CONSIDERING CULTURE

CASTE SYSTEMS

Throughout history, humans have been put into caste systems. A prominent example is the Hindu caste system in India. The United States does not have a caste system as such, but throughout U. S. history millions have been placed in categories that have branded them inferior. Blacks, Chicanos, and Native Americans are some example of such branding. What impact do you think such branding has on the individuals who belong to racial classes? What are some consequences of making someone feel inferior?

father shave in the morning. He's not sure why he's doing it, but he likes the look on Dad.

During the third stage, a child goes beyond imitation to **role-playing**. Here the toddler has some idea that she's playing a role when she steps into her mother's high heels and carries her mother's purse. She's gone beyond imitation to a partial understanding of role-playing.

In the final stage, **symbolic role-playing**, the child (let's say he's a boy) can practice roles in his mind as a way to test how those roles operate in the real world. He doesn't have to go through the steps of playing the role but can imagine acting like his father in a social situation.

George Herbert Mead (1934) emphasizes the importance of roles in shaping the self-concept. If a 4-year-old girl, say, plays a nurse and gets feedback from one or both parents that such a role is good, she'll likely repeat the experience. But if she starts playing the role of truck driver and receives a message that "Girls don't drive trucks" she learns that she should find some other role.

THE RESIDUAL SELF-CONCEPT

William Wilmot (1987) uses the phrase "residual self" to describe the lingering self-image brought on by years of conditioning from significant other people such as parents and peers. Each person carries into any given encounter recollections about self-worth forged by past experiences. He or she measures these recollections against the situation of the moment. Wilmot (p. 5) describes the steps:

1. You enter a situation with a residual self-concept.

2. Your behavior is experienced by others; their interpretation of your behavior influences their behavior.

3. You interpret (attach meaning to) the others' behavior.

4. You view yourself as you think others do based on your meaning for their behavior.

5. When necessary, you reconcile the two views of yourself: (a) the residual self-concept and (b) the number 4 above. You arrive at a slightly revised self-concept which is a new residual of the two meanings. And the process continues.

At the age of 21, Louise may be the student body president of her college and can usually walk into a meeting with serenity and confidence. But somewhere in the back of her brain a small voice whispers that she's a loser, because her older brother kept using that word for three straight years when they were both preadolescents. A male at the meeting gives her the same look as her brother did when he was putting her down. This reaction, in turn, affects her fluency, and she uncharacteristically stumbles over some words.

The **residual self-concept** can often motivate people to **self-monitor**. According to Hamachek (1992), a high self-monitor is someone who can read a situation and project whatever image is required. Louise, for example, might stumble momentarily because one male in the audience reminds her of her brother. But if she is a high self-monitor, she can get right back into character as the smooth, poised president. She knows the role she is supposed to play and normally can play it when she needs to. She's good with other people because she can adapt quickly to the circumstances she finds herself in. A low self-monitor, in contrast, can play a limited range of roles. Such a person acts pretty much the same way in almost every circumstance and finds it hard to adapt to changing conditions.

A certain amount of self-monitoring can be helpful. If you know you need to present a certain professional image in a job interview, you dress, act, and talk in a way that will help you get the job. You don't want to act the same way during the interview as you would with a group of friends on Friday night after three beers. If you want to impress a potential romantic partner, you might want to think about the kind of person you want to project—at least in early encounters. A problem can occur when high monitors never step out of the roles they want to play, thereby robbing others of seeing them as they really are most of the time.

THE SELF-CONCEPT IS MULTIFACETED

The self-concept is a relatively stable set of perceptions you carry about yourself, and has a number of different facets. These include how you look, how bright you think you are, your kind of personality, your set of talents, and your perceived inferiorities or liabilities. Steve may think of himself as a skilled athlete but a poor math student. Marsha may believe she's a good writer but not a graceful dancer.

You can also divide your self-concept into categories such as social, moral, intellectual, and physical. Everyone has a social self and some definite ideas about how well he or she does in social situations. Frank may be quite confident walking into a room full of strangers, while Diane dreads the same experience. Diane may think of herself as highly moral, while Frank believes he's a reprobate. Frank thinks he's more intelligent than most, while Diane has her doubts about how smart she is. Diane likes the way her body looks, while Frank would like to trade his in on a new, huskier model.

Very few people like everything about themselves. Even those whom others might consider unusually bright or attractive may want to be even more bright and attractive than they are. Yet, some who might be considered "plain" or

THE EXPERIENCES OF SELF-ESTEEM

Here are some self-talk statements that can characterize high, medium, or low self-esteem.

HIGH SELF-ESTEEM

"I consider myself a valuable and important person. In many ways I'm at least as good as other people of my age and education. I'm regarded as someone worthy of respect and consideration by people who are important to me. I'm able to exert an influence on other people and events, partly because my views are sought and respected and partly because I'm able and willing to present those views. I can control my actions and have a good understanding of the kind of person I am. I enjoy new and challenging tasks and don't get upset if things don't go well at first. The work I do is generally of high quality, and I expect to do worthwhile and even great work in the future."

MEDIUM SELF-ESTEEM

"I like some things about myself but some things I don't like. I wish I could change my looks and would prefer to be more intelligent than I am. I'm OK around people I consider my peers or inferiors but get nervous around those who are smarter or more attractive than I am. I expect to do reasonably well in life and hope to get into a profession that will make me happy. Most people respect my views, but I really don't like it when people present ideas that are counter to mine."

LOW SELF-ESTEEM

"I don't think I'm very important or likeable, and I don't see much reason for anyone else to like me. I'm not sure about my ideas and abilities and think that other people's ideas are better than mine. Other people don't pay much attention to me, and given how I feel about myself, I don't blame them. I prefer to stay on safe ground. I don't expect much from myself in the future. I don't have much control over myself, and expect that things are going to get worse rather than better."

Now check your own level of self-esteem on the following scale. How much do you think your level affects your personal happiness and your relations with other?

10	High
9	
8	
7	
6	
5	Medium
4	
3	
2	
1	
0	Low

Most people check in around 5 on a scale of 1 to 10. Parts of them they like, parts they'd like to change. A self-score of 7 or 8 is a very strong self-concept, and people who fit into this category are usually confident and successful.

One of life's great satisfactions is achieving a goal that is important to us.

who have an average I.Q. are quite satisfied with the way they are. They don't have any desire to change.

Some people have strong self-concepts. They like the way they are. Although they recognize some liabilities, they don't dwell on them. They focus on their strengths. At the other end of the spectrum are people who like very little about themselves. They dwell on their own flaws and constantly "see their glass" as half empty rather than half full. If friends compliment them, they don't believe the compliment. They reason that no one can really mean such positive comments.

SELF-CONCEPT AND THE SELF-FULFILLING PROPHECY

Self-perception often plays a strong role in how successful people are. Rosenthal and Jacobson (1968) describe the "**self-fulfilling prophecy**"—the notion that how you think about yourself often shapes how you'll act in certain situations. Scott is a college graduate who enters an interview with the conviction that the interviewer won't like him because he believes he can't express himself clearly. So he stumbles over his words—and then the prospective employer *does* think of him as inarticulate. His view of himself helped determine his performance. Sharon, in contrast, may be nervous about her interview but if she consistently maintains a strong self-image, she'll play down her fears and nervousness and focus on her strengths.

Focusing is crucial in maintaining a healthy self-concept. Suppose both Scott and Sharon fear they'll go blank when the interviewer asks a question. Scott suddenly forgets what he was going to say and immediately focuses on the fact that he's forgotten his material and that the interviewer is now staring at him. He concentrates on the panic and the feeling of helplessness. Sharon, however, has the same experience. She's forgotten her material, but she immediately thinks, "Don't telegraph this message to the interviewer. Play it cool and get back to what you were talking about." Scott rivets his mind on the panicky realization that he's looking embarrassed. Sharon does the same briefly, but she concentrates on the material and the interviewer rather than her embarrassment.

Even though people can think faster than they can speak, the human mind can focus on only one thought at any given instant. Steve thinks, "I'm doomed"; Sharon thinks, "OK, I've forgotten, but I'll get back on track. The interviewer won't know the difference if I stay calm and remember where I was."

THE SELF-CONCEPT AND COMMUNICATION WITH OTHERS

How you view yourself has a lot to do with how you relate to others. According to Missildine (1963), the "inner child of the past" still lingers in the memory of the adult and continues to influence the adult's behavior. In one sense, this "child" joins every interpersonal encounter to one degree or another. Missildine (p. 54) actually claims that there are four people in the marriage bed:

> Each of the four has a distinctive and individual feeling about being there. In this way, the "inner child of the past" of both man and wife plays an important part in their sexual relationship. In most instances where there is embarrassment, shame, humiliation, resentment, guilt or sexual exploitation, there is a "child of the past" dominating the sexual scene.

Generally, people who like themselves tend to like others and feel confident around them. Those who don't care much for themselves often don't like others either. People generally feel most loving toward others when they feel good about themselves. If Marcel likes the way he looks and is comfortable about his personality, he can forget about himself and focus on somebody else. But if he dwells on his negative traits, he is not nearly as likely to reach out to others. He may spend hours worrying about whether his girlfriend or his buddies really like him.

REFLECTED APPRAISAL

Charles Cooley (1912) first coined the term **"reflected appraisal"**—a concept that means people define themselves in terms of what others have said about them. Because people are used to doing so, it's difficult to critically analyze the validity of what others say. Most children are true believers in what their parents tell them and rarely doubt their word in the early years. This is a hard habit to break. Even adults tend to sculpt their self-concepts by what others say about them. If Jane is in a relationship with Mark, she's very affected by what Mark says about her good and bad points. Let a good friend point out a flaw in your character and you will most likely feel stung. Let a romantic partner express deep love, and you may become ecstatic.

At some point, everyone thinks about the roles and images other people give him or her and decide that the images are either accurate or inaccurate. The seventh-grader whose parents tell him that he is a "klutz" may make the school basketball team and decide his parents were wrong. The college student who has heard from her sister that she is unattractive may hear comments from suitors that are just the opposite and conclude that she *is* attractive.

RAISING SELF-ESTEEM THROUGH SUPPORTIVE LANGUAGE

Have you noticed that other people's long-term attractiveness comes as much or more from personality and warmth than it does from physical looks? You usually make a judgment about someone's attractiveness in the first half minute or so based on physical looks, but that perception changes depending on how the person relates to you. If someone is friendly and outgoing and builds you up, his or her attractiveness increases. If physically handsome people, however, project an image of aloofness, indifference, or hostility, their attractiveness often decreases. You usually find attractive others who simply *like* you. This in turn strengthens your self-esteem. You tend to avoid those who are either indifferent to you or put you down.

> *The greater part of our happiness or misery depends on our dispositions and not on our circumstances.*
>
> MARTHA WASHINGTON

COMMUNICATING SKILLFULLY

Most couples who enjoy a healthy relationship find great satisfaction in the other, but each is also able to feel comfortable alone. Think about two people you know who have an unusually strong union. Now consider if they fit the concept just stated. On reflection, have they achieved a good balance between togetherness and separateness?

CONSIDERING CRITICAL THINKING

HOW VALID IS CRITICISM?

Think back on two of the unkindest comments anybody ever made about you. When you consider them in hindsight, were they true, false, or exaggerated? Did you believe them, or did you carefully consider whether they were valid? If you did believe them completely, how did they affect you? For example, if someone called you "really stupid" in the fifth grade, did the comment have an impact on your schoolwork? For the next week, monitor every comment someone makes about you. Consider whether there is evidence to back the claim the person is making about you. For example, if a roommate says, "You're lazy," is the statement true, false, or exaggerated? What evidence is there to support any of the three possibilities?

Drawing by
Modell; © 1986
The New Yorker
Magazine, Inc.

"His brother, on the other hand, didn't have a serious bone in his body."

Martin has a poor self-image. He's met George, a man he wants to impress. As he gets to know George, he reveals more about himself. Sometimes Martin talks about his accomplishments. At other times, he reveals some of his failures. Martin makes his successes sound greater than they were: "I scored 24 points a game in high school basketball" (he actually averaged 12 points a game). He also plays down his negative traits: "The reason I'm depressed at times is because my father never brought me gifts when he came back from a trip. I've always resented that." (His dad regularly returned with gifts for all his children.) How do you think Martin's distortions will affect his relationship with George over the long run? Why is it important to tell the truth during the development of a relationship?

WAYS OF STRENGTHENING THE SELF-CONCEPT

It took years to store the data that forms a self-concept, and it takes a long time to change for the better, too. Unlike working with a computer, people can't push a "delete" button in their central nervous systems and wipe out all past memories. Recall the scale that measures self-image: 10 indicates a very positive image, and 1 is very low. If you had to pick a number that reflects your own self-image, what would it be? A 4, a 7, an 8? And if you want to improve your self-image, how can you do it? Here are some techniques others have used to strengthen their self-concepts:

1. *Reflection.* Take five to ten minutes daily to sit quietly and dwell on your positive traits; for example, intelligence, ability to get along with others, and athletic skills. Focus on your successes in the areas you've decided to think about. Recall that you were able to succeed despite some initial fears. Apply that same kind of thinking to any upcoming event you find challenging. Tell yourself you plan to face any difficulties and overcome them.

2. *Vivid imagery.* Use your imagination to see a scene before it occurs. Such a scene might include a conversation with a difficult co-worker, a talk with a good friend who is going through a tough time, or a dreaded encounter with a parent. Imagine the scene vividly and rehearse what you plan to say. Anticipate the very worst that could happen, and then imagine how you would deal with the worst-case scenario. Then imagine how you want the scene to turn out.

Feedback we receive from others shapes our self-concept, no matter what our age.

3. *Constructive self-talk.* Words shape your perceptions and thinking. Examine your use of words in reference to yourself. If you wrote down five adjectives to describe yourself, how many would be positive and how many negative? It would be unrealistic to use nothing but positive language in describing yourself, but do try to make the ratio 4 to 1 in favor of positive over negative. For example, as you anticipate a difficult conversation with someone, tell yourself, "I'm calm, prepared, poised, smart, and a little nervous."

4. *Keep a sense of humor about yourself.* If you take yourself too seriously, you're bound to find it hard to live up to your expectations. Humor has the double advantage of relieving tension and raising self-esteem. One psychiatrist has a card taped to his bathroom mirror that reads, "This person is not to be taken seriously." Good advice.

THE POWER OF HABIT

The four suggestions just described work best when they're applied together and become habits. Horace Mann has described a habit as a series of threads that, tied together, form a cable that is difficult to break. Mann's principle applies to both bad and good habits. If Jane has been in the habit of exercising daily, it's fairly easy for her to put on jogging shoes and go out and run, even if it's raining. But if she hasn't exercised, it's hard to take the first steps. The beginning stages of changing a habit are the toughest. If John has been eating junk food, his body at first rebels when his mind tells him he needs to eat more vegetables, fruit, and fish.

THE IMPORTANCE OF ATTITUDES ABOUT SELF

The longer I live, the more I realize the impact of attitude on life. Attitude, to me, is more important than facts. It is more important than the past, than education, than money, than circumstances, than failure, than successes, than what other people think or say or do. It is more important than appearance, giftedness or skill. It will make or break a company...a church ...a home. The remarkable thing is we have a choice every day regarding the attitude we will embrace for that day. We cannot change our past...we cannot change the fact that people will act in a certain way. We cannot change the inevitable. The only thing we can do is play on the one string we have and that is our attitude. I am convinced that life is 10% what happens to me and 90% how I react to it. And so it is with you...we are in charge of our attitudes.

CHARLES SWINDOLL

Reflection, vivid guided imagery, positive self-talk, and a sense of humor reinforce each other. Reflection can help you focus and control your thoughts. Vivid guided imagery can help you rehearse difficult situations in advance. You can play out scenarios before they happen and rehearse what you want to do. Constructive self-talk can help you reframe the words you use. Strong, reality-based language can replace negative words. A sense of humor can lighten even the most difficult circumstances.

Practicing these steps on a regular basis takes some discipline, but the rewards are worth the effort. The word *discipline* is not popular. It may conjure up visions of children being punished or military recruits going through boot camp. But *discipline* comes from the Latin and means "learning." In *The Road Less Traveled* (1978), Scott Peck says, "Without discipline we can solve nothing. With only some discipline we can solve only some problems. With total discipline we can solve all probems" (pp. 15–16). People who accomplish important things in life usually do so because they're mentally disciplined enough to take the steps to change when they need to. This is especially important in resculpting the self-concept. Because messages of self-worth have taken so long to build up, it takes a strong dose of mental discipline, especially at the beginning, to change a sagging self-esteem into one that is strong and can carry someone through difficult situations.

Discipline requires a firm resolution to change, followed by the steps necessary to bring about the desired change. People who succeed have a specific plan and then follow it. For example, if you want to raise your grade-point average (GPA) from a 3.1 to a 3.3, you might plant in your mind a firm resolution to change. Then do whatever it takes to reach your goal. List the specific steps needed to bring your plan. If you conclude that the major reason for failing to achieve the desired grade point is procrastination, then examine why that happens. You may discover that you've been in the habit of putting things off until the night before a paper is due. Or you might have set aside a certain amount of time to study but almost always find that you waste half an hour before you get going.

A change of habit works best when you focus on the benefits of the change you want to make. If a student has vowed to earn at least a 3.3 GPA the current term, she imagines the benefits she'll gain as a result. Such benefits could include a better chance of getting into the graduate school of her choice plus the personal satisfaction of knowing she has done something difficult and succeeded. When she gets discouraged, she recalls that image and plunges ahead.

Changing from a less desirable to a better habit is especially difficult at first. For example, if you've converted from a typewriter to a word processor, you know that the learning process can be frustrating. Let's say you're used to typing papers on a typewriter. A friend tells you about the advantages of a word processor. You determine you're going to learn, and start writing your next term paper on a computer. You start reading the owner's manual, type a few keys, and ask friends for advice. You're frustrated for the first week and tell yourself that you can type the paper twice as fast as you can get it done on the word processor. Then you recall that learning anything new often takes longer at first, but over the long run will save you a lot of time. The same applies to practicing the techniques described earlier for strengthening your self-concept. In turn, a healthier self-concept can make you feel better about yourself and should enhance your interpersonal relationships.

LOOKING BACK - LOOKING FORWARD

The self-concept is the collection of attitudes built up over the years. Each person's sense of self develops over a period of years through feedback from significant people. Their self-concepts can influence the relationships people have with others: Four specific methods for strengthening the self-concept are (1) reflection, (2) vivid imagery, (3) constructive self-talk, and (4) a sense of humor. In Chapter 5, we look at ways that self-disclosure and rhetorical sensitivity can affect relationships with others.

REVIEW TERMS AND CONCEPTS

self-concept 78	role-playing 80	self-fulfilling prophecy 83
self-esteem 78	symbolic role-playing 80	reflected appraisal 85
personification 79	residual self-concept 81	
imitation 79	self-monitor 81	

PUTTING THEORY INTO PRACTICE

FOR DISCUSSION:

1. Do theorists put too much emphasis on the way early childhood shapes adult experiences? Is it too easy to blame adult behavior on upbringing and therefore to not take as much responsibility as one should?

2. What is the place of willpower in changing a negative or weak self-image? If you decide to improve your self-concept, why can't you simply make the decision and do it?

3. Do humans tend to focus more on criticism than on praise? If you receive ten compliments and one put-down, do you think much more about the put-down than the compliments? Why or why not?

SKILL BUILDERS:

1. Get together in small groups, and discuss the place of feedback from grade school peers on your self-concept. Without feeling obligated to "reveal all," share with other members of your group how you felt when you were either criticized or praised. Then talk about what you have done to deal with some of this early feedback from peers.

2. Write down five adjectives that you believe describe you right now. How many are positive, and how many are negative? Then write down what you plan to do to get a higher ratio of positive to negative labels.

3. Take some time out in class to try the following exercise: Begin by picking some difficult but achievable challenge you face next week. Such challenges could include a tough exam, a meeting with a difficult person, or a speech you have to give in class. Then for ten minutes do the following: Start by focusing on your strengths ("I am bright, confident, good with people," and so on). Spend about four minutes concentrating on these strengths. Don't let any negative thoughts intrude. Now imagine the challenging situation in advance. See the place, and/or the people involved. Rehearse how you're going to deal with the difficulties that will probably occur. Imagine the worst that could happen. How would you deal with the worst? Now imagine the best that could happen. How will you deal with that possibility? Now see yourself in control. Finally, repeat to yourself some positive phrases such as "I'm confident, in control, and able to handle this situation."

FOR EXTENDED STUDY

Missildine, W. (1963). *Your inner child of the past.* New York: Simon & Schuster.

This book provides some helpful insights about how and why your childhood still affects the way you feel about yourself as an adult. The author goes on to explain how the child you were can sometimes have profound impact on the people you relate to as adults.

Peck, S. (1978). *The road less traveled.* New York: Simon & Schuster.

This book is not for everyone, but thousands have found it very helpful in solving problems. Dr. Peck shows how facing problems and addressing them with discipline can bring far more satisfaction in the long run than avoiding them. He has excellent sections on love and spiritual development.

Siegel, B. (1986). *Love, medicine and miracles.* New York: Harper & Row.

Dr. Siegel is a physician who discusses the importance of attitudes in patients who are struggling with physical illness. He provides some specific methods for getting the mind to help influence how the body feels.

Letting people in is largely a matter of not expending energy to keep them out.

HUGH PRATHER

Developing Relationships: Small-Talk, Self-Disclosure, Rhetorical Sensitivity, and Confirmation

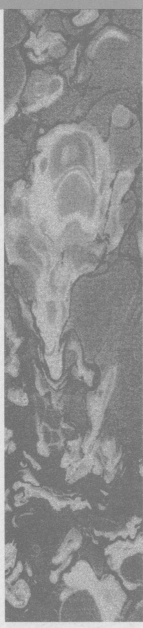

OBJECTIVES

After reading this chapter and taking part in class activities, you should be able to

- Explain the importance of "small talk" as a conversational skill in initial encounters.

- Define self-disclosure, and explain the factors influencing its use in interpersonal relationships.

- Explain the Johari Window model and define each of the four windows.

- Describe, from the social penetration perspective, the roles played by breadth and depth of information in developing relationships.

- Describe the role of rhetorical sensitivity as a behavioral choice in relational development.

- Define the concepts of confirming and disconfirming communication and their roles in relational development.

Cognitive Map 5

Developing interpersonal relationships

Conversational skills in initial encounters
1. First moves
2. Small talk

Uncertainty reduction and interpersonal style

What is self-disclosure

Self-disclosure in relationships

Self-disclosure and self-knowledge

Social penetration theory

Why not self-disclosure?

Rhetorical sensitivity
a. Noble self
b. Rhetorical reflectors
c. Rhetorical sensitivities

Social confirmation
Disconfirming responses
Confirming responses

THINK ABOUT A "GOOD" RELATIONSHIP you have developed. Where did you meet the person? How were you introduced? Who spoke first? What was your first impression of the person? Was she or he warm and friendly, or uncomfortable and maybe even disinterested? How did the other see you? How did the relationship continue from the first encounter? Did you work at the same place or have a class together? What did you have in common? How did you know? Were you "fast friends" from the beginning, or did you think you had little in common with him or her? Can you remember a time with the person in which you talked and exchanged dreams, goals, ideas, or information with the person freely and comfortably? If so, did it strengthen the relationship or at least make it better defined? As we discuss material on self-disclosure, rhetorical sensitivity, and confirmation, think through the impact of each on your relationships.

In this chapter, we discuss the concept of conversational skills and interpersonal style in developing relationships. To be effective interpersonally, people must consider who they are, what roles they play, and what expectations they hold for relationships—then they select the combination of communication skills (strategies) that works for them. As authors, we cannot prescribe what is good for you. There is no magic prescription (a pill to take) or "cook book" for being an ideal interpersonal communicator. Instead, we'll present some alternative strategies to consider. Your goal is to think critically and select the ideas you want to test—to add those that work well for you to your interpersonal style ("toolbox") of communication.

We've only just begun.

CONVERSATIONAL SKILLS IN INITIAL ENCOUNTERS

How do relationships begin? We asked you in the beginning of this chapter to recall how one of your relationships began. In Chapter 1, we discussed the developmental perspective of interpersonal communication and noted that initial contact with others is impersonal rather than personal, by its very nature. Did the relationship we asked you to recall start off impersonal? If it did, that was typical communicative behavior for this stage. During the first few moments of interaction with the new person, you were assessing him or her on the basis of physical appearance and her or his first comments. If these first few moments were satisfactory, you may have begun to trade small talk or what Powell calls "phatic communion."

First Moves

For better or for worse, when someone meets someone else for the first time, both develop impressions of each other that influence the chances this relationship has for growing—or not. As noted in the chapter on perception, much of the information people receive comes through nonverbal cues such as physical characteristics, clothing, and posture, among others. Often, if this stage in the relationship is successful, the pair moves to the next stage through conversation.

In the conversation, because neither person knows much about the other, both rely on cultural norms and sociological data and have what DeFleur and his associates (1993) calls **scripted** conversations. Like a film or play script, they tend to recite lines heard in other initial conversations: "Hello, how are you?" "Fine" Even if the respondent is *not* fine, the scripted and expected answer is "Fine." Through the script, both are saying, "I see you and recognize you as another person." To a degree, the words are unimportant—the attitude and acknowledgment of each other's presence carries the effect. In conversations with new acquaintances, people generally talk about superficial information such as the weather, sports, or some factual, nonopinionated material. Another term for this kind of conversation is **small talk**.

Small Talk

Many people claim to dislike small talk and see it as trivial or a waste of time. However, small talk is an important interpersonal skill. The fact is, interpersonal relationships develop by moving through this phase of small talk. Small talk is a social skill that allows for the time to get to know another person by talking about nonthreatening, safe subjects. If you have difficulty maintaining small talk, it is helpful to remember some of the following:

1. Remember the other person's name. Knowing, using, and remembering a person's name, tells that person that he or she matters to you. You like it when people remember your name. When someone tells you his or her name, listen closely and perhaps even have him or her spell it out. Rehearse it a few times in your mind, and associate it with something familiar. In conversation, use the other person's name whenever possible.

2. To effectively initiate a conversation, it's important to make eye contact. Eye contact lets the other person know you are interested in him or her, it's an important skill in small talk. However, you don't want the eye contact to be perceived as a stare. Staring not only is impolite but also can be perceived as threatening. Also, some cultures, such as Hispanics and Japanese, are taught,

Small talk is an important but often devalued interpersonal skill. Without small talk, relationships have difficulty developing.

as a sign of respect, not to look someone directly in the eyes. During communication, members of these cultures tend to concentrate on the lower part of the face.

3. Try to be open and immediate in your nonverbal communication. In Chapter 7 we discuss nonverbal communication in detail. Here we want to point out that in initial encounters people want to convey interest and liking through both verbal and nonverbal messages. To do so, it is helpful to use such nonverbal cues as smiling, head nodding, leaning forward, and using open body positions. These cues communicate not only physical closeness but also psychological closeness.

4. Try to get the other person to talk about him- or herself. People tend to like others who show interest. Ask safe questions such as "Where are you from?" and follow up on them with others. Follow-up questions show you have been listening and helps you avoid random topic switching.

5. A general rule of small talk is that it should stay light and positive. Delving into personal topics or disclosing very personal information may actually threaten the other person. Keep the conversation positive by avoiding criticisms and complaints, no matter how minor. If you discuss negative perceptions about others, or the awful traffic, or how over-worked you are, you may be perceived as someone with a negative attitude.

Practicing small-talk skills is important and helpful for initiating and developing relationships. If the small talk is unsuccessful, you will have difficulty developing relationships any further. If, however, the small talk is successful and you want the relationship to develop more interpersonally, you need to reduce uncertainty about each other.

UNCERTAINTY REDUCTION AND INTERPERSONAL STYLE

Remember that Chapter 1 discussed how all people develop a certain interpersonal style. Your personality, culture, and society all affect who you are and how you communicate. We also mentioned that the degree of interpersonalness in relationships develops over time, through the process of uncertainty reduction. An important element of your communication style is what strategies you use to develop your interpersonal relationships. Your relationships grow more interpersonal as you know more psychological information about another person and you can predict his or her communication responses and explain his or her behaviors. Part of your interpersonal style, then, has to do with gathering information about others. Two particular approaches useful in developing relationships are self-disclosure and rhetorical sensitivity.

People respond to people who respond.

ANONYMOUS

SELF-DISCLOSURE

Theory and research shows that **self-disclosure** is one of the most effective strategies for learning about another person. When you're willing to share personal information about yourself with others, it's common for others to share with you. In other words, self-disclosure is usually **reciprocal**. If I want to learn more about you, then I have to be willing to share parts of my personal self with you. Culbert (1967) defines self-disclosure as "an individual's explicitly communicating to one or more persons information that he believes these others would be unlikely to acquire unless he himself discloses [shares] it." Self-disclosure is not storytelling or sharing secrets, but rather is revealing how you are reacting to the present situation and giving any information about the past that is *relevant* to the other person's understanding of your current reactions. Self-disclosing in relationships was championed by humanistic psychologist Carl Rogers, who stressed the importance of understanding self and others through self-disclosure, feedback, and sensitivity to the disclosures made by others. Rogers believed that weak relationships are characterized by inhibited self-disclosure.

Self-disclosure theory suggests that if you want to know something about someone, rather than ask him or her a question, you should volunteer some information about yourself. Your listener will respond with information about him- or herself. If you make a self-descriptive statement such as "I'm Sarah O'Brien and I'm majoring in communication studies at Boston College," you have engaged in a level of self-disclosure. According to psychologist Sydney Jourard, you could expect a statement like the one just made to be reciprocated by your listener. However, self-disclosure occurs at different levels of personalness, so generally speaking, disclosure is reciprocated at the levels at which it is initiated. In his book *The Transparent Self* (1971), Jourard suggests that in ideal interpersonal relationships people allow others to experience them fully and are open to experiencing others fully. Jourard and others have done extensive research on self-disclosure, and Stephen Littlejohn (1992) notes several of their research findings:

1. Disclosure increases with increased relational intimacy.

2. When rewarded, disclosure increases.

3. Disclosure increases the need to reduce uncertainty in a relationship.

4. Disclosure tends to be reciprocal.

5. Women tend to disclose more than men.

6. Women disclose more with people they like; men disclose more with people they trust.

7. Disclosure is regulated by norms of appropriateness.

8. Attraction is related to positive disclosures but not to negative disclosure.

9. Positive disclosure is more likely in nonintimate or moderately intimate relationships.

10. Negative disclosure occurs with greater frequency in highly intimate settings than in less intimate ones.

As these findings indicate, many variables influence disclosure. In relationships, people need to be conscious of the impact and appropriateness of self-disclosures. Let's turn to these factors now.

Self-Disclosure in Relationships

Although self-disclosure theory represents a normative theory—that is, the theory tells us how we *ought* to communicate—some contingencies still apply. Appropriate self-disclosure

1. Is not random, but is ongoing

2. Is reciprocated

3. Concerns what is going on between and in people at the present

4. Creates a chance for improving the relationship

5. Takes account of the effect it will have on the other person

*How can I know
what I think until I
hear what I say?*

E. M. FORSTER

Although you build relationships by sharing information with others through disclosure, at times you don't want to share with others. From the chapter on perception, recall that people base many perceptions on past experience. If experience suggests that you not trust someone, then you probably will not self-disclose. Trust is important because self-disclosures have an impact on the listener and consequences for discloser. There is always an element of risk. Think of times you've chosen not to reveal information about yourself to another person. What kept you from choosing to share the information?

SELF-DISCLOSURE AND SELF-KNOWLEDGE

To communicate with someone, you must be aware of your own motivations. Self-knowledge or self-awareness is helpful in self-disclosure because what you choose to share with others is your true understanding of self. Self-knowledge is the content of self-disclosure. To increase your self-awareness, it may help to look at the models found in Figure 5.1 (Luft, 1970).

This model is named the **Johari Window** after its originators, Joseph Luft and Harry Ingram. The model is an attempt to illustrate there are certain things you (or anyone) know about yourself and other things you don't know. Also, there are things others know about you and things they don't know. In the beginning of a relationship, when you don't know much about the other person and vice versa, the model looks as it does in Figure 5.1(a). After the development of a close relationship, the model might look more as it does in Figure 5.1(b). There are exceptions to this because you're not equally open with all people, even though you may have a long-term relationship. For example, you might be much more open with a close personal friend than with a parent, even though you presumably have known your parent all your life. In essence, you tend to disclose different kinds of information in different relationships. Generally speaking, however, the more closed or defensive you tend to be, the more you keep information from others and therefore have a larger hidden or closed area. The more you are open to the feedback of others, and the more comfortable you are in letting others know you, the larger the free or open window is.

Self-disclosure is one primary system for enabling people to get to know each other. Still, as Littlejohn (1992) suggests, some people tend to disclose more than others (women more than men, although that is not true in all cases) and *what* is disclosed is also very important. "What is disclosed" is at the core of Altman and Taylor's "social penetration theory" and John Powell's "five levels of communication."

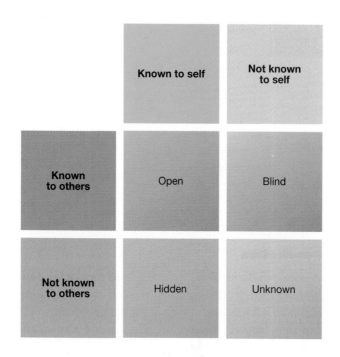

(a)

FIGURE 5.1

The Johari Window
(a) The Johari Window
(b) Early stages in a relation-
   ship
(c) A developed interpersonal
   relationship

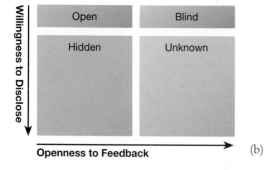

(b)

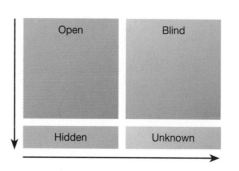

(c)

COMMUNICATING SKILLFULLY

JOHARI WINDOW EXERCISE

Draw a Johari Window for four different relationships in your life. The size of each window is up to you but should be based on how willing you are to let the other person know you and how open you are to feedback on how he or she sees you. Decide if you're satisfied with this degree of openness. In small groups, share these windows and—with out necessarily sharing the name of the person your drawings represent—explain your level of satisfaction and what you could do to change it if you were not satisfied.

CONSIDERING ETHICS

Form small groups (four to five students) in the class. Discuss the following questions:

1. How can we be honest without being potentially hurtful?

2. When does saying nothing actually imply something?

3. What role do "white lies" and equivocation (talking around an issue) play in self-disclosure?

4. When asked a direct question, are we obliged to answer honestly? Is lying or deceit ever ethically defensible when it comes to self-disclosure? *Develop a set of ethical guidelines for self-disclosure, and share them with the rest of the class. With the whole class, seek to reach consensus about these ethical guidelines. Is it difficult or easy to do so? Why?*

In order to see, I have to be willing to be seen.

ANONYMOUS

Social Penetration

Irwin Altman and Dalmas Taylor (1973) have proposed the **social penetration** theory, establishing a model (Figure 5.2) in which communication is rapid and broad at superficial levels of information, but gets increasingly slower and more limited in areas such as emotions and self-esteem. Altman and Taylor believe that disclosure is a gradual, developmental process.

Perhaps the easiest way to understand this model is to visualize it as a dartboard. The concentric circles represent the various layers of the personality. The outermost ring is superficial but has many items, usually factual in nature. A statement such as "I'm John, and I play the banjo" would be at this level. Moving toward deeper layers of personality, the items become fewer but represent more personal ideas, beliefs, or emotions. If you talk about your religion or feelings, you are approaching these inner rings. The innermost circle, or

FIGURE 5.2

Social Penetration Model
SOURCE: ALTMAN & TAYLOR (1973), P. 304.

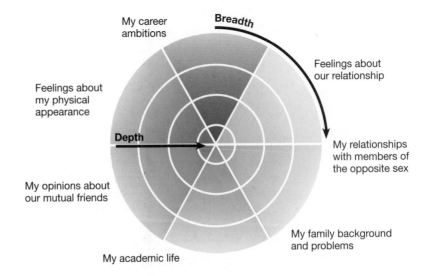

CONSIDER THIS CONNECTION

An interesting note here is that the depth dimension of personality has some similar connections to E. T. Hall's proxemic (personal space) theory, which you'll encounter in

Chapter 7. Hall claims people's use of space in interpersonal relationships radiates outward in concentric circles. He suggests that we attempt to protect our vulnerability by establishing ever-widening boundaries or layers. Hall argues that

interactions are arranged along boundaries of intimate (closest space), acquaintance, social, and public. These categories correspond to the amount and quality of disclosure in Altman and Taylor's core through superficial levels (see Figure 5.3).

bull's-eye, symbolizes the "fundamental, core characteristics of personality that relate to and influence peripheral items" (Altman & Taylor, 1973). This intimate core is composed of a few items such as a person's self-concept and basic values.

Besides the concentric circles, a dartboard is also divided into triangular sections. These triangular divisions are the substantive areas of personality that Altman and Taylor label *categories*. According to their model, personality is organized in two ways: the depth dimension ranges from superficial to intimate layers, and the breadth dimension groups similar personality items into a variety of categories. In other words, people divide their interests into major topics such as family, work, hobbies, and so on.

Altman and Taylor (1973) propose that "social interaction is generally predicted to proceed only gradually and systematically from superficial to intimate

FIGURE 5.3

Concentric illustrations of Hall's model and Altman & Taylor's

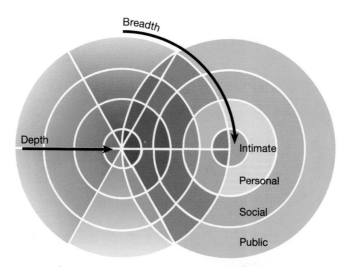

Social penetration model   Hall's proxemic zones

topics." When you first meet someone, conversation does not begin with fundamental, personal topics but with biographical facts such as your name, and so on. If a relationship continues to develop, topics become more intimate. A continuous relationship provokes exploration of different categories to broaden the areas of conversation and explore similar interests. According to Altman and Taylor, in a casual relationship you may share much breadth of information with the other person, but not much depth. In an intimate relationship, you share both breadth and depth of information. This depth factor represents the greater "interpersonalness" that typifies the developmental view of interpersonal communication.

This developmental hierarchy is also explored by John Powell (1969), who argues that communication takes place on five levels (see Figure 5.4).

Powell labels the first or outer level as "cliché" conversation, in which interactions are limited to biographical detail and polite compliments. The second level is limited to factual reporting of impersonal information. The third level is exploratory in nature. Here, you reveal more personal information and cautiously test your listener's receptiveness. Powell calls the fourth level "emotional communication," in which people exchange uniquely personal feelings. The innermost or core level Powell calls "**peak communication**." Powell believes people accomplish nearly complete disclosure and empathy at the peak level. Although this depth of communication may exist between close friends or relatives, its level of mutuality is embodied in the ideal marriage. At this peak level of communication, self-disclosure touches the core of personality—it is both deep and broad, intimate and mutual. The first two levels of Powell's model typify interactional, impersonal interaction, while the later three stages of disclosure represent "transactional" communication, in which people share uniquely personal feelings and experiences. Powell believes that what level you use in communication with others is situational and momentary—that is, in conversation you move from level to level depending on a number of factors such as the subject being discussed, emotional climate, with whom you are speaking, and so on. At one moment you may be speaking

FIGURE 5.4

Powell's Five Levels of Communication

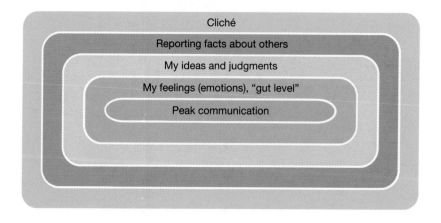

generally and using clichés; at another moment, you may be sharing your emotions.

Thus several key theorists have suggested a developmental view of self-disclosure and interpersonalness. However, as mentioned earlier in the chapter, self-disclosure theory grew out of humanistic psychology and much of the research was based on people who were seeking some form of psychotherapy. From a psychotherapeutic viewpoint, self-disclosure helps people accept themselves and be open to others. Many theorists in communications have rejected self-disclosure as necessary to develop interpersonalness in relationships, and we turn to them now.

Why *Not* Self-Disclose?

In his book *Crazy Talk, Stupid Talk* (1976), Neil Postman warns *against* "saying what's on your mind" and "expressing your feelings honestly." Woody Hays, a famous former football coach at the Ohio State University used to like to say, "When you pass the football, three things can happen and two of them are bad!" Similarly, many people in the field of interpersonal communication believe that when you self-disclose, several things can happen, and many of them are bad. Can you think of some negative outcomes of self-disclosure?

In *Why Am I Afraid To Tell You Who I Am?* (1969), Powell discusses both our rational and irrational fears of self-disclosure. Self-disclosure is not a universal value and does not represent an interpersonal communication panacea. Because self-disclosure is not always appropriate, people may turn to another interpersonal style for developing interpersonal relationships, called "rhetorical sensitivity."

RHETORICAL SENSITIVITY

An alternative concept to that of self-disclosure in developing relationships and gaining knowledge of other people is "rhetorical sensitivity." This idea grew out of the work of Roderick Hart and Don Burks (1972) and was a critique of self-disclosure theory. Self-disclosure is uncomfortable for many, and perhaps more importantly as Arthur Bochner (1984, p. 608) has said, "...There is no firm empirical basis for endorsing unconditional openness. A critical examination of the evidence suggests at most, a restrained attitude toward the efficacy of self-disclosure." Communication theorist Stephen Littlejohn (1992, p. 112) says, "for these theorists, effective communication does not arise from blatant openness and disclosure but from sensitivity and care in adjusting what you say to the listener."

In essence, self-disclosure is a risk and can have negative consequences. Rather than bringing people closer together, it could potentially have the opposite effect. Can you remember a time someone shared something per-

*Things are seldom what they seem,
Nonfat milk masquerades as cream.
Externals don't portray insides,
Jekylls may be masking Hydes.*

ANONYMOUS

When is wearing a mask helpful in a relationship? When is it harmful in a relationship?

sonal with you and rather than bringing you closer to that person it made you want to distance yourself from him or her? Hart's work suggests an alternative approach to effective communication that can be applied to interpersonal communication development and is based on research in communication rather than on humanistic psychology. Hart believes that communication requires an adaptive approach to others that balances one person's self-interests with the interests of others. For Hart, the effective interpersonal communicator adjusts his or her communication by taking into account the beliefs, values, and mood of the other person. You don't give up your own point of view or values in this approach, but find the best way to communicate your ideas given all circumstances.

CONSIDERING CULTURE

The notion of self-disclosure as a necessary ingredient for developing strong, healthy interpersonal relationships is not accepted in many cultures. The Japanese believe it is better to put on a "good face" rather than displease their lis-

tener or guest by being honest and open. It is not unusual for a Japanese student studying in America to actually say yes they understand and will do something, when in fact they did not understand and don't have a way of doing what has been requested of them.

For Japanese people, maintaining harmonious relationships is more important than reporting your feelings and thoughts. Form small groups in class, and list other cultures that would find the process of self-disclosure acceptable or unacceptable in early stages of relationships.

COMMUNICATING SKILLFULLY

Divide the class into small groups. Reread the section on the three traits Hart described. Each group should generate a role-play situation centered around a conflict. Here's an example: You and another person are supposed to meet at the library to work on a project. You go to the library at the time decided on but your partner never shows up, and you leave feeling angry. The next day you see each other in the commons area and start to talk about what happened the night before.

Role-play this situation in front of the class. Alternate roles being noble self, rhetorical reflector, or rhetorically sensitive. Have the class guess which trait you were role-playing.

Back in your groups, discuss how it felt to communicate from each trait type. Which type are you predominantly: noble self, rhetorical reflector, or rhetorical sensitive? Think about communication situations where you have used these different styles. Discuss which style you use most and which style you appreciate most in others. Why? Discuss possible steps of developing a rhetorically sensitive interpersonal style.

Building on the research of Darnell and Brockriede (1976), Hart and Burks (1972) have suggested three general types of communicators: (1) noble selves, (2) rhetorical reflectors, and (3) rhetorically sensitives. **Noble selves** don't adjust their communication strategies for others and do stick to their personal ideals. **Rhetorical reflectors** are people who, unlike noble selves, mold themselves to others' wishes and do not have any particular scruples to follow. Between these two extremes are the **rhetorically sensitive** individuals, who have a concern for self and others, and take a situational attitude. Littlejohn (1992) outlines five attributes of rhetorical sensitivity:

1. Rhetorically sensitive people accept personal complexity; that is, they understand that each individual is a composite of many selves.

2. Such people avoid rigidity in communicating with others.

3. The rhetorically sensitive person seeks to balance self-interests with the interests of others, a sensitivity called *interaction consciousness*.

4. Rhetorically sensitive people are aware of the appropriateness of communicating or not communicating particular ideas in different situations.

5. Such people realize that an idea can be expressed in many ways, and they adapt their message to the audience in the particular situation.

In a study of rhetorical sensitivity administered to over three thousand students at 49 universities, Hart, Carlson, and Eadie (1980) found that each person has varying degrees of all three types but that a given type predominates.

Some of the variables that affect which type you are include philosophical, geographical, and cultural forces; and/or family background, ethnic group, and religious orientations.

In many ways, the description of a rhetorically sensitive individual sounds like an ideal trait. Hart, Carlson, and Eadie (1980) believe the three traits they describe are genetic and therefore inherently part of one's interpersonal style. However, because rhetorical sensitivity provides a set of principles they could in fact be used in interpersonal relationships to achieve more effective communication. We believe rhetorical sensitivity can be used as a behavioral choice useful to gain knowledge of others and therefore further develop relationships. Adapting a more rhetorically sensitive communication style would help to make people aware of communication contexts, the uniqueness of individuals, and the selection of the most appropriate way to express needs, interests, and ideas to others.

As your interpersonal style develops through strategies of self-disclosure or rhetorical sensitivity, whether or not your relationships continue often depends on your feelings of being recognized as a unique and valuable person by your partner. This feeling of recognition and acceptance is called **confirmation**.

Drawing by Eric Teitelbaum; © 1990 The New Yorker Magazine, Inc.

"If something is bothering you about our relationship, Lorraine, why don't you just spell it out."

CONFIRMATION

The philosopher Martin Buber (1965) wrote,

> The human person needs confirmation....An animal does not need to be confirmed, for it is what it is unquestionably. It is different with [the person]. Sent forth from the natural domain of species into the hazard of the solitary category, surrounded by the air of chaos which came into being with him, secretly and bashfully he watches for a Yes which allows him to be and which can come to him only from one human person to another. It is from one [person] to another that the heavenly bread of self-being is passed.

When you form a relationship with another person, you don't intend to lose your identity. When "I" becomes "you and me," and "you and me" becomes "us," you still need to see yourself as an individual. A relationship implies an **interdependence**—not *in*dependence but *inter*dependence. To feel interdependence, each person in a relationship needs to feel a sense of personhood. That is, each matters, each can influence and be influenced by the other and each can help and be helped by the other. Continued relational development requires a sense of confirmation by the other.

People feel confirmation in their relationships when their partners treat them with respect (recognizes their personhood) and positiveness. In an article called "Patterns of Interactional Confirmation and Disconfirmation," Kenneth Cissna and Evelyn Sieburg (1981) describe three clusters of disconfirming responses and three clusters of confirming responses in interactional patterns. The types of responses people get from others gives them confirmation or disconfirmation. Let's look at disconfirming responses first.

Disconfirming Responses

Disconfirmation is a pattern typified by ignoring someone's communication or presence. The disconfirmer is saying, either with or without words, that this person and his or her ideas are not worth giving time or consideration to. The three major types of disconfirming responses include indifferent responses, impervious responses, and disqualifying responses.

An *indifferent response* is typified by denying the existence or relationship with the other person. This can be done by denying his or her presence; avoiding involvement by using impersonal language, avoiding eye contact or physical contact, or other nonverbal "distancing" cues; or by rejecting communication by responding in ways that are unrelated or only minimally related to what is being said.

An *impervious response* is one that shows a lack of awareness of another's perceptions. This type of response is disconfirming because it denies what one person really feels or believes. When you're negatively challenged for what you believe or told you don't really mean something that you said, you are receiving an impervious response. Responses such as the following all show imperviousness:

"Don't say that, I know you don't mean it."

"How could you make such a big deal over that?"

"That's stupid for you to feel that way."

These statements raise doubts about the other person's way of experiencing life. They discount the other person's view of reality.

Disconfirmation by *disqualifying responses* is made up of two types: speaker disqualification and message disqualification. Speaker disqualification may be verbal or nonverbal and consists either of a direct attack, blame, criticism, name calling, and so on, or of sarcasm, a heavy sigh, or a "Tsk" when the person speaks. Speaker disqualification sends the message of worthlessness. Message disqualification takes place when someone makes a statement, but is ignored or answered in only a very tangential way. An example of a disqualifying response might happen in a small group when one member makes a comment to the group, and another member of the group responds by rolling his or her eyes and sighing. Such nonverbal behavior sends the signal "Not you and your stupid ideas again!"

Confirming Responses

Confirming responses serve to socially validate people in their relationships and although not as specific as disconfirming responses, center on the three main clusters of recognition, acknowledgment, and endorsement. Like disconfirming responses, they're communicated by a combination of verbal and nonverbal behaviors.

Recognition is expressed by the degree to which partners physically attend to each other. This attention may be expressed through eye contact, minimal physical space, touching, or language that speaks directly to your partner. Recognition messages say that you respect your partners and value their attempts at communication and interdependence.

When you *acknowledge* another person, you do so by making direct and relevant responses to his or her communication. This does not mean that you necessarily agree with your partners, but that you actively listen and respond directly to their ideas, feelings, and emotions. In responding in this manner, you not only acknowledge the importance of the other person to you, but you also help facilitate clear communication between you two.

The last confirming type of response is *endorsement*. Cissna and Sieburg (1981) suggest that "this cluster includes any responses that express acceptance of the other's feelings as true, accurate, and okay." In essence, endorsement is saying, "I will let you be who you are" without any justification or analysis.

In this chapter, we have pointed out two possible strategies to gain the knowledge necessary to develop interpersonal relationships. In a very real sense, we have been talking about how everyday encounters may or may not develop into fully developed interpersonal relationships. As noted in the beginning of this chapter, to be effective interpersonally you must first consider who you are, what roles you play, and what expectations you hold for your relationships. Then you must select the combination of communication strategies (in this case self-disclosure, rhetorical sensitivity, and confirmation) that work for you as part of your interpersonal style. These theories are useful because they let people make informed choices in developing relationships. Perhaps some of your relationships will grow because of reciprocal self-disclosure and others will grow because of rhetorical sensitivity. Although we have contrasted self-disclosure and rhetorical sensitivity, perhaps you'll be able to use them in unison.

A goal for you in this chapter was to select those ideas you want to test and, for those that work well for you, to add to your interpersonal style ("toolbox") of communication. In essence, we're writing a confirming message: you're an important and unique individual who can critically think through the ideas we've presented and select and practice the ones that fit your interpersonal style in your everyday encounters. In adapting these strategies to your style, consider the following three factors:

1. *Context.* It is important always to be aware of the context of communication and to be aware that relational development can be hurt from ignoring

COMMUNICATING SKILLFULLY

With a partner, identify a relationship in which you have felt confirmed and another where you felt disconfirmed. What kinds of statements made you feel that way? Looking at these same relationships, identify to what degree you engaged in sending confirming and disconfirming responses. What could you have done to change the disconfirming relationships?

Confirmation—recognition, acknowledgment, and endorsement—allows us to be socially validated and grow in our interpersonal relationships.

CONSIDERING CULTURE

RELATIONAL ANALYSIS

Either as a class activity or individual activity, watch a feature film and study the confirming and disconfirming messages between any two lead

characters. *A couple of classic films that might be fun and lead to insight, are* Casablanca *or* Who's Afraid of Virgina Woolf? *Films like* Thelma and Louise *or* When Harry Met Sally *might also*

work well. After watching the film, discuss the use of confirming or disconfirming communication between the characters. What did this contribute to the degree of interpersonalness between the characters?

context. Pushing relational development in a work context may not only hinder the quality of work but may perhaps be perceived as sexual harassment. Context always plays a factor in the kinds of interaction and types of information that are appropriate to share with others.

2. *Goal.* When you intentionally communicate with another, it is important to be aware of what you would like to achieve. Do you want, in fact, a interactional relationship based on sharing a breadth of information about your interests and mutuality, or do you want a relationship that is more interpersonal and characterized by a depth of information and honesty? If you're seeking an interpersonal relationship, you need to be aware that relationships tend to grow slowly over time, and you must not force artificial self-disclosure. Are your goals and that of your partner reciprocated? If you clearly recognize your goal in communication, it will be easier to select the communication strategy that works best for you.

3. *Receptivity and responsiveness.* Communication implies a sharing of information or to use (international communication expert) Sam Keltner's words, "commangé." Regardless of your understanding of communication context and goals, an interpersonal relationship will not grow and develop unless both parties are receptive and responsive to each other. You can't *make* another person have an interpersonal relationship with you. Reception and responsiveness is communicated by your sending and receiving confirming messages.

LOOKING BACK - LOOKING FORWARD

In the last chapter, we examined the process of perception and how one's perception of others affects the kinds of judgments one makes regarding personality, ideas, and values. We discussed how withholding judgments allows people to consider secondary information and gain more accurate perceptions—a key to successful communication.

In this chapter, we've examined strategies that help build and maintain effective interpersonal relationships.

In the next chapter, we'll look at language and symbolic behavior. Many theorists believe that the human capacity for language is the most unique characteristic of our species. Language allows people to share perceptions with others through symbol creation and usage. However, language also presents people with certain pitfalls that can hurt attempts at communication. In Chapter 6 we'll explore these issues in depth.

R EVIEW TERMS AND CONCEPTS

P UTTING THEORY INTO PRACTICE

FOR DISCUSSION:

1. There has been much discussion about the difference between men and women when it comes to openness and self-disclosure. Why do you think the differences exist? Is the situation changing by generation?

2. If you have the chance to watch a feature film video in the course you're taking, contrast the communication climate in your classroom with those in *The Paper Chase*, *Children of a Lesser God*, and *Dead Poet's Society*. What role do confirming or disconfirming messages play in each? What impact do grading and other forms of evaluation play in this regard?

SKILL BUILDERS:

1. With a partner, discuss how you react in situations where you feel you have to disclose personal information about which you feel

uncomfortable. Do you use "white lies" or vague language? What are the ethics of honesty in these situations?

2. Discuss in class, or write a short paper that illustrates the "social penetration" theory in action. Analyze a present or former relationship that shows how the levels of depth and breadth increased and brought you closer in an interpersonal sense.

3. Using the following Self-Disclosure Inventory, complete the questionnaire regarding the kinds of information you are comfortable sharing about yourself with others. In dyads or small groups, discuss the kinds of things you were comfortable disclosing.

4. Create an original list of "rules" for self-disclosure in close, intimate relationships (based on your experience and observation of others). Compare your list with those of your classmates. Do you agree with each other's lists? What would you add? Leave out? What role do you believe culture and ethnicity play in your comfort with self-disclosure?

Self-Disclosure Situations Survey

This is a survey of a number of different situations that people sometimes find themselves in. Our aim is to find out more about the way people react to the variety of situations presented here. One way in which various situations differ is in terms of how willing people are to reveal personal information about themselves in those situations. In some situations, a person may be willing to express personal information in such a way that the others truly understand where that person stands in terms of his or her feelings and thoughts regarding any topic. In other situations, a person may be willing to discuss only certain topics, and only on a superficial level, if at all.

This survey lists twenty different situations to see how willing you would be to reveal information about yourself in each specific situation. Indicate how willing you would be to disclose personal information in each situation. Imagine yourself in the situation, and then ask yourself how revealing you would generally be.

To record your reactions to a situation, use the numbered scale. Select the number that best indicates the degree of self-disclosure with which you would be comfortable in the situation, and put that number in the parentheses beside the number of the situation. Use this same numbered scale for all your answers.

In the numbered scale, only the numbers at the far left and far right (1 and 6) have been described. However, use any of the numbers that best represent your reaction to the situation. The numbers from 1 to 6 are to be understood as indicating gradually increasing degrees of willingness to disclose at a personal level in that situation.

1	2	3	4	5	6
"I would be willing to discuss only certain topics, and on a superficial level only, if at all, in this situation."					"I would be willing to express, in complete detail, personal information about myself in such a way that the other person(s) truly understand(s) where I stand in terms of my feelings and thoughts regarding any topic."

Here is the list of situations. Imagine yourself in each situation and then indicate, using the numbered scale, the degree to which you would be willing to disclose. Please be sure to answer each item. After completing the survey, form small groups and discuss your responses and those of other group members. Report your group findings to the whole class.

SELF-DISCLOSURE SITUATIONS

_____ 1. You are on a blind date.

_____ 2. You are having dinner at home with your family.

_____ 3. You are sightseeing with a tour group in Europe.

_____ 4. You are sitting next to a stranger on an airplane.

_____ 5. You are with the family of a friend.

_____ 6. You are in a coffee shop with some casual friends.

_____ 7. You are being introduced to a group of strangers.

_____ 8. You are a member of an encounter or sensitivity group.

_____ 9. You are at a party with some friends.

_____ 10. You are in the library with a friend.

_____ 11. You have picked up a hitchhiker while driving.

_____ 12. It's evening and you are alone with your boyfriend or girlfriend in his or her home.

_____ 13. You are applying for a job as a public relations consultant.

_____ 14. You are in a discussion group on human sexuality.

_____ 15. You are at a restaurant with your date.

_____ 16. You are meeting your girlfriend or boyfriend's parents for the first time.

_____ 17. You are eating lunch alone and a stranger asks if he (she) may join you.

_____ 18. You are taking a walk in a park with your girlfriend or boyfriend.

_____ 19. You and a friend are driving to Atlanta.

_____ 20. You are on a picnic with friends.

FOR EXTENDED STUDY

Berg, J. H., & Archer, R. L. (1983). The Disclosure–liking relationship. *Human Communication Research, 10,* (Winter).

This article is written for the serious student or scholar and is a good review of research on self-disclosure and attraction.

Jourard, Sydney. (1971). *The transparent self.* New York: Van Nostrand Reinhold.

In this book, Jourard describes how people can gain full health and personal development when they have the courage to be themselves.

Powell, John, S.J. (1969). *Why am I afraid to tell you who I am?* Chicago: Argus Communications.

Powell's book is an easy read that takes a humanistic look at self-disclosure in our relationships

Language is an expression of who we are and what we give value to.

M. A. K. HALLIDAY

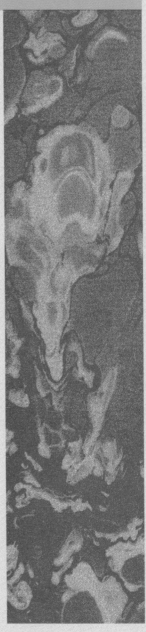

Language:
Negotiating Reality

After reading this chapter and taking part in class activities, you should be able to

- Explain the importance of language in interpersonal relationships.

- Describe the relationship between language and experience.

- Explain how knowledge of constitutive and regulative rules affects the coordinated management of meaning (CMM) with others.

- Explain the importance of using language with sensitivity to others, with clarity of expression, and with flexibility in attitude and meanings.

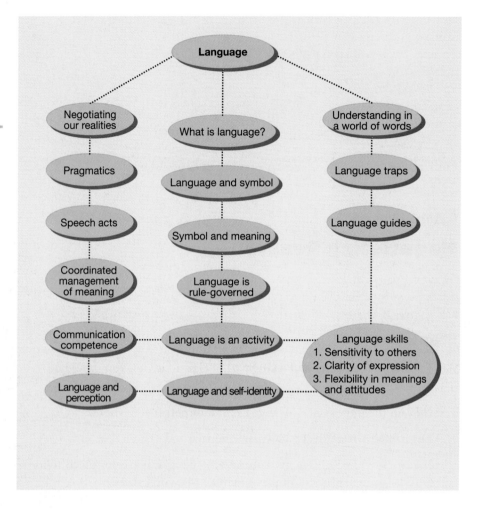

AS THE QUOTE FROM LINGUIST M. A. K. HALLIDAY at the beginning of this chapter points out, language is important. Language has a powerful, magical, even mystical quality about it. Language is how you share your internal world with others—how you negotiate realities in daily life. When infants start to utter their first words of "Mama" or "Dada," parents respond with smiles of ecstasy. When children begin to try out two- and three-word sentences, parents begin to feel they have the beginnings of a "young Einstein." Eventually, the child also begins to realize there are some words he or she isn't supposed to say because they are "bad words" (taboo words).

Children also learn that some words are to be said as part of rituals (*please* and *thank you*). Some words are to be said with respect or reverence, like *God.* You learned as a child that you need to mean what you say and even stand up for it if necessary. You learned that some people speak "funny." When you hear others speak, it may be an exotic-sounding foreign language, or perhaps just different from yours in slight ways (accent, dialect, jargon). You actually started to judge other people by the way they talk. You learned that some people are allowed to say words you were told never to use (sometimes the taboo words are said by the very people who lay down this rule!) and if you say certain words you are pledging your honor (oaths and promises). You learned you can make up "private" languages with your friends, and you learned you can make people laugh or make people cry with words. You can hurt others and be hurt by others by saying certain things.

What gives language such unique power in human affairs? This question has probably been asked from the time humans first spoke. Language has been a phenomenon that has intrigued people's understanding of themselves as members of the human community. And, language continues to be studied by philosophers, linguists, psychologists, and other communication scholars. Human understanding of human behavior is intricately linked with knowledge of language. The early Greek writings of Socrates, the mid–1900s views of Wendell Johnson and S. I. Hayakawa, or the current writings of the new post-modern, post-Cartesian philosophers such as Martin Heidegger or Hans-Georg Gadamer, all identify the use of language as perhaps humankind's greatest accomplishment. In his book *The Third Chimpanzee* (1992), University of California at Los Angeles physiologist Jared Diamond discusses how language was the "missing ingredient" that changed primitive humans into more complex beings 40,000 to 100,000 years ago and distanced them from apes. Before speech was developed, humans were not much different from apes and didn't have sophisticated tools. This capacity for language allows people to work

Are you speechless?

cooperatively with others by being able to talk about ideas or events not in their presence. Through language, people form, maintain, and end interpersonal relationships.

Why is language so central in human relationships? In this chapter, we look at several theories about the use and role of language and explore several keys to developing communication competence and "negotiating reality with others."

WHAT IS LANGUAGE?

Among the various theories of language, two strands are prominent in the field of communication. One looks at the centrality of the symbol in communication, and the other is **language** as an activity that requires the understanding of certain kinds of rules to use language. Let's look at each of these strands in some detail.

Language and Symbol

Although no one can clearly define where or how language began, it is clear that the human capacity to modify, shape, and share their world through language is part of what makes them human. This is our "**semiotic potential**." Semiotics is the study of the use of signs and symbols as people construct, reconstruct, and even deconstruct their world with others (Fiske, 1982). To the degree you connect with others, symbolically speaking, you are reaching your semiotic potential. To be human is to use symbols. According to rhetorician Kenneth Burke (1968, p. 16),

> [Hu]man is
>
> the symbol-using [symbol-making, symbol-misusing]
>
> animal
>
> inventor of the negative (or moralized by the negative)
>
> separated from his [or her] own making
>
> goaded by the spirit of hierarchy (or moved by the sense of order)
>
> and rotten with perfection.

In this passage, Burke offers his perspective on the centrality of symbol use in human behavior and describes how language can link people together through the rhetorical use of identification. At the same time he suggests that the use of symbol, or language, is a two-edged sword because it also can create problems. Anthropologist Edward Sapir (1949, p. 220) once said about language, "(it) is the most massive and inclusive art we know, a mountainous and anonymous work of unconsious generations. It is the best show that man puts on." Through language, the internal world becomes externalized. Through symbols, people share their realities and negotiate meanings with others.

What is a symbol? Often people use the terms *sign* and *symbol* interchangeably. However, they represent a different order of understanding to the semiotician or linguist. Essentially, a **symbol** is something that refers arbitrarily to something else, while a **sign** points something out. An example of a sign is that if you see smoke, you may assume there is a fire—in this case, then, smoke is a sign of fire. An example of a symbol is the word *cat*. The word *cat* can *stand for* a little, black, furry creature, but it *is not* a cat. You can easily combine other letters to form a word that represents the same small, black, furry animal. To that extent, *language is arbitrary*. You can create any new symbols you want. With the exception of onomatopoeic words like *shush*, the sound of the word has no connection to its meaning. Think about several new lines of cars that have appeared over the last few years and how their manufacturers created new words (symbols) to name them. They tried to capture in symbolic form, words that would convey a feeling or attitude of power or strength or freedom. *Geo, Lexus, Integra, Prelude, Maxima, Camry, Saturn*—what do these words mean when attached to a car? Everything and nothing. They are merely arbitrary combinations of sounds and letters used to promote a product and give it an identity. The manufacturer hopes the choice of a symbol gives it an identity you will want to buy!

Symbol and Meaning

Semantics is the study of meanings. Meanings do not reside in objects but are determined by receivers. You can look in the dictionary for the definition of a word, but when you want to know its meaning, you have to listen and see how

Sound familar?

people use it. Without use, language lacks meaning, by itself. Communication teachers often explain this concept by saying "Words don't mean, people do!" Perhaps one of the most insightful characterizations of meaning was put forth in 1923 by C. K. Ogden and I. A. Richards. Figure 6.1 shows their diagram of the relationship between words and the things they signify.

In their book, *The Meaning of Meaning* (1923), Ogden and Richards make the point that the relationship between the word and the thing it refers to is arbitrary, and therefore they use dotted lines between "Word" and "Referent" in the diagram. The lines between "Word" and "Thought" and "Thought" and "Referent" are solid because they see this relationship as direct. As a member of a particular culture, you come to use common symbols and share common meanings for your experiences. Hayakawa (1939, p. 31) writes, "The first of the principles governing symbols is this: The symbol is NOT the thing symbolized; the word is NOT the thing; the map is NOT the territory it stands for." Ogden and Richard's model helps show that meanings are in thoughts or references that people have, not in the referents themselves. There is nothing spicy about the word *spaghetti*; there is nothing painful in the word *pain*. In sharing symbols and meanings, you negotiate your reality with others. When you talk with someone you are sharing your perceptions, your sense data about both your internal and external world.

Language Is Rule Governed

Although symbol usage is arbitrary, language is also rule governed. The rules of language have to do with what letters can be combined with others to form words, and what words can be placed with others to form sentences. These are the rules of syntax and grammar. Without the use of these rules, speech and writing become individualized; then, instead of clarifying ideas, people obfuscate them and are no longer engaged in effective symbolic behavior. People use symbols so they can share with others. When their utterances (or sentences) are indecipherable to another, they are misusing symbols. Remember, a major function of language use is to link people together.

Language Is an Activity, a Behavior

All people are surrounded by language. From the moment you're born, you hear language and as you grow you begin to see language as well. You live in a world of words. As Stewart (1990, p. 52) says, "Language isn't simply a list of nouns, but an *activity*, a living process that is happening all around us, literally from the moment we are born to the day we die."

To say that language is an activity or a behavior means that people learn language not by imitating others but by taking an active role in developing their semiotic potential. The infant hears and plays with language at its mother's breast or in the crib. During this activity, the infant is not only learning symbols but rules—rules of syntax and grammar, and even rules of interpersonal communication. The rules of interpersonal communication include when to talk and when to listen; what is a question and what is a statement; who are *we* and who are *you*; how to express feelings, and so on. Through this learning of language, people begin to recognize the interpersonal functions that language serves. According to Halliday (1973, p. 133), these functions include "the grammar of personal participation; it expresses the speaker's role in the situation, his persona; commitment and his interaction with others." Through learning interpersonal functions of language, people both adopt a role or set of roles, while accepting (or rejecting) those that are assigned them; they express their own judgments, own attitudes, own personalities, and in so doing exert certain effects on the receivers. The learning of language is in no way a passive, imitative process but an active social process of discovery.

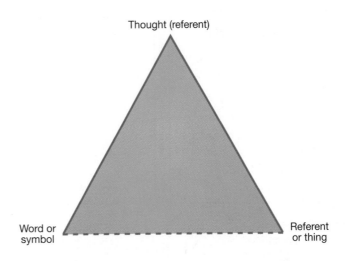

FIGURE 6.1

The triangle of meaning

Language and Self Identity

Basil Bernstein (1967) identifies certain "critical socializing contexts" in which the interpersonal use of language plays a key part in the transmission of culture to the child. In studying the ordinary talk between parents and their children, Bernstein discovered how culture and sense of self are passed on in the seemingly insignificant conversations of what parents and children talk about and how they talk to each other. One of Bernstein's findings was the notion of how language and social class are typified by what he describes as **elaborated** or **restricted codes**. Elaborated codes he associates with middle-class speech in homes and schools. These codes are generally longer, grammatically complex, and flexible. He associates restricted codes with lower- or working–class homes and says they may be acceptable in homes or with peers, but is not adequate for other circumstances. He describes restricted codes as grammatically simpler, with shorter sentences, and limited use of impersonal pronouns. Bernstein's work has been extended to studying speech patterns in

DILBERT reprinted by permission of UFS, Inc.

professions and in other social settings, and he now suggests that certain occupational jargon also can be considered restricted code. For example, a computer specialist might talk about "RAM," "K," and "gigabytes."

In this sense then Bernstein suggests that restricted codes do not exclusively indicate social class difference, but rather an economy of language for "in-group" behavior. That is, language can be used to indicate who is a member of the group and who is not. For Bernstein, the learning of our culture and largely the learning of self–identity are enmeshed in the language web.

The concept of self varies from society to society and language to language. In the United States and western European cultures, language emphasizes the self as an individual. In Chinese language, the self is seen as a sub–element of family and society, and in native African, Australian, and Indonesian languages the self is considered a part of nature. To a great extent, language becomes a crucial influence on the nature of culture and the notion of self. Your self–concept, your very self–identity is linked to your language. When someone criticizes your language such as grammar, dialect, or accent, you may feel this is an attack and may respond defensively. You respond defensively because in many ways "your language is you" and you perceive such criticism as an attack on your self or identity. Although society may have preferred styles of grammar and pronunciation, "language is self." This becomes a very important issue in intercultural or interethnic situations, where there may be a tendency to judge another person's education or background on their language use. In Chapter 12, we discuss culture and ethnic communication considerations in depth.

> *Speak, that I may see thee!*
>
> SOCRATES OR
> BEN JONSON

NEGOTIATING REALITIES

Although language can be thought of as a system of symbols, this view is somewhat simplified. Look back at Figure 6.1 and notice that the triangle of meaning is made up of how people label things with nouns. However, language is made up of more than nouns. As you learn and use language, you

CONSIDERING CULTURE

As described earlier, language and self-identity are closely related. Immigrant children often feel torn between the language of home and the language of school. In Richard Rodriguez's book Hunger of Memory: The Education of Richard Rodriguez (1982), he describes growing up as a Mexican American in Sacramento, California, in the 1950s and 1960s. Speaking English at school but Spanish at home, he experienced periods of alienation at school using English, but warm comfort at home when he was being spoken to in Spanish. He writes,

> A family member would say something to me in Spanish and I would feel especially recognized. My parents would say something to me and I would feel embraced by the sounds of their words. Those sounds said: I am speaking with ease in Spanish. I am addressing you in words I never use with los gringos. I recognize you as someone special, close, like no one outside, you belong with us. In the family. (p. 15)

are engaged in a meaning-building activity. Stewart (1992) suggests that language is an activity that you take part in from your time in your mother's womb until the day you die. He refers to this process as "languaging." He proposes that all people simmer in a sort of "linguistic soup" all their lives, and in this soup they create meanings. When discussing meaning, Stewart uses the metaphor of the potter's wheel. If you've seen the film *Ghost*, you might remember the scene where the two main characters share a potter's wheel as they are constructing a clay piece (of course, at the same time they are engaging in relational messages!). Try to picture a potter's wheel with you on one

Negotiating Reality

side and someone you are communicating with on the other side. Both your hands and those of the other person are stretched out to the pottery wheel and intertwined, shaping and molding the clay. The clay represents the use of words to express thoughts, and hands that shape the clay represent negotiating meanings with a partner. From this process, meanings become manifest; people negotiate their reality by actively taking part in this "languaging."

To take part in this activity, you need to understand some of the pragmatics of language; that is, what you are using language to accomplish. Searle (1969) has labeled what people intend language to do **speech acts**. Examples include acts such as requesting, questioning, warning, threatening, declaring, and so forth. You might be asking yourself, "How do I know how to interpret speech acts and where and how to use them?" Let's turn to that topic now.

COORDINATED MANAGEMENT OF MEANING

W. Barnett Pearce and Vernon Cronen (1980) have suggested that people learn through observation and practice. They see communication as "social action best studied as a process of creating and managing social reality—rather than a technique for describing objective reality" (p. 61). They have called their theory the **coordinated management of meaning** (**CMM**). The theory explains that you know how to use language not because you have labels or a series of nouns, but because you follow rules that tell you how to understand and produce speech acts.

According to CMM theory, there are two kinds of rules: (1) **constitutive rules**, which tell you how to recognize speech acts, and (2) **regulative rules**, which identify in any given context the speech acts that are appropriate or not. Communication theorist John Stewart (1990) uses a sports metaphor for discussing these two kinds of rules of talk and suggests that constitutive rules define the game itself; for example, are you playing volleyball or golf? These rules consist of legal and illegal hits, the size of a court or course, the kind of ball, and so on. When you use language, certain rules define whether you are playing the game "greeting," or "telling a joke," or "requesting" something. If on greeting someone for the first time you said, "Can I have your car keys?" you would be breaking the rule for what constitutes a "greeting."

Regulative rules tells you what speech acts are appropriate given your goals and your understanding of the context. Again, using Stewart's sports metaphor, regulative rules guide you in how the game is played, not what the game is. If you were greeting someone, you might just say "Hi" or shake hands. You might just nod or give the person a hug. You might bow or salute. All would be a form of "greeting."

Pearce and Cronen (1980) believe that each person has acquired a cluster of constitutive and regulative rules. This gives him or her the power to interpret other people's acts and to translate these meanings into felt obligations to perform actions of their own. When two people manage to coordinate their systems of regulative and constitutive rules, they are running like a smooth engine. But what happens when you don't mesh and your clusters of rules clash? Turning back to Stewart's "potter's wheel metaphor" again, picture one set of hands squeezing too hard and elongating the clay while the other set of hands keeps slipping off the clay. Perhaps an example might be helpful here. Let's say you are out with someone you're relating to romantically and you say, "I love you." Let's describe this speech act as "love talk." As you understand the rules of love talk, what would be an appropriate response? "I love you too," or "Me too," or (suggest your own) "_____." What if their response was "Well, I hate you"? Or how about "Have I told you what I got on my interpersonal communication exam?" These responses would break the regulative rules of the speech act. Sometimes people break the rules unintentionally and sometimes intentionally. In any case, the use of rules shows competence in communication.

COMMUNICATION COMPETENCE

The ability to understand and use constitutive and regulative rules is called pragmatics or **communication competence**. Pearce and Cronen (1980, p. 187) see communication competence "as a person's ability to move within and among the various systems s/he is co-creating and co-managing." It is not always easy to communicate appropriately. Can you remember a time when you said something, that was totally inappropriate for the speech act that was taking place, or the context of the communication? If you've ever seen the movie *When Harry Met Sally*, you might remember the scene where Billy Crystal and Meg Ryan are traveling together from Chicago to New York. Coming into the city of Toledo, Ohio, they are having an animated conversation about what attracts women to men and men to women. Just as they are about to enter a diner, Billy says to Meg, "Well, that settles it, you have never had good sex!" Meg is startled and doesn't answer immediately; a moment later, she enters the diner and in a rather loud voice blurts out, "I have too had good sex!" Immediately there is silence in the diner as everyone stops talking and eating to look at the women who just said she's "had plenty of good sex." The context for this speech episode changed from the privacy of a car to a public setting. It changed from one receiver to many. Meg Ryan is embarrassed, and the audience gets a hearty laugh. However, since your life isn't a movie, you hope not to make such mistakes. Part of mastering communication competence is being able to accurately recognize context.

The use of language in interpersonal communication is a complex and rule-bound process. When you learn the rules well, relationships are often

No one when he uses a word has in mind exactly the same thing that another has, and the difference, however tiny, sends its tremors throughout language… All understanding, therefore, is always at the same time a misunderstanding…and all agreement of feelings and thoughts is at the same time a means of growing apart.

WILHELM VON HUMBOLDT

England and
America are two
countries sepa-
rated by the same
language.

GEORGE
BERNARD SHAW

smoother and more rewarding. If you misunderstand contexts or have inadequate sets of rules, your relationships can be frustrating and marked by conflict
and tension.

LANGUAGE AND PERCEPTION

People use language to describe what they perceive in their environment. Anthropologist Benjamin Lee Whorf (1959) and his teacher Edward
Sapir discovered a very important connection between language and perception that became known as the Whorfian thesis or **Sapir-Whorf hypothesis**.
The hypothesis can be expressed as "language is culture, and culture is con-
trolled by and controls language." The essence of this hypothesis is that
"Language determines reality." That is, what you believe you sense is largely
dependent on your having language to describe or label your sense data. The
hypothesis is stated in both the "hard form" known as *linguistic determinism*, as
just described; and in a "soft form" that says "Language influences reality,"
known as *linguistic relativity*.

The importance of the Sapir-Whorf hypothesis is that what you believe to
be real is based on the language you habitually speak. When you come into
contact with a speaker of another language, you are in fact coming into contact with a person who has another reality, another world view. Sapir suggests
that the more distinctly different the language of a speaker, the greater the difference in realities. By way of example, then, a U.S. speaker of English would
have a greater understanding and sharing of world view with a British speaker
of English than with a speaker of German. But since both English and German
are Indo-European languages, these speakers would share more world view
than they would with a speaker of Japanese, because Japanese is not part of the
Indo-European group. The English use the words "moving staircase" for the
American word *escalator*. Most Americans would easily understand what a
moving staircase is. If different language groups use similar-sounding words,

CONSIDERING CRITICAL THINKING

THE SAPIR-WHORF DEBATE

There has been much
debate in the fields of
communication, linguis-
tics and anthropology
about the validity of the

Sapir-Whorf hypothesis,
particularly in the hard
form of linguistic deter-
minism. However, the
hypothesis has not been
disproved. Divide the
class into two groups.
Ask one group to develop
at least three arguments
to support linguistic

determinism, and ask the
other group to develop
three arguments to dis-
prove linguistic determinism. Hold a class debate
between the two groups.
What are the results?
Which side do you now
support? Why?

anthropologists con-
clude that these lan-
guages have a com-
mon origin (see
Figure 6.2). By way
of example, if you are
in France and want a
coffee "with cream"
you would ask for a
cafe au lait, in Spain a
cafe con leche, and in
Italy a *cafe latte*. The
cat we spoke of ear-
lier in the chapter
would be *chat* in Paris
(French), *katze* in
Berlin (German),
katte in Stockholm
(Swedish), and *kot* in
Gdansk (Polish).

A friend who was
in the Peace Corps
during the 1960s tells
the story of a situa-
tion in Africa in
which this idea of
language, perception,
and reality played a

*What will it be? Columbian?
French Roast? or
Decaffinated?*

significant role in the law courts. Because the country had been colonized by
the British, the citizens used both English and tribal language. If someone
were taken to court, it could make a difference between guilt or innocence if
he or she were tried in an English speaking court or a tribal language court. In
the history of the country, tribal people would migrate from place to place
depending on seasons and the availability of food and other resources. During
the periods of migration, the tribes would help themselves to food and other
resources, because there was no concept of private ownership of "natural"
resources. But after colonization, the British tried to reduce these tribal migra-
tions and passed a law making it illegal to "steal" food and other resources
while moving from one part of the country to another. If someone was caught
"stealing" and his or her case was heard in English, he or she would receive a
fine or be jailed. However, if someone's case were heard in a tribal language
court, he or she would be set free because the language had no word for
"stealing." There was no concept of stealing "natural resources," therefore no
crime was committed.

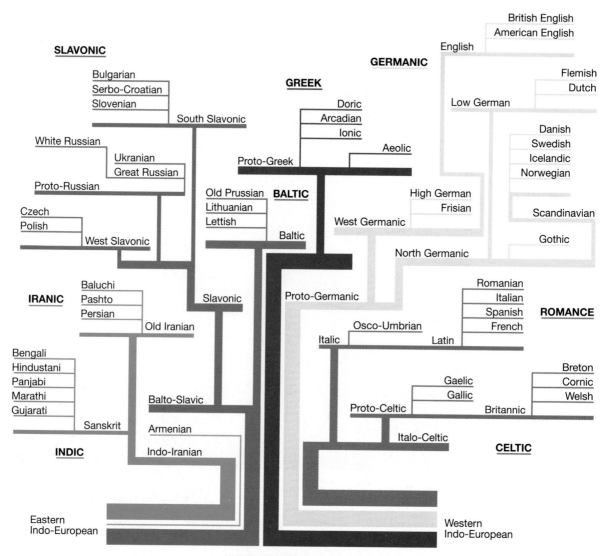

FIGURE 6.2

"The Language Tree"

Languages, then, are not totally translatable to other languages because ideas, realities, are embedded in a specific language. John Keltner (1973, p. 31) uses the example of the French word *s'engager* when he talks about the importance of involvement in interpersonal communication:

> to engage oneself, to promise, to take upon oneself; to enlist; to entangle oneself, to get involved. To say "Je m'engage!" means more than our English "I am engaged" or "I am involved" or "I am committed"—the French expression incorporates all these and even more.

CONSIDER THESE TRANSLATIONS

SPECIALIST IN WOMEN AND OTHER DISEASES

One of the 84 known subcategories of humor is the commercial sign written in a language not native to the country in which the sign is found. A recent list of prime examples has been making its way through the computer networks; allegedly, its origin is an Air France memo.

It's hard to know how real these signs are. Almost certainly many have been shortened or rephrased to make them funnier; a few may be outright inventions. Nevertheless, as any traveller knows, this art form does exist.

Nor of course, are English speakers innocent of provoking the same merriment in the other countries. One only has to remember the million dollar campaign that introduced Coca Cola to China a few years ago. Its proud slogan, emblazoned everywhere trumpeted: "Bite the wax tadpole."

Thus and herewith:

From a Tokyo hotel: "Is forbidden to steal hotel towels please. If you are not a person to do such a thing is please not to read notis."

In a Bucharest hotel lobby: "This lift is being fixed for the next day. During that time we regret that you will be unbearable."

In a Yugoslavia hotel: "The flattening of underwear with pleasure is the job of the chambermaid."

On the menu of a Swiss restaurant: "Our wines leave you with nothing to hope for."

In an advertisement by a Hong Kong dentist: "Teeth extracted by the latest Methodists."

In a Belgrade hotel elevator: "To move the cabin, push button for wishing floor. If the cabin should enter more persons, each one should press a number wishing floor. Driving is then going alphabetically by national order."

In a Rhodes tailor shop: "Order your summer suit. Because is big rush we will execute customers in strict rotation."

In an Austrian hotel catering to skiers: "Not to perambulate the corridors during the hours of repose in the boots of ascension."

In a Bangkok temple: "It is forbidden to enter a women even a foreigner if dressed as a man."

In a Norwegian cocktail lounge: "Ladies are requested not to have children at the bar."

In a Copenhagen airline office: "We take your bags and then send them in all directions."

In an Acapulco hotel: "The manager has personally passed all the water served here."

On the menu of a Polish hotel: "Salad a firm's own make; limpid red better soup with cheesey dumplings in the form of a finger; roasted duck let loose; beef rashers beaten up in the country people's fashion."

In a Zurich hotel: "Because of the impropriety of entertaining guests of the opposite sex in the bedroom, it is suggested that the lobby be used for that purpose."

A sign posted in a German park: "It is strickly forbidden on our black forest camping site that people of different sex, for instance, men and women, live together in one tent unless they are married with each other for that purpose."

On the door of a Moscow hotel room: "If this is your first visit to the USSR, you are welcome to it."

In a Macao store: "Sorry! Midgets will always be available tomorrow."

From a brochure from a car rental firm in Tokyo: "When passenger of foot heave in sight, tootle the horn. Trumpet him melodiously at first, but if he still obstacles your passage then tootle him with vigor."

The headline from this column, by the way, is a sign outside a doctor's office in Rome.

SOURCE: JON CARROLL, "A SPECIALIST IN WOMEN AND OTHER DISEASES," SAN FRANCISCO CHRONICLE, MONDAY, JULY 30, 1990. COPYRIGHT © BY SAN FRANCISCO CHRONICLE. REPRINTED BY PERMISSION.

Learn a new language and get a new soul.

CZECH PROVERB

In many ways, the limits of your language are the limits of your world. A monolingual person (a person who speaks only one language) perceives the world in a more narrow fashion than a person who is bilingual or multilingual. With each language, you add to your semiotic repertoire. In essence, you add another view of reality to your understandings. Your skills of understanding others in intercultural settings are greatly enhanced through language learning.

In the day-to-day use of language, as in the African example mentioned earlier, you can find many instances of the fact that how you label something makes a difference in how you perceive it. If you say, "I hate" something, it is different from saying, "I don't like it." If you call someone an "administrative assistant" instead of a secretary, it not only changes your own attitude and behavior but also can change the way the person sees him- or herself. A few years ago, one of us had an employee who for purposes of job classification was titled a "data entry clerk." Her work was very detailed, and the title had little to do with her tasks. However, because she could not pass a personnel "words per minute" typing test, her title had to remain a "data entry specialist." When a loophole was discovered that allowed her to be reclassified to "program assistant," her work improved dramatically, her attitude grew more positive, and even her test anxiety was reduced. On the very next occasion that the typing test was administered, she passed with no problems. Language influences self-concept and therefore behaviors and attitudes. In the *Art of Talking to Yourself and Others*, (1987, p. 19), Bud Hazel, co-author of this book and a professor of communications at Gonzaga University, gives the following example of how language can shape behaviors and attitudes:

> During World War II a young bride from New Jersey went with her soldier-husband to a military base near the edge of a California desert. Because her husband was heavily involved in military training exercises, she rarely saw him. To make matters worse, she lived in a primitive shack near an Indian village. The heat was intense and a constant wind blew sand over everything. Her only companions much of the time were the Indians who couldn't speak English. After awhile her loneliness became intolerable and she wrote to her mother. In the letter she said she could take no more and wanted to come home. In a few days, she received a reply. Her mother reminded her of an inscription on an old family heirloom: "Two men looked out from prison bars. One saw mud, the other saw stars." These words transformed her. During the next few days, she repeated them often to her self. She began to see the desert as a place of subtle but marvelous beauty. She made friends with the Indians and started taking lessons in pottery and weaving. The young bride became immersed in their culture and every day would discover beauty in her environment. A series of words strung together from a family heirloom had helped dramatically change her perception.

Think of some labels that have an impact on you. For example, what is the

CONSIDERING ETHICS

For the most part, reframing can be positive if it helps people to take a more optimistic outlook in our daily lives. However, someone can use this same technique to manipulate others. Let's say someone you respect sees you on the sidewalk at the university and tells you that he needs to see you later in the day because he has a real "opportunity" he thinks you will be interested in. This person knows you as a hard-working, inquisitive student. You're flattered that he has thought of you for this opportunity and can't wait to see him later that afternoon. Finally, when you meet up and talk for awhile, he tells you that this "opportunity" is for you to buy something from him to start your "own" home-based business. If he had mentioned this to you earlier in the day, you would never have even gone to see him. You would have just told him you're not interested in sales. Was he being unethical by reframing the purpose of the appointment and calling it an opportunity? Can you think of other examples of this kind of situation? What ethical guidelines would be most appropriate in such interpersonal situations?

difference between a test and a quiz? How does going out on a "date" differ from going "with" someone? How does saying your calculus class is "the pits," differ from saying your calculus class is "a challenge"? What if your professor asks you if you would be interested in a job for "no pay" or offers you an unpaid "internship"? In each case, the change in terms has an impact on thinking. This process of changing thinking by changing terms is called *reframing*.

We have been discussing two particular views of langugage in the field of communication. The first, you'll remember, looks at the centrality of symbol use to language, while the other focuses on the rules a person must understand to take part in the transaction of communication. These two views, although different, are highly compatible. The first involves signs and symbols as artifacts or acts that refer to something other than themselves; the second relates to the use of language to generate and negotiate meanings. Both contribute to an understanding of interpersonal communication as meaning-centered activity that is accomplished through an understanding of symbols as well as the rules that govern their use.

Unfortunately, although language is a very flexible instrument of communication, it is not without problems. Language can be ambiguous ("It was an 'interesting' play"), it can be obscure ("Are you taking the 'Excursions in Math' class?"), and it can hurt ("Boy, are you dumb!"). In order to show how to avoid certain language traps, we now turn to an area of study called general semantics.

> *Only those who are wise to words are the wise to whom words are sufficient.*
>
> WENDELL JOHNSON

UNDERSTANDING IN A WORLD OF WORDS

The field of **general semantics** has provided some insights into dealing with the multiple meanings in language. In the 1930s, Alfred Korzybski wrote a book entitled *Science and Sanity* ([1933] 1955) and started the Institute of General Semantics at Lakeville, Connecticut. *Saturday Review* magazine has called *Science and Sanity* one of the most important books of this century. The essence of this work and other prominent scholars such as S. I. Hayakawa, Wendell Johnson, Abraham Mazlow, F. S. C. Northrop, and J. Samuel Bois (who were in the International Society of General Semantics) was to explain what words and meanings impart to values and human welfare. In *Semantics and Communication* (1985), communication professor John Condon points out that general semanticists study not only symbol-referent relationships, but also the behavior and results of language habits. Research in the field of general semantics has contributed much to the understanding of the role language plays in interpersonal communication. The three most practical ideas here are language traps:

1. Language is not neutral.

2. Words are at various levels of abstraction.

3. People use language in habitual ways.

Let's look at each of these propositions in detail.

LANGUAGE IS NOT NEUTRAL

When you take your language for granted, you may presume everyone thinks the same way you do, or uses words to mean the same thing you do. When people respond to words differently from you, you might think of them as strange, wrong, or uneducated. Condon believes a more sophisticated approach to language is to assume very little. Language reflects your attitudes and values and as such conveys a point of view. When people use language differently from the way you do, it's because their experiences are different from yours. Their experiences are not right or wrong, but different. As psychologists Albert Hastrof and Hadley Cantril (1954, p. 133) have said, "It is inaccurate and misleading to say that different people have different 'attitudes' concerning the same 'thing.' For the 'thing' simply is *not* the same for different people whether the 'thing' is a football game, a presidential candidate, Communism, or spinach."

WORDS ARE AT VARIOUS LEVELS OF ABSTRACTION

Some words are more specific than others. Semanticists have emphasized that the higher levels of abstraction are from sense data, the greater the possibility of confusion between sender and receiver. To illustrate language and levels of abstraction, general semanticist S. I. Hayakawa ([1933] 1964) created the "abstraction ladder."

Look at the abstraction ladder in Figure 6.3, and you will see that the ladder applies a number of different descriptions to the same person, event, or thing. At the bottom or lowest level of the ladder the description is at the molecular level. As you move up the abstraction ladder, the descriptions are of what you see, what words are said, colors or other descriptors, of the actual sense data you are experiencing when you encounter this person, event, or thing. As you reach the highest levels of the ladder, you move away from sense data once again and begin to generalize. The abstraction ladder helps you to be aware of the level of language you are using and the degree of specificity you want. There are times to be specific, and there are times to be abstract. Knowing which to be, in any given social setting, is important. Usually, however, the higher you move up the ladder from recognizable sense data descriptions, the more likely your statements and responses become misleading. Let's take a few

FIGURE 6.3

Ladder of Abstraction

7th level	"Transportation"	The word "transportation" is a very high level of abstraction leaving out almost all characteristics of my black convertible.
6th level	"Land transportation"	When my black convertible is referred to as "land transportation" still more of its characteristics are left out.
5th level	"Motor vehicle"	"Motor vehicle" stands for even fewer characteristics—only those my black convertible has in common with buses, trucks, tractors, etc.
4th level	"Car"	"Car" stands for only those characteristics which my black convertible has with other cars.
3rd level	A label: "My black convertible"	"My black convertible" is the name we give to the level 2 object. It merely stands for the object leaving out many characteristics.
2nd level	The car we see and touch	The car we see, not the word but the object itself, omits many characteristics of the "process car."
1st level	The car as a changing atomic process	The infinite and ever-changing characteristics—consisting of atom, electrons, etc. as science would define its makeup.

Read up from 1st level

words that represent high-level abstractions such as *freedom* or *love*. When people use a word that has a high level of abstraction, they often confuse others. Some people use the word *love* extremely frequently and easily. They say things like "I loved the book," "I love cold weather," "I love chunky peanut butter," or "I love birds." Others find the word so powerful and full of commitment that they can barely say it at all.

In relationships, the meaning of the word *freedom* has caused battles to be fought and relationships to wash up on the rocks. What does *freedom* mean? Freedom to do what? Freedom from what? When you use words at this level, you might think you agree with the person with whom you are communicating, when in fact, you don't. You might be misleading your receiver, when in fact you weren't trying to. Once, in giving a weekend retreat to work on interpersonal relationships, I (one of the authors) was asked by a prospective student, "Will it be intense?"

I responded, "Well, it will be somewhat intense, it depends on what you give to the process."

The student then said, "Well, if it's intense, I'm not going."

I asked, "What's wrong with intense?"

She replied, "I'm just not very comfortable sleeping in 'tents.'" The misunderstanding was about "intense" and "in tents." If we had never brought our discussion down to lower levels of abstraction, we would have thought we agreed on an idea.

PEOPLE USE LANGUAGE IN HABITUAL WAYS

To say that people use language in habitual ways means that although people have an infinite number of words that they can string together to form sentences and express thoughts, language is so much second nature to people that they generally find themselves repeating words, sentences, and ideas. This is the redundant feature of language. But, because the use of language follows habitual practices, they often forget that logic is embedded within the structure of language. In order for people not to take language and its inherent logic for granted, general semanticists offer suggestions for guiding the use of language:

1. *To me.* Remind yourself that your reactions are "inside-your-own-skin" images, and may not reflect reality or what is "out there." Remember that your realities are not necessarily what others are experiencing. When describing your experiences, it is helpful to begin the description "To me…"

2. *To what degree.* Avoid either–or thinking, and be aware of many values involved in an issue. Experiences are not black and white, good or bad,

but are made up of many shades of gray. When you can remind yourself of this fact, you may stop trying to convince others that there is only one way, one reality, and be open to the reality of others.

3. *Etc. Etc.* (or *Et Cetera*) is the name of the journal of the Society of General Semantics and represents a key concept—that people can never know or say everything about a subject. Remember that what you know is limited by several factors of time, place, information, and so on, and at another time there may be a different point of view or information available.

4. *Dating.* Dating reminds people of the fact that things change, that life is a process. If you attach dates to what you say or hear you'll be more likely not to assume the idea is fixed forever. You are not the person you were in 1975 or 1980 or 1990. By mentally attaching dates to events, people, and things, you will be reminding yourself that things and people change.

5. *Plurals.* The "process" world is very complex. There are causes rather than one cause, aims rather than one aim, and methods rather than one method. Thinking in plurals helps people to recognize the complexity of events in daily life and avoiding easy answers and simple solutions when they are not realistic.

6. *Indexing.* No two events or people are absolutely alike. Think in terms of indexing. When you don't index, you get in trouble with the language by stereotyping. In stereotyping, you take one characteristic of a group and apply it to all members of a group. An example might be to say something like "All jocks are lazy" or "All Italians are good singers" or "Teachers are bookworms." Even when you leave out the "all," as in the teachers example, the "all" is still implied. Indexing helps you remember that Susan and Christine are both athletes or "jocks" but they are not alike. Jock $_1$ is not Jock $_2$, is not Jock $_3$, and so on. Tony may be Italian but may not be a good singer, and Mrs. Washington is a teacher who prefers the outdoors to a library. Indexing helps you to remember that each person is an individual and every event is different.

7. *Hyphens.* Avoid talking as if things could be separated; such as mind and body, or ends and means, and so forth. Remember the process nature of the world and events, and see how things are linked together. When people separate the process world into discrete elements, they end up with false perceptions of reality and therefore false dichotomies.

8. *Quotation marks.* Think with quotation marks around words to be reminded of the difference between the words and the objects to which they refer.

9. *Delayed evaluation.* When you do not judge too quickly, your opinions

COMMUNICATING SKILLFULLY

Look over the preceding list of language suggestions from the general semanticists. Try to recall one or more situations where your use of language got you in "trouble." Which of the preceding ideas would have kept you from falling into the language trap? Discuss your conclusions in small groups.

will tend to be less rigid. The tendency to evaluate people, circumstances, and events leads people into unnecessary conflict. When people remain open to other analysis, new data, and alternative explanations, they are more open to others.

In applying these propositions to interpersonal transactions, you can (1) *use humor* whenever possible and avoid a grim, demanding, one-up-manship way of delivering a message; (2) *operate with trust*, recognizing the great difficulties that exist in trying to communicate with yourself and with others. Give your best to the task and assume that the other person involved is equally responsible. And (3) *go easy*—avoid challenges and criticism. Use suggestions and questions to promote learning. Criticism, even implied, can blight a desire to learn. It promotes defensiveness that blocks effective interpersonal communication.

At the beginning of this chapter, we said we would discuss the nature and function of language and symbolic behavior in social intercourse, and present several language skills to help you "negotiate your reality with others." The preceding sections of this chapter have helped to explain the complexity of language. This complexity and versatility of language make it the best tool for linking up with other people. You use language to name, to make contact, to play with others, to bring the out-of-sight to the present, to gain a cultural and social identity, to find out, to explain, and to persuade. But to use language to its greatest human potential, you must also be aware of how it can lead you astray. We would now like to turn to what we see as three primary skills in the use of language in interpersonal contexts. These three skills are (1) sensitivity to others, (2) clarity of expression, and (3) flexibility in meanings and attitude.

SENSITIVITY

When giving and receiving messages, seek to be sensitive not only to your own language choices but also to those of others with whom you are interacting. When you receive a message from someone else, remember the difference between both of your languages, experiences, and realities. When meanings clash remember that meanings are in people, and search for levels of understanding rather than areas of seeming disagreement. When levels of word usage are abstract, be sensitive enough to seek clarification by providing feedback.

Avoid judging another person just because his or her language, dialect, or accent is different from or the same as yours. Stereotyping another person can lead to communication breakdowns. Maintaining sensitivity to others is an important interpersonal language skill.

CLARITY

In message construction, make messages complete and choose symbols or words carefully. As we said earlier in the chapter, there are so many ways even simple words can be misunderstood. To be understood, you need to share with receivers as much information as possible about your perceptions, feelings, and ideas. There is, however, a point where you can say too much—give too much information. At this point you'll notice your receiver start to fadeout and pay less attention to you. Giving too much information can create a negative effect in the attempt to be clear.

Another language skill that helps clarity is to be able to express your thoughts in different ways. If your receiver does not get your message in one way, then perhaps an alternative approach might work. This pattern of redundancy in your messages also helps to reinforce what you're saying.

To help achieve clarity, whenever possible, you need to "talk the same language" as your receiver. By "talking the same language," we do not mean to say you should mimic them or try to behave like them. That kind of behavior would make you look phoney and ridiculous. By "talking the same language," we mean that we're aware that words operate at a number of levels of abstraction and that people should try to use those levels that parallel their listeners' level of abstraction. If we were writing an English book for fourth-graders, for example, we wouldn't use the words "literary genres" in discussing different types of stories. Instead, we would aim the language at the audience's level and talk about the different "kinds of stories" they have read. In interpersonal interactions, too, people need to use those words that make most "sense" to their receivers.

FLEXIBILITY

Flexibility in language usage and understanding is important. As the general semanticists mentioned before emphasized, either–or attitudes are to be avoided. A good suggestion is to think in terms of "sometimes," "possibly," "normally," and "now and then." Such words as "always," "never," "all," and "none" can cause problems. "Allness" language makes people tend to think in set, rigid patterns in which they fail to distinguish what is unique in each case, and do not allow for change.

If you honestly examine all the misevaluations and misinterpretations that occur in your life because of reactions to words, you may be able to minimize many semantic problems. With awareness, and a desire to improve semantic responses, you can become more effective interpersonally.

LOOKING BACK - LOOKING FORWARD

Thus far we have explored the foundations of interpersonal communication, and examined the core role language plays in developing people's sense of self and their cultural identity, and in linking people interpersonally with others. In the next chapter you will see how nonverbal behavior and language becomes a "communication package." It is the combination of these two instruments of communication—language and nonverbal behavior—that help people reach what we have described in this chapter as their "semiotic potential."

REVIEW TERMS AND CONCEPTS

language
124
semiotic potential
124
symbol
125
sign
125
semantics
125
elaborated codes
127

restricted codes
127
speech acts
130
coordinated manage-
ment of meaning
(CMM)
130
constitutive rules
130
regulative rules
130

communication
competence
131
Sapir-Whorf
hypothesis
132
general semantics
138

PUTTING THEORY INTO PRACTICE

FOR DISCUSSION:

1. Words and meanings change over time. Identify words that you now hear less often than when you were a child. Identify examples of what you might consider "new" words. How do these words identify people of any particular group?

2. What happens when you don't know the rules for a new "speech act" that you haven't ever experienced? How might you learn such a rule set without a firsthand experience?

SKILL BUILDERS:

1. Form small groups, and identify new terms you have become familiar with since you have been in college. Discuss: have these new terms given you any different perspective or appreciation for the subject?

2. As discussed in the chapter, words are ambiguous partially because of the different levels of abstraction. Recall a misunderstanding you've recently had over different interpretations of a word. Using that word, create an abstraction ladder for it. Bring your abstraction ladder to class and share it, pointing out to the class at what level, according to your ladder, you were speaking during the disagreement.

FOR EXTENDED STUDY

Hazel, Harry. (1987). *The art of talking to yourself and others.* Kansas City: Sheed and Ward.

This short book includes practical guidelines for looking at the impact of intrapersonal language in people's relationships with each other.

Hayakawa, S. I. (1978). *Language in thought and action.* New York: Harcourt, Brace, Jovanovich. (Original work published 1933)

An excellent introduction to general semantics. The material includes illustrations, exercises, and applications.

Rodriguez, R. (1982). *Hunger of memory: The education of Richard Rodriguez.* New York: Bantam Books.

An excellent personal account of Rodriguez's memories of growing up in two cultures, two languages. Clearly presents the notion "The limits of my language are the limits of my world."

We respond to gestures with an extreme alertness and, one might say, in accordance with an elaborate and secret code that is written nowhere, known by none, and understood by all.

EDWARD SAPIR

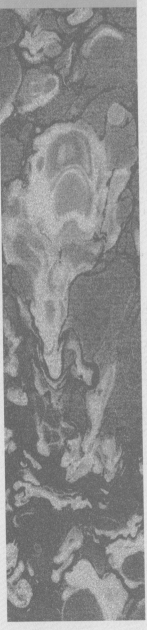

Nonverbal Behavior in Interpersonal Relationships

OBJECTIVES

After reading this chapter and taking part in class activities, you should be able to

• Explain how nonverbal communication functions with verbal communication in interpersonal relationships.

• Distinguish between nonverbal behavior and nonverbal communication.

• Explain why it is almost impossible to avoid communicating nonverbally in interpersonal relationships.

• Identify bodily movements that convey meanings consistent with and contradictory to verbal messages.

• Analyze your own nonverbal skills and those of others to increase understanding in interpersonal relationships.

Nonverbal
behavior

Nonverbal
communication

Characteristics

Nonverbal
skills

Functions

Nonverbal
repertoire

Sensitivity,
Receptivity

Paralinguistics
Kinesics
Proxemics
Haptics
Physical
characteristics

Accurate
comprehension

Sending clear
messages

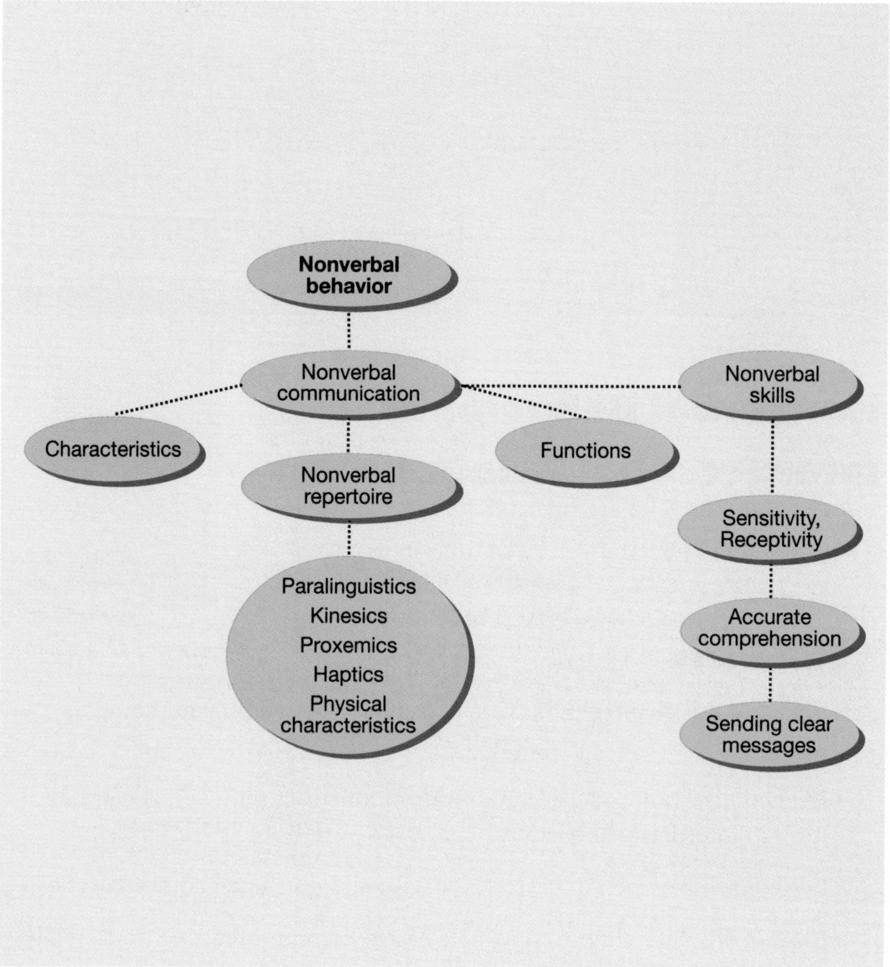

PEOPLE HAVE LONG BEEN AWARE of the importance of nonverbal communication. And yet how or why nonverbal communication can be so powerful has remained somewhat a mystery. Nonverbal communication has been one of the most fascinating areas of communication research because it helps give meaning to behaviors often outside the level of consciousness. Communication researchers have made major advances in unlocking the role of nonverbal behavior in social interaction, particularly in interpersonal relationships. In this chapter, we want to help you increase your understanding of the sig-nificance of nonverbal behavior as part of your total "communication package" or your "semiotic potential" as described in the last chapter. We'll examine various perspectives, characteristics, and forms of nonverbal behavior and offer several skills you can master to avoid sending unintentional or incongruent messages. We'll also offer skills to help develop sensitivity, accuracy, and comprehension in receiving nonverbal messages.

WHAT IS NONVERBAL BEHAVIOR?

What meanings do the following expressions have for you?

- "Actions speak louder than words."

- "You're a bad liar."

- "A picture is worth a thousand words."

All are common expressions; "folk wisdom" about the everyday use of, and believability in, the power of the nonverbal. But what constitutes the nonverbal, and is there a difference between nonverbal behavior and nonverbal communication?

Recall that interpersonal communication is an everchanging transactional sharing that develops between people who are finding meaning with each other and come to know one another better as their relationship tends to move from impersonal to personal. **Nonverbal communication** includes a wide range of phenomena. The way you sit, dress, and comb your hair (or don't), all communicate something about you. Many male professors wear ties when they teach, but male students usually wear ties only for job interviews. With few exceptions, female professors rarely wear summer shorts to teach, yet fall, spring, and summer find shorts on many female students. How does the way you "package" yourself send messages to others? Without necessarily intending to, and without using words, your choices of clothing, grooming, and posture, consciously or unconsciously communicate to people around you.

Nonverbal then, quite simply put, means "not words." The definition of the word *nonverbal* says, "It does not pertain to, or is not in the form of, words." Communications professor Judee Burgoon (1989) defines nonverbal communication as "those attributes or actions of humans, other than the use of words themselves, which have socially shared meaning, are intentionally sent or interpreted as intentional, are consciously sent or consciously received and have potential for feedback from the receiver." Because it's difficult to always recognize whether people are intentionally or unintentionally sending a message, we've chosen to use the words **nonverbal behavior** instead of *nonverbal communication* and have slightly altered Burgoon's definition for this reason. Considering the total impact of nonverbal phenomena, it seems more appropriate to consider the more all-encompassing term *behavior* as more ideally suited to the total magnitude of the interaction. This is consistent with the work of Richmond and his colleagues (1987) in their book *Nonverbal Behavior in Interpersonal Relations*. For this reason, we give the term *nonverbal behavior*

Behavior is action—communication is the generation of meaning.

preference in this discussion. Our definition of nonverbal behavior is "those attributes or actions of humans, other than the use of words themselves, which have socially shared meaning, and have potential for feedback from the receiver."

Nonverbal behaviors, then, are the signals, intentional, or unintentional, without the use of words, of any given sender. These signals become communication when people perceive and interpret them—that is, they create meaning. If I'm tapping my foot and no one sees, that's a nonverbal *behavior*. If you see me tapping my foot and attach some meaning to this action (I'm happy, or in a hurry, and so on) my behavior has become *communication*. Richmond and his colleagues (1987) point out that people can engage in nonverbal behavior when they're alone or with someone else, but they can engage in nonverbal communication only in the presence of someone else who chooses to interpret their behavior as messages and assign meanings to them.

Although we have separated verbal and nonverbal behavior into two chapters, it must be acknowledged that, as distinguished nonverbal researcher Ray Birdwhistell has shown, trying to separate nonverbal and verbal messages ignores the true relationship and understanding of verbal and nonverbal behavior. The separation of this material into two chapters is primarily for your convenience, as the reader. Later in this chapter we discuss the relationship of verbal and nonverbal behavior by linking them together, as part of our "communication package."

Trends in the Study of Nonverbal Behavior

Over the last twenty years, the academic study of nonverbal communication has grown. Two best-seller books, Fast's (1970) *Body Language* and Nirenberg and Calero's (1971) *How to Read a Person Like a Book*, established nonverbal communication as a popular subject. In fact, Mark Knapp (1990, p. 129) says,

> When Julius Fast's best-seller *Body Language* hit America's bookstores in 1970, you could count on one hand the number of colleges and universities courses entirely devoted to the subject of nonverbal communication. In less than 20 years, this course has become a staple curricular offering in most departments of communication.

Unfortunately, books such as these, although very popular, tried to offer a short-cut to gain an understanding of human motivation and interaction. The authors provided an oversimplified view of nonverbal phenomena and saw understanding nonverbal messages as "reading someone's mind," rather than understanding someone's messages. Our emphasis in this chapter is to examine nonverbal behavior to show the complexity of the subject, and at the same time to build skills at sending clear nonverbal messages and understanding other people's nonverbal messages.

Nonverbal messages can be carried over multiple channels of sight.

The Importance of Nonverbal Behavior in Relationships

We've stressed before that understanding others is a crucial concern in interpersonal relationships. It follows that nonverbal elements of messages must be understood. Psychologist Albert Mehrabian has suggested that more than 65 percent of every message is transmitted through the nonverbal channels of sight, sound, touch, taste, and smell. When you speak to another person, he or she is getting multiple messages from your eyes, body posture, facial expression, and distance from him or her, to name a few factors.

THE COMMUNICATION PACKAGE: YOUR SEMIOTIC POTENTIAL

The nonverbal modes of communication constitute, along with verbal skills, what we call the "communication package," (see the cognitive map in Chapter 4) and are part of the "semiotic potential." In *Learning How to Mean* (1975), M. A. K. Halliday explains how children come to understand nonverbal messages first, and later verbal messages, as they are overlaid like transparent pages showing the vessel and bone structures in an anatomy book. Because these two primary modes of human communication are laid, one over the other, they can never be completely separated. In learning to understand and use both verbal and nonverbal signs and symbols (semiotics), your potential as a symbol user starts to be realized. This development continues over your lifetime and shapes what we refer to as the "**communication package.**" This is illustrated in Figure 7.1.

An understanding of the communication package can be gained from research in a number of disciplines, including anthropology, linguistics, psychology, sociology, semiotics, and speech communication. Because the human capacity for symbol using is so central to an understanding of human development and behavior, it has merited inquiry from many disciplines. This chapter has been written from the multidisciplinary perspective on nonverbal behavior and interpersonal relationships

CHARACTERISTICS OF NONVERBAL COMMUNICATION

What constitutes nonverbal phenomena? We've already said that it's difficult to separate verbal and nonverbal phenomena. But for purposes of clarification, you can think about the nonverbal as all nonlinguistic aspects of interaction that influence the messages you get, or seem to get, from another person. These messages may include facial expressions, body movements, distances between interactants, vocal qualities, and other associated voice elements. Nonverbal phenomena can be characterized in very different ways from the ways we characterize verbal communication.

1. *Nonverbal communication is ongoing.* Words are discrete, separate, digital signals that have little or no meaning in part or without being spoken completely; but nonverbal signals are ongoing, visible, and often difficult to manipulate. You can choose to stop talking, but you can't stop behaving. Watzlawick, Beavin, and Jackson (1967), stated this communication principle as "We cannot not communicate."

2. *Nonverbal communication can be intentional or unintentional.* Just as the Communicating Skillfully experiment may have shown, because nonverbal signals are visible they're beyond ready concealment or manipulation. Whether you try to send a signal or you stay silent with a neutral expression on your face, a receiver still interprets your uninterrupted stream of behavior. The receiver may interpret this expression as bored or disinterested. The communication takes place in the reception and interpretation of the message.

3. *Nonverbal communication is the primary mode for expressing* **emotions.** In 1872, Charles Darwin wrote a classic book titled *The Expression of Emotions in*

FIGURE 7.1

The Communication Package

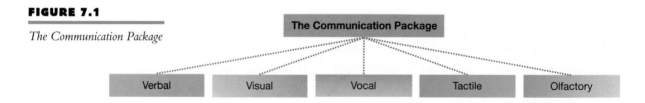

Man and Animals. Darwin's book was the beginning of the scientific era of study of nonverbal communication. Where early studies of facial expression were for the study of rhetoric, elocution, or acting, Darwin's work was concerned with innately linked emotional expression and survival values. Darwin saw facial expression as genetically transmitted and therefore universal. Research by Ekman and his colleagues (1967) has supported the notion that some body movements, including facial expression, are biologically determined. Although people talk about their emotions from time to time, they more often express feelings nonverbally. When people ask, "Is something wrong?" "What is the matter?" "Why is he so upset?" and so on, they're generally reacting to nonverbal expressions.

4. *Nonverbal communication is **ambiguous**.* Although some have tried, no one has written a definitive dictionary on nonverbal communication, because nonverbal messages are ambiguous—can mean several different things, depending on such factors as context, culture, personality, and so on. Some people get very quiet when they're happy. Others express happiness through smiles, shouts for joy, and even tears. To have any success at understanding another's nonverbal signals, you need to remember the factors of context ("What are the surrounding events in which I am getting this message"), culture ("Are my cultural understandings and those of the sender the same?"), and personality ("Have I been around her enough to recognize her idiosyncratic behaviors?"). The next time someone accuses you of being defensive because you've crossed your arms across your chest, remind them of this principle. (However, be prepared for a defensive reaction!)

5. *Nonverbal communication adumbrates social interaction.* The term to **adumbrate** means to foreshadow or to partially disclose. In social interaction, one characteristic of nonverbal communication is to foreshadow or give cues to what should happen next. When someone reaches out a hand to you, that is usually a cue for you to also reach out, in order to shake hands. The intricate rules for social interaction are laden with nonverbal adumbrative cues. Adumbrative cues are learned primarily through observation, and therefore

COMMUNICATING SKILLFULLY

Have one member of the class stand in front of the group without speaking for one minute, and ask the person to try not to communicate. Ask the rest of the class to observe during this time and to write down any messages they get from the person. What messages did you get? Was the person able to not communicate?

COMMUNICATING SKILLFULLY

Using the following list of emotions, select several items that seem difficult for you to express. Take turns expressing them nonverbally to the class, and see the different interpretations the class makes of the same expression.

fear	*sureness*
security	*anxiety*
hate	*exhilaration*
love	*joy*
approval	*success*
rejection	*failure*

What emotions were easy to express and recognize? Which ones were difficult? Why?

when people are in a new situation they are not always sure of the cues. New situations can include such things as working at a new job or traveling in a foreign country with different cultural norms. Take as an example, the social setting of a first romantic kiss. Because intimate behavior such as kissing is somewhat tension producing to begin with, people sometimes miss subtle cues such as angles of head position or moving closer as signals of "permission" to kiss.

When people miss these nonverbal cues, they don't or can't follow through. People who are reticent or shy often miss such adumbrative cues. Adumbrative cues often operate outside awareness. Some examples include greetings and behavior in receiving lines and at grocery checkout stands. It is important to recognize that adumbrative cues occur at both the interpersonal and small-group levels of communication. The success of asking your parents to borrow the car, negotiation sessions between employer and union, and peace talks between nations depend on the ability to recognize adumbrative cues that indicate not only how you should proceed, but—sometimes more importantly—also when.

THE FUNCTIONS OF NONVERBAL COMMUNICATION IN SOCIAL INTERACTION

As mentioned before, your ability to communicate nonverbally is part of your semiotic potential. Some writers, such as rhetorician Kenneth Burke (1968) or linguist George Trager (1965), have suggested that this ability to manipulate symbols makes human beings unique. Because verbal and non-

In a routine communication context like a grocery "check out" line, there are many adumbrative cues which guide our communication.

verbal symbols are somewhat inseparable in social intercourse, what specific functions or purposes do the nonverbal instruments serve? To understand the concept of functions, it might be useful to think of an analogy. For example, one function of a pen is to write; the function of a typewriter is to type; the functions of a refrigerator are storage and cooling. In the same way, the functions of nonverbal behaviors can be identified. Philosopher of language Ludwig Wittgenstein (1958), discussing how language can be used to perform certain tasks, offers a toolbox metaphor:

> Think of the tools in a tool-box: there is a hammer, pliers, a saw, a screw-driver, a rule, a glue-pot, glue, nails, and screws. The functions of words are as diverse as the functions of these objects. (And in both cases there are similarities). Of course, what confuses us is the uniform appearance of words when we hear them spoken or meet them in script and print. For their application is not presented to us so clearly.

The toolbox metaphor can be used in an analysis of nonverbal behavior, because it is possible to look at movement or vocal stress and see the function of such behavior. Linguists, philosophers, anthropologists, communication theorists, and psychologists have all given consideration to the functions of language and nonverbal behavior for some time. According to Ekman (1969), the primary functions of nonverbal messages are: repeating, substituting, complementing, accenting, and contradicting. Let's take a look at each of these.

1. *Repeating.* When you tell someone directions to another house down the block and around the corner and point in the same direction, you're repeating your verbal message. When you wave to a person driving away from the house and say, "Bye-bye," you are repeating the message.

2. *Substituting.* A shrug of a shoulder or raised eyebrows can be a response to the question "What's up?" These movements are substituting for a verbal response such as "Not much." In social situations where it might be inappropriate to speak, people often use this substitution function. In a crowded room at a party, for example, it is socially unacceptable to call across the room to your friend and say, "I'm tired or bored, so let's go." However, by making eye contact with your friend, miming a yawn, and nodding your head toward the door, you can accomplish the same task.

3. *Adding detail or complementing.* The detail or complement function of the nonverbal embellishes and adds richer meanings to verbal messages. If you tell someone you love him and hug him at the same time, you're complementing your verbal message. The same is true when expressing anger. Generally when you're angry you not only express with your words but reinforce your anger with your facial tensions. In fact, many books on assertiveness suggest that attempts at assertiveness often fail because of the lack of consistency between words and behaviors. If you ask someone to quiet down a little so you can study but say it in a way that indicates that if he can't you'll just go somewhere else to study, you probably won't get his compliance. The primary reason is

COMMUNICATING SKILLFULLY

Form small groups, and have each group give a presentation to the class that shows each of the five functions just listed. Use as many different forms of nonverbal communication as your group can think of.

that these complementing behaviors most often signal attitude, and in this case you indicated it is not very important for them to be quiet. All students have experienced the professor who asks for questions, but nonverbally signals that he or she really doesn't want to hear any.

4. *Accenting.* Like complementary behaviors, accenting adds details, but more specifically emphasis. Accenting can also be accomplished by vocally stressing a certain spoken word ("It wasn't *my* fault you were late"). Even when you write messages, and use all UPPER CASE, or underline, or add a slew of exclamation points, you're sending distinct nonverbal messages!!!!

5. *Contradicting.* Often people send contradictory, or as psychologists refer to them, incongruent or double messages. Expressions such as "You say one thing and then do another" or "You talk out of both sides of your mouth" are attempts to describe this behavior. When someone asks you, "What's wrong?" and you answer with downcast eyes and a barely audible voice, "Nothing," you're sending an incongruent, contradictory message. Sometimes you may send these contradictory messages because you feel both ways. Sometimes you do this because you want the person to work harder to get the "real" message, and sometimes you send these double messages unintentionally. Examples of unintentional double messages might include a half smile with a small "Thank you" to someone who gives you a gift that you already have, or appearing very nervous during a job interview even while expressing your confidence to do the job.

When people receive double messages, they tend to pay more attention and to believe the nonverbal message more than the verbal message. The quantity of information that comes through the nonverbal channels of voice, eye behavior, gesture, and posture overpower the verbal message, even when they're subtle.

These five functions of nonverbal communication operate through the various communication channels of voice, body movement, physical space, and others. Let's look at these now.

THE NONVERBAL REPERTOIRE

You communicate nonverbally through the tools in your communication package. Although you're born with the capacity to communicate, it is your development and use of these tools that allow you to reach your semiotic potential. The first tool we'll discuss is paralinguistics, because it is so closely associated with speech communication.

Paralinguistics

Paralinguistics or paralanguage means "with language" or "accompanying speech." Perhaps an easy way to understand paralanguage is by thinking about not *what* you are saying, but *how* you are saying it. If you say, "*How* are you today?" with the emphasis on "*How*" or "How are you *today*?" with the emphasis on "today," you have changed the meaning of the question through your tone and inflection. David Crystal (1975) says paralanguage is a bridge between nonlinguistic forms of communicative behavior and the central areas of "verbal" linguistic study—grammar, vocabulary, and pronunciation. Sometimes called the "greasy" parts of speech because they are hard to pick out, write down, or even name, they consist of such things as hesitations, vocalizations, and so on. Paralanguage can include laughing, crying, tsking, sighing, as well as pitch, articulation, rhythm, resonance, tempo, volume, yelling, whispering, moaning, whining, belching, yawning, and vocal segregates (noises made to take the place of words) such as "uh," "uh-huh," "uh-uh," "shh," and other clicks, snorts, and sniffs. Some writers in the field of nonverbal communication have referred to the study of paralinguistics as "vocalics" or "voice messages." These writers are usually concerned with those aspects of your voice that influence the receiver's perception of the speaker. Many voice qualities, such as breathiness, orotundity (clear, deep, resonant, perhaps even pompous or bombastic), and nasality, have been studied to see what effect they have on listeners. In a major study entitled "The Relationship of Selected Vocal Characteristics to Personality Perception," D. W. Addington (1968) reported his findings. See Table 7.1.

Given Addington's research on stereotypical perceptions of voice qualities, members of both sexes might want to avoid nasality; males should emphasize orotundity; and females might like to increase their rate and pitch variety. In face-to-face interaction, other physical features such as facial expression and body posture have a mediating effect on the message your voice projects. For example, if you sound irritated but you're smiling, your listener may get a mixed message. If you're smiling, your vocal tone is friendly, and your body looks relaxed, your listener is getting a consistent message rather than a contradictory one. We're not going to tell you what kind of speaking voice you should use. We simply want to emphasize that the tone and inflection of your voice in itself carries a message. An awareness of all the nonverbal and verbal messages you transmit at any given moment can help make you a better communicator.

Kinesics and Eye Behavior

Kinesics, or body movements including eye behavior, are another part of your nonverbal repertoire. The term kinesics was coined by Ray Birdwhistell (1955). Birdwhistell studies nonverbal behavior from an anthropological perspective. That is, he looks at the role communication plays in how humans adapt to their culture, and he is also interested in studying how a combination of musculoskeletal movements carry meaning to a receiver. Much like a linguist studies various parts of language such as morphemes, phonemes, syntax,

Nobility and dignity, self-abasement and servility, prudence and understanding, insolence and vulgarity, are reflected in the face and in the attitudes of the body whether still or in motion.

SOCRATES,
XENOPHON,
MEMORABILIA III

TABLE 7.1

PERCEPTION OF PERSONALITY AND VOCAL CHARACTERISTICS

Vocal Cues	Speakers	Stereotyped Perceptions
Breathiness	Males	Younger, more artistic.
	Females	More feminine, prettier, more petite, more effervescent, more high strung, and shallower.
Thinness	Males	Did not alter listener's image of the speaker.
	Females	Increased social, physical, emotional and mental immaturity; increased sense of humor and sensitivity.
Flatness	Males	More masculine, more sluggish, colder, more withdrawn.
	Females	The same perception as held for males.
Nasality	Males	A wide array of socially undesirable characteristics.
	Females	The same perception as held for males.
Tenseness	Males	Older, unyielding, cantankerous.
	Females	Younger, more emotional, feminine, high strung; less intelligent.
Throatiness	Males	Older, more realistic, mature; sophisticated; well adjusted.
	Females	Less intelligent; more masculine; lazier; more boorish, unemotional, ugly, sickly, careless, inartistic, naive, humble, neurotic, quiet, uninteresting, apathetic. In short, "cloddish and oafish," according to Addington.
Orotundity	Males	More energetic, healthy, artistic, sophisticated, proud, interesting, enthusiastic. In short, "hardy and aesthetically inclined," says Addington.
	Females	Increased liveliness, gregariousness, esthetic sensitivity, proud and humorless.
Increased rate	Males	More animated and extroverted.
	Females	The same as for males.
Increased pitch	Males	More dynamic, feminine, variety, aesthetically inclined.
	Females	More dynamic and introverted.

and grammar, Birdwhistell examines various elements of body motion that occur in different combinations and classifies them as kines, kinemes, kinesic markers, and so on. Birdwhistell describes his task as isolating structural meaning by studying body motions in social context—as they are happening in day-to-day experiences.

Psychologists Paul Ekman and William Friesen (1975) extended Birdwhistell's work and turned it in another direction. They argued that there are basically five types of body expressions: (1) emblems, (2) illustrators, (3) regulators, (4) affect displays, and (5) adaptors.

EMBLEMS

Emblems are usually gestural equivalents of a word or phrase. For example, the phrase "Come here" can easily be replaced by the familiar motion of bringing the open hand and arm toward the chest in a repeated motion. The "peace" or "victory" sign made with the fingers are also examples of emblems. The Japanese perform a bow to show polite-

In interview situations, we try to communicate competence and confidence. We do this through our mode of dress, our grooming, posture, rate of speech, gesture, and facial expressions, to name a few nonverbal modes.

ness or respect. Emblematic movements most frequently occur when the verbal channel is blocked. A ground controller can gesture a pilot into the proper position when the engine noise makes oral communication impossible. In

CONSIDERING CRITICAL THINKING

Independently of other classmates, read the following scenario and decide who you would hire and why. Form small groups. Discuss your answers with your group. See if you or any member of the group wants to change answers after the group discussion. If so, why? If not, why not? What role does nonverbal communication play in your answers?

Scenario: Two people apply for the same job (dealing with customer complaints), and you're the interviewer. The first applicant is smartly dressed, has a GPA of 2.8 with a communication major, and answers questions carefully. The second is not as sharply dressed, speaks with a foreign accent, and has a GPA of 3.8 with a business major. Presume that the primary qualification for the position is the ability to talk to a variety of people and deal effectively with their complaints. Whom would you hire based on the information you have?

CONSIDERING CULTURE

WHAT YOUR TONGUE MAY REALLY BE SAYING

On a conscious level, the human tongue is regularly put to a wide variety of useful purposes: it licks postage stamps, demolishes ice-cream cones and also performs a major function in the delivery of that staccato sputter of derision known as the Bronx cheer, or rasberry. In Tibet, when one hill tribesman encounters another, the two exchange greetings by protruding their tongues, much as two Westerners might wave or shake hands.

Now, however, a team of evolutionary biologists at the University of Pennsylvania has completed a five-year study of how people use their tongues at the unconscious level. Their major finding seems to be that the unconscious display of the tongue is a universal sign of aversion to social encounter—a sign that is used alike by all races, and also by such other primates as orangutans and gorillas.

Drs. W. John Smith and Julia Chase, assisted by graduate student Anna Katz Lieblich, first studied displays at Philadelphia's Mulberry Tree Nursery School. There, they noted that toddlers tend to show their tongues when they are engrossed in difficult tasks, such as finger painting or climbing over obstacles, and also when they are involved in awkward social situations, such as receiving a scolding for misbehavior. This suggested to Smith that the action indicated a desire to be left alone, so he decided to test the hypothesis by trying to provoke tongue showing.

Adults: Smith stationed himself in the path of a 4-year-old girl who was running a repeated route from room to room, and caught her eye as she approached him. The girl averted her eyes and protruded her tongue. She repeated this behavior four times. But on the sixth curcuit, now sure that Smith would not grab her, the girl showed no hint of her tongue.

The biologist then made the unobtrusive observations of tongue-showing among the general public in Philadelphia and in Panama. They found that it occurred among adults in exactly the same settings as with children. Adults show their tongues during tasks requiring intense concentration—when making a tricky shot a pool, for example, or backing into a small parking space— and also in socially threatening situations, such as being interrupted in conversation. Extending the study further, Smith and his colleagues watched a number of gorillas and orangutans at close quarters, with identical results. For although the apes tended to show their tongues more prominently than did humans, the circumstances involved either complex tasks such as peeling bananas with their toes, or unpleasant situations in which the apes were scolded for fighting. On a conscious level, apes also use their tongues to eat ice-cream cones.

many cultures, the larger number of obscene words in everyday speech suggests a greater inhibition against vocalizing certain phrases than against using gestural equivalents. The referent for many emblems is purely arbitrary; as an example, twirling the forefinger around near you temple to indicate that another person is insane has no visual connection with the concept of madness or with the acts of the insane.

Emblems, like language, are learned in everyday social interaction and for the most part are culturally specific. When we say "culturally specific," we mean that gestures are learned in the process of becoming part of a culture. The same gesture may mean something quite different in another culture. For example, the American use of forefinger and thumb placed together to make the "OK" sign is an obscene gesture in other cultures. Sogon and Masutani's (1989) comparative research of Japanese and Americans shows that "emblematic gestures" (like the Japanese bow) vary across cultures and are directed to those who belong to the same culture.

ILLUSTRATORS

Illustrators are directly linked to speech because these actions illustrate what is being said orally and for the most part are intentional acts. People speak rhythmically, and also gesture in time to vocaliza-

Gestures are ambiguous and change their meaning from culture to culture. Does this gesture mean"OK," "aero," or is it a sexual vulgarity?

tions. A gesture can add emphasis to a particular part of a phrase. Illustrators also express logical relations or directions and spatial relationships. In fact, in difficult communication situations—such as describing the size or shape of something—people tend to use more illustrators and are frustrated in certain situations where they can't be used,—when talking on the phone, for example (Rutter, 1986). Movements in which people point to an object to which they are verbally referring to are illustrators. Some illustrators—acts that designate or depict—can stand alone, without verbal support. However, other illustrators—those emphasizing rhythm or relationship—can only be understood in connection with the verbal message. Ekman (1969) suggests that people learn to use illustrators through imitation, and because illustrator's are socially learned, they are socially variable. Ekman's point is that illustrators are culturally specific behaviors and their use and nature vary among different cultures.

REGULATORS

Regulators are actions that serve to control oral interaction between two or more people. "They tell the speaker to continue, repeat, elaborate, hurry up,

There was speech in their dumbness, language in their very gesture.

SHAKESPEARE,
WINTERS TALE

Without the use of gestures such as pointing, the task of giving directions becomes much more ambiguous.

become more interesting, less salacious.... They can tell the listener to pay special attention, to wait just a minute more, to talk, etc." (Ekman, 1969, p. 69). Recent research in communication refers to this behavior as "turn taking." Common examples of regulators would include head nods for "Keep going" or, on the telephone, saying "Uh-huh" for the same purpose. Most regulators, like illustrators, can't be understood apart from the verbal messages being exchanged. Leaning forward or backward, breaking eye contact, and raising your eyebrows can all be classified as regulators.

AFFECT DISPLAYS

Affect displays are body expressions that reflect the emotional state of the communicator. Because facial expressions are the principal way most humans convey their feelings, a face that shows anger, fear, or disgust is displaying an affective state. However, as Knapp (1990b) has said, "the whole body can also be read for global judgements of affect; for example, a drooping, sad body." Like the body movements discussed in the previous categories, affect displays are not tightly bound to verbal expressions. Furthermore, affect displays tend to be less consciously controllable than the previous types. For example, people may often seem to know how others feel, or ask, "What's wrong?" because of affect displays they observe. However, because people often try to manage the impression others have of them (impression management), people try to mask their own affect displays. Examples include beauty contestants or job applicants smiling to mask their exhaustion or anxiety. Or someone might mask hurt at an insult or joy at being dealt a good hand in poker. In fact, the term "poker face" has been coined for not letting emotions show in a card

Used by permission of the estate of Michael ffolkes.

"That was unkind, darling. When their mouths turn up at the corners they wish to be friends."

game or in any social context. Think of times people have read your affect displays when you were unaware your affect showed. Now think of a time you needed to mask your "true" emotional state.

ADAPTORS

The last classification, for Ekman and Friesen, is called an **adaptor**. Adaptors are movements, learned in childhood, that are part of a patterned activity. Adaptors are more difficult to define and are open to more speculation than most other gestures. Eisenberg and Smith (1971) suggest that an individual (say a man) who wipes his mouth on the back of his hand during a conversation is committing an action that was once part of a grooming pattern he was trained to follow; as an adult, he's now using this isolated movement to relieve stress or to "put on a better face." There are three types of adaptors: (1) *self-adaptors*, such as hair brushing, remnants of a learned activity toward one's own body; (2) *alter (stress) adaptors*, or movements learned in the process of interpersonal relations such as restless movements of hands and feet, because of anxiety; and (3) *object-adaptors*, such as using a tool such as a pencil, gestures that indicate rearrangement of the environment. Each of these kinds of adaptor movements is theoretically performed without one's awareness. They're not generally noticed or, at least, commented on by others. Eisenberg and Smith suggest that to the trained eye, however, adaptors indicate much about someone's socialization experience and emotional state. When people are talking together, their use of adaptors can be a distraction from really engaging in communication.

An area of kinesic behavior not mentioned so far is eye behavior. Let's turn to that now.

Nonverbal Communication

(or Power to the Pupil)

Eye say, eye say, eye say,
Let's throw linguistics away.
Just look into these eyes
Observe the pupil size,
They'll tell you when to fight and when to play

Pupils generate the heat
Hearts begin to miss a beat
Interactions start to thrive
And people really come alive
When pairs of pupils in vibrant silence meet.

Cast aside the MPI
For extroverts can surely lie
Adopt the seeker's role
Into the window of the soul
Behold the wonders of the telltale eye.

ANONYMOUS

EYE BEHAVIOR OR GAZE

Have you ever heard the expression "Your eyes are the windows to your soul?" Or, perhaps you've heard of someone giving someone "the evil eye." Eyes are powerful signaling devices. When the eyes of two people meet, there is a special kind of communication. The term eye contact or mutual **gaze** is often used to describe this kind of visual interaction or visual reciprocity. Mutual gaze can be used as a "regulator" in conversations, and it can be used to signal something directly to another person. In North American culture, mutual gaze can indicate interest, caring, and attentiveness. Anthropological linguist Mary Ritchie Key (1975, p. 86) reports that "deaf persons are insistent on eye contact in interactions; they depend heavily on kinesic movements to supplement the 'conversation.'" **Gaze avoidance** can also be meaningful and indicate a psychological distance, insincerity, or even shame. Sociologist Erving Goffman (1963) calls gaze avoidance in crowded elevators and other places where a relationship must be kept at a distance "civil inattention." **Gaze aversion** refers to the practice, common among people in normal conversation, of looking at the speaker or receiver at times and at other times looking away.

Whether or not to look someone straight in the eye, and for how long, is a product of your culture and the context of your encounter. In many cultures, it's considered a sign of respect to avoid mutual gazing with someone who is older or more important than you are. In fact, even in mainstream U.S. culture, a direct stare is considered a social offense to be avoided. The stare can be interpreted as an invasion of someone's privacy, or even as a threatening gesture, commonly referred to as a "predatory gaze."

An important side note on eye behavior in relationships is the study of eye pupils. When you're attracted to someone, your pupils dilate (expand) and you become relaxed. When you're angry with or dislike someone, your pupils constrict (grow smaller). Research indicates that, all other things being equal, this eye behavior will be reciprocated for distances up to about four feet away. People are attracted to large pupils. The stereotype that people with "beady" eyes are untrustworthy may come from this perception.

Proxemics

A fourth part of your nonverbal repertoire is your use of **proxemics**, or personal and physical space. Closely linked to kinesics or body movements, *proxemics* is a term coined by cultural anthropologist Edward T. Hall. Hall (1968) defined proxemics as "the study of how man unconsciously structures microspace—the distance between men in daily transactions, the organization of space in his houses and buildings, and ultimately the layout of his towns." Of primary interest in interpersonal communication is face-to-face interactions. Hall is most widely noted for his contribution of personal space or the distances people keep away from others in social interaction. In his book *The Silent Language* (1959), Hall points out that people know what distance to maintain between themselves and others in a given situation. He lists eight interaction or "comfort zones" for middle-class Anglo-Americans (see Table 7.2)

Hall believes the space you leave between yourself and others affects the type of vocal message you send and the character of your communication. At *intimate distance,* your voice is soft; more information is carried through the channels of hearing, smelling, and touching; and you're probably speaking confidentially or intimately. At the *personal distance* range, you're generally talking about personal subject matter with low volume. At *social distance,* you might be sharing public information and speak in full voice. And at *public distance* you would speak in a full or loud voice and be addressing a group. All these distances reveal relationship.

Hall said these distances apply to middle-class Anglo-Americans. This is a key point because Hall's work as a cultural anthropologist made it clear that the

TABLE 7.2

HALL'S PROXEMIC DISTANCE

Intimate distance, close	Touching or contact
Intimate distance, far	6 to 8 inches
Personal distance, close	1 1/2 to 2 1/2 feet
Personal distance, far	2 1/2 to 4 feet
Social distance, close	4 to 7 feet
Social distance, far	7 to 12 feet
Public distance, close	12 to 25 feet
Public distance, far	25 feet or more

amount of space people leave between themselves and others is to a great extent culturally determined. Two Mexican men might greet each other with an *embrazo* (embraces) and then proceed to walk arm and arm. Two Egyptian men might do something very similar. But general American protocol conditions men to keep a personal distance of about 1 1/2 feet between them. The term "general American" is used here because as a multicultural society with continual new immigrants, the social distance norms for Americans are greatly influenced by gender, racial and ethnic cultural traditions. Hall believes that some cultures are contact cultures, while others are noncontact cultures. Depending on your cultural upbringing, you carry these distances into your social interactions.

Although many writers popularized and continue to quote Hall's study on proxemic distances, Hall believes they have misunderstood the concept. In his later writings (1964, 1966), he makes the point that it is less the concern of proxemics to measure distances between interactants than it is to understand the use of the senses to regulate these distances. The basis of proxemic behavior on the interpersonal level should be viewed as "a constellation of sensory inputs that is coded in a particular way" (1968). So for Hall proxemic behavior is a *system* of interrelated variables and it is understanding of these variables that helps improve social interaction in interpersonal communication. These variables include

1. *Gender and posture identifiers.* These variables indicate the gender of interactants and whether they are standing, sitting, squatting, or prone.

2. *Sociofugal-sociopetal axis.* Social interaction quality may be affected by the extent to which interactants face each other squarely or at divergent angles.

3. *Kinesthetic factors.* These factors affect the distance from one person to another in terms of the potential for touching.

CONSIDERING CULTURE

List as many examples as you can of gender, ethnic, national, or cultural group differences in nonverbal behavior. Two ways to find differences are (1) interview members of different ethnic groups or international students to find out how they see themselves communicating differently from other groups; and (2) ask outsiders of your own group to tell you their perceptions of how your group behaves nonverbally.

CONSIDERING ETHICS

Two students (one male, one female) in an interpersonal communication class are carrying out an experiment involving Hall's proxemic zones. They hypothesize that North Americans will feel pressured if a stranger invades their "intimate zone." To test the hypothesis, they enter various elevators and stand as close as they can to a few people (mixed gender) who are riding with them. The people who are objects of the experiment are obviously uncomfortable but the two students justify their approach on the basis of learning more about the proxemic zones. Do they have the right to make someone else uncomfortable in the interest of their own education?

4. *Touch code*. This code regulates the amount and kind of touching that takes place during interaction.

5. *Visual code*. This code regulates the amount of visual contact during interaction, from eye-to-eye contact to gazing off into space.

6. *Voice loudness*. Interactions are affected by the intensity of a person's voice during an interaction.

7. *Thermal code*. This code regulates how much conduction of thermal radiation or heat from an interactant's body is acceptable.

8. *Olfaction code*. This code filters the detection of undifferentiated body and breath odors.

For Hall, these factors operate together and are the prime factors that influence interactants' personal use of space. They also reflect the degree people like, dislike, or feel neutral about others in interpersonal settings. Hall (1975, p. 59) said, "The mistake is that culture isn't just one specific thing that you can pinpoint and define. Rather, culture is a series of interrelated systems, all of which affect each other."

Breaking the Rules

Although Hall's work suggested that use of personal space follows certain social norms, Burgoon and Hale (1988) have suggested that there are times people should break the social norms. In their study of immediacy, that combination of nonverbal behaviors that convey physical closeness and involvement with others, they write (1988, p. 58) "There are circumstances under which violations of social norms and expectations may be a superior strategy to conformity." One of the most intriguing of Burgoon's findings (Burgoon & Walther, 1990) is that violating social norms such as distance can be perceived as negative or positive depending on the attractiveness of the communicator. That is, if you perceive a person as attractive, using characteristics such as gender, personality, physical attractiveness, reputation, status, and future interaction as indicators, their violation of distance norms may actually increase your personal evaluation of the person in a positive direction. As Griffin (1991, p. 66) writes in *Communication Theory: A First Look*, "Burgoon is convinced that for rewarding relationships, a distance of too close or too far is better than spacing that's 'just right.'"

Territoriality

A subarea of the study of proxemics is **territoriality**. Territoriality is concerned with the tendency to use fixed geographical space as one's own territory or untouchable space. Just as other animals mark off or scent "their" space, so do humans. This can be seen in examples such as your Mom or Dad's chair at the dinner table or in areas of your dorm room that are off limits even to your roommate without your permission.

Generally speaking, there are three basic territorial zones. Primary territories are those you call your own, such as your work area, or your room, or perhaps your car. Secondary territories are those you don't own but you've occupied or you're had associated with you. Examples of secondary territories include a seat in the classroom you usually choose to sit in or *your* table in the student union. Public territories are open to anyone to use and include public parks, malls, restaurants, and such.

In interpersonal relationships, the use of these various territories can signal status as well as ownership. The size and location of territory indicates status. People who are perceived as higher-status individuals may enter a lower-status person's territory, while the opposite is not allowed. The president of the university might come right into the office of one of the deans, but the dean would probably never walk into the president's office without seeking permission. Also, in class a professor might sit in on a group of students working on a small-group project, but the students could not do the same thing to a group of professors.

Haptics or Touching Behaviors

A fifth element in your nonverbal repertoire is **haptics**, or touching behavior (see Figure 7.1). As mentioned before, touching behavior—like proxemics—is to a great extent culturally determined. However, touch is one of the first learned forms of communication. In fact, if babies were not born with touch sensors in their lips and mouth they would be denied the very source of life. Touching behavior is important in a child's early life development, in adolescent behavior, and in both middle and old age. In fact, many new studies on touch describe the absence of being touched as a primary concern for health in the aged. Touch can be comforting and a natural sedative for those feeling distress. It can be playful, congratulatory, and athletic in nature. On the down side, touch can be manipulative and abusive when used in exploitive or inappropriate ways in the home and at work.

Several interesting patterns of touching frequency have been noted in interpersonal relationships. In Judith Hall and Ellen Veccia's article, "More 'Touching' Observations: New Insights on Men, Women, and Interpersonal Touch" (1990), they note that in interpersonal relationships

- Males and females touch each other intentionally with equal frequency.

- Under 30, males touched females more than vice versa; over 30, the reverse was true.

- Members of male-male dyads touch each other much less than members of female-female dyads.

- Mixed-sex dyads are much more likely to touch than same-sex dyads.

Look at the findings of Hall and Veccia, and consider how accurate their research would be for you. Their figures are not prescriptive; that is, they do not suggest how much we *should* touch others. If you find this research doesn't fit you, think through some reasons why that is true. Discuss some of your ideas about this with a classmate or friend. Touch is a natural behavior between human beings, and being able to positively give and receive touch is a key element of the competent communicator. Recognizing your comfort level with touch in various relationships is an important awareness to develop.

Physical Characteristics

Certainly physical characteristics are part of nonverbal communication. If they were not, few people would voluntarily pay large sums of money to a plastic surgeon to alter some part of their anatomy, or to the weight loss industry to help them get slim. Among physical characteristics are body shape and size, general attractiveness, height, weight, skin and hair color or tone, and body and breath odors. Gender plays a strong role in perceptions of and research on physical characteristics.

The influence of body shape on interpersonal perception was first explored by W. H. Sheldon (1954) in his book *Atlas of Man: A Guide for Somatyping the Adult Male at All Ages.* This work was concerned with a person's physical similarity to the three extreme varieties of male physique as shown in Figure 7.2.

Sheldon classified men into three basic **somatypes** or body shapes. The three somatypes were called (1) **endomorph**, soft, round, and fat; (2) **mesomorph**, bony, muscular and athletic; and (3) **ectomorph**, tall, thin, and fragile. Although Sheldon's work received much scientific criticism, several

Black people are communal by culture. They prepare communally. They dance, they play games communally. That slap on the hand you see…means something to those brothers. It means something to the brothers in the stands. It means something to the brothers who are watching the TV sets.

HARRY EDWARDS

FIGURE 7.2

Sheldon's Somatypes

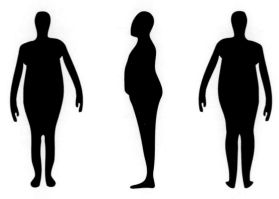

A. The endomorph: Soft, round, fat.

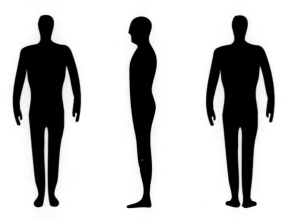

B. The mesomorph: bony, muscular, athletic.

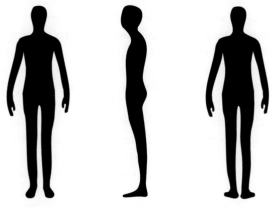

C. The ectomorph: tall, thin, fragile.

TABLE 7.3

Somatypes and Temperament Characteristics

Endomorphic	Mesomorphic	Ectomorphic
dependent	dominant	detached
calm	cheerful	tense
relaxed	confident	anxious
complacent	energetic	reticent
contented	impetuous	self-conscious
sluggish	efficient	meticulous
placid	enthusiastic	reflective
leisurely	competitive	precise
cooperative	determined	thoughtful
affable	outgoing	considerate
tolerant	argumentative	shy
affected	talkative	awkward
warm	active	cool
forgiving	domineering	suspicious
sympathetic	courageous	introspective
soft-hearted	enterprising	serious
generous	adventurous	cautious
affectionate	reckless	tactful
kind	assertive	sensitive
sociable	optimistic	withdrawn
soft-tempered	hot-tempered	gentle-tempered

researchers went on to test the validity and have confirmed many of his conclusions. One such study, conducted by J. B. Cortes and F. M. Gatti (1965), connected certain temperament patterns with these somatypes. The temperament characteristics are listed in Table 7.3.

What do these body shapes and temperaments have to do with nonverbal communication and interpersonal relationships? If the link could be clearly drawn from this work, it would seem that the way you are perceived and the way you perceive others would be greatly influenced by such stereotypes. Look at the three figures and temperament lists. How realistic do you think they are? How influenced are you in forming first impressions by other people's physique? What about their height? Skin color? If you can be aware of the information you use to form first impressions of others, you can be aware of the possible influence on your relationships.

As for Sheldon's work, although many studies have tried to link physical characteristics with certain personality types, so far no clear link has been established. Physical attractiveness and perceived temperament appear to have more to do with self-esteem, attractiveness to others, and projection of favored characteristics on those to whom one is attracted.

COMMUNICATING SKILLFULLY

From magazines, gather some current pictures that suggest different physical characteristics (age, weight, wealth, education, sex, and so on). In small groups, discuss what these people are like, and what it would be like to visit them. Your stereotypical responses can provide food for thought and discussion.

Artifactual Communication

Artifactual communication include all those artifacts or elements you add to your body, such as earrings (how many, where placed, how long), watches, necklaces, eyeglasses (how long you spend at the optometrist mirror until you find the frames that are "you"), hairpieces, wigs, eyeliners, perfumes, and other cosmetic devices. Other artifacts that act as extensions of self can include the car you drive, the way you decorate your room, the "name brand" sweat shirt or athletic shoes you wear. These extensions act as nonverbal status symbols.

We've been discussing basic areas of nonverbal behavior. Now we would like to turn to specific nonverbal skills for you to consider as part of your communication repertoire. At the beginning of this chapter, we said we would like you to gain an understanding of the significance of nonverbal behavior as part of your total "communication package." In examining the various perspectives, characteristics and forms of nonverbal communication, we hope you've gained this understanding. Although knowledge of these areas is a worthy accomplishment in itself, as a liberal arts student you'll want to use this knowledge to improve the quality of your communication. So the question you might be asking yourself is "What can I do with all this information?"

We would like you to consider using three primary skills—sensitivity, receptivity, and accurate comprehension—in your nonverbal communication with others. These three skills deal with receiving and sending nonverbal messages. The reception skills you need to enhance are being sensitive to nonverbal messages, and accurately comprehending them. As a sender of nonverbal messages, the skills to master are to control your nonverbal messages and to avoid sending unintentional or incongruent messages.

SENSITIVITY, RECEPTIVITY, AND ACCURATE COMPREHENSION

To be an effective communicator, you need to become receptive to nonverbal cues in understanding someone's total series of messages. It's also important to recognize the various modes or repertoires of nonverbal components if you are to accurately comprehend them. In a now famous series of studies, Robert Rosenthal (1974) and his colleagues at Harvard University conducted a test called the Profile of Nonverbal Sensitivity (PONS). The PONS Test was a film in which emotions were expressed by actors; only part of the body would be shown, or the voice would be altered to tone qualities only. This test was administered to subjects in the United States and many other countries.

Rosenthal's early research on the Pygmalion effect and self-fulfilling prophecies led him to believe that much communication is wordless and that

CONSIDERING CULTURE

In their article "Identification of Emotion from Body Movements: A Cross-Cultural Study of Americans and Japanese" (1989), Shunya Sogon and Makoto Masutani indicated that both Americans and Japanese could recognize the expressions of the emotions sadness, fear, and anger but that Japanese subjects could not identify contempt or disgust. The authors believe this is due to cultural differences in the two countries. Japanese people suppress feelings of disgust and contempt because it is a serious breach of custom to express these emotions directly. The suppression of these feelings is important to success in life. In the United States, people are taught that it can be bad to suppress emotions because it keeps them from being honest in relationships. Can you think of other examples of intercultural differences in the expression of emotions? How might these differences affect contact between international students and U.S. students at your college? How might these differences affect business and government relations between countries?

some kind of nonverbal communication was the medium through which one person's feelings and ideas were transmitted to another. Rosenthal was interested in finding why some people were more effective and clearer in their "sending" and "receiving" powers. He wanted to know what kinds of senders influence particular receivers most effectively.

Rosenthal's findings proved both enlightening and provocative because they showed that females are better at detecting nonverbal cues. Females at all ages, from third grade through adult, detected nonverbal messages better and more accurately comprehended them than men (Rosenthal et al., 1974).

The results were not hopeless for men, however. The differences between the sexes narrowed and even reversed themselves among men in certain jobs or training for certain occupations. These occupations included teachers, psychologists, mental health workers, and workers in the visual arts. An important point from the Rosenthal study is that people can learn to "read" nonverbal cues more accurately by building sensitivity skills. Also, the study showed that nonverbal sensitivity was somewhat independent of general intelligence. In other words, someone can be extremely bright, but "thick as a brick" when it comes to nonverbal awareness. Someone can be of average intelligence but have excellent sensitivity to others' nonverbal signals.

Kelly-Dyreson, Burgoon, and Bailey (1991) also found that females are superior to males in their accuracy of reading nonverbal messages. Their research led them to three conclusions:

1. Females are superior to males in nonverbal sensitivity.

2. Accuracy is greater in decoding kinesic channels (movement) than the vocalic channel (paralanguage—how something is said).

3. Stress may have some negative impact on decoding emotional expression.

CONSCIOUS FEEDBACK

As mentioned in earlier chapters, a key to accurate comprehension and understanding nonverbal messages is the same key for understanding all interpersonal communication—namely, seeking and giving feedback. Since nonverbal communication is nonspoken, it takes tact and poise to bring a nonverbal message to the conscious verbal level. That is, when you receive a nonverbal message you might need to ask the person you are interacting with if in fact the message you received is the message he or she sent.

ATTITUDE

Recent research by Manusov (1990) suggests that attitude also influences how sensitive and receptive people are in interpreting nonverbal signals. To a great extent, the degree to which you're satisfied with a relationship influences how you interpret your partner's nonverbal communication. If you're very happy with your partner, you'll interpret his or her nonverbal behavior as positive or "relationship enhancing." If you're less satisfied with your partner, you interpret their nonverbal behavior as negative and create "distress-maintaining" causal explanations. For example, if you think you have a good relationship with someone, you might perceive his or her lack of eye contact with you as a sign of shyness or coyness. It might actually increase the partner's attractiveness. However, if you're unhappy with your relationship, you might perceive these same behaviors as indicating disinterest in you and a way your partner is avoiding contact. When it's not possible to seek or give feedback, people can be trained to more accurately "read" nonverbal messages. The "Putting Theory into Practice" section of this chapter provides several activities you can use to sharpen your reception skills. However, your attitude or sensitivity remains key.

SENDING NONVERBAL MESSAGES WITH CLARITY

In all communication, the sender of the message has the responsibility to be as clear as possible and to seek feedback, to find out what the receivers are getting. As a sender of nonverbal messages, controlling your nonverbal messages is not possible 100 percent of the time because so much of behavior operates outside the level of awareness. However, because it's so important to avoid sending unintentional or incongruent messages, carefully attending to interactions can eliminate or at least correct inadvertent messages. As you gain knowledge about your total communication package, you need to check and match your nonverbal message to your verbal message whenever possible. Ask, "What part of my nonverbal repertoire is best for this certain type of communication? Should I use illustrative gestures when giving a message? Do my body movements add clarity or distract from my message? Will I convey warmth and caring by standing closer and perhaps touching you?" Knowing which nonverbal mode to use is every bit as important as carefully selecting the words. However, as we said in Chapter 1, there are no clear set of rules on which nonverbal mode to use. As a communicator, be mindful of the context of communication in deciding on appropriate communication strategies. The "Putting Theory into Practice" section lists several skill builders designed to increase your clarity in sending nonverbal messages.

As you get better at recognizing others' nonverbal signals, tune in more carefully to your own nonverbal signals, and seek feedback from others about the nonverbal messages they are getting from you, your nonverbal competence will increase to the point that you simply will not make many nonverbal "slips." This is not to say your actions will lack spontaneity and are totally rehearsed, but rather that you've developed sensitivity, receptivity, and accurate comprehension. Like a good athlete, your skills will become second nature and be appreciated and recognized by others. Nonverbal competence pays a high reward in avoiding misunderstandings, enhancing our self-esteem, and gaining the esteem of others.

LOOKING BACK - LOOKING FORWARD

In the chapter just completed, you've gained a clear understanding of the significance of nonverbal behavior as part of your total communication package. You've examined various perspectives, characteristics, and forms of nonverbal communication and have been presented with several skills you can master to avoid sending unintentional or incongruent messages while at the same time developing your sensitivity, accuracy, and comprehension as a receiver of nonverbal messages.

Chapter 8 explores the role of listening in our relationships and offer you some skills you may want to try in improving your listening abilities.

REVIEW TERMS AND CONCEPTS

PUTTING THEORY INTO PRACTICE

FOR DISCUSSION:

1. Divide the class into small groups, and have members of the groups discuss three ways they might increase their sensitivity to nonverbal communication. Each group should report back to the total class the ideas generated.

2. What are the advantages and disadvantages of distinguishing between nonverbal behavior and nonverbal communication? Write your own definition of each, and share with the class. After the class members share their definitions, discuss what the definitions had in common and what was different.

SKILL BUILDERS:

1. Each student should bring to class a magazine advertisement. In small groups, analyze the nonverbal messages in the ads. What are the communication goals suggested by the ad?

2. Show a fairly popular television commercial in class, with the sound

off. Have the class analyze the nonverbal communication in the commercial. How has the commercial used time, space, and action to achieve communication goals?

3. If your classmates include dance or theater majors, or some members who enjoy performing, ask them to demonstrate a story or theme through dance and pantomime.

4. Discuss in small groups the nonverbal forms of rejection and alienation that may occur in the class itself. Expand the discussion to the campus and the community. Suggest possible ways to handle the nonverbal signals of rejection and alienation.

5. If some members of the class like photography, ask them to create a story without any words. This can be done with prints, slides, or video.

6. Listen to one of your professors' lectures. How does he or she use vocal qualities to emphasize points in lectures. How do vocal qualities contribute to how he or she feels about the topic? What other voice qualities contribute to your understanding or enjoyment of the lecture? Record your experience and share it with your class.

7. Try this with a classmate you don't know well. On a sheet of paper, make three inferences about the other's personality based on the person's physical characteristics. What aspects of physical characteristics were primarily used to make inferences about each other? What other appearance cues (dress, hair style, posture, and so on) contributed to these impressions? Discuss with your partner the impact of these kinds of inferences on your communication with others.

FOR EXTENDED STUDY

Burgoon, Judee K., Bueller, David B., & Woodall, W. Gill. (1989). *Nonverbal communication: The unspoken dialogue.* New York: Harper & Row.

A very valuable contribution to the field of communication, with coverage on many aspects of nonverbal communication. The book is very thorough and supported by research.

Eibl-Eibesfeldt, Irenaus. (1989). *Human ethology.* New York: Aldine/De Gruyter.

Science students might particularly find this book stimulating. Derived from the first wave of evolutionary thinking about human behavior, this book represents a capstone summary of Eibl-Eibesfeldt's research and views on nonverbal communication. The research is presented in rich detail with extensive cross-cultural data that by themselves makes the book valuable.

Hall, Edward T. (1959). *The silent language.* New York: Fawcett Books,

> *An anthropologist reveals how we communicate by our manners and behavior. Hall's initial work in proxemics is explored in both a practical and theoretical sense.*

Hall, Edward T. (1977). *Beyond culture.* Garden City, NY: Anchor Books.

> *This book is written in a popular and colloquial manner. It extends Hall's theories of proxemics and provides a good understanding of the manner in which culture conditions people to perceive their world in certain predetermined ways.*

Henley, Nancy. (1977). *Body politics: power, sex, and nonverbal communication.* Englewood Cliffs, NJ: Prentice-Hall.

> *Henley is a social psychologist who takes a feminist stand on how gender differences influence nonverbal behaviors and power.*

Key, Mary Ritchie (Ed.).(1980). *The relationship of verbal and nonverbal communication.* New York: Mouton.

> *An excellent collection of essays that explore the connection between language and nonverbal communication from the development of communicative behavior through theoretical approaches to human interaction.*

Montagu, Ashley. (1986). *Touching: The human significance of the skin,* (3rd ed.). New York: Harper & Row.

> *Classical review on the importance of touch in the development of human relationships.*

Richmond, Virginia P., McCrosky, James C., & Payne, Steven K.(1987). *Nonverbal behavior in interpersonal relations.* Englewood Cliffs, NJ: Prentice-Hall.

> *A very thorough work that presents nonverbal behavior as a multidisciplinary study.*

*We have two ears
and only one
tongue in order
that we may hear
more and speak
less.*

DIOGENES (320 B.C.)

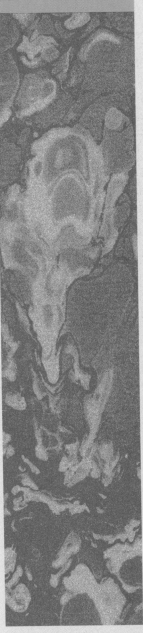

Listening

OBJECTIVES

After reading this chapter and taking part in class activities, you should be able to

- Compare and contrast hearing and listening.

- Distinguish the four kinds of listening necessary for effective interpersonal communication.

- Explain why listening is so hard.

- List ineffective ways people listen.

- Describe ways you can improve your listening skills in interpersonal relationships.

HOW MANY TIMES have you heard someone give you a message and then later you discovered you missed the meaning? For example, a friend might tell you that she'll meet you at 7 in "our usual place" for a study session. You caught the "usual place" and "study session," but you didn't grasp the time. Since you've met at 8 for the last four times, you assumed the session would be held at 8 again. You show up to discover that you're an hour off.

Such situations happen all the time. For most people, misunderstanding is a greater problem than disagreement. A lot of misunderstanding occurs because people may *hear* a message but not listen to it carefully enough to get the full meaning. In his classic book, *Are You Listening?* Ralph Nichols (1957) shows how many college students are not good listeners. Test yourself. During the last class you attended, how much time did you listen so that you could recall the material presented? Maybe you're the exception, but many college students listen to less than half of the lecture material and then forget half of that within a short time. The result: students listen with a 25 percent level of listening effectiveness. If much of the material for exams comes from lectures, then poor listening habits can cost you dearly in frustration and poor grades.

LISTENING AND INTERPERSONAL COMMUNICATION

Poor listening can also impair interpersonal communication. Messages often get missed because one or both parties in a conversation fail to grasp what the other was saying. They're not really listening to each other. In this chapter, we examine four kinds of listening used in interpersonal communication:

1. Informational

2. Empathic

3. Critical

4. Dialogic

We then discuss some problems many people have in listening effectively, and suggest some skills you can develop to listen better. Practiced on a regular basis, these listening skills can make your interpersonal communication richer and more satisfying.

Listening in a conversation is as important as talking.

How Does Listening Differ from Hearing?

The word *listening* comes from Middle English and means "to attend closely." If you really listen to someone, you pay close attention to his or her words and ideas. Listening is different from hearing. **Hearing** is a physiological process that includes your middle ear absorbing sound waves and then transferring them along neural pathways to specific parts of the brain. You can hear people talking in the background at a party, but you may not attend to what they're saying. Your ears pick up the sounds of voices but you're not listening to their comments. Hearing is a necessary prerequisite to listening but is only part of the process.

Early studies by Paul Rankin (1929) and more recent research by Barker and others (1981) confirm that we listen more than we talk during most encounters. Listening is a vital part of the communication we carry on during an interpersonal relationship. How well you listen can often mean the difference between a union that is highly satisfying and one that is mediocre or even tragic. Let's look now at the four kinds of listening that can occur during the communication process.

Listening effectively during a lecture takes discipline.

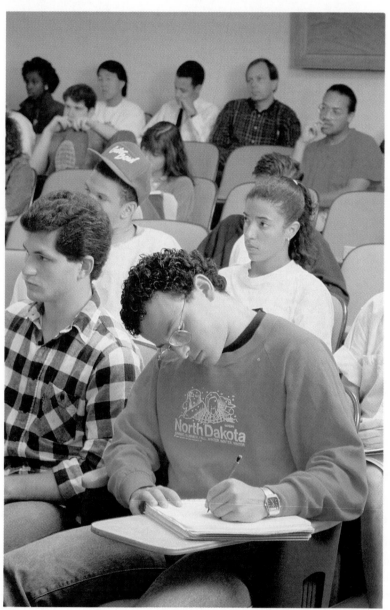

INFORMATIONAL LISTENING

The most obvious kind of listening is **informational**. If you're taking a calculus class, you work hard to understand the equation the instructor is explaining. If your best friend has been in an accident on a deserted road and is trying to give you directions on how to find him, you try to make sure you have all the facts. Listening for information is highly important for you in both these situations. You know that just one piece of incorrect information can lead to your missing something in the lecture or cause you to make a wrong turn and not find your friend.

Most experts on listening make a distinction between **active** and **passive listening**. As an active listener, you put in great effort to understand the information being presented to you in the calculus class or by your friend over the phone. In passive listening, you may hear the words and understand a few ideas, but little more is happening than the voice vibrations from the speaker striking your middle ear and getting sidetracked somewhere on the neural path to the brain. Passive listening may happen for a number of reasons—you're tired, the material presented is boring, or you want to think about something other than what you're hearing. You may, on occasion, *choose* to listen passively, because you've heard the material many times before or you really need to think about a problem.

POOR INFORMATIONAL LISTENING

The following types of poor listening can interfere with effective communication.

Pseudo-listening

Most college students have developed the ability to fake attention during classes. Most professors are probably relieved that students don't always let them know when they've drifted off into some personal fantasy. Such a revelation could be distracting for someone giving a lecture. Faking attention means that you may be gazing at the instructor and telegraphing the impression that you are absorbing every bit of information. You really may be thinking about anything from Saturday's game to what you're going to eat tonight for dinner. Most people engage in **pseudo-listening** at some time during a lecture or conversation. Very few of us can constantly focus on what a speaker or a conversation partner is saying.

LISTENING IN LECTURES

In a now famous experiment, Professor Paul Cameron of Wayne State University tried an experiment to test how well students really listened to a lecture. During a college psychology course he was teaching, Cameron had a gun fired at random intervals.

He then asked students to let him know what they were thinking about each time the gun went off. Here is what he found:

- *Twenty percent of the students—both men and women—were thinking erotic thoughts*

- *Twenty percent were recalling something from the past*

- *Eight percent were thinking about religion*

- *The rest were worrying, daydreaming, or thinking about food*

On the average, only 20 percent were paying attention to the lecture with only 12 percent engaged in active listening.

Tuning Out Because Speaker or Topic Is Boring

Most people will listen to a conversation or a talk because the speaker is intriguing or the subject is interesting. In the best circumstances, the speaker is outstanding and the subject is exciting. Some people compel our attention. Their voice is vibrant, and they project a dynamism that is hard to ignore. They could talk about irrigation systems and make it interesting. Unfortunately, such people are relatively few. You may begin your school day with a history professor who can captivate and keep your attention with dramatic lectures on the French Revolution. The next period, you attend a lecture by someone whose speaking style is as dry as dust. Or you may want to really listen to someone who has a personal problem. But as much as you try, you find it hard to listen to the other person's tale of woe, especially as it goes on and on.

Most of us can understand why people tune out to this kind of discourse. But we pay a price for doing so. At the very least, listening to a lecture will almost always help students succeed on exams and learn the material better. And if you really listen to the person with the problem, you may be giving just the support needed to work through the troubles.

Wasting the Differential Between Thought and Voice Speed

You can think three to four times faster than you can talk. On the average, you speak between 100 and 150 words per minute. You can _think_ at around 400 words per minute. The differential between thought speed and voice speed can either be a liability or an asset. It's a liability if you allow yourself to get distracted and off the track. It's a great asset if you absorb the information you're hearing, consider it, formulate an answer, and express that answer clearly. Let's say Sam and his father are having a heated conversation about how much money Sam needs during the school year. His dad reminds him that he spent more money the last academic year than he had budgeted, and wants him to keep a tighter rein on his finances. Instead of listening to everything his father says—no easy task—Sam recalls similar conversations like this from years ago. He dwells on how frustrated he felt then and now. He also prepares in his mind a response to his father's concerns. He has the capability to listen to everything his dad says, prepare an answer, and express it. But he finds it easy to get distracted and either thinks about something from the past or spends his time preparing his answer without listening to what his father is really saying.

BETTER WAYS TO LISTEN FOR INFORMATION

Ideally, you would listen to everything you hear, but you know that's impossible. Good listeners, however, use techniques that help them absorb the material they hear. Here are some of their methods.

Focus on Key Points Instead of Remembering Facts

You're not alone if you find it difficult to listen to and remember all the facts during a lecture or conversation. You're given so much information that your mind gets overloaded. A better approach is to focus on key points. If the speaker is organized, try to find the key ideas being presented. For example, let's say you've missed two classes because you were sick. You go see a professor or teaching assistant to get the information you need for an exam. During the course of the conversation, your teacher outlines three major problems Confederate soldiers faced at the end of the Civil War:

1. A devastated homeland in the southern states

2. Virtually useless money

3. A strong feeling of defeat for a cause the Confederates thought was right

You can use those three as categories and let the facts fit under each one. You'll have a hard time if you try to remember all the different pieces of information presented during the session unless you fit them under the categories. If you keep breaking down the categories, you have a much easier chance of retaining the information. Suppose under the heading of "devastated homeland," the professor breaks down the material to

a. Plantations destroyed

b. Homes ruined

This approach is similar to trying to grasp the key ideas of a book. If you're reading a book for pleasure, you start with page 1 and go all the way through. But if you would like to learn the contents of the book, you're better off to start with an overview. Are there three major sections? How are the chapters broken down according to categories? Under each category, what are the key points? Breaking down ideas according to some kind of organized form is a lot easier to remember than trying to remember the 200 isolated facts.

Exploit Thought/Voice Speed Differential

The 4-to-1 differential between thought speed and voice speed can be a great asset if you use it well. You can find key points in a dialogue. You can detect the feelings of the speaker. You can discern whether he or she is being straightforward, ironic, humorous, or serious. You can apply your critical thinking skills to see if what is being said is reasonable. And you can do all this in an instant if you use your time well. For example, if a friend tells you that she is seriously thinking about dropping out of school to get married, you can glean the information she provides, empathize with her point of view, and evaluate whether what she says makes good sense.

Use Effective Methods of Remembering

Treatises on memory have existed at least since the time of Cicero and the first century b.c. Three methods of **remembering** that are particularly helpful are association, imagination, and repetition. Let's look at each one.

ASSOCIATION

From listening comes wisdom, and from speaking repentance.

ITALIAN PROVERB

People remember better when they link things together. If I asked you to tell me about a movie you've seen in the last three weeks, you would have very little trouble recounting it because you would string together the series of images that make up the plot. The opening of the film leads to the next part, and the rest of the plot unfolds all the way to the conclusion. If you wanted to know this chapter for an exam, you would be well served to break it down to the organization we're using: We've discussed listening in interpersonal communication, and are explaining four kinds of listening. We focus on problems and some better ways to listen.

IMAGINATION

With your imagination, you can remember vividly the details of something you've already experienced. Abstract ideas are like Teflon—they don't stick easily. Imagination, however, is like Velcro—it sticks. Take the example of the movie we mentioned. Try to recall what the main characters looked like. What was the most graphic scene? How did the movie end? If you use your imagination, you can recapture the images in your mind. You apply the same technique to remembering any material you want. Even for abstract ideas, you can form a vivid image. Suppose you want to remember Aristotle's concept of logical argument. If you merely memorized that logical argument refers to reasonable arguments supported by evidence, the material will be hard to recall later. But you could imagine a court case where an attorney used specific evidence to show that the accused could not possibly be placed at the scene of the robbery.

Words low on the abstraction ladder are easy to remember because they're vivid. If I asked you to imagine what Barbara Streisand or Bruce Springsteen look like, you could probably immediately call up an image of each singer.

REPETITION

Association and vivid imaging help people to remember, and so does repetition. If you needed to know the plot of a Shakespearean play—*Hamlet*, for example—you would start off by getting the key parts of the plot and then you would try to graphically see a version of *Hamlet*. You might want to refer to Mel Gibson's portrayal of Hamlet as the anguished prince of Denmark. After you have gone through the association and imagination, now repeat the process three or four times. Notice that the sequence is locked in your mind.

EMPATHIC LISTENING

A second kind of listening is **empathic**—a skill that can be of great value during an interpersonal encounter. When you listen empathically, you try to understand what the other person (let's say a woman) is saying, and try to feel as she feels. You make an effort to get inside her perceptual world to see and feel how she experiences something. For a time, you try to leave behind your own way of looking at the world, to see hers. If a classmate confides to you that she's crushed over the grade she received on an English paper, you might try to grasp her emotional frame of reference. You make a conscious effort to understand vicariously her sense of disappointment. For another example, let's say you go home on vacation and your 10-year-old brother tells you how afraid he is of a bully at school. Rather than immediately giving him advice to take boxing lessons, you try to see his fears from his point of view.

We use the word *try* to emphasize that it is impossible to completely lay yourself aside. As John Stewart (1990, p. 195) says,

> "Laying aside yourself" is as literally impossible as lifting yourself by your ears—or your own bootstraps. So you may well decide to focus on the other person and to do your best to sense her meanings or feel his happiness, but these efforts will always be grounded in your own attitudes, expectations, past experiences, and world view.

Some people get very close to experiencing how the other party feels, but no one can feel exactly the same way as another.

TYPES OF POOR EMPATHIC LISTENING

There are at least three ways people can fail to be good empathic listeners. Let's look at these.

Being Unwilling to See the Other Side

One of the most common faults of empathic listening is an unwillingness to look at a situation from somebody else's perspective. You see the world from your viewpoint because you're locked into your own background, attitudes, and ways of perceiving outside events. This is especially true in a conflict situation. Suppose you've been in a minor traffic accident, and you firmly believe the other person is at fault. It's hard to start a conversation by looking at the fender-bender from the other person's position. Similarly, if you get into a discussion about a volatile topic such as abortion or racial issues, it's not easy to see a viewpoint other than your own. But if you _begin_ by trying to see and feel from the other's perspective, your communication will almost automatically be better. Much destructive conflict comes from an unwillingness or an inability to look at the other person's side of an argument. Think of the last time you had a disagreement with someone. Did you begin by trying to get inside the other person's feelings and perceptions? In the end, you may not agree with what the other person is saying, but at least you have heard him out and have tried to appreciate why he feels the way he does.

Not Listening with Support

Empathic listening does not demand that you agree with the other person's position, especially if after careful listening you really don't. But not to show any empathy toward someone else may stop effective communication before it has a chance to start. During the delicate phase of closing a sale, an adept salesperson may not agree with the customer's position. For example, someone is thinking about buying a house but has balked at the amount of the mortgage payment per month. The realtor could argue with the customer by showing him that he could afford the payments if he really wanted to. Such a response

LISTENING IS HARD

A young psychiatrist had recently opened his practice and often rode up the elevator with a man who had been a psychiatrist for many years. In the morning, both looked fresh. At the end of the day, they often rode down together. The young psychiatrist noticed that his older colleague looked just as fresh at the end of the day as he did at the beginning. He himself felt and looked exhausted from the day's counseling sessions. One day he said, "I don't get it. You and I come in the morning both looking rested. By the end of the day, I'm completely wiped out and you look as relaxed as you did in the morning. How do you listen, listen, listen all day long and finish looking the way you do?" The older psychiatrist responded, "Who listens?"

Drawing by Shanahan;
© *1989 The New Yorker*
Magazine, Inc.

however, would serve to turn off the customer and ensure that the deal would fall through. If, however, the realtor began by empathizing and showing support for the other person's viewpoint, she has a much better chance of closing the sale. She may say, "I fully understand that $750 per month is more than you had in mind. I would feel the same way myself, since I'm careful with my money. But I want to point out that if you can stretch your budget, you'll have a better investment. In the long run, you'll make more profit than if you put your money into a savings account." She may then go on to point out the benefits of buying a house in a market that has been strong for the past two or three years and gives every indication of staying strong. She *begins* by listening supportively to the other side and then presents her point of view.

Being Too Empathic

If responding with no support is one fault of empathic listening, getting overly involved is another. Professional counselors are usually skilled empathic listeners, but they don't get so absorbed in a patient's problems that they lose all sense of objectivity. For example, someone talks to a counselor about how difficult his roommate has been during the past two months. He proceeds to tell the counselor that he is so angry at the roommate that he wants to throw

> *True listening, total concentration on the other, is always a manifestation of love.*
>
> SCOTT PECK (1978)

all the roommate's belongings out the sixth-floor window of their dorm room. The counselor can empathize with the young man's anger but for him to become totally involved to the point that he *agrees* with the action is not really going to help the situation. Listening empathically does not mean that you become totally immersed and agree with everything that is said. You try to feel how the other person feels and you try to see the situation from the other's perspective, but you withhold judgment until you've heard everything the other person says.

IMPROVING EMPATHIC LISTENING

The following methods can help you listen better with empathy.

Paraphrasing

Robert Bolton (1979, p. 51) defines **paraphrasing** as "a concise response to the speaker which states the essence of the other's content in the listener's own words." When you paraphrase, you try to listen carefully to what the other person is saying and then repeat the gist of what you heard. Paraphrasing needs to be done carefully. If you've ever talked to someone who parroted back what you just said, you probably found that reaction irritating. If, however, someone occasionally summarized what you said to make sure he or she heard your message right, you probably found that response supportive.

Keeping Some Objectivity

Even though empathic listening is an effective communication tool, people need to keep a sense of objectivity when dealing with others. Just as good counselors listen to the thoughts and feelings of a client, they also listen to see if what's being said makes sense. Counselors keep some objectivity so they can make judgments about what can be done to solve their patient's problems.

CRITICAL LISTENING

Even when you have absorbed the information from somebody else and empathized with their feelings, you should still examine the validity of what they're saying. **Critical listening** means you consider the ideas that you both are discussing, to see if they make sense. Very few people are logical all the time. If people look back on conversations throughout the day, they would have to admit that some statements were not logical, were not backed with evidence, and didn't make sense.

CONSIDERING CRITICAL THINKING

Your 17-year-old brother has just finished a one-week session with a group that promotes itself as religious. He goes into great detail telling about how caring the members are. He then tells you that the leaders advocate that their young followers quit school and join the group for at least one year. You make every effort to be empathic to what your brother is saying, but the more he talks the more suspicious you become about the religious group. How would you apply informational, empathic, and critical thinking skills to handle this situation?

In Chapter 2, we discussed critical thinking as a way to help make intelligent decisions based on reason rather than emotion. When you listening critically, you try to discern whether what you're hearing makes sense, so you can make an intelligent response. Let's say you work in a shoe store during the summer months and someone (say, a man) brings back a pair of shoes that have obviously been worn for a long time. The customer looks you straight in the eye and swears he's had the shoes for two weeks and they've fallen apart. Your sense of reason tells you that the person is lying, but you also remember that your manager has emphasized that salespeople should take back any returned item no matter what the condition or how wild the story that accompanies the return. You might think, "OK, this person is not leveling with me and is trying to put over a fast one. But I know that to challenge him on the return would not be good business and would violate my manager's instructions. Therefore I'll bite my tongue, smile, and give him a new pair."

Most court systems require that attorneys back their arguments with evidence. Such a demand by judges ensures the best chance of getting at the truth in a case and ultimately achieving justice. The prosecution has to prove, beyond a reasonable doubt, that a defendant is guilty as charged. Assertions aren't enough in a court case. As we've seen before, anyone can make an assertion: "O'Reilly's has the best food in town." "Women are naturally smarter than men." "Harvard is the best academic institution in the United States." All three statements are unproven. O'Reilly's may indeed be the best restaurant in town, but we should seek proof either by testing the food or by demanding some evidence to back the claim. It's easy to accept assertions at face value without testing whether what we hear is true.

ROADBLOCKS IN CRITICAL LISTENING

Listening critically is not easy. Here are some obstacles to careful listening.

PERSONAS ARE POWERFUL

A few years ago, fifty-five psychologists, psychiatrists, and social workers gathered to listen to a speech by Dr. Myron Fox of the Albert Einstein University. When they were asked after the presentation to critique Dr. Fox's presentation, audience members made comments like "excellent," "extremely articulate," and "warm." Each person who took a survey reported that she or he had learned something from the talk, which was entitled "Mathematical Game Theories as Applied to Physical Education." Three college professors carried out the experiment because they wanted to know if profes- sionals could detect an eloquent phony. Dr. Fox was really an actor from California who had been given a glowing introduc- tion before he spoke on his "area of expertise." His talk was in fact a potpourri of abstract phrases and meaningless jargon.

SOURCE: HAZEL.
(1989, P. 129.)

Focusing on Status Rather Than Ideas

In their book *Persuasive Communication* (1987), Bettinghaus and Cody summarize the research done on the power of status in influencing others. People often tend to listen less critically to others who have either high status or low status. If someone is presented as an expert on a topic, people may let their critical guard down and assume that because that person is an expert, his or her claims must be correct. Conversely, if someone who is not considered an expert makes a statement, some may dismiss it out of hand.

Falling for "Doublespeak"

Another fault of poor critical listening is failing to recognize doublespeak for what it is—an attempt to hide the truth with acceptable language. George Orwell first coined the term in his book *Politics and the English Language*. People who use doublespeak try to soften harsh realities by using soft and ambiguous words. Doublespeak often shows up in government documents and political speeches. Howard Kahane (1988, p. 128) offers some examples of doublespeak used by the U.S. government during the Vietnam War:

A concentration camp is called a "pacification center."

Bombing is labeled a "protective reaction strike."

Off-target bombings (usually involving civilians) are termed "incontinant ordnances."

Killing is called "termination."

Being Overly Critical

We advocate that you carefully listen to what you're hearing to see if ideas have logical validity and evidence to back claims. One extreme, however, would be to logically dissect every statement to see if it has validity. Some people demand proof for everything. If you challenged everything your partner said and asked for proof, you could ruin a relationship. No one likes to have his or her ideas constantly dissected and exposed to the light of logical validity. Like everything else between humans, a certain amount of **critical listening** can help people figure out the false from the true, or distinguish invalid from valid arguments. But this analysis can be overdone. Few reactions interfere with a good relationship more than someone who critically analyzes every aspect of a subject or a person.

One of the authors remembers two debaters—a woman and a man who were dating each other. Their conversations were extensions of their arguments during debates. Everything the other said was subjected to proof and refutation. These two may have liked the intellectual stimulation of challenging each other's ideas, but for most of us the critical approach in everything would quickly wear thin.

Making Incorrect Inferences

An **inference** is a logical leap from evidence to a conclusion. In making inferences, people look at an experience and then draw a conclusion about what caused that experience. For example, Walt walks into his dorm room after a long, hard day and gets into bed. He finds his sheets are shorted. Walt immediately concludes that his friend Mort did the evil deed because a week ago Mort told him he would "Get even" for the prank Walt pulled on him—substituting shaving cream in a Twinkie he was eating. Walt may be right, but he could be jumping to conclusions or making a shaky inference. In the U.S. court system, an attorney must usually present not just one piece of evidence, but a case. A case is a whole series of data that ultimately leads to a probable conclusion.

CONSIDERING ETHICS

A friend comes up to you and says, "I really shouldn't tell you this confidential piece of information, but I want you to know anyway." Is it alright for you to listen to such information when the person telling you about it has used the word confidential? If your answer is no, why do you say that? If your answer is yes, please justify your response according to some of the ethical guidelines already discussed in the book.

Failing to Look for Supporting Evidence

Closely allied to an erroneous inference is the failure to demand evidence for claims that others are making. We're not suggesting that every statement anyone makes should be judged according to the criteria of sufficient evidence. But never to demand evidence or proof can put you in peril. For example, Marie has been in a relationship with Rich for two years. Rich has been demeaning and rude as well as irresponsible in showing up for promised appointments. Marie has forgiven him more than ten times after he promises to reform. But each time he shows no evidence of really wanting to change and reverts to his old obnoxious ways. If Marie never demands proof, she can get severely hurt in the long run. Seeking evidence does not mean she uses a district attorney style of questioning. It means that she watches carefully and weighs Rich's behavior over a period of time.

BETTER WAYS TO LISTEN CRITICALLY

We've discussed some flawed ways people listen critically. Let's look at some suggestions for sharpening critical listening skills.

Checking for Supporting Evidence

As we've already said, we're not suggesting that you should subject every statement to the glare of critical thinking. But we do recommend that as you listen you look for support for what you're hearing. If someone (let's say a man) you're getting to know talks about how dependable he is and constantly demonstrates that he is just the opposite, such evidence is useful to you. You may want to end the relationship, change it, or at least talk about your perceptions that the other person says one thing and does another. To be blind to this inconsistency can get you into situations that can harm you.

Making Sure Reasoning Is Cogent

Someone who is cogent makes statements that are logically convincing and are backed with some evidence. If Patrick asks Jennifer to marry him after a whirlwind one-month courtship, Jennifer might ask herself whether this suddenness makes sense. Is one month long enough? Have the two had a chance to develop their relationship so it develops into something long-lasting and stable? Have they talked the matter through carefully and thought about the consequences?

Insisting on Correct Inferences

The principle "Insist on correct inferences" is closely related to the previous two, but the focus is on looking at data presented and then making warranted conclusions. To use a previous example, let's say Rich gets specific with Marie by promising to change. And he does change for a week. Then he says, "See, I can change." One week is a good start but it's not enough evidence to warrant that he really has changed.

DIALOGIC LISTENING

An important fourth kind of listening for interpersonal communication is **dialogic listening**. John Stewart (1990) refers to dialogic listening as "sculpting mutual meanings." Stewart gives credit to his colleague Milt Thomas for the sculpture metaphor. Recall the example we used in Chapter 6 on language. We asked you to imagine each partner in a conversation sitting on opposite sides of a potter's wheel. One person works with the other to shape a piece of sculpture. Together, they share pieces of clay and work together to produce a combined work of art. Thus, two people engaged in dialogic listening work to mold their conversation as they carry it on. Some of our best interpersonal exchanges are dialogic. Two people communicating well with each other do much more than transmit and register what the other says. They build together what Stewart calls "chunks" of conversation. Through a process of talking and listening, they refine ideas that weren't clear when they started. In a dialogic pattern, they shape, reinforce, and revise each other's thoughts until they understand each other and gain new insights as a result. Let's say Rhonda and Bob have been engaged for three months with the wedding scheduled for a week from Saturday. The church has been reserved, invitations sent out, and the big reception planned down to the last *hors d'oeuvre*. But Rhonda has some serious reservations about whether she should go ahead with the ceremony. She knows her parents had a big wedding in the same church and then divorced twenty years later. She doesn't want that to happen to her and Bob. After calling her fiancee to tell him her fears, the two sit down to talk at her house.

Their conversation is much more than a mutual exchange of information. Bob might start by saying, "I'm crushed. I thought we had this all worked out." Rhonda replies, "I know we did but I can't help how I feel. This is a big step—I don't want to make the same mistake as my parents." Although each will transfer information and try to empathize with the other, the heart of the conversation is their dialogic exchange. If they really listen to each other, they will build on each other's thoughts and feelings. Stewart says that dialogic listening has at least four features: a focus on "ours" instead of "mine"; open-endedness; the tendency to speak "in front of" rather than "behind" the other person; and "presentness." Let's look at each one of these features.

"Ours" Instead of "Mine"

Bob could continue his conversation with Rhonda by saying, "How can you do this to me? My parents have invited all our relatives. My friends are going to think I'm a fool if you drop me just before the wedding." His response might be considered natural, but he would be speaking from his perspective rather from one that includes his fiancee. Or Bob could say, "This really bothers me, but I want to begin by hearing why you feel the way you do." In the second example, he would be starting to engage in dialogic listening. He would want to see the situation from an "ours" perspective because the problem affects both of them.

Open-ended and Playful

Dialogic listening is also open-ended and playful. Open-ended means that the participants are not sure where the conversation will lead because they're building it together. This quality involves a certain amount of tentativeness because the participants do not have preconceived notions about the outcome. Let's say Rashad is talking to Cindy. These two met a week ago and there was immediate mutual attraction. Since then, they have been spending a lot of time together getting to know one another. They have chatted about their various backgrounds. They've told each other what they like and have discussed a range of ideas from their favorite sports figures to why men and women are so different. If they have a disagreement about men and women being different, their conversation is characterized by receptiveness to the other person. In dialogic listening, they also demonstrate a playful quality. They're talking about a serious subject, but they don't stay serious all through the dialogue. One may kid the other—"So how long have you been a chauvinist?" They don't quite know where their conversation will lead but they enjoy building it together. They may influence each other to change a point of view previously held. They're happy to come to the same insights after some discussion.

In Front of Rather Than Behind

The third aspect of dialogic listening is that the communicators listen "in front of" one another rather than focusing on "what is behind them." Stewart defines listening "behind" as trying to find out what's behind the words, eyes or the mind of the conversation partner. For example, a counselor will listen carefully to a patient in an effort to glean insights about the patient's internal psychological state. With dialogic listening, in contrast, the two partners focus

Conversations can be a joyful give and take, especially when the participants practice dialogic listening.

on their mutual sculpting of meaning. As Stewart puts it, "You concentrate on the verbal and nonverbal text the two of you are building." Let's say Rashad is trying to decide what kind of person Cindy is—is she more extroverted than introverted? Could she have some personality quirks that he would be uncomfortable with? Listening from that perspective would be listening behind or "psychologizing." Rashad is trying to find out "where Cindy is coming from." But if Rashad and Cindy are working on what's "in front of" them, they try to build new ideas together with no intention of gathering what they might consider as useful information. This does not mean each accepts without critical evaluation what is being said, yet their emphasis is not on psychoanalyzing or critiquing, but on building the conversation together. Recall the potter's wheel example at the beginning of this section. Each person on the other side of the wheel is contributing clay to build the final product. Together they shape and mold the clay into something they both find satisfying.

Presentness

The final aspect of dialogic listening is "presentness." The partners focus on the here and now as they build their meaning rather than on the past or future. They may think about the past and anticipate the future but neither is their primary emphasis. If Rashad and Cindy are listening dialogically, they try to be present to the other to absorb each other's ideas and to "massage" (work through) those ideas.

If you practice dialogic listening, you approach each conversation with an open mind. You know in advance that anything comes from the conversation will be a product of both of you. You don't focus on gathering information so you can somehow use it against your conversation partner later, but try to carve out meanings together. You rejoice in the building of new ideas as a team rather than as an isolated individual.

LOOKING BACK - LOOKING FORWARD

In this chapter, we have discussed four kinds of listening—informational, empathic, critical, and dialogic. If you listen for information, you try to absorb what the other person is telling you. If you listen empathically, you try to see things from the other person's point of view. Listening for information and listening empathically should not prevent you from carefully weighing what you're hearing to see if it makes sense. You do not give up your critical thinking powers as you listen to a conversation, nor do you go to the opposite extreme of critically analyzing everything someone else says. Dialogic listening involves two people trying to build meaning together through chunks of conversation.

In the next chapter, we look at close relationships. We emphasize that while each close union is unique, certain patterns characterize the way people develop their relationships. The journey continues as we look at the kind of relationships that can create deep satisfaction when they work well. We also examine some of the pitfalls that can invade and harm a close union.

REVIEW TERMS AND CONCEPTS

hearing
183
informational
listening
184
active listening
184
passive listening
184

pseudo-listening
185
remembering
188
empathic listening
189
paraphrasing
192

critical listening
195
inferences
195
dialogic listening
197

PUTTING THEORY INTO PRACTICE

FOR DISCUSSION:

1. Why is it so difficult to juggle all four kinds of listening during a conversation?

2. Why is pseudo-listening so prevalent? What steps can both partners take to avoid pseudo-listening?

3. Show how dialogic listening also contains informational, empathic, and critical listening.

SKILL BUILDERS:

1. Break into groups of three. Two of you should take opposite sides of a controversial issue, such as abortion, gun control, banning smoking in public places, and so on. The third person observes the other two. The two engaged in a discussion should spend about one or two minutes preparing an argument for their point of view. After the brief preparation, one person states his or her argument to the other. The other can respond either by attempting to refute or by presenting his or her own argument but only after paraphrasing to the satisfaction of the other what was heard. The third person acts as timekeeper, to make sure the participants talk for one minute. After about seven minutes, the class should get together and listen to reports from the observer about what happened.

Here are some questions to keep in mind during the report: Did the two really listen to each other, or did they seem to be preparing their own arguments without really listening to what the other was saying? Did the participants influence each other to change an opinion? Did each seem to empathize with the other's point of view, or did they hold steadfastly to their own?

2. Think about a problem—imaginary or real. (No one should feel pressured into revealing a real personal problem.) Then divide into dyads. The first person should spend two minutes recounting the problem while the other tries to listen empathically. The one listening should try hard to focus on the feelings and perceptions of the other person. Then reverse the process. The speaker becomes the listener who tries to listen empathically to what the other is saying. After about ten minutes, get back together as a class. Each person should discuss how hard it was to try to get into the perceptual framework of the other. If you found it hard, explain why you thought it was so difficult.

3. Break into dyads and pick a topic that interests both of you. As best you can, carry on a dialogic conversation. Recall the elements that characterize such a dialogue—"ours" instead of "mine," open-ended and playful, being "in front of," and presentness. Then hold a class discussion about how easy or difficult it was to carry on a dialogic conversation. If you did manage it, what rewards were there for each of you?

FOR EXTENDED STUDY

Nichols, R. A. (1957). *Are you listening?* New York: McGraw-Hill.

This is the classic book that helps people become more aware of the need to listen better. Nichols provides practical ways to listen better for information.

Stewart, J. (Ed.). (1990). *Bridges, not walls: A book about interpersonal communication.* (5th ed.). New York: McGraw-Hill.

This is an excellent series of essays about interpersonal communication. Stewart's own essay on dialogic listening is especially useful as it relates to the material discussed in this chapter

To have a friend is to be honored. To have a love is to be happy. To have a love for a friend is to be truly blessed.

ANONYMOUS

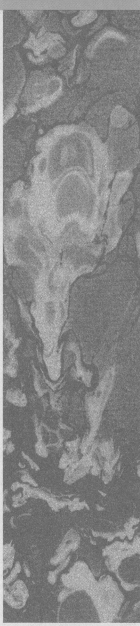

Close Relationships

OBJECTIVES

After reading this chapter and taking part in class activities, you should be able to

• Describe the similarities and differences between intimate relationships and friendships.

• Explain why humans enter and stay in close relationships.

• Describe how close relationships develop.

• Distinguish between constructive and destructive forms of conflict in close unions.

• Identify some of the stages people go through in ending close relationships.

• Identify some choices that will enhance rather than hinder close unions.

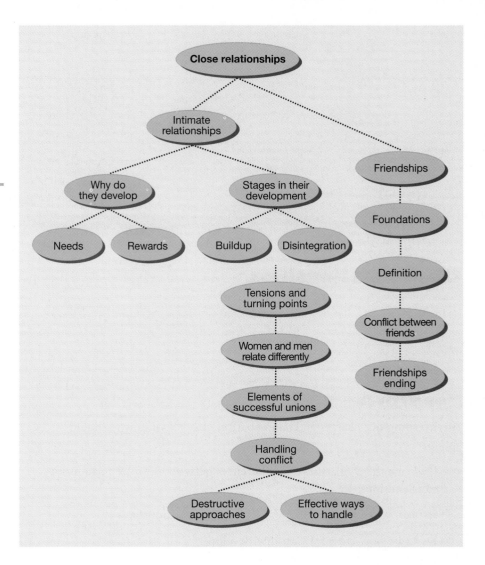

Cognitive Map 9

THE TWO QUOTATIONS ON the opposite page reflect the feelings of two women. One, by poet Elizabeth Barrett Browning, expresses her strong love for a man who helped her change from a reclusive invalid to a woman with a strong zest for life. The second statement typifies the kind of conversation that takes place every hour somewhere in the world.

Few of us would argue that close relationships with others bring great happiness and sometimes cause intense pain. You would probably agree that your life takes on its greatest meaning when you have someone you love deeply and who loves you the same way in return. That special person can be a spouse, a lover, parent, child, or a close friend. In this chapter, we examine close or intimate relationships as an important dimension of interpersonal communication. We go on to discuss how long-term romantic unions and friendships develop, why they often contain elements of conflict and change, and suggest some ways to make them better. We then show how they some-times break down and end.

INTIMATE RELATIONSHIPS

The word *intimate* comes from the Latin "intimus" and means "innermost." In an intimate or close union, two people share their innermost thoughts and feelings with each other.

Intimate relationships are those that last over a long period of time, involve a high degree of self-disclosure and contain strong affection. They can be romantic and/or sexual but need not be. Such relationships can occur between partners in married couples, lovers, best friends, or family members.

How do I love thee? Let me count the ways.
I love thee to the depth and breadth and height my soul can reach…

ELIZABETH BARRETT BROWNING

Her eyes misting, she looked at him and said, "I don't know how to put this, but I feel our relationship is not working and I think we should end it. I'm sorry if this hurts."

Sometimes intimate relationships happen quickly, but usually they take time to develop and mature. Think back on the best and most enduring relationship you've ever had. How long did it take to blossom? How long did it last or, is it still going? Did it—or is it still—progressing through discernible stages?

Close relationships for most people are the most important form of inter-personal communication in their lives. Someone may interact with hundreds of others and be adept at dealing with a wide range of people, but he or she places priority on those unions that allow the most sharing. In Chapter 4, we discussed self-disclosure as a major element of interpersonal communication. Humans have to trust someone else before they reveal much about themselves other than the superficial. A major tenet of this text is that people rarely, if ever, reveal *everything* they believe, think, and feel to another human. With a few people, however, you "share your soul." You trust that person so much that you tell him or her almost everything about yourself. Most people have only a few others who would qualify as "intimates" or even close friends. They may have many acquaintances and colleagues, but only a small number are allowed into the inner sanctuary of private thoughts, hopes, and fears.

WHY DO CLOSE RELATIONSHIPS DEVELOP?

Steve Duck (1973) notes that humans filter information over a period of time to discover others who match them in attitudes and personality. People gather information about others to see if they want to become relative strangers, colleagues, friends, or even lifelong partners. Consider those people you tend to "click with." Is it because they're the best-looking in your view, or because they affirm you and have attitudes that are similar to yours? Thousands

Sharing thoughts and interests characterize close relationships.

of people come into your life. Both you and they make choices about how much or little each of you wants to interact. If you're attracted to someone else, but the other person doesn't reciprocate, you usually stop promoting the relationship after a time because you don't enjoy rejection.

Needs

Human needs often propel people into close relationships. Communication expert William Schutz (1958) maintains that humans have three fundamental needs: inclusion, control, and affection. These three **interpersonal needs** help explain why many people seek close unions.

The need for *inclusion* is the need to interact with others and to be part of their group. For example, Martin joins five different clubs on campus because he enjoys doing things with other people. He also has a crowd in his dorm room most evenings. He is a socializer who is happiest in a group. The need for *control* is each person's need to shape the behavior of others. Eileen, for example, is a "take charge" person who always volunteers to chair any committee being formed. She likes being a shaker and mover of others. *Affection* is the amount of fondness or tender feelings you have for others or want them to have for you. When you say that Loraine is a very affectionate person, you may mean that she likes to give and get hugs, or conveys unusual warmth in her voice.

Although all people share the same drives, some have greater needs in one area than another. One person may want lots of people around, while another likes privacy. The one who likes privacy may want to establish and maintain close, highly affectionate relationships with just a few people, while the other enjoys casual unions with many. One may need a great deal of control in a relationship while the other wants very little. For someone else, affection is the key ingredient that matters—he or she wants *one* person in the world who really loves him or her unconditionally.

Schutz's theories are important in predicting how long a close relationship might last. If two people are strongly attracted to each other romantically and sexually, but have vastly different needs for inclusion, affection, and control, their union may cool dramatically once the romantic and sexual attraction tapers off. Yet two people in a close relationship may have somewhat differing needs for inclusion, control, and affection but complement each other. Complementary relationships are those in which one partner supplies what the other lacks. Sharon may like greater control in her marriage to Frank. He gladly gives her the control because *his* greatest need is inclusion. He really doesn't mind that she "takes charge" in most situations.

Rewards and Relationships

If inclusion, control, and affection are catalysts for seeking close relationships, rewards keep the relationship going. Although a few altruistic mortals will give their all with no expectation of getting anything in return, most people are willing to give themselves only if they get something back. Thibaut and Kelley (1959) propose a **social exchange theory** to explain why people forge and stay in close relationships. Partners continually weigh the consequences of their relationship by looking at the relative rewards and costs of continuing a marriage, a romantic liaison, or a close platonic union. Most people will put up with a few flaws and idiosyncrasies if they receive rewards in the bargain.

CONSIDER THIS: DO OPPOSITES ATTRACT?

*D*o opposites attract? The answer seems to be—yes, but they don't always do well once they become intimates. Brian may be drawn to Betsy's quiet, methodical manner while she finds his outrageous extrovert behavior "a blast" for awhile. But let the relationship mature over time, and what was once perceived as a strong point turns into an irritant.

Some people are attracted to others who have traits or qualities they lack. Randy may be outgoing and artistic, and doesn't mind a messy apartment. He may find Maria very appealing because she is an engineering major who always keeps a tidy room. Maria has the qualities Randy lacks. Extroverts often pair up with introverts. The "good girl" may be drawn to the "bad boy" because he does the things she wouldn't do. The attraction may stay for a time, but over the long haul, we're usually more comfortable with those who are like us than with those who are different.

Such rewards could include the knowledge that the other person really loves you, overlooks some of your flaws, or is never boring to be with. People may be attracted to someone who affirms them at their core. Few people seek out or stay with someone who constantly puts them down or who continually ignores them.

Some will stay with a close union only if the rewards exceed the cost. One reason for the high divorce rate in North America is the realization by many couples that they can choose to get out of a marriage if they perceive that they're giving more than they're getting or if the rewards found at the beginning are no longer there.

Stages in Close Relationships

We've looked at the reasons why people form intimate relationships. Let's examine some of the discernible stages that many unions follow. Love at first sight or instant attraction between two people occurs occasionally, but is not the norm. Mark Knapp (1984) has divided these stages into two categories—development and disintegration—with five phases for each category. The first five illustrate how relationships blossom while the last five show how they can unravel.

RELATIONSHIP DEVELOPMENT	RELATIONSHIP DISINTEGRATION
Initiating	Differentiating
Experimenting	Circumscribing
Intensifying	Stagnating
Integrating	Avoiding
Bonding	Terminating

Let's look at the first five stages. Later in the chapter, we'll examine the last five when we discuss how some relationships end.

Initiating is the first meeting of two people who see the happy possibility of cultivating a close union. The setting may be a classroom or a supermarket. This first stage is loaded with small talk like "Is this weather cold or what?" or "Can you believe how those Broncos rallied in the last quarter?" As they move through this ritual, each party measures the other in terms of attractiveness, compatibility, and potential rewards. Each asks, "Is there something here for me? Should I move this further?"

Experimenting involves both participants probing to see if the relationship should go further. The small talk usually continues as the two start assessing each other to discover if they have something in common. If the attraction is strong, so are the interests and experiences they seem to share at first. Each

"I've had a lovely evening, Keith, and may I say that I found you every bit as caring, sensitive, warm, witty, emotionally available, open to commitment, eclectic, values-rooted, stable, cultured, centered, fit, sincere, adventurous, unglitzy, down-to-earth, spontaneous, and fun as your ad promised you would be."

may be pleasantly surprised to learn that the other also plays tennis, likes Bach, tolerates big cities, and owns a dog named Ruff—or at least has a cousin who knows someone with a dog by that name. Differences are usually ignored as the two get on the same wavelength.

Intensifying is the process of two people finding ways to get even closer. They may both use "we" instead of "I" during conversations. They may wear the same T-shirts they bought together at the county fair. They might miss the daily phone call if one of them forgets to make it. One may declare her or his love for the first time. One might show signs of jealousy if the other plans to have lunch with an old boyfriend or girlfriend. Each normally goes down deeper into the iceberg of self-disclosure. This stage can happen gradually or within a span of a few days, depending on the couple and their desire for increased intimacy. Relatively few relationships advance to this stage.

With *integrating*, the fusion of partners becomes more pronounced. Gifts of greater value are exchanged. Events are planned around each other's schedule. Neither minds if the world now recognizes them as a couple. The two may refer to "our song" or "our favorite movie" or "our special restaurant." They may start making plans for the future together. Either or both may talk about getting married.

The term *bonding* refers to the pair formalizing their union, usually by way of a contract. They may rent an apartment together or get married. They make public commitments. They're happy to take out a marriage license and go through a ceremony with witnesses. They're glad to sign away their freedom because life with the other is the most important experience each can imagine.

TENSIONS AND TURNING POINTS

The patterns just described help account for some predictable phases as a relationship develops. Even during these stages, however, intimates forge their own unique union as they try to sort out and define their particular relationship. Leslie Baxter (1990) describes these changes as *dialectic tensions*. The word **dialectic** comes from the Greek and means "a clash of opposites." The Greek philosopher Socrates prodded his students to argue opposite ideas as a way of learning. The German philosopher Georg Wilhelm Friedrich Hegel used the term to explain how major ideas clash throughout history. Karl Marx, the major theorist for communism, applied Hegel's term to explain how social movements clash with each other to form the next combined or synthetic movement. Baxter contends that tensions clash in a relationship, explaining changes that occur. She divides the dialectic into three tensions.

The first is the clash in each person between autonomy and connection.

CONSIDERING ETHICS

Sandi has been seeing Ed for four months, and both have gone through the first four relational stages. Ed would like to go beyond "integrating" to "bonding" and has told Sandi he plans to buy an engagement ring. Ed has been a generous suitor, taking Sandi to expensive restaurants and buying lavish gifts. Sandi puts him off with comments like "I love you but I'm uncomfortable thinking about marriage until after I finish law school in two years." Her statement is true, but she's not telling Ed the whole story. She's also interested in Steve and has been seeing him on the side as a "good friend," with the possibility that their relationship could blossom into something more romantic. She hesitates to level with Ed because she really does like him and enjoys the gifts. She's afraid that if she reveals all, Ed will either drop her or be moody for a week—something she hates in other people. Does Sandi have an obligation to tell Ed the whole truth? What ethical principles would you use to support your answer?

Autonomy is the desire to retain independence while *connection* is the need to bond with someone else. Bob, a college senior, may want to be independent from Diane, his fiancee, but he also may want to get closer to her. She lives in their hometown 500 miles away. He is torn between forming new friendships with women on campus and his devotion to Diane. He may try to reduce this tension a number of ways: (1) tell Diane about it and take her advice on what to do; (2) not mention it to her, but make sure he keeps any new relationship within the bounds of friendship only; or (3) decide to confine his friendships to males.

Bob's dilemma brings up a second tension—openness and closedness. The term *openness* refers to how much you want to reveal to your partner, and *closedness* is the drive to keep some thoughts to yourself. Bob wants Diane to know most of what is going on in his life but he hesitates to share everything with her. He may be hesitant to tell her about Judy, the bright and friendly sophomore he studies with two nights a week. He fears she may object to his actions, and he also wants to preserve his right to do what he believes is best in getting good grades.

A third tension Baxter describes is the pull between *novelty* and *predictability*. Novelty is the desire to experience anything new while predictability is the need to know that life follows some orderly patterns. Bob may like the stability of his relationship with Diane. He knows he can call her every third evening and she will be there for him—a symbol of her steadiness in every other part of their relationship. He also yearns for occasional surprises—something he rarely gets from Diane.

The way Diane reacts to these three tensions also affects the changes in her relationship with Bob. She may be very pleased, thank you, with the connectedness of her union with Bob. She doesn't want to be autonomous. She also shares practically everything with her husband-to-be and sees no reason to hide anything. She may like the stability of an ordered life and feels uncomfortable with surprises. Thus the tensions clashing within each person also affect their relationship with each other.

"Why Can't a Man Be Like a Woman?"

Diane's desire for greater connectedness, openness, and predictability underscores the clash of relating styles between men and women. Deborah Tannen (1989) struck a respondent chord when she wrote *You Just Don't Understand*. Basing her conclusions on rigorous research in linguistics, Tannen shows that men and women's social conditioning is so different that it seems as if the two sexes were raised in different cultures. Women are brought up to feel comfortable about intimate relationships. It's OK for women to talk about being hurt or angry. Men are supposed to hold back such reactions. According to Joseph Pleck (1975), men are trained to be social but not intimate. The difference is significant. Boys share many activities like sports, but they get the message early that competition and being strong is more important than close friend-ships. As a result, according to McGill (1985) only one male in ten has a close male friend to whom he divulges his innermost thoughts.

Women are usually comfortable expressing highly personal thoughts to female and male intimates, while most men express their emotions to women rather than to other men. Men's conversations with each other revolve most often around sports and sex but not relationships, whereas women can glide easily from conversations about work or politics to feelings and relationships.

These differences add variety and joy to a close relationship, but they can also cause frustration and heartache. According to sociologist Gerald Twomey (1982), only about 10 percent of people who stay married find their union one of the most satisfying features of their life. Twomey (p. 77) maintains that another 20 percent are happy some of the time, with the rest either bored, unhappy, or staying together for the sake of the children.

You can view these conclusions in two ways: (1) many marriages are unhappy and (2) the 10 percent represents thousands of couples who have found deep satisfaction in their marriages. We suggest that the happy couples follow a discernible pattern in relating and that this pattern helps account for their successful unions. Satisfied couples seem to emphasize five elements in the following order of priority:

1. Shared values

2. Friendship

3. Temperamental compatibility

4. Romantic attraction or "limerance"

5. Sexual attraction

In the North American culture, items 4 fand 5 often take precedence over the first three. Romantic and sexual attraction become the magnets that draw many couples together, but these two strong forces often fail to produce lasting happiness in a close union. The most satisfied couples seem to recognize the force of romantic and sexual attraction, but emphasize shared values, friend-ship, and compatibility as they develop their relationship. Partners in a success-ful union recognize that romance and sexual appeal are powerful but are also short-lived by comparison with the other three. Let's look at each of the five in more detail to further develop the thesis that the proper blending of these components can generate the most lasting satisfaction.

Sexual Attraction

Of all the categories, sex takes the least explanation. This natural and domi-nant human desire intrudes early on virtually all romantic relationships. Either a couple gives in to the urges soon or makes a decision to defer sex until sometime later for reasons that range from religious to practical. Those who start having sex soon *feel* like they're drawn together intimately—and of course they are, on a physical level. The problem, however, often becomes one of substituting sexual closeness for psychological intimacy. Because sex is so high voltage and is so physically intimate, couples often mistake it for a deeper and more enduring closeness. In physical intimacy, couples share their bodies. In psychological closeness, couples share their souls. They reveal much to the other about their hopes, fears, and flaws. She tells him secrets she would tell no one else. He lets her in on his private world as he does with no other.

Romantic Attraction

If sex ignites and propels a relationship, so does romantic attraction. Romantic love or **limerance** is a right-brain activity characterized by feelings of euphoria—and sometimes sudden depression if the lover believes that the beloved does not feel the same way. Physical symptoms can literally include a faster beating heart, sweaty palms, and a surge of hormones. Life takes on a new, exciting perspective, as the two in love now believe that everything from sunsets to porcelain pelicans are beautiful. Researchers Berscheid and Walster (1985) contend that while limerance is strong, such intensity wanes after awhile. Most people fall and stay in love from between six months to two years. The problem is not with falling in love but believing that this phenomenon will last forever. If two people are in love and are sexually attracted to each other, the combination by itself often becomes the reason for advancing their relationship.

The cultivation of sex and limerance can often mask problems a couple might be having. At the very time two people need the most freedom to realistically see if their union has the potential to bring long-lasting satisfaction, sex and limerance can make them ignore potential trouble areas that will inevitably emerge later. Our purpose is not to denigrate romance, but to suggest that it must be assimilated into the entire fabric of a relationship to be most fulfilling over the long run.

Compatible Temperaments

Isabel Briggs Myers and Katheryn Myers (1976) are a mother-daughter team who have devised a test that helps people place themselves in four different personality categories: extrovert, introvert, sensors, and intuitives. Personality types can also include hard-driving "A" types and the more laid-back "B" types (Vancevich, Matteson, & Gamble, 1987). Labels such as "optimists" and "pessimists" can also describe individual temperaments. In a close relationship, some people have personalities similar to their partners and others are quite opposite. She may be an artist (sensory–extrovert) and he may be an engineer (introvert–intuitive).

One partner who lacks certain traits—neatness, mechanical ability—may admire and be attracted to someone who has those qualities. As mentioned before, most people prefer over the long run to be close to others who are more like them than different. The old saying is true that "familiarity often breeds content." Opposites can start rubbing each other the wrong way after the initial attraction wears off.

Couples Who Are Friends

Ask any couple in love if they're also good friends and they'll look at you as if the question is ridiculous: "Of course—we're great friends." Few would be so honest to say, "No, we're not really friends. We're in this relationship primarily for romance and sex." We'll discuss friendship in greater detail later in the chapter, but we want to address this element as one of the most important components of a strong, close union.

One way to test the depth of friendship for a couple in love is for them to ask themselves if their friendship with each other has the same characteristics as their friendship with someone they've called their best friend over a long period. Do they trust each other without reservation? Can they confide and know the other will keep secrets? Would each be there for the other if she or he was sick for a long time? Would they still really care about the partner if he or she gained or lost a lot of weight? Do they support the other during tough times? Do they tell each other the truth?

Shared Values

Shared values are those qualities each person believes are most important in human living. Two people in a close relationship who share values would hold the same world view. One couple might believe that their most important goal is to amass as much wealth as possible. Another couple might think that material possessions are not crucial to their happiness and instead seek a simple life that focuses on helping the poor.

Still other couples hold opposite values. If one is strongly religious and the other is an atheist, they don't share the same values. If one believes that a lavish lifestyle is the way to happiness but the other thinks that keeping things simple and helping the homeless is important, they have different values. One may believe in marriage "until death do us part," while the other believes in marriage until passion and romance start to fade.

Discussion of values often gets delayed during courtship. Inevitably, though, such issues come up and need to be dealt with if a couple have any hope of staying happy. A potential marriage mate need not be questioned on the first date about what he or she thinks is important in life, but it is a good idea to talk early about values. If a couple find their values are poles apart, each partner should anticipate how those values will clash down the road. Two atheists might be happy together, but an atheist matched with a devout Jew or Christian is in for some troubled times.

We believe that careful integrating of all five elements offers the best chance for success in a long-term relationship. Realizing that limerance and sexual attraction will fade to some degree may discourage the couple in love, but accepting of this fact will produce a better union over the long run. The couple can enjoy the glow of the romantic stage but at the same time build on a foundation of shared values, compatible temperaments, and deep, lasting friendship.

CONFLICT IN CLOSE RELATIONSHIPS

I f love is a key part of every intimate relationship, so is conflict—an experience Hocker and Wilmot (1991, p. 12) describe as "an expressed struggle between at least two interdependent parties who perceive incompatible goals, scarce rewards, and interference from the other party in achieving their goals." Many perceive conflict as abnormal and harmony as normal. Some see conflict as always messy and unpleasant. Like so many other human experiences, conflict can be destructive or productive depending on how the participants handle the problem they have. Let's discuss some types of conflict resolution to get a better idea of what seems to work best in solving problems people have with each other.

Destructive Approaches

AGRESSION

Aggression is the effort to solve a problem between two parties by using power and violence. The 1991 war between the United States and Iraq illustrates, on a global level, what happens in a destructive conflict. Saddam Hussein decided to invade Kuwait and make it Iraq's nineteenth province. Most leaders in the world were angered by the aggression and called for Iraq's immediate withdrawal. President Bush was the most vocal in making this demand. The United States was partially dependent on Iraq, not only for its oil but also for the potential influence Saddam could exert in the Mideast. Both parties perceived scarce rewards from doing what the other wanted and viewed the other as interfering in achieving their goals.

The immediate outcome of that struggle is well known: when Saddam did not accept Bush's demand for withdrawal, the United States and other U.N. nations went to war and forced Iraq to leave Kuwait. In this case, military power brought at least a temporary solution to the problem.

Although the consequences may not be as tragic in lives lost, many interpersonal conflicts are solved with power and aggression. For example, two

CONSIDERING CRITICAL THINKING

Sheri is a good friend of yours. After a long search, Sheri has met the person who has turned her dreary days into magical nights. His name is Phil, and Sheri has never fallen for anyone so quickly or so hard. Sheri tells her friends that Phil is bright, is a witty conversationalist and shares her love of wind-surfing, hard rock, and dog shows. After they go together for three months, Phil proposes marriage. Sheri says yes but soon starts noticing some red flags. Phil blows up over small problems, has gone to church with Sheri three times before announcing that he doesn't believe in God, and asks her to consider working for two years while he finishes graduate school. Sheri is still very much in love and wants to stay in the relationship, but is not sure about marrying Phil. She asks you for advice. What would you tell her?

teenage brothers have an expressed struggle. The younger one says, "You took my shirt." The other responds, "Yea, and I'm not going to give it back." They're interdependent because they live in the same house. They see giving in to the other's demands as producing little reward, so they duke it out until the older and stronger one wins. You may have seen the movie _War of the Roses_. Kathleen Turner plays the wife and Michael Douglas the husband in a marriage that begins well enough but turns into an escalating power struggle. Wife and husband are interdependent during the stormy divorce because they want as much of their mutual property as they can get. Each sees the other as a deterrent to achieving what each wants. Although the film is fictitious, the pattern of increasing violence is not. Many intimates deal with their disputes by resorting to power and aggression with results that are as tragic as they are ineffective.

AVOIDANCE

The opposite of aggression is avoidance, which can be defined as backing away from a conflict. Let's say that Dave and Georgia married before finishing their degrees and are now in their senior year. Dave hates conflict. When he was small, he watched and heard his parents battle far into the night. He vowed he would not fight with his wife but would always speak with courtesy. Georgia, however, grew up in a loving family where laughs echoed through the house but so did some angry words. When a problem occurs, Dave backs off because he doesn't want a battle—even of ideas. He has prided himself on being the "negotiator" at school, the person who always smoothed things over.

Although his efforts at peacemaking are praiseworthy, in the long run he can hurt the marriage by avoiding issues that need to be addressed. Like a medical malady that gets worse without treatment, relationship problems tend to fester and build up unless both parties face and then work through them.

BLAMING

When people blame, they place the responsibility of conflict on the other person. They may admit playing some role in the blowup, but mostly people believe the other person is at fault. But placing all or most of the blame on the other party doesn't work very well, because the target of the blame is so busy protecting shattered self-esteem. If someone tells another he or she has done something wrong, that person often musters defenses rather than listen objectively to the criticism. Fortunately, many people will accept responsibility for conflicts they help create. They know it usually takes two to start and continue an argument.

PLAYING GAMES

Eric Berne (1964) maintains that when intimate relationships break down, the parties often resort to "games." Just as in athletic games, relationship games are played according to rules and rituals that produce winners and losers. One

Most couples experience some conflict in their relationship. The method each employs to resolve the conflict is crucial to a satisfactory or unsatisfactory outcome.

game is "gunny sacking" (or burlap bagging, or even croker-sacking, depending on your region). In **gunny sacking,** one or both partners ignore grievances but hold them in for a time. Eventually, one or both blow up after the pressure builds. For example, Margaret loves her father but does not like his irritating habit of using sarcastic humor to put her down in front of relatives at family reunions. Margaret takes his gibes for a few months, but then blows up when her father engages in what he considers a very mild form of kidding.

Another game is "Going for the Achilles heel." In a close union, partners come to know well the other's weaknesses. During a fight, one party may be tempted to lash out at the other's most vulnerable trait. The attacker has the advantage of letting off steam, but as with the tactic of blaming, most people recoil and protect themselves when attacked where it really hurts. In one episode of the long-running TV comedy *All in the Family*, Archie Bunker greets his daughter Gloria and son-in-law Mike after their return from a married couples' workshop. He hears them refer to the "game" they've just learned about, called "going for the Achilles heel." When he asks what the term means, Mike explains, using Gloria as an example. He points out that Gloria feels inferior because she has only a high school education while Mike is a graduate student. When his friends come over, she perceives herself intellectually inferior. Nostrils flaring, Gloria goes for Mike, telling her dad that Mike is a mooch who doesn't like paying rent to stay in her father's house.

Aggression, avoidance, blaming, and playing games are often used in conflicts between intimates. Besides wounding, they rarely work in strengthening a relationship. In most cases, these tactics weaken unions. Conflict, however, can contribute to the strengthening of a union if handled well. Let's look at why and then examine three ways to deal with the inevitable friction found in most close relationships.

Advantages of Conflict

Knapp and Vangelisti (1992) list four benefits that can come from conflict between two people:

1. Conflict can produce a greater understanding of the two parties and their relationship.

2. Conflict can clarify the similarities and differences between them.

3. Conflict can help the two learn better methods for handling future conflicts.

4. Conflict can reveal areas where communication can be strengthened.

Intimates who resort to aggression, avoidance, blaming, and game playing are often unhappy and bewildered. They don't know why their relationship isn't working. People who use effective approaches are usually far more satisfied with their union.

EFFECTIVE WAYS TO HANDLE CONFLICT

So what are some methods used by couples who deal with their conflicts constructively? Let's look at three ways that work.

See the Problem from the Other's Side

One of the best ways to deal with conflict is to start by seeing things from the other person's point of view. This approach goes against the grain because people tend to do just the opposite. Each usually comes from a different background and thus looks at issues from a different perspective. No two people share at all times the same moods and perceptions.

When you begin by looking at the other's point of view instead of only your own, you have a much better chance of solving a conflict. Let's say Todd and Mark were close friends in high school and decide to room together in college. Todd has always prided himself on his neatness. Even during his teens, Todd kept his room tidy, despite derisive comments from his friends.

From the first day the two close friends started sharing the same room, Mark tossed his clothes on the floor. He also left the bathroom in shambles every morning for three days in a row. Todd's first tendency is to blast Mark's penchant for sloppiness. He strongly believes that neatness is next to godliness. Mark is not godly.

If Todd begins by trying to see the situation from Mark's perspective, he has a much better chance of converting him than if he starts with the angry outburst and righteous indignation. Todd does not like his wayward roommate's sloppiness, but he realizes that by trying to see things from Mark's perspective, he'll have a better chance of coming to an acceptable compromise.

Listening

Listening carefully is one of the best tools for handling conflict. In the last chapter, we described four types of listening. All four can be applied effectively in conflict situations. If you practice informational and empathic listening skills, you gather the facts you need to negotiate successfully and also relay the message that you want to understand the other person's perspective. In the preceding example, if Todd tells Mark, "Look, I have a problem with our living arrangement. I like things to be tidy, you don't. I'm not blaming you, because you have a right to live the way you want. But can we talk about it? I want to hear where you're coming from." This approach may persuade Mark to consider the impact of his style on his roommate. It has a much better chance of soothing the conflict than a snide comment or hostile outburst.

You can also apply logical listening skills to a conflict situation. Just because Todd listens carefully for information and empathizes with his roommate, does not mean he has to accept Mark's ideas. He may listen carefully to get the information and may try to see the situation from Mark's perspective. He may also conclude that his roommate's proposal is unreasonable. For example, if Mark says, "OK, you like the place tidy and I don't. What if I clean the room one Saturday and you take care of it the next Saturday?" That proposal has not solved the problem, since the room will inevitably get messy throughout the week. Todd may respond by saying, "I appreciate your offer and respect your right to live the way you want, but what about the room during the week? Can we solve this in a way in which we're both happy?"

Finally, the two could help ease the conflict by practicing *dialogic* listening. Recall that dialogic listening demands building together chunks of conversation or sculpting mutual meanings. Todd and Mark would thus focus on "our" problem instead of "your" problem. Each would discuss the situation with an open mind and do so in a somewhat playful manner. They would stress "in front of" conversations instead of "behind" each other. Recall in the last chapter that "in front of" means the two participants try to shape their own script as they go. Neither tries to figure out where the other is coming from but each looks for ways to sculpt a solution they both find acceptable. Rather than Mark trying to "psych out" Todd ("What is he *really* trying to do here?"), Mark accepts Todd's words at face value.

Finally, in dialogic listening the two would be "present" to each other. Rather than place much emphasis on the past or future, they would focus on the conversation as it develops in the here and now. Each would think, "What can I do right now to help bring this problem to a solution we can both live with?"

Mutual Problem Solving, or Principled Negotiating

Participants in a conflict have a much better chance of solving a dispute if they look at the situation as mutual problem solvers rather than antagonists who each must win. Fisher and Ury (1991) have devised a procedure that helps each person in a conflict focus on the other side's interests. In *Getting to Yes*, they describe three styles of dealing with conflict: soft, hard, and principled.

In the soft approach, either one or both participants are friends and are reluctant to do anything to harm their relationship. They make concessions they shouldn't. They change their position easily if they think their union might be threatened. Either or both will accept losses if they believe the acceptance will preserve their friendship. They yield easily to pressure. Like the nonassertive style, the "soft" approach leaves at least one of the parties dissatisfied with the outcome.

Participants in the hard approach see the other as an adversary and want a victory rather than a negotiated settlement. Either or both dig into their stated positions, make threats, distrust the other, and look for only one answer to their problem. For them, the conflict is a clash of wills rather than a dialectic of ideas.

In the principled approach, the two are problem-solvers who want to settle the conflict on the idea level. To do so, they focus on the other party's interests and not on stated positions. They realize that conflicts often can't be solved with one answer so they explore a number of options that will please each of them. They both want to reach a solution in an efficient and friendly way.

Prime Minister Menachem Begin of Israel and President Anwar Sadat of Egypt are examples of two people who were able to come to a peaceful solution in 1978 by sitting down and carving out a peace treaty that came to be called the Camp David Accord. Rather than staying entrenched in their positions, each focused on the other's interests. Israel was concerned about security while Egypt wanted its sovereignty back. To help the other achieve his interest, Sadat agreed to withdrawing tanks far back from Israel in the Sinai, while Begin granted Egypt its right to fly its own flag wherever it wanted in the Sinai (Fisher & Ury, 1991).

In their book *Getting Together: Building Relationships as We Negotiate*, Fisher and Brown (1988) show how the method just described can be applied to close unions. The authors recommend that participants listen carefully to each other, deal with the issues, and work as constructive problem solvers who will both benefit from an amicable solution.

The methods described for dealing with conflict are not guaranteed to always work. However, practiced on a regular basis they have a much better chance of succeeding than the angry outburst or violence. Also, two people in a close relationship will solve their conflict faster precisely because they are closely bonded. If the two really care about each other, they can have an argument and get over it rather quickly. The same argument between two colleagues or students who share little or no affection can produce long-lasting animosity. For example, Ben and Sue are happily married and have an argument over money. The two of them can get over their conflict in fifteen minutes with no lingering animosity. Let's say, however, that Ben has a fragile relationship with his brother-in-law Mort and has the same heated exchange with Mort at the family picnic. The identical conversation could produce resentment that might last for years.

We have discussed effective and ineffective ways to handle conflict in close relationships. Intimates who use effective methods have a better chance of sustaining their union than those who don't. Two people who resort to the ineffective methods described are more likely to end a close relationship. When that happens, the couple usually follows the recognizable stages Mark Knapp (1990) describes.

The hero riding off with the heroine into the sunset makes a happy ending in many westerns because viewers assume that the two will marry and will never be separated until one dies. But the sad reality is that many intimate relationships do end before either party dies: marriages break up, close partnerships dissolve, and best friends decide not to see each other any more. How does it happen? Mark Knapp lists the five stages of relationship breakdown. Although not every union that ends follows this exact pattern, many do.

FIVE STAGES OF RELATIONSHIP DISINTEGRATION

Differentiating is the stage where at least one person starts focusing on differences in the relationship instead of similarities. Lisa and Manuel have gone through the five stages of relationship development: they've initiated their union, have experimented with small talk, have intensified with deeper revelations about love and caring, have bonded by letting the world know that they should be considered a couple, and then enjoyed a "honeymoon" period that lasted for seven months. During this time, both were busy building their careers. Then something happened: the union started to unravel. What they formerly saw as endearing traits, they now see as irritating flaws. While they were forging their union, they focused on all the admirable qualities of their partner. Now they find more blemishes than virtues. In the struggle between interdependence and independence, independence starts to take over. Instead of reveling in how alike they are, as they did before, they notice their differences. Either or both start feeling pressured and make comments like "I need more space."

The next stage is *circumscribing*, a word that comes from Latin and means to "draw a line around" or "restrict." Lisa and Manuel may limit their conversations to everyday business instead of talking about their disintegrating union.

They may tiptoe around each other and discuss only those topics they know won't hit a nerve for either one. During the "coming together" stage, they delighted in sharing secrets and talking about the wonder of their unfolding romance. Now they go through their daily routine in silence. Manuel buries himself in the paper while Lisa spends more time than ever working on her clients' tax returns. If they go out in public, they put on a good show of togetherness for their friends and clients, but as soon as they're alone, they talk little or revert to silence.

The term *stagnating* describes the stage where little or no motion takes place. Like a stagnating pond, Lisa and Manuel's union stands still for a time. Their relationship does not move forward. They continue to live together because "we need the combined salaries to maintain a decent standard of living in this depressed economy." Life is not fun in their apartment. Conversations together at the dinner table—if they have dinner together—are as superficial as they are boring.

"This next one goes out to all those who have ever been in love, then become engaged, gotten married, participated in the tragic deterioration of a relationship, suffered the pains and agonies of a bitter divorce, subjected themselves to the fruitless search for a new partner, and ultimately resigned themselves to remaining single in a world full of irresponsible jerks, noncommittal weirdos, and neurotic misfits."

Avoiding is the process of withdrawing. When the stagnation becomes too much, Lisa or Manuel—or both together—may start taking steps toward dissolution. He may move out. They may agree on a trial separation. They may be more blunt in the way they talk to each other: "We've got to do something about this situation. We're both really unhappy." Either or both may communicate their thoughts in less direct ways: "I can't come home for the next three nights because I'm swamped at work." The purpose in this stage is to move the relationship toward its inevitable end.

Terminating is the final step in which partners formally or informally break off their relationship. Often there is a "dumper" and a "dumpee." Maybe Lisa wants to end their union but Manuel doesn't and tries to dissuade her. Or they may both decide to call it quits. The termination may be abrupt or gradual. The way partners break up depends on how intimate their relationship has been. Cody (1982) found that the closer the relationship, the greater was the obligation of the one ending it to justify such a step. If a relationship hasn't moved very far toward intimacy, one partner simply withdraws from the other. If the union has been a little more intimate, one partner usually asks that the couple see less of each other. If the union has been even closer, the partner trying to break off will try to do so in a way that will assuage the other's feeling. In the closest relationships, the partner seeking the dissolution will show grief over the parting.

Any given couple may skip one or more of the disintegration stages Knapp describes. Or two people may go from stagnation back to bonding and revive their sagging union. Every relationship is unique and, as such, resists getting put into clear-cut categories. But the stages are useful in showing how relationships form and sometimes unravel.

Our purpose in discussing these phases is not to demoralize but to share some research about what can happen when a relationship comes to an end. Sometimes, a close union goes on for a number of years and then ends because both parties want it to. Neither regrets the time together or the emotional investment. Each is satisfied that the union brought satisfaction and then ended. Neither has any real regrets. Other close relationships, however, might have been saved if the two people had a better knowledge of how the stages evolve. If you know what could and often does happen when you let the process take its natural course, then you're more likely to do whatever is necessary to keep the relationship strong and vibrant. The best intimate relationships, including marriages, demand work: they rarely happen because partners "lucked out" and found soulmates who were completely compatible. The same applies to other intimate unions such as friendship—the subject we discuss for the remaining part of the chapter.

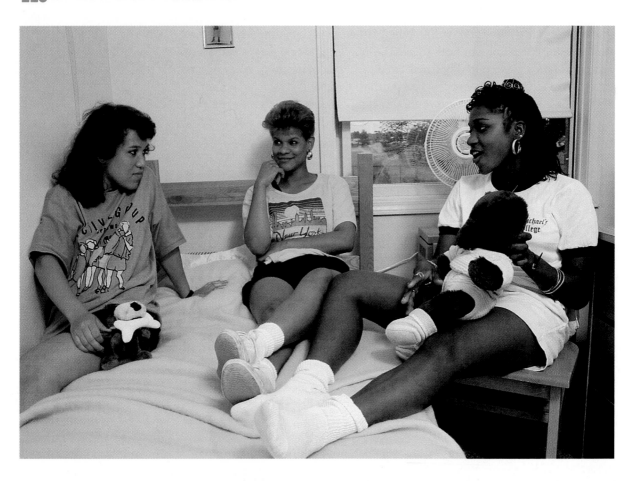

Close friendships provide some of life's greatest joy.

FRIENDSHIP

We define **friendship** as a close union between two people who know each other well and who share a strong affection. Close friendships produce some of life's greatest joys. From toddlerhood through the teens into adulthood, most people cherish good friends who are there for them and who do not judge them harshly when they fail. Friends offer support when it's needed and genuinely care about each other.

The intimate kind of relationships discussed before in this chapter are somewhat similar to friendship, but they're also different. Many passionate relationships often last as long as each partner stays healthy and keeps his or her physical attractiveness. With friends, feelings of attraction are not the glue that binds. Plenty of social rituals exist for marriage and family, but few exist for friendships. Friendships are much easier to end than marriages or family relationships. Friends don't have to go through a legal divorce to announce that their union has ended.

Foundations of Friendship

Friendships are also different from certain close unions because they're voluntary. Very few people choose their families, but almost all can choose their friends. Other people rarely force their friendship others. And friendships can often survive periods of absence. "Friends for life" can have intense activity for two years and then not see each other for six months and pick up the relationship right where it left off. Just as differences exist between intimates and friends, there are also some similarities.

Partners in both unions begin by finding things in common—interest in sports, music, studies, books, etc.—and move through some of the same stages. Friends, like lovers, begin by revealing positive elements about themselves and when they establish trust, move on to talking about negative traits. Friends have fun together. They like sharing jokes and cartoons. They're on the same wavelength. They seek out each other because they enjoy the other's company.

Friendships can be broken down into at least two categories: close and superficial. When we say we're going to the football game with "friends," we usually mean casual acquaintances whose company we enjoy but with whom we have not established a deep, close relationship. Most of us also have one or two close friends. We may not share our secrets with the eight people we run around with, but we will share such intimate thoughts with a special friend we trust. Argyle and Henderson suggest six characteristics that distinguish close from superficial friendships. Close friends

1. Stand up for the other person when they're apart

2. Share news of success with the other

3. Show emotional support

4. Trust and support each other

5. Volunteer to help when there is a need

6. Try to make the other happy when the friends are together

Conflict Between Friends

Anyone who has ever had a "best friend" or a "really good friend" also knows that friends can occasionally have arguments. Such conflicts can be generated by violation of trust, misunderstanding, or incompatible goals. Let's say Traci and Maureen have been best

We are not evil, inadequate or incompetent when our relationships fail. It may have been that we were simply overconfident about them, not adequately prepared for them or unrealistic in our expectations of them. Not all relationships are right. As long as values change, insights expand, human façades remain inpenetrable and human behavior unpredictable, we will make mistakes.

The very measure of a good relationship is in how much it encourages optimal intellectual, emotional and spiritual growth. So, if a relationship becomes destructive, endangers our human dignity, prevents us from growing, continually depresses and demoralizes us—and we have done everything we can to prevent its failure—then, unless we are masochists and enjoy misery, we must eventually terminate it. We are not for everyone and everyone is not for us.

LEO BUSCAGLIA (1984, P. 15)

CONSIDERING CULTURE

Studies by Gudykunst and Ting-Toomey (1987) suggest that Americans are far more ready to reveal a great deal about themselves than Japanese. Assume that someone you know well—an American—has struck up a friendship with someone from Japan who has been studying in this country for one year. The person you know is very frustrated because she likes her new friend but finds that the Japanese student is reluctant to tell much about herself. Your friend has opened up by revealing a great deal about herself and can't understand why the new friend won't reciprocate in kind. Based on the research by Gudykunst and Ting-Toomey, what would you tell your friend? What suggestions might you make for solving the problem of uneven revelations?

Friendship always benefits; love sometimes injures.

SENECA

friends since grade school and have made it a point to spend holidays together whenever possible. Traci started going with Frank four months ago, and the romance has progressed steadily. Traci announces that she and Frank will spend Thanksgiving together by going to meet Traci's parents. Maureen feels jilted, even though she has her own boyfriend. She's spent the last three Thanksgivings with Traci and finds it hard to accept her exclusion this time. Her mind tells her that this arrangement is understandable, but her emotions make her feel rejected.

Can this situation be worked out? Yes—and with greater ease than a conflict between fellow workers. Loving intimates or close friends have the advantage of a bond that helps them get over conflict faster and better than colleagues or strangers. Good friends also know the other better and can thus gauge reactions more easily than can two people working in the same office or attending the same college.

Why Do Some Friendships End?

You're fortunate indeed if you have one friend who has always been there for you. You know that you can be separated from a good friend for six months and then can renew the bond with a long-distance call. You also know that a number of friendships end for a variety of reasons. Two roommates may have shared much during their three years in the same residence hall, for example, but after graduation different jobs in cities half a continent away make it hard to stay in touch.

Some friends may have a serious falling out and even though they reconcile to a degree, their friendship is never the same. The breakdown might have resulted from a variety of causes. One may have changed, and the other stayed the same. One might take on a new set of values that the other can't or won't accept.

"'Tis better to have loved and lost than never to have loved at all" is a well-known statement. Like many famous aphorisms, it has lasted because it contains a comforting insight. Whether you are still working on friendships or have ended some of them, they all have made your life richer in the long run. Part III looked at the elements of interpersonal dialogue—self-disclosure, language, nonverbal elements, and listening. This opening chapter of Part IV

LOOKING BACK - LOOKING FORWARD

focused on close relationships between intimates and friends. We discussed some research studies that give you a better idea of why close unions develop, how they often go through recognizable stages and how they sometimes break down. We offered some ideas for you to consider that might help you make intelligent choices about how to improve your own relationships.

The next chapter examines another kind of close relationship—interpersonal communication in families. As you continue this journey, reflect on your own family to rediscover what was right about it and some of the problems that made it less than perfect. You can't change the past or reinvent your unique family, but you can learn from the positive and negative experiences you've had. Such reflections can enrich the family you belong to now or the one you might help form in the future.

REVIEW TERMS AND CONCEPTS

intimate relationships
207
interpersonal needs
208
social exchange
theory
209

dialectic
212
limerance
215
shared values
216

gunny-sacking
219
friendship
226

PUTTING THEORY INTO PRACTICE

FOR DISCUSSION:

1. Divide into groups of three to five. Discuss what you believe are the qualities of an outstanding close union. Such a union could be a marriage or a live-in relationship. Pin down the three most important elements you believe would contribute to the best intimate unions. Such qualities could include trust, deep affection, or shared values. Then list

the two most destructive forces that erode close relationships. Report your findings to the class, and then discuss ways to foster the strong qualities and eliminate those that are destructive.

2. Conduct the same exercise for friendships. Re-examine the six qualities of close friendships listed on p. 227. Do you agree with the six or would you substitute other qualities? Then go on and talk about those elements that hurt friendships. As suggested in the preceding exercise, report back to the class and hold a discussion on ways to enrich friendships and methods for weeding out harmful factors.

SKILL BUILDERS:

1. Think of a film that focuses on disastrous close relationships. For example, *War of the Roses* is the story of a married couple who can't reconcile their major differences. *Looking for Mr. Goodbar* depicts a young woman who continuously gets herself in unions that hurt her. Why do the characters fall into the traps they do? What could they have done differently?

2. Consider a film that depicts two people who struggle to build a strong, positive relationship and finally succeed. What did they do to overcome some of the obstacles they encountered along the way? Two examples are *Dying Young* and *Prince of Tides*. Why did the union of the main characters survive, despite difficulties?

3. You've heard the phrase "Love is blind." If love is blind, especially during the first stages of relationship development—initiating, experimenting, intensifying, and integrating—what makes this true? If it is true that most people during the formation of a close union see virtues, rather than flaws in the beloved, what can you do to prevent "blindness"?

4. List four conflicts that have taken place between nations over the past five years. What led to the conflict? How was it settled? Now compare global conflicts to personal ones you have either experienced or observed. Discuss the major similarities and differences between the global and personal examples. What can you learn from a global conflict that you can apply to a personal one?

5. Consider some of the best close friendships you've ever had. What made these unions succeed? How did you and your close friend work through the inevitable problems that emerged in any close union? What made the friendship so satisfying for both of you?

6. You can't change the past but you can learn from it. Think back on a close relationship you've had that dissolved. In retrospect, you wish it

hadn't, but it has. What insights did you gain from the dissolution that could help you maintain a current close union or help you succeed in a future one?

OR EXTENDED STUDY

Fisher, R., & Ury, W. (1991). *Getting to yes: Negotiating agreement without giving in*. New York: Penguin.

This is a practical manual on ways to handle conflict. Fisher has co-authored another book (with Scott Brown) that applies the "principled" approach to interpersonal relationships. The book is Getting together: Building relationships as we negotiate (New York: Penguin, 1988).

Tannen, D. (1990) *You just don't understand: Women and men in conversation*. New York: Ballantine.

Dr. Tannen is a linguist who explains clearly, with numerous examples, why women and men relate differently to each other.

Wilmot, W. W. (1987). *Dyadic communication*. (3rd ed.). Dubuque, IA: Brown.

A thorough examination of all kinds of conflict. Wilmot demonstrates styles of conflict and suggests some strategies for people who want to work through them.

The happiest moments of my life have been the few which I have passed at home in the bosom of my family.

THOMAS JEFFERSON

10

Family Interpersonal Communication

OBJECTIVES

After reading this chapter and taking part in class activities, you should be able to

- Describe the family from a systems perspective.

- Explain the functions of family communication.

- Identify a variety of ways in which "rules" govern communication behavior in families.

- Distinguish among several patterns of family interaction.

- Describe steps in managing conflict.

- Describe several communication-related issues that face "nontraditional" families.

Cognitive Map 10

HAPPY CHILDHOOD MEMORIES…family vacations…Sunday dinners…the family pet…birthdays…holiday celebrations…and so on. For many people, these things trigger pleasant thoughts about family life. For others, the idea of family life may not be so rosy. For some, stressful divorce, conflict, and fighting may be the most vivid recollections. As these people look back to younger days, they may remember being amazed at others talking about "having fun" with their family.

What descriptive words come to mind when you think of the word *family*? Do you imagine your own family, or other families? When you think of "a family communicating," do you have recollections of what you may consider healthy communication relationships?

Whether the notion of family conjures up smiles or frowns, the inevitable fact remains—everyone has one. Many people are seeking answers to the

numerous communication problems afflicting families today. Others are seeking a greater understanding of the functions and roles of families as they grow and change. Because interpersonal relationships and communication are fundamental to the survival of families, we have devoted an entire chapter to giving greater insight into the workings of families and the powerful influence that communication has on family life.

Dolores Curran, who wrote the book *Traits of a Healthy Family* (1983), conducted a study in which she asked 551 teachers, doctors, family counselors, youth club leaders, religious advisors, and other professionals to identify traits typical of a healthy family. The results focused on the ability to communicate as the most highly rated quality.

This chapter explores the qualities and communication styles families share. Although there are certainly "ideal" patterns of family communication, conflict is inevitable. Therefore, as we examine the roles of family members and the communication skills people develop as a result of family membership, we'll also delve into the ways individuals deal with conflict that either help or hinder communication. We'll discuss the role of family in developing members' self-esteem and the family's influence on value formation. Lastly, the idea of family as a "system" with its own unique characteristics, challenges, and opportunities provides a launching pad for the development of relationships and a support system that continues to grow and change throughout life. Let's begin by taking a look at the family from a systems perspective.

While there are many definitions of the "family," traditionally a family has been described as "a social group composed of children and their parents."

THE FAMILY SYSTEM

n recent years, many definitions of the term *family* have emerged. Psychologists, sociologists, and communication experts would be hard pressed to find a definition they all agreed on. Many definitions include such traditional notions as "blood related" or "bonded in marital union." Others would go beyond a "multigenerational" systems definition (Yerby, Buerkel-Rothfuss, & Bochner, 1990) to suggest that the notion of family encompasses a broader range of relationships to include such groups as organizations or clubs where people may describe themselves as a "family." Of course, this less conservative view would then include groups of people who interact on an interpersonal level and share some kind of personal commitment to each other. According to Webster's Dictionary (1989), a family is "a group of persons of common ancestry; a group of individuals living under one roof and under one head; a social group composed of children and their parents."

The concept of the family as a system has been explored by many communication theorists. According to Hall and Fagen (1956), a system is "a set of objects together with relationships between the objects and their attributes." If those objects are people, one of those attributes would be communicative behavior (Bavelas & Segal, 1982). In their article, "Family Systems Theory: Background and Implications," marital and family therapists Janet Beavin Bavelas and Lynn Segal further define the family as a system,

> a special set of people with relationships between them; these relationships are established, maintained, and evidenced by the members communicating with each other. In general, any human interactional system can be defined as "persons-communicating-with-other-persons." Note that even this simplest definition of a system has the effect of putting the "objects" in the background and bringing their relationships to the foreground. Moreover...insofar as family relationships endure, they form patterns over time, and it is this patterning over time that is the essence of a family system. (p. 102)

The **family system** approach looks at the family as an entire unit, rather than as the sum of its parts, with the individual parts of the system relating to one another and affecting the whole. As Beebe and Masterson (1986) suggest, the systems theory approach takes a holistic perspective.

If we consider the family system as a whole unit, then there are parts or extensions of the family that we would call **subsystems.** These may be temporary or more permanent dyads or subgroups that are part of the whole (or part of the larger family unit). For example, your parents would be considered a husband-wife subsystem. If you have any brothers or sisters, we could say that the children are a subsystem of the larger family unit. The interpersonal subsystems become even more complex as the family unit grows larger (Galvin & Brommel, 1991).

Let's explore some other characteristics of the family as a system, to provide insight and understanding about ways to improve the overall quality of family life.

Family as an Open System

The family is an **open system**—it is affected by external factors. It is not a closed unit that does not interact with its environment. Across the disciplines, an "open system" means that the unit is influenced by and influences its external environment. Many theorists note that much of the stress that families face today is due to external pressures, or forces outside the family unit. Perhaps you can relate to a few of the following examples of these external forces that have an impact on the quality of family life: jobs held outside the home, membership in religious and/or social organizations, the fluctuating economy, your neighborhood and/or community, and even cultural norms. There are obviously many more environmental influences; one that everyone who is reading this book can relate to is school. You could probably think of all sorts of ways that your obligation to go to school is affecting your family life. Some of you may be away from home and have very little immediate contact with your family. Others may be going to school full or part time while holding a job to support your family. When you have a major exam coming up and you still have to work your normal number of hours at your job, your family may feel the effects of the pressures impacting you, and a chain reaction sets in. You may be stressed out, you take it out on a member of your family, and he or she does the same to yet another member of the family.

As you look at your families or your friends' families, it helps to be aware of both the internal and external influences that affect family life. The healthy family can distinguish between what is going on within its own system and what is coming in from the external environment. Let's move on and take a look at some of the functions of family communication.

FUNCTIONS OF FAMILY COMMUNICATION

Families are unique in their ways of doing things, interacting, and just plain functioning. Although families probably share many common functions, their ways of going about doing what they do and how they communicate may vary in a variety of ways. In this section we look at the **family communication functions** that emerge as families grow and change.

CONSIDERING COMMUNICATING SKILLFULLY

View several television sitcoms (such as Married With Children, The Simpsons, Home Improvement) *that involve families. Can you identify some of the external influences these families face? How do television families differ from your experiences in real families?*

Family members often seek one another for support on an emotional level.

Support

Families offer **support** in a number of ways. Some are immediately apparent, and others may not even be generally thought of as "support" on a less obvious level. Although people can't always count on their families to be supportive, for the most part families provide social support and intimacy to their members. When you can't count on your friends, you can usually count on your family (at least some member). Just from being a member of a family, you have a sense of belonging that can be found through no other comparable source.

Families provide a source of support by contributing a feeling of intimacy. Intimacy can be displayed in three common ways: physically, emotionally, and intellectually (Adler & Rodman, 1991). You've seen families whose members appear very close on a physical level, sharing hugs and kisses quite naturally and openly. You've probably also seen families whose members rarely display any outward signs of affection or physical attention, but who probably are quite supportive on an intellectual or emotional level.

In addition to providing social support, the family plays a fundamental role in developing members' self-concept, self-esteem, and value formation.

Personality and Identity

Whether a child is reared in a single- or a two-parent family environment, the family is the main source for identity formation. Of course, the ways in which people view themselves will vary according to the kind of experience they had growing up in their own particular homes and their own unique communication environment. Recall that your self-concept is really your view of yourself, and self-esteem has to do with how you feel about that view. Your family strongly influences both of these constructs because you spend so much time with the family in your formative years. In families where communication is healthy and supportive, members grow up feeling positive about themselves. As a result, they project a positive self-concept in other relationships. Conversely, children who begin their lives in a communication environment where they feel they are burdensome or a source of family troubles usually have a very negative view of themselves. Of course, as you venture out and increase your contacts through other significant relationships your self-concept may shift, but the initial foundation is often difficult to alter.

Value Formation

People who write books about raising families and dealing with children often talk about **value formation.** Just as your self-concept is influenced greatly by your experiences in your own family, so is your value system. Through a variety of communicative behaviors, parents convey to their children their understanding of what is desirable or important. Parents typically instill the values they experienced in their own families of origin. Certain family values are passed on through the generations. For example, a family where a college education is deemed important will promote this goal in a variety of ways. This value can be conveyed through the kinds of reading materials provided in the home, what kinds of educational activities the family participates in, and the daily encouragement family members receive from their parents about their efforts in school.

Family traditions, rituals, and celebrations also convey a sense of values to members. In some families, it is traditional to celebrate individual accomplishments (awards, recognition, good grades, and so on). This reflects the importance of success for these families. Even bedtime rituals can be a source of value formation. If a child is given individual attention and time for conversation with one or both parents with a bedtime story and a brief chat before the light goes out, the child comes to feel he or she is valued as an individual.

Of course, not all family values are necessarily positive in their outcomes. For example, in some families the goal of winning or being the best at whatever you set out to accomplish might be a desirable value. But if members are encouraged to achieve these goals no matter *how* they achieve them (perhaps through hurting others in the process or by being dishonest), the value becomes tainted.

You've seen how communication within families greatly influences the development of self-concept and value formation. While all this is happening, families are also discovering ways to manage daily activities and the normal routines of everyday life. Let's focus now on how family communication affects everyday functioning.

Family Communication and Everyday Life

No two family members share the exact same talents or experiences. So it's helpful, as family members work together to "survive" everyday life, if they can communicate effectively to make life a little more efficient and pleasant. For example, some families have a message or bulletin board through which they share their comings and goings, maybe appointments, so that other members of the family know of their whereabouts. That may seem like common courtesy, but for some who are too busy or simply don't care, the lack of communication can cause unnecessary chaos. In some families, unlike the traditional stereotypes, the dad may be the master chef and really likes doing dishes, so it makes more sense that he assumes those duties while others help with homework or other chores. If some children are old enough to babysit their siblings, this built-in convenience provides another means of mutual support for busy families.

Some typical functions of family communication, then, are to offer social support, to help form personality and identity, and to deal with the practical events of everyday life. Now we'll discuss family roles, rules, and interaction patterns.

FAMILY ROLES, RULES, AND INTERACTION PATTERNS

Gender and Roles

Let's begin this section by looking at gender and roles in the family. After completing the "Considering Critical Thinking" discussion, you might be curious about how these designated sex roles have come to play such an important part in social interaction. First let's define the term **role** as it relates to family communication. Roles are socially determined sets of expected, patterned behaviors that individuals assume as they occupy a position in the family. Beebe and Masterson (1986, p. 86) write,

> While there is considerable debate over the origins of sex roles

CONSIDERING CRITICAL THINKING

In small groups, discuss some of the female and male role-specific duties and understandings you can recall as being important in your family while you were growing up. For example, were there certain chores that only males were required to do, such as mowing the lawn or taking out the garbage? Did females have more leeway when it came to expressing emotions through tears? Were certain displays of affection OK between family members of the same sex, but discouraged with the opposite sex?

Did you ever rebel and try to change or break some of those "rules" or expectations? What were the consequences? As you look back on these situations, do you now interpret some as unhealthy or too restrictive?

(are there basic genetic differences between men and women that tend to make women more nurturing, men more aggressive, or are these traits developed socially?), there is general agreement that social interaction is, at least, in part, responsible for sex-role identity. The expectations your parents held for you, the activities in which they encouraged or discouraged you, and their verbal and nonverbal communication with you have all influenced your perception of "appropriate" sex roles.

In addition to families, there are, of course, other influences on sex role development such as religious and social groups, school, everyday interactions with peers, and the media. (In Chapter 13, we'll further explore the notion of media and its influence on interpersonal communication.) For example, even television has provided us with role models of families. From the Cleaver family on *Leave It to Beaver* to the Cunninghams on *Happy Days* to shows like *The Simpsons,* television has shown us the joys and trials of assuming certain sex roles and the influence of family communication on their formation. Many of us can identify with these popular programs. Of course, as discussed later in this chapter, there are many new norms (rules for behavior) for the composition of the family unit, such as single-parent families, two members of the same sex raising children together as a family, and so on. Of the many external influences that affect sex role formation, family communication is the strongest.

Family role functions pivot on role expectations—the unwritten **rules** that families (and society) have established for men and women. From expected patterns of behavior, to responsibilities about running the household, to psychological or personality-related expectations, many sets of rules guide—and confuse—us. Feldman (1982) has generalized psychological dimensions of male and female roles (see Table 10.1). How might such generalizations affect family communication? A lot depends on the cultural background and influences of individual families. For example, in some families the "rules" are very clear about what men and women are supposed to do or not. In the 1992 movie *The Prince of Tides*, Tom, played by Nick Nolte, has flashbacks of growing up in a family with extremely strict role expectations. In one scene, he is reprimanded and humiliated in front of his brother and sister as his father suggests that Tom's crying is a female behavior. His father even goes on to tell him to go put on a dress. Many of us can probably think of examples of our own or other people's families where role expectations and "rules" have a profound impact on family communication.

In families where communication patterns are considered healthy, individuals are allowed to be flexible in their roles. They understand that as people mature and times and circumstances change, so do the rules. By letting others be flexible in their roles, you let them adapt to situations and assume new roles.

As you've been reading about gender and roles, you might have thought about some of the roles you assume within your own family. If you think about it, the list could be rather lengthy. For example, you might be a woman who is a daughter, a wife, a mother, a sister, a teacher, a friend, a student, a cook, a housekeeper, and so on. In a contemporary view, many of these roles need not be linked to either sex specifically. In many traditional families, how

Television has shown many versions of the "typical" American family and the roles members display.

TABLE 10-1

COMMON BELIEFS ABOUT FEMALE AND MALE ROLES

The Female Role

Women are expected to be (or allowed to be) the following:

1. Home oriented, child(ren) oriented

2. Warm, affectionate, gentle, tender

3. Aware of feelings of others, considerate, tactful, compassionate

4. Moody, high-strung, temperamental, excitable, emotional, subjective, illogical

5. Complaining, nagging

6. Weak, helpless, fragile, easily emotionally hurt

7. Submissive, yielding, dependent

The Male Role

Men are expected to be (or allowed to be) the following:

1. Ambitious, competitive, enterprising, worldly

2. Calm, stable, unemotional, realistic

3. Strong, tough, powerful

4. Aggressive, forceful, decisive, dominant

5. Independent, self-reliant

6. Harsh, severe, stern, cruel

7. Autocratic, rigid, arrogant

SOURCE: FELDMAN (1982, P. 355).

ever, there are more defined "rules" with regard to sex role expectations. We suggest that neither the contemporary view nor the traditional view is ideal. Rather, whatever works in the individual family to help in healthy functioning is best.

Clear expectations regarding role behaviors make for successful family communication. Family members need to realistically assess their expectations of each other and understand each others' perspectives. Communication about what members should or shouldn't do is essential. When expectations are unclear or unrealistic, stress and frustration surface and satisfaction with family life decreases. For example, if a boy comes home from school with a note from his teacher describing his fighting behavior on the playground and immediately has some favorite privilege taken away from him by his parents, he may

Through their choice of cloth-ing and actions, children will model their own roles after their parents and other adult role models.

become confused. His understanding of what it means to be a "real man" is to defend himself when being verbally or physically attacked. He understood that by the very fact that he is his father's son, he was to behave "like a man" in all circumstances. Perhaps his parents had never made the expectation clear that there are times and places where this kind of behavior is not appropriate. Whose fault is it that this incident occurred? It really doesn't matter who is at fault: the fact remains that expectations were unclear.

Role expectations are an important key to understanding communication within families, but "rules" govern sex role behaviors. Communication "rules" are not limited to role expectations. As we'll see in this next section, rules are important for understanding how families operate.

CONSIDERING CULTURE

In small groups, discuss the findings in Table 10.1. Describe how you think a member of the opposite sex would react to these generalizations. How many of these do you agree with? Do you see any of these as being specific to any particular culture(s)?

Family Communication "Rules"

Most families probably don't sit down over a family meeting and write down a list of official rules for conduct and communication within their household. In fact, the discussion may not ever take place on a formal level, but through daily interactions and through the socialization process, family members come to understand their own set of unwritten rules. Some rules are explicit; for exam-ple, "We will always go to church on Sunday morning"; "The last person to use the shower wipes it down"; "No one is allowed to talk on the phone while the family is eating dinner." But most rules are never officially expressed. In other words, families have "rules" that govern expressions of affection and intimacy like "Never kiss Dad. Hugs are OK sometimes, but a handshake is preferable, especially if people who aren't family members are in your presence." These "rules" suggest what topics are appropriate to discuss in front of the children and what topics are taboo; for example, never talk about money problems in front of the children. Some "rules" reflect appropriate responses to extreme emotions: it's OK to cry, but laughing at someone else's mistake is unacceptable. Shimanoff (1980, p. 83) suggests that rules "may function to regulate, interpret, evaluate, justify, correct, predict, and explain behavior." As family members partake in and observe interaction episodes within their own families, they discover these rules.

Rules serve many functions in the family system. They help families maintain a sense of stability and predictability. Rules guide family members' behavior and help to avoid chaos. Perhaps you've observed a family more than once that appears to have very few, if any, rules (explicit or implicit). You've seen firsthand how interactions and everyday comings and goings can get out of hand. Some may describe this kind of family behavior as dysfunctional. Furthermore, if people fail to understand the rules of their families, they may find themselves in situations of misunderstanding, frustration, and conflict.

Later in this chapter we explore conflict in families and offer some suggestions and examples of effective conflict resolution and healthy communication patterns. First, let's see how families come to understand each other and develop an identity through their own unique patterns of interaction.

Interaction Patterns

As discussed in the previous section, families share certain rules for behavior that provide them with a sense of stability and predictability. Families also communicate through a variety of patterned interactions. Communication involves the creation of shared meanings. Families, then, create their own unique meanings through repetitive interaction patterns. We have already seen how family communication rules influence interaction patterns, so now let's look at other areas of communication behavior that will help us understand how family meanings emerge.

According to Bochner and Eisenberg (1987), family-of-origin influences reflect the experiences one has growing up in the family (or families) and are the earliest and most powerful influences on one's personality. Galvin and Brommel (1991, p. 56) further suggest:

> The term **family-of-origin** refers to the specific experiences one encounters while growing up, which reflect both a unique combination of (1) multigenerational transmissions and (2) ethnic/cultural heritages represented with the family of origin.

In other words, most families pass on their traditions and patterns of interaction from generation to generation without even being aware that they are doing so. In other situations, the intent is quite purposeful. For example, most families develop their own vocabulary that is unique to that particular family

CONSIDERING CRITICAL THINKING

Prepare a list of at least ten "rules" that you can recall from your own family experiences. Then form small groups and compare your lists. Make a master sheet with all the rules on them, and categorize them according to explicit or unstated. Which do you find more of? Why do you think this is?

and understood best by its own members. These words can usually be traced back through the generations to find the original reference. When two people marry, they are merging the learned interaction patterns they have been developing all their lives. If there is a wide discrepancy between the couple's family-of-origin behaviors, communication breakdowns are inevitable. After-meal family rituals are examples of this. In some homes, it is customary to clear the table and completely clean the kitchen before retiring to the living room to watch TV or simply visit with each other. In other homes, the custom is to relax at the table or in a more comfortable setting and share in conversation, leaving the clean-up for a later time. If you come from a home where the first example is more familiar and your spouse is used to the latter, the communication patterns in your new family system can be greatly (even negatively) affected.

Ethnic or cultural heritage can greatly influence family interaction patterns. Think about the other people in this class. Do they all come from similar cultural backgrounds? Do you think they all share the same rules for interaction that you do with your own family? Probably not. People come from a variety of ethnic backgrounds. As a result, they also come from countless family experiences. For some, the rules for interaction were gender or role related. The head of the household was typically the father or the eldest male, and certain responsibilities were connected with this role. For others, the gender or role responsibilities might become confusing if the family is being raised by a single parent because the mother or father may perform duties that are generally expected to be performed by someone of the opposite gender. The film *Mr. Mom* (about a working mother and stay-at-home father) depicts such confusion. Furthermore, when the mother is not only the sole breadwinner and head of the household, she may expect to provide the emotional support and wisdom that her mother and grandmother (and so on) provided for her family as she was growing up.

Family interaction patterns develop over time and are influenced by a number of factors. Although it is not always easy to pick out obvious differences among families, it is easier to observe the flow of communication between members of a family. Family communication networks establish certain rule patterns.

Family Communication Networks

The term "family communication networks" refers to such interaction patterns as who talks to whom and about what. A network determines the two-way flow of messages from one family member to one or more other members or significant others outside the family (Galvin & Brommel, 1991, p. 67).

In their book *Family Talk: Interpersonal Communication in the Family,* Beebe and Masterson (1986) suggest four different communication networks typically used by families (see Figure 10.1). The first is described as the **chain network**,

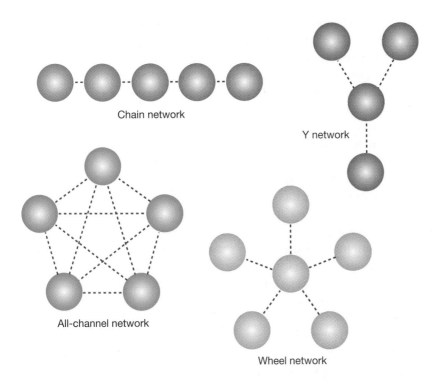

FIGURE 10.1

Communication Network Types

Chain network

Y network

All-channel network

Wheel network

which consists of family members passing on information from one person to the next, one at a time until the message reaches its intended destination. In some families, age determines the direction of the chain. For example, one of your authors, the youngest child of three, recalls being the last one to receive a message from the siblings before being the one to make a request to the designated parent. Of course, there were also "rules" about which parent one asked depending on the type of request. Usually the request was one that the older siblings knew was a real long shot, but might have a chance if the "baby" of the family approached them. A potential problem the chain network faces is much like the game of Telegraph, where a message gets passed through a series of players. Typically some level of distortion adds to or detracts from the original intention of the message. Thus, communication breaks down.

Similar to the chain network is the **Y communication network**. In this pattern, one member of the family serves as the gatekeeper, controlling the flow of messages from one person to another.

For example, perhaps the father is working late and one of the children needs a message conveyed to him. The mother may serve as gatekeeper, sending the message as she deems appropriate after the father has had a chance to unwind on his return from work. Of course, there are no guarantees that the child's message will be relayed as intended. This becomes another potential problem.

A third communication pattern is called the **wheel pattern** and is characteristic of families with a strong decision-making, central figure in the middle. In this scenario, family members rarely use each other as channels of information; rather, they deal directly with the center of the wheel (the decision maker). Imagine what it must be like to be in the center of the wheel, expected to literally hold a family together. Such expectations can be rather consuming and exhausting.

A last communication network is the **all-channel network** in which all family members freely exchange messages with each other. Because communication is allowed to flow in all directions, decisions are typically more effective because all members have had an equal chance to discuss them. Feedback provides the strength for this network pattern. A potential problem with this network is that it can allow for disorganized communication with messages flowing in all sorts of directions, leading to chaos.

Family communication networks change as families change their membership. Furthermore, families are not restricted to using just one network. Just as many rules guide what to talk about and when to talk, unwritten rules guide the choice of networks for transmitting information among family members.

The key to understanding and successfully using family roles, rules, and interaction patterns is effective listening. As you recall from Chapter 8, listening encompasses the notion of feedback, which is crucial for successful interpersonal communication. Taking time and having the patience to wait your turn (no matter where you are in the communication network) will help alleviate frustration and chaos and in turn lead to greater interpersonal understanding.

Learning about family roles, rules, and interaction patterns provides important insights into family relationships. These insights show that families are far from perfect. Human beings argue, disagree, and fight. Learning to manage interpersonal conflict in families can lead to greater satisfaction with family life. This next section focuses on conflict and provides suggestions for managing, rather than avoiding conflict, as you strive for healthy communication in your families.

CONFLICT: UNAVOIDABLE, INEVITABLE, AND MANAGEABLE

We begin this section with an important qualifier. Although we hope to provide insights regarding stress and conflict in families, we can't promise magic formulas for eliminating them entirely. The best we can do is to offer suggestions for *coping* with stress and *managing* conflict. With that in mind, let's begin by looking at some sources of conflict in family life.

In the last chapter, we offered Wilmot's definition of conflict as an expressed struggle between two people. Conflict can also be defined as a disagreement between or among individuals. The word *disagreement* tends to denote a negative meaning for most people. Like Wilmot, Borisoff and Victor (1989) suggest that instead of accepting and perpetuating the negative meanings derived from the word *conflict*, people begin to recognize the positive aspects of it.

One of the first myths to eliminate is that conflict is absent in families where communication is healthy. If conflict is *never* present, then people are probably avoiding each other or simply not communicating honestly and openly. Psychologist Carole Wade suggests that "The happy family knows it can't always be happy." She says (1992, p. 99),

> The difference between a generally happy family and one that doesn't work well is that the happy family will admit to problems and even seek outside help when necessary. The members trust their bonds to be strong enough to hold them together through difficult times. In a crisis, they are willing to be honest and negotiate with each other. By contrast, families in serious trouble sometimes work overtime to preserve a false façade of harmony. Therapist Michael Nichols tells of a family that was so intent on enforcing phony togetherness that they were "like an arthritic piano player: They could only strike chords of agreement; they were too glued together to play individual notes."

The roles, rules, and interaction patterns families use tend to take steps toward effective conflict resolution, to escalate problems, or to avoid conflict altogether. Many family conflict episodes result from unmet or unrealized expectations. For example, the costs and benefits of remaining in a family situation must be in balance for members to feel satisfied. In many cases, people stay together in the family unit as long as the costs do not outweigh the rewards. If one member is verbally or physically abusive to one or more other members of the family (obviously a serious conflict), then the affected party (or parties) may justifiably feel compelled to leave. The pain simply outweighs the benefits, unless a cycle of dependency has developed whereby the family "functions" dysfunctionally, as is true for many families.

Just as an imbalance of costs and rewards can fuel conflict, so can misunderstood or unfulfilled role expectations. More and more, with two parents working outside of the home while also raising children, families are experiencing a variety of role conflicts. Traditionally certain expectations were placed on the mother (cooking, cleaning, laundry, and so on) and others on the father (empty the garbage, yard work, car maintenance, and so on). Partners are beginning to challenge these role expectations and each other in the attempt to make sure they both do their "fair share." Conflicts surface when individuals do not want or cannot fulfill the expectations their roles demand.

You can probably think of all kinds of destructive conflict you have either observed or experienced; it may be more difficult to come up with examples of constructive conflict. In this next section, we'll discuss the notion of constructive conflict and offer suggestions for managing conflict.

Constructive conflict teaches a lesson to use in future conflict situations. Many lessons can be learned about striving for effective conflict resolution—managing conflict—that can lead to healthy communication among family members.

A first guideline is to attack the issue, not the person. Far too often people make generalized statements about another person and actually cause conflict to escalate because they have not been specific enough about the issue that is really the source of conflict.

Along the lines of the first guideline, stick to one issue at a time. You know how easy it is to verbally let loose with "machine guns," blasting the other with as many "bullets" as you can to make sure you are on the winning side. This leads to the next suggestion for managing conflict: Strive for a win-win situation. This means that you are not going into a conflict situation looking for one winner. If one person is the winner, naturally the other is the loser. Further, if you fight with the goal of winning, you may find out that in the end neither party wins. Both may end up losing. Depending on the severity of the issue, the consequences could be final.

Another guideline that cannot be highlighted enough is to listen and confront actively. The first part of this suggestion for managing conflict has to do with active listening. You know all too well how easy it is to get caught up in thinking of your next argument while paying little attention to what the other person is saying. You may be missing a very important point of agreement, but you were so busy preparing your rebuttal that you completely missed the point. By confronting actively, you assertively offer your position instead of assuming that the other person knows your stance or using the silent treatment to convey a message. Productive, active confrontation (keeping the previous tips in mind) lends to healthier, happier conflict resolution.

By taking responsibility for your thoughts and feelings, you're promoting a more honest and open exchange of ideas. Saying things like "I feel" rather than "Everybody thinks" or "So-and-so says" helps you take more responsibility for your words and actions. As a result, you'll think more carefully before you act.

Another tip for managing conflict constructively is to use direct and specific language. Focus on the here and now rather than on what the person did or said two months ago. (Focusing on the past is like the "machine gun" attack above.) Use descriptive language and focus on observable behavior. Try not to presuppose motives. For example, you might find yourself confronting someone by saying, "You forgot to tell me to return that phone call to your mother so I would look like I didn't care!" Presupposing motives can get you in big trouble.

Lastly, use humor for relief, not ridicule. Sometimes couples can see the ridiculousness in their positions if they can step back and laugh at the situation (*not* at each other). People can get so caught up in the desire to be right or to win that they fail to see the lighter side of a situation. However, if humor is used sarcastically to ridicule another, the conflict will move that much further away from resolution, and may just add another issue to an already loaded agenda.

When families experience difficult times because of stress and conflict, it's easy to focus only on the negative. In contrast, if you look at conflict situations as opportunities for growth in learning and understanding you'll find you experience more satisfaction from your family relationships.

As we began this chapter, we provided some definitions and assumptions about what a family is. However, our discussion would not be complete if we neglected to mention that there is no such thing as the "typical" American family. As we conclude this chapter, we'll briefly look at other family forms.

THE TYPICAL FAMILY IS NOT SO TYPICAL

Take a look at today's popular magazines or the newspaper, and you will find all sorts of depressing statistics and predictions about the state of the family. Television perpetuates the image that the happy family is the middle-class two-parent family with children (and maybe even grandchildren) rounding out the picture. What is wrong with this? This is not reality. In this section we explore some specific family forms and discuss some of the communication-related issues that naturally accompany these family types. We look at three that are currently most common: single-parent families, step-families, and homosexual partners and gay and lesbian parents.

Single-parent families consist of one parent and one or more children. There is no requirement regarding marital status—the parent may be divorced, single because of the death of a spouse, have an adopted or foster child, or have been deserted by the other parent. The single-parent family population makes up one-quarter of all families with children.

Single-parent families face many communication problems that result from other stress-producing factors. Typically, single-parent families face more economic difficulties than two-parent families. Economic stress often leads to interpersonal conflict. Furthermore, the effects of divorce or death on children can be varied. Effects on happiness and self-concept can be temporary and even eliminated if families have a support system from either their own family or support groups made up of people in similar situations.

Step-families or blended families are families made up of two adults and the children of one or both of them. Often a step-family is made up of what used to be two single families. As the step-family is formed, there is a lot of room for conflict and stress as any change in a family's lifestyle might bring. The potential for conflict revolves around many of the same issues discussed earlier in this chapter: role expectations, rules, and patterns of interaction. Two families with their own unique roles, rules, and network systems are merged and expected to function as one new unit. Now questions may arise such as "Who is in charge of discipline? Whom do we ask for money? What about

MORE NONTRADITIONAL FAMILY UNITS

Guy, Chair, Three-Way Lamp

A Woman, Her Daughter, Forty-four
My Little Ponies

The Troy Triplets and Their
Personal Trainer

Two Guys, Two Gals, Two Phones,
a Fax, and a Blender

Drawing by R. Chast;
© 1992 The New Yorker
Magazine, Inc.

space and territoriality in the family home? How much time do I get to spend with my real mom (or dad)?" These are just a few issues that could lead to misunderstanding and unclear expectations if they are not openly and honestly discussed.

In addition to single and step-families, more and more families are being headed by **same-sex couples** and homosexuals. Perhaps this is not such a new phenomenon; maybe it's just being recognized more. According to Galvin and Brommel (1991), same-sex couples are considered a family form because of society's growing recognition of the existence of long-term committed relationships within the gay community. Furthermore, a turn toward more monogamous relationships has developed in response to the AIDS crisis.

Communication consequences within same-sex family relationships are vast. The most notable, though, have to do with the acceptability or appropriateness of talking about their lifestyles. Often there is little social support and, as a result, gay families can feel isolated from heterogeneous couples. In addition, the parents in same-sex relationships often find it difficult to talk to their children about their choices in relationships. Role-related conflicts do not seem to emerge as frequently in same-sex relationships as they do in heterosexual relationships, although income is of far greater importance for establishing dominance in male homosexual relationships than in lesbian couples. So the issues about which heterosexuals disagree may not be similar to those of same-sex families.

Conversely, same-sex couples *with children* find themselves facing issues similar to those of heterosexual couples with children. Perhaps families with children face many similar problems as they see their children through various stages of growth and development.

Other family forms could be explored, but our focus in this chapter is mainly on looking at communication within the family. As research continues, we will find more and more documentation and insights into what used to be considered not-so-typical family forms.

LOOKING BACK - LOOKING FORWARD

In this last section we've been exploring some very specific kinds of interpersonal relationships. In Chapter 9 we looked at the close relationships we share with intimates and friends. We examined particular communication problems as well as means for improving communication in those relationships.

In this chapter, we focused specifically on another kind of close relationship that is influenced strongly by interpersonal communication—that of the family. We've seen that interpersonal communication within the family poses its own unique challenges and rewards. Although you may not always be able to change your family, you might come to understand your family better if you learn more about the functions and patterns of family communication.

In the next chapter, we look at interpersonal communication factors in our professional relationships. Increased understanding of interpersonal relationships with families, friends, and even the working environment can lead to increased communication satisfaction in each of these areas.

REVIEW TERMS AND CONCEPTS

family system 236	roles 240	all-channel network 248
subsystems 236	rules 241	single-parent family 251
family communication functions 236	family-of-origin 242	step-family 251
open system 237	chain network 246	same-sex-couples 253
support 238	y communication network 247	
value formation 239	wheel pattern 247	

PUTTING THEORY INTO PRACTICE

FOR DISCUSSION:

1. Which of the suggestions for managing conflict do you find most beneficial for you? Which would be more difficult for you to practice? Why do you think that is?

2. Traditional gender roles continue to change with the times. What specific gender role behaviors that are acceptable today might have been unspoken in our parents' generation?

3. If you could change one thing about the structure, roles, or rules of your family, what would it be and why? How might you apply effective interpersonal communication skills to the situation you chose?

SKILL BUILDERS:

1. Review the section on family communication networks. Then diagram the networks of communication most specific to your family. Draw in all participating family members. Once this is complete, analyze the networks: have you diagrammed an example of effective communication strategies? How might you re-draw the diagram to illustrate more successful relationship strategies?

2. Find a partner, and choose a common interpersonal problem that typically leads to conflict in a family. Role-play the situation, using some of the specific techniques suggested for managing conflict. Note how many of the techniques you used in your conversation.

3. Pay attention for one week to the variety of television shows that involve families. Categorize the shows according to family form. In other words, list which ones exemplify a single-parent household, a "traditional two-parent" (male and female) household, and so on. What are the trends? Do you think television is painting a realistic picture of families of today?

4. Interview one of your grandparents or a friend's grandparents. Explain to them what is meant by family communication "rules." Ask them to recall some rules that applied to their family. Then ask them to compare the rules to what they consider the rules of their descendants. Do they think the rules have changed? Are there some rules specific to their family that they see being passed on through the generations?

FOR EXTENDED STUDY

Satir, Virginia. (1972). *Peoplemaking*. Palo Alto, CA: Science and Behavior Books.

A thorough look at the stages of development and the importance of improving family communication. A family therapist, Satir capitalizes on key notions discussed in this chapter as well as many others.

Beebe, Steven A., & Masterson, John T. (1986). *Family talk: Interpersonal communication in the family*. New York: Random House.

This book provides a particularly useful unit on "improving family communication skills." Although it is not prescriptive in nature, it does offer some practical and helpful tools.

Nichols, M. (1984). *Family therapy: Concepts and methods*. New York: Gardner Press.

Nichols includes a focus on communication as key to family therapy, with an emphasis on clarifying communication. This book gives insight into early methods of therapeutic approaches to improving family communication.

Carter, B., & McGoldrick, M. (1988). Overview, the changing family life cycle: A framework for family therapy. In B. Carter & M. McGoldrick (Eds.), *The changing family life cycle* (2nd ed.). New York: Gardner Press.

The focus of their writing is on change in the family life cycle. They present a model depicting stressors that reflect family anxiety and its effects on the family system.

The workers are the saviors of society, the redeemers of the race.

EUGENE DEBS (1905)

11

Professional Relationships

OBJECTIVES

After reading this chapter and taking part in class activities, you should be able to

• Explain why the professional workplace requires special interpersonal communication skills.

• Identify some communication patterns that characterize superiors and employees.

• List and distinguish four leadership styles.

• Describe conversations typical of employees.

• List some techniques successful companies use in relating to their customers.

• Describe how the "grapevine" works in an organization and explain how it can both help and hinder effective communication.

• Define the function of small groups in organizations.

• Define a successful meeting.

• Describe some kinds of interviews used in organizations, and conduct a successful interview.

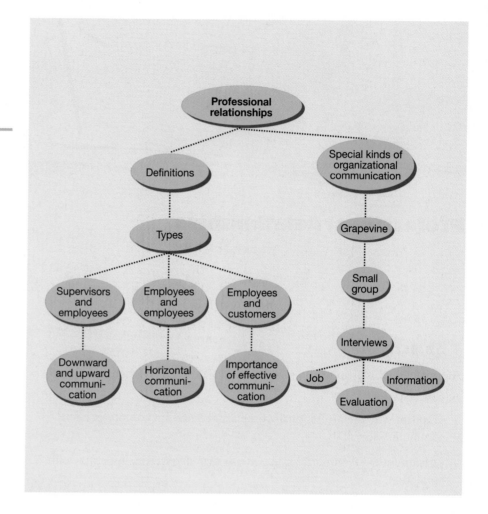

AARON GETS UP ONE MORNING in a bad mood. Within five minutes, he starts an argument with his wife, Alice. She knows that the day before Aaron received word from his boss that his performance as an accountant was not up to par and that he needs to improve if he wants to keep his job. Alice loves her husband and tolerates his harsh words. She fixes him a special breakfast and kisses him before he heads off to the office.

Despite his improved mood prompted by his wife's loving reaction, Aaron runs into a fellow accountant named Phil. Phil immediately starts criticizing Aaron for the way he did a client's income taxes. The two have a shaky relationship anyway, and Phil's comments hit a nerve, especially in light of yesterday's evaluation session with Aaron's boss. Aaron says, "Look, I don't need to hear your garbage today. I'll take care of clients as I see fit, and I don't want

It usually takes different skills to communicate effectively with someone at work as opposed to close, trusted intimates.

any more interference from you." Phil retorts, "You've got it, buddy. I was only trying to help but I'll make sure I stay away from now on. You're way too touchy." The two don't speak to each other for three weeks. When they finally do, their conversations are icy and have an edge.

Why could Aaron have almost the same kind of conversation with a loving wife that he did with a colleague and produce results that were so negative and different? For starters, the very fact that Aaron and Alice enjoy a solid and loving union makes it far easier for them to overcome the inevitable conflicts that invade any relationship. They have also become sensitive and used to each other's way of operating, because they've lived with each other for some time.

So far in this book, we've discussed a number of interpersonal communication theories and practices. In this chapter, we focus on an environment that demands a special set of communication skills—the professional workplace. What people can often get away with at home, won't wash in a professional setting. Co-workers normally don't develop the kind of bond that allows them to trust as much as do intimates or good friends.

WHY WORK RELATIONSHIPS DIFFER FROM OTHER KINDS

People sometimes develop close relationships on the job, but more often they don't. Recall any job you've had. Did you choose your workmates, or did a supervisor assign you to interact with people who were complete strangers? Unlike a relationship you've formed with a friend, you normally don't get to choose your fellow employees. As a result, such relationships are fragile. If you've dealt with the public, you know you have little choice over who walks in to do business with your company. You're expected to be courteous to a wide range of customers. You've probably heard the phrase "The customer is always right." Most businesses have to operate by this principle. To do otherwise would alienate customers, influence them to stop doing business with a company, and relay the message to friends to boycott your company. This delicate relationship with fellow employees and customers presents special problems. Let's look at some of the factors that impact the work environment.

COMMUNICATION CLIMATE

The term "**communication climate**" refers to the interpersonal tone in an organization. Is the place friendly, cold, inviting, or stiff? Do employees feel valued or tolerated? In *A Great Place to Work*, organizational expert Robert Levering (1988) describes the positive communication climate that characterizes top companies. Climate in an organization is like weather climate: Some locales are pleasant and mild; others are harsh and uninviting. Many are somewhere in between. For example, recall a job you liked because the climate or atmosphere was pleasant. Now remember one where the mood was negative and few people looked forward to going to work.

Charles Redding (1972) states that communication climate is largely a product of employee perceptions, especially in how employees view the quality of their relationships at work. Redding suggests five elements that help account for a positive communication climate. The five are

1. How much support employees get, especially from their superiors

2. How much influence they have in decision making

3. What kind of trust they have in the messages of colleagues

4. The candor of messages

5. The clarity of performance goals

All these factors affect **organizational communication**. If you've worked for a company that enourages open and candid feedback, you're much more likely to express your views and get involved in projects. If your supervisor doesn't like feedback, you're not about to give it—or at least you would be reluctant to give it.

Communication climate affects supervisors as well as nonsupervisors. Kline and Boyd (1991) found that job satisfaction for presidents, vice presidents, and middle managers was related to the communication climate of their workplace. Presidents experienced the highest job satisfaction, depending on the organization's structure, context, and climate. The structure shows how formal or informal a company is. Context includes such factors as the size of the organization and extent of automation. Each of these elements can affect interpersonal communication. If you've worked for a small company with an informal way of doing things, you probably found it easier to talk to others. If you were part of a very formal organization with strict rules, most likely you found communication more difficult.

For vice presidents and middle managers, climate was even more important than structure or context. The climate can make vice presidents feel their input is important and that their colleagues respect their work. For many, climate is more of an incentive to work than a paycheck.

ROLES IN THE WORKPLACE

Workplace roles have to do with behaviors employees are either assigned or take on in a work environment. In the last chapter, we explained the place of roles in the family. Now we turn to a discussion of how *roles* can impact the work environment. Gary Kreps describes roles as "the recurring behavioral patterns that individuals engage in within social systems" (1990, p. 170). Most organizations have supervisors and employees. Each is expected to play the role assigned. An employee doesn't usually go into a boss's office, prop his feet on the desk, and say, "So, Eileen, when do we get a raise around here?" As a supervisor, Eileen wouldn't normally approach an employee and say, "I really don't know what to do about asking the president for an increase in our budget. Would you tell me what to do?"

Roles can be broken down further to *formal* and *informal*. A formal role is one a company assigns to an employee. Such roles could range from president to janitor. An informal role is one the company doesn't assign, but that plays a big part in the communication climate. The president may be morose and dim-witted but got the job because he's the founder's son. The janitor, in contrast, may be bright and witty, but has chosen a job that carries little pressure. The president may be perceived in the informal role of dour dim-wit while many employees see the janitor as a closet intellectual and company wit.

Other informal roles could include nurturer, counselor, healer, and supporter. Both formal and informal roles play into the mix of how people interact with each other. Madeline may be a supervisor, but she's also someone her staff can come to talk about personal problems. Jess, however, might be the personnel manager but has the reputation of being a loner who never likes to deal with personal problems.

TRY THIS

Think back on the best place you've ever worked. Then consider the worst. What were the differences between the two? Did the best have some of the elements Redding describes? Did the worst place lack some or all of these elements? Did other factors help account for why you either liked or did not like your workplace?

A successful manager needs a wide range of communication skills to lead well.

WORK RULES

Besides roles, organizations also have *rules*. Schall (1983) describes rules as "tacit understandings (generally unwritten and unspoken) about appropriate ways to interact (communicate) with others in given roles and situations." Most companies have a set of formal rules about dress and behavior; and many may implicitly also demand adherence to informal rules. For example, Brian may know from the first day on the job that he should wear a suit and arrive at his office on time. It may take him a little longer to realize that his company expects him to work overtime without pay on occasion. He could jeopardize his employment if he violates either or both the formal and informal rules. As an extreme case, let's say he follows the rules for two months, but then gets fed up with what he perceives as the overly formal structure in his company. So one day, fifteen minutes late, he shows up in jeans and a checkered shirt and goes directly to his supervisor to complain about the two nights he had to work late. Brian has violated both written and informal rules. This in turn could cost him his job.

LEADERS IN ORGANIZATIONS

If climate and roles are important in the professional workplace, so is the kind of leadership supervisors display. Effective leaders help create a positive organizational climate. A good manager can make a job a joy. A tyrant on a power trip can make the job a nightmare. Jablin (1979) suggests five elements that characterize effective supervisors:

1. The best ones talk easily to their staff.

2. Good supervisors are excellent listeners who are willing to act on suggestions they hear from subordinates.

3. Instead of ordering or demanding, they ask or reason with employees to get what they want.

4. They're sensitive to the needs of their employees.

5. They disseminate information readily. If a change is coming, they let employees know and give reasons for the change.

Noted expert Gerald Goldhaber (1990) states that the most important factor in job satisfaction for employees is the relationship each has with a supervisor. He goes on to cite six qualities that exemplify top bosses: praising subordinates, understanding of an employee's job, trusting, offering warmth, being honest, and allowing the freedom to disagree. All these qualities contribute toward a leader's style.

LEADERSHIP STYLES

Leaders come in all types and styles. The style each leader uses has a direct impact on interpersonal relations with employees. Let's look at four styles leaders can use and then discuss how these **leadership styles** can affect interpersonal communication. The four styles are autocratic, bureaucratic, persuasive, and participative.

Autocratic

In the autocratic leadership style, someone leads primarily by command and the force of personality. Given authority by a higher power, the autocratic tells people what to do and often how to do it. He or she solicits little or no feed-

> *Reason and judgment are the qualities of a leader.*
> TACITUS
> (ABOUT A.D. 100)

back from subordinates. This in turn, often leaves the autocratic leader alone in making decisions. For example, assume that Stan comes from a military background and has often heard his father bark out commands. He believes this style works, even though he found it unpleasant at times, so he follows the same path as his dad. Now he's been appointed the manager of a small accounting firm and starts ordering employees around. He's convinced that unless he begins by showing power, his subordinates won't respect him. He's cordial but distant in relating to his staff. His well-educated employees resent his abrasive manner and talk to him only when they have to.

The autocratic style has some advantages and disadvantages. Employees are reluctant to give honest feedback, so often an autocratic leader has to make decisions alone. Also, morale can be low if the leader is overly abrasive and hard to work for. Yet some workers like a no-nonsense manager who lets them know what they need to do to get the job done.

Bureaucratic

Bureaucratic leaders go "by the book." If they can't find the solution to a problem in the company manual, they feel lost. Their style is characterized by adherence to rules, and they expect followers to do likewise. This kind of leader comes across much like the autocratic type, but rather than leading through the force of personality, they rely on rules.

The bureaucratic leader carries some of the same advantages as the autocrat. Employees know where they stand at all times. Some people like the clear sense of direction the bureaucratic leader provides. But there are also disadvantages to this style. Many situations come up that demand more than adherence to a policy manual or a set of rules. Most workers prefer someone who can adapt her or his style to the situation or to them individually. The strict bureaucrat can't do that.

Persuasive

Persuasive leaders try to motivate followers rather than tell them what to do. They solicit feedback and often act on what they hear. They make the final decision about a problem themselves but they do so with the help of their staff.

Like the other two styles, the persuasive approach has advantages and disadvantages. Most employees tend to work with more enthusiasm when they've contributed to a project or when a leader has asked for their help. Persuasive leaders usually produce more teamwork because everyone feels more involved in projects at hand.

On the down side, the persuasive approach takes more time than the previous two. To get feedback, the leader often has to ask for it in the form of meetings or communiques. The persuasive style also presumes that the leader is skilled in motivating. Not all leaders have the ability to inspire followers.

And even if one leader has the skill, certain employees are not always receptive to this approach. Some would rather have an autocratic leader tell them what to do and how to do it.

Jessie Jackson is a good example of a persuasive leader.

Participative

A final leadership style is the participative style. The leader using this approach gets everyone to pitch in on a problem that requires decision making. She or he tries to get as much input as possible before the group decides on the solution to a problem by consensus. This approach is similar to the persuasive style except that the members and the leader make the final decision together.

The advantages of the participative style are the same as for the persuasive style. Employees are more enthusiastic because they contribute directly to getting a job done. They often have greater self-esteem because they help make decisions. But this approach has some of the drawbacks of the persuasive style. It takes extra time, and some people would rather not assume the responsibility that participation demands.

The obvious question by now might be "So which style is the best?" And the answer might be just as obvious: "It depends on the ability of the leader, the employees themselves, and the situation." As with other aspects of interpersonal communication, there has to be a fit between the leader and followers. If some employees want and need an authoritarian leader, a manager might practice that style. If a group is self-motivated and experienced, its members might do better with a persuasive or participative leader. A group of young army reserves might be best served by an autocratic master sergeant during boot camp. Experienced vice presidents in a business might respond better to a persuasive or participative leader.

The persuasive or participative leader comes closest to modeling the traits listed by Jablin (see p. 263). But even autocratic or bureacratic leaders can get a positive response from followers if they are perceived as having the best interests of their staff in mind. For example, movies for years have depicted the tough master sergeant with the heart of gold. Usually played by John Wayne or Clint Eastwood, the autocrat trains his troops so they'll be ready for battle, not because he craves power. He usually shows his soft-heartedness by rescuing one of his men during a firefight. As in other interpersonal relationships, one person in a dyad will often tolerate conflict if he or she believes the other cares about him or her.

DIRECT COMMUNICATION

We've looked at leadership styles. Let's now examine the flow of communication in an organization.

Downward Communication

The term "downward communication" refers to messages traveling from leaders to subordinates. A boss writes a memo to employees explaining why the purchasing office will be moved from the third floor to the basement. A manager meets with her sales staff on Monday morning to let them know what quota of cars she expects them to sell. A president calls his vice president to let him know he's displeased with the clutter in the conference room after last Saturday's Christmas party.

Smith, Richetto, and Zima (1972) found that downward communication has been studied more than any other element of formal communication.

Chase (1970) showed that downward communication is often ineffective for four reasons:

1. Information is inadequate.

2. Methods of transferring the information is inappropriate.

3. Information gets distorted as it is filtered downward.

4. Messages frequently follow a pattern of dominance (leader) and submission (follower).

These conclusions underscore the interpersonal communication problems subordinates experience in professional organizations. If employees don't receive the information they need or the data get distorted on their way down, morale suffers and frustration sets in. Pace and Boren (1972) describe the inaccurate filtering of downward messages as **serial reproduction.** You're already familiar with serial reproduction if you've been in a group that passed a message on from member to member. By the time the message reaches the final person, it has changed—often dramatically. This is easy to understand. Recall Chapter 3 on perception. Each person filters a message through her or his perceptual frame. The more people involved, the greater the chance for distortion.

Upward Communication

The term "upward communication" refers to messages subordinates relay to superiors. Not surprisingly, such messages are not as frequent as communication from the top down. What may be surprising is the tendency of subordinates to distort messages, depending on the effect they want. Krivonos (1976) points out that subordinates often tell their bosses what they think the bosses

COMMUNICATING SKILLFULLY

Play a game of **serial communication.** Break into groups of between five and seven. Then one of the group should write a message, something like "Women are far better at communication than men because they're brought up differently. Women are conditioned to estab-lish relationships while men are taught to compete." Construct a message that has enough controversial elements to make it easy to misconstrue. Then repeat the message orally to another member of the group. That member should pass it on to someone else until everyone has heard it. The last person should tell the class the message he or she heard. Then discuss why the communication broke down. If the message was basically the same by the time it reached the last person in the group, what accounts for the accuracy? Finally, discuss why serial messages can be easily misinterpreted in a professional environment.

want to hear. They also tend to limit or withhold information if they believe the information will make them look bad. For example, Darrell may send his boss Marilyn a report about the success of the annual fall company computer conference. He highlights the projects that went well—meals were on time, the conference rooms were ready, speakers appeared when they were supposed to, and so on. Darrell neglects to report that the new computer system didn't work and that Darrell forgot to pick up the keynote speaker at the airport, forcing her to take a cab. The preceding scenario is understandable, because employees often operate through fear that their jobs may be in jeopardy unless the boss views them in a favorable light. Darrell's report may backfire against him if his superior learns from someone else about the less flattering aspects of the conference.

Horizontal Commnication

"Horizontal communication" is the flow of messages among employees who have equal status within an organization. Nurses in the pediatrics department of a medical center talk to each other about the needs of their patients. Members of an English department at a community college share ideas about ways to save time in correcting a large batch of student papers.

Communication professors Wayne Pace and Don Faules state that horizontal communication occurs for six reasons (1989, pp. 111–112):

1. To coordinate work assignments

2. To share information on activities and plans

3. To solve problems

4. To gain common understanding

5. To negotiate differences

6. To provide interpersonal support

Pace and Faules (1989) refer to communication between segments within an organization as "cross channnel" communication. To the preceding example, a member of a community college English department speaks with another English teacher in the faculty lounge about student papers. An hour later she talks to a member of the speech faculty about a co-sponsored project. The pediatric nurse discusses a certain medicine with someone from the pharmacy.

Members from various segments have an obvious need to talk about matters of mutual concern and often they do. But some of the problems with horizontal communication among department members can be even worse with people from different departments. Such problems include a lack of trust and a competition for limited resources. The speech instructor, who is willing to cooperate with an English faculty member in the morning, may deliberately

CONSIDERING CULTURE

One well-known example of horizontal communication is the use of quality circles. American W. Deming introduced the process to the Japanese shortly after World II, and within the past few years, companies in the United States have applied it to improve the quality of their products.

Probably the best-known example is the automobile industry. Instead of letting supervisors and designers on their own determine how to build a car, the workers who assemble the parts meet on a regular basis to offer their views on how to improve the product.

According to the magazine Consumer Reports, *Japanese cars* overall are still superior to American automobiles. Do you believe the quality circle approach has helped U.S. companies catch up with the Japanese in the production of cars? Are there other factors that might help explain why U.S. auto manufacturers are closing the gap?

withhold information from that same person in the afternoon if they're both applying for a similar grant.

EMPLOYEE COMMUNICATION TO CUSTOMERS

An area that has received special attention in the past few years is the interpersonal communication between employees in an organization and the customers or clients they serve. Peters and Waterman (1982) in their now classic book *In Pursuit of Excellence: Lessons from America's Best Run Companies*, re-emphasized the importance of customer service for companies that wanted to survive in the 1990s. It should have been obvious that a strong concern for clients was a must for businesses that wanted to succeed. But apparently many organizations have ignored the need for superior customer service.

Recall a recent experience you've had with a representative of a college, a store, or a restaurant. How did you feel about the way you were treated? Did you perceive that you were someone special to the employee, or did you get the impression that you were a nonentity who had to be endured? The same principles we've discussed in this book about the needs of affection, inclusion, and control apply in professional settings as much as they do in intimate relationships. But there is a difference. In a close union, you can survive a conflict with relative ease if your relationship with the other person is strong. The same is not true in an employee/customer relationship. If customers perceive they're treated with indifference or rudeness, they usually will not tell the salesperson how they really think—they'll stop doing business with the company.

We've mentioned before the old adage that the customer is always right.

THE QUIET CUSTOMER

In his book *How to Win Customers and Keep Them for Life,* Michael LeBoeuf (1987, p. 11) includes the following letter under the heading "Are 'Nice Customers' Ruining Your Business"?

I'm a nice customer. You all know me. I'm the one who never complains, no matter what kind of service I get.

I'll go into a restaurant and sit quietly while the waiters and waitresses gossip and never bother to ask if anyone has taken my order. Sometimes a party that came in after I did gets my order, but I don't complain. I just wait.

And when I go to a store to buy something, I don't throw my weight around. I try to be thoughtful of the other person. If a snooty salesperson gets upset because I want to look at several things before making up my mind, I'm just as polite as can be. I don't believe rudeness in return is the answer.

The other day I stopped at a full-service gas station and waited for almost five minutes before the attendant took care of me. And when he did, he spilled gas and wiped the windshield with an oily rag. But did I complain about the service? Of course not.

I never kick. I never nag. I never criticize. And I wouldn't dream of making a scene, as I've seen some people do in a public place. I think that's uncalled for. No, I'm the nice customer. And I'll tell you who else I am. I'm the customer who never comes back.

REPRINTED BY PERMISSION OF THE PUTNAM PUBLISHING GROUP *FROM HOW TO WIN CUSTOMERS AND KEEP THEM FOR LIFE,* BY MICHAEL LEBOEUF. COPYRIGHT © 1988 BY MICHAEL LEBOEUF, PH.D.

The reason for such advice is simple: companies can't afford to alienate customers, even if the customer is wrong.

THE GRAPEVINE AS A COMMUNICATION CHANNEL

Up to now, we've discussed relationships at work. We turn now to other factors that make interpersonal communication unique in a professional setting. One of the more intriguing is the grapevine. The **organizational grapevine** can be described as the informal channel that carries messages from one person to another. Unlike formal channels—memos, letters, and reports—the grapevine has a power of its own.

Scholars have conducted a number of research studies on the grapevine. Goldhaber (1990) summarizes some of the key findings:

1. *The grapevine is fast.* Someone in production shares with a colleague that an employee in the marketing department is getting a divorce. Not constrained by the more formal channels of having to write a memo, the listener calls a friend in the production department to convey the news. The word then spreads throughout the company.

2. *The grapevine transmits rumors.* Closely related to the first observation is the grapevine as the conduit of rumors. With no restrictions about checking for evidence, virtually anyone in an organization can start a rumor. Joanne thinks she hears a manager say something about a raise for a few but not for everyone and concludes that some of the employees in her department will get salary freezes for the next year. She passes on this information to Hal, who spreads it around the tenth floor. It finally filters back to the manager who made the comment Joanne heard. The manager then has to write a memo, squelching the rumor and assuring employees that they'll all get raises. He then tries to understand why the rumor got started and concludes that a comment he made must have sparked the rumor.

3. *The grapevine is generally accurate.* Despite what many believe, the grapevine is often more accurate than formal channels. Goldhaber explains that many managers believe the grapevine is highly inaccurate for the following reason. When inaccurate information is conveyed through the grapevine, it's usually dramatic. (For example, an employee might say, "I've heard we're all going to get fired next week.") The dramatic, in turn, is easier to remember. But for the most part, the grapevine is on target.

4. *The grapevine provides both a gauge of employee sentiment and a cathartic outlet.* If a boss really wants to know what the morale in the department is like, he or she doesn't seek information through a formal survey. Instead, the boss finds out the prevailing sentiments being transmitted through the grapevine. What is being said in the coffee room? What are the latest rumors? Are they positive or negative?

The grapevine has advantages and disadvantages. Gibson and Hodgetts (1991) list a number of these benefits:

1. It acts as a sounding board to help employees let off steam.

2. It helps improve the social life of an organization because employees can share news and gossip with each other. As a result, people become better team players.

3. It helps convey messages not transmitted by formal channels.

4. It helps get work done. If employees operated only through formal channels, they might stop working once a manager was out of sight.

On the other hand, the grapevine has some disadvantages. These include

1. A degree of error occurs, even though the grapevine is 75 to 95 percent accurate.

2. Employees sometimes create self-serving facts rather than report the truth.

3. Unlike formal channels of communication, no one has to take responsibility for information relayed through the grapevine.

4. Messages are often delivered inaccurately.

Although there could be a form of the grapevine in families, especially ones with an authoritative leader like a forceful father or mother, the grapevine is found mainly in organizations. Like other communication channels, an understanding of its advantages and disadvantages can help you communicate better in a professional setting.

SMALL GROUPS

Another important structure found primarily in professional organizations is the small group. We define a small group as a collection of employees who gather for a specific purpose. Various types of small groups might help explain this definition. For example, people in a company may meet to discuss a new policy manual and learn how to apply it to their job. This is called a *learning* group. Another group assembles during the noon hour once a week to play chess or to talk about a new best-seller. Their purpose is enjoyment or self-enrichment. This is a *social* group. A third type is the *encounter* group. Pioneers in this movement are Carl Rogers and Curt Lewin, who saw the encounter group as a vehicle for people to help solve their personal problems. Thus, fifteen workers experiencing great stress on the job might meet every Wednesday evening. Their purpose is twofold: they gain emotional support from each other and, through discussion, glean insights they could not get on their own. A fourth kind of small group in an organization is the *problem-solving* group. In this format, professionals come together to pool their collective expertise and to use their critical thinking skills to solve a problem outside the domain of any one individual. For example, Julie may be a participant in the "stress encounter group" on Wednesday evening. On Thursday morning, she walks into a problem-solving session to help the company increase sagging sales. The corporation president has asked Julie to be a member of the latter group because she has ten years of experience in selling and a sterling track record in sales, and because the other members respect her insights. Her purpose on Wednesday night is to help herself cut down on the stress of holding down a full-time job as sales manager and juggle her life as a wife and mother. On Thursday morning, her goal is to help the company solve a problem that is cutting into profits.

Small groups in an organization are often formed on the assumption that many heads are better than one in solving a problem. Rarely do chief executives try to solve problems alone. They try to assemble the best associates they can find. They normally pick people who have experience, are knowlegeable, and can cooperate with others in the group.

Suppose morale is a problem with a manufacturing company. Most of its employees believe that management takes them for granted, does not listen to their suggestions, and refuses to give them the wages they deserve. The president ignores the problem for awhile, but finally a delegation of workers convince him the situation is daily getting worse. He calls together his staff and some experts to address the problem. His staff includes two vice presidents, a director of personnel, and his administrative assistant. He brings in a management consultant and someone holding a doctorate in psychology. For two hours, the seven members of the group look at the problem, discuss desired outcomes, and decide on solutions. Such solutions could include the following:

1. The president holds a general session with all employees and tells them he's heard their concerns and wants to take steps to solve the problem.

2. The president sets up a series of meetings with employee representatives and members of management to find satisfactory solutions.

3. The president announces a series of pay incentives for employees.

Ideally, all small groups would function like the team just discussed. But research by Irving Janis and others underscores that groups often make worse decisions than individuals do. We've used the word *groupthink* before in this book. Janis describes groupthink as a drive toward consensus by groups with little attention to critical thinking. It's difficult to go against the grain of what a group is deciding. Once members establish norms (ways of behaving that groups adopt), an individual finds it hard to deviate from that norm. Suppose the group just described followed a norm that the president was not to be contradicted, even though he said he welcomed suggestions that were contrary to his. If members have learned over time that the president met any disagreement with a frown, most would keep from disagreeing. This in turn can often lead to a lack of the critical analysis needed to solve problems.

One way of understanding why some groups function well as problem-solving teams and others fail is to examine how groups come together and start developing. Most scholars divide group dynamics into four stages. One of the easiest models to remember was developed by Tuckman (1965). He divides the stages into forming, storming, norming, and performing:

1. *Forming.* In this first stage, members are getting together and finding

Ideally, problem-solving group members contribute their best thinking and expertise toward finding workable solutions.

out what tasks they're supposed to accomplish. They're also staking out their positions in the group. How does each one want to be perceived by the others? Who is going to have the most influence in the discussion? Do I feel comfortable with these people? Can I work in harmony with them? An example would be a group of accountants meeting for the first time to suggest ways to streamline returns around income tax time. During this first phase, the members try to discern how others might accept them and their suggestions. They usually want to know what tasks the group is supposed to accomplish. They may talk about procedures for accomplishing those tasks.

2. _Storming._ This is one of the most important stages because members can experience conflict on at least two levels. They can clash on the maintenance or interpersonal level or on the task or idea level. Two people in the group may be competing to be the emergent leader. As a result, they resent each other. This is an interpersonal clash on an emotional level and could inhibit the group's goal of solving a problem. A healthier and more productive clash would include a critical analysis of ideas each member presents. This task-level conflict can help the group make decisions based on sound reasoning. In general, conflicts on the emotional level tend to be destructive, while those on the idea level tend to help a group make intelligent decisions.

3. _Norming._ If the group members have been able to either avoid or solve interpersonal conflicts, they move toward becoming an effective

decision-making group. At this stage, they share ideas while working as a team to solve whatever tasks they have. For example, a group of nine quality control workers in a car manufacturing plant might decide on what kind of quality they want in the automobiles that roll off their assembly line. Are they striving for quality in the engine, the body, the interior, or all these items? They may have established the healthy norm that each is allowed to express an opinion about a car model without fear that the ideas will be rejected.

4. *Performing*. Assuming the group has gone through the first three stages unscathed, members concentrate on getting their jobs done well. To

Drawing by Joe Mirachi; © 1988 The New Yorker Magazine, Inc.

"Then it's official. The Hell no's have it."

extend some of the examples used before: for a president's cabinet, the task is to improve morale. The accountants work to find a more efficient way to streamline their returns at tax time. The quality control group focuses on ways to make their car as good or better than that of their competitors. Even though the group may not have resolved every interpersonal conflict, they feel comfortable enough with each other to disagree and engage in critical thinking.

Rarely does a group follow the exact order of stages just presented, but most groups go through the stages to some degree in their deliberations. If serious interpersonal problems have occurred during any of the four phases, the group may have a hard time achieving its goals. Such problems could include power struggles between members, a reluctance to speak out for fear of being put down or an inability to distinguish idea or task clashes from those on the interpersonal or maintenance level.

Successful Meetings

One barometer of an effective group is its handling of a meeting established either to solve a problem or make a decision. How many meetings have you attended that took twice as long as they should and got very little accomplished? Millions of meetings take place each day in the United States because they provide the logical format for sharing expertise and gaining mutual insights.

Successful meetings rarely happen by chance. They're a product of careful planning. Meetings that work usually include the following elements:

1. A leader sends out a well-developed agenda to participants to let them know in advance the subjects for discussion.

2. Each member does homework on her or his portion of the agenda.

3. Each member anticipates in advance the subjects that will be discussed.

CONSIDERING CRITICAL THINKING

You have been elected to a student body council position and are now attending your first meeting of student officers. Stan has been chosen as student body president, over Hal. Their campaign has been a bitter one, especially since the two didn't like each other to begin with. As the meeting proceeds, it becomes clear that Hal is undermining virtually everything Stan tries to do. If Stan suggests a proposal, Hal argues against it. If Stan is against something, Hal is for it. You're the only one in the group who knows the depth of animosity Hal holds for Stan. Later, after the meeting is over, what could you do to bring these two rivals at least into a friendly working relationship?

4. Once the meeting begins, leaders and members move through the discussion topics with efficiency.

5. All members deal with ideas on the task rather than on the maintenance level—although they don't avoid attention to socioemotional needs.

6. Besides following the agenda, the group uses a discussion process to make sure they critically examine ideas and avoid "groupthink." One such example is the reflective thinking agenda mentioned in Chapter 2.

7. Members listen carefully to each others' ideas and build on those ideas.

INTERVIEWS

A final type of interpersonal communication unique to the workplace is the interview. Let's examine three kinds of interviews you might experience in a professional setting: the job interview, an employee evaluation interview, and the information-collecting interview. Each type requires special interpersonal skills from both interviewer and interviewee. Each has a more clearly defined goal than most ordinary conversations.

The Job Interview

Perhaps no other communication event, other than a marriage proposal, can have more far-reaching impact than the job interview. Ironically, college students can spend thousands of dollars and hundreds of hours earning degrees, and yet can have their fate depend on how well they conduct themselves in the short time of an employment interview.

Unlike most other interpersonal conversations, the successful job applicant needs to prepare in advance. A strong interview is a combination of a polished conversation and a speech. Like a well-prepared speech, the job interview takes careful preparation and a clearly defined opening, middle, and closing. Let's look at each of these.

Advanced preparation virtually always requires a first-rate résumé. The professional résumé is a delicate blend, giving a potential employer enough of your good points to want to hire you but not so many that you come across as bragging. For the most part, the résumé is a factual account of your professional experience. Nighswonger (1991) describes the ideal résumé as one that contains the following characteristics:

1. Your work history, in clear, concise language

2. A well-organized structure to display those strengths that would help you do well the job you're seeking

3. A clearly stated career objective with a specific explanation of how this objective matches what the employer wants

You also include your address, phone number, education, and hobbies, and indicate that you will be happy to supply references on request.

The résumé should normally be one page. Occasionally the "one-page rule" can be broken if you really need to give a prospective employer more information. The key is to remember that employers read numerous résumés and the easier you make yours to read, the better impression you'll make.

When appropriate, you should also bring examples of your work that could be relevant to the job you're seeking. For instance, if you're applying for a position that requires advanced writing skills, you would be well served to bring samples of your writing. If you're seeking a job with the U.S. Forest Service, you could bring slides of projects you've completed while you worked in the summer for the National Parks Association.

Effective job interviews take careful planning and well-honed interpersonal skills.

How you dress is another key factor in the advance preparation needed for a successful job interview. Experts agree that both men and women should be well dressed and carefully groomed. If the company dress is more formal than casual, interviewees would want to dress the same way. Even if you are interviewing for a company, such as Hewlett Packard, that allows more informal clothing, you will still want to dress up. You may not wear a suit, but neither would you walk into the

WHAT NOT TO DO IN A JOB INTERVIEW

Columnist Jim Kershner of the *Spokane* Spokesman-Review *(January 17, 1990) recounts some true stories of job applicants who interviewed less than effectively. He then goes on to make some tongue-in-cheek recommendations about what not to do during the employement interview.*

THE TRUE STORIES:

One man dozed off and started snoring during the interview.

One woman announced at the beginning that she hadn't had lunch and went on to eat a hamburger and french fries during the interview.

Another person brought her large dog to the interview.

Someone else interrupted to call his therapist for advice on answering specific questions.

WHAT NOT TO DO DURING THE INTERVIEW *[Kershner's advice]*

DO NOT:

Toy nervously with a handgun.

Drink repeatedly from a flask.

Demonstrate your skill at juggling.

Hold your head in your hands and moan.

WHAT NOT TO SAY:

"Wow. There are some big words on this application."

"Does your health plan cover sex change operations?"

"Technically, I wasn't fired from my last job."

"Can I check with my mother on that?"

interview with jeans and a khaki shirt, even though you've seen Hewlett Packard employees dressing that way at work.

THE OPENING

Since first impressions are important in any interpersonal encounter, the opening is especially crucial for the interviewee. How you carry yourself and how you greet the interviewer will have a lasting impact. During the opening, you normally smile, shake hands, and engage in casual conversation on a subject that often has nothing to do with the interview. Topics could include observations about the architecture in the office, the friendly people you've met already, or the weather. After a short time, the one in charge usually outlines the format of the interview and you begin answering questions.

THE MIDDLE

Interview questions can be either factual or a seeking of your opinion. For example, you may be asked to expand on the information you've included in your résumé. Two minutes later, the interviewer may want to know your philosophy of effective management. A question is well answered when you've given the interviewer the material he or she wants in a concise way.

You may find an interviewer will ask you a variety of questions. Dennis

Gouran, Larry Miller, and William Weithoff (1992) have provided a list of the kinds of questions you may encounter:

1. A *primary question* is one that introduces a new topic. For example, the interviewer may switch from finding out more about your employment background to asking for your philosophy about teamwork.

2. A *secondary question* is one that follows a primary question: "You've said you believe strongly in teamwork. Could you give us some examples of how you've practiced this philosophy in past jobs?"

3. Subcategories of primary and secondary questions are the *probe* and *mirroring* questions. An example of the probe is: "Good—go on." A mirroring question is much like a paraphrase: "Let me make sure I understand your position on teamwork. You're saying that there are times when teamwork can be a detriment rather than an advantage?"

4. Other types of questions are open and closed. With an open question, the interviewer does not limit you in your answer: "Take a few minutes to tell us what you would do if two of your employees called in sick and you had to get some important orders out in an hour." Notice that while the question is specific, you can answer it any way you want. With a closed question, you're more constrained: "Would you have a problem with working overtime twice a week if we needed your services?"

5. Two other forms are neutral and leading questions. With a neutral question, you're quite sure the interviewer is not looking for a desired answer: "We can give you a choice of two offices—one painted beige and the other light yellow. Which color would you prefer?" With a leading question, you conclude the interviewer would like to hear one response: "Do you have any problem with helping out with projects like the annual Christmas party or the summer picnic?" You know that the wrong answer would be: "I don't like social events" or "I'll do my job, but don't ask me do anything I'm not paid for."

6. A final type of question you may encounter is the loaded one. A loaded question is one that contains inflammatory language: "We've heard that you don't like working with people over 50. If that's true, how will you get along with our personnel who are over that age?" Some employers will purposely throw you a curve to see how you can handle it. This is relatively rare, but it can happen.

The job interview is a unique interpersonal communication encounter because the stakes are high, especially for the interviewee. It is really an accelerated form of communication. The participants have very little time to develop a relationship, because most interviews last less than an hour. As the interviewee, you don't have the luxury, as you might in other relationships, to show your weak side. You know you must present your best face if you want to get the job. The interview is unique also because it uses the question as its primary form of communication. Therefore, it's crucial to prepare carefully for an interview. Such preparation includes assessing the right clothes for the company and the occasion. You must also anticipate any questions that might come up, including loaded ones. It helps to practice with someone else who can ask the questions and evaluate your responses. This is even better if you videotape such a session and then examine the tape carefully as if you were someone other than yourself. How did this person—you—handle the questions? How much at ease did you seem, despite some nervousness? Were your answers clear and crisp, or vague and wandering? If you and your partner notice flaws in the presentation, how will you correct them?

You should also have some of your own questions ready if the interviewer asks, "Do you have any questions?" This is an opportunity to let him or her know that you've prepared carefully for the interview. For example, you could say, "I read in your company policy manual that you place a strong emphasis on personal initiative. I believe in that also. Would you mind giving me a couple of examples of employees who have practiced personal initiative?" You should also feel free to ask questions to give you information you could not otherwise get from the company manual, or data that were not covered during the interview."

THE ENDING

The conclusion serves much the same function as the opening: your purpose is to end on a pleasant note and to thank the interviewer for the opportunity to apply for a job with the organization.

The Employee Evaluation Interview

A second kind of interview is the employee **evaluation interview**. Most organizations routinely require that supervisors sit down with their staff members to give them feedback on their performance. This standard ritual can cause anxiety for both the interviewer and interviewee. Supervisors rarely enjoy giving employees bad news about their performance, even when the information is valid. Few employees savor the anticipation of getting negative comments from a boss.

Here are some guidelines that can help make the experience less frightening and more productive:

For the supervisor

1. Begin in a warm and positive way.

2. Tell the employee the purpose of the interview; for example, to give some feedback about performance so that strong points can be bolstered and flaws trimmed.

3. Start by telling the staff member what you like about the job he or she is doing.

4. Be as specific as possible in pointing out shortcomings. For example, if someone is often late, rather than say, "You have a real problem getting to work on time," say, "Three days last week, you arrived at least fifteen minutes late. Do you want to talk about that?"

5. Discuss concrete ways to improve.

6. End on a positive note.

For the person being evaluated:

1. Start with the attitude that no one is perfect and that feedback, both positive and negative, will improve your performance.

2. Greet the interviewer in a warm, positive way.

3. Listen carefully to the feedback.

4. Discuss practical ways you intend to use to improve strengths and eliminate weak points.

5. Thank the interviewer for the assessment.

Evaluation interviews can be valuable for both parties for a number of reasons. Employees receive data that can help them improve job performance. Such improvement is often linked to promotion and merit pay. Supervisors, for their part, can get better work from staff members. If conducted well, the interview can help cement the relationship between the two participants.

The Information-Gathering Interview

A final kind of interview is one designed to gain information for a specific project. Such information-gathering interviews can include but are not limited to newspaper articles, scholarly investigations, and opinion polls. Unlike a written survey, which can be distributed with no contact between questioner and information giver, the oral interview requires contact either by phone or in person.

The key to successful information gathering is planning. Most people are quite busy and often see the interview as infringing on their time. Therefore, the interviewer needs to begin by explaining specific goals, posing carefully crafted questions, and using efficient recording methods. For example, the interviewer might say, "I really appreciate your taking this ten minutes to give me information. I'm doing a survey for an interpersonal communication project, and I'm trying to get some data on how happily married couples deal with conflict. I have seven questions and would like to record your answers, if that's alright with you."

All three types of interviews are unique forms of interpersonal communication. The job and information-gathering interviews don't assume that the participants have already established a relationship. In fact, most participants haven't met each other before the interview. Job and evaluation interviews can create stress because the interviewees are being judged by the interviewers. On the positive side, an awareness of interview dynamics and a mastery of communication skills can help you achieve some important goals such as getting a job or improving your performance at work.

LOOKING BACK - LOOKING FORWARD

In this chapter, we've examined a particular kind of communication environment—the workplace. We explained why interpersonal relationships between colleagues is often more fragile than those between good friends or intimates. We emphasized that peers often don't share the same solid bond that loved ones do. We discussed communication climate, work rules, and employee roles. Then we went on to explain different styles of leadership and showed how these styles can affect followers. We looked at upward, downward, and horizontal communication patterns that occur among supervisors, employees, and customers. And we studied some special kinds of communication that happen more often in organizations than they do in families. These include the grapevine, small groups, and interviews.

In the next chapter, we focus on two important issues—culture and gender. Either or both of these elements can affect a work environment or a close relationship like a marriage or a family.

REVIEW TERMS AND CONCEPTS

communication
climate
260

organizational
communication
260

leadership styles
263

serial reproduction
267

organizational
grapevine
270

evaluation interview
281

PUTTING THEORY INTO PRACTICE

FOR DISCUSSION:

1. Why is it so important to know the business practices of other countries—say Germany, Japan, or Russia—if you are going to interact professionally with people from those cultures?

2. Given your past experiences, what would you avoid in the future when you participate in an employment interview? What would you do again that worked in the past?

SKILL BUILDERS:

1. Given your own experience of different jobs, draw a profile of the boss you believe did the *best* job of leading employees. What qualities made him or her succeed? Recall the *worst* supervisor you've had. What qualities did this person have that made him or her so difficult to work for? Now draw a profile of the kind of supervisor you would like to be if you were in a position of authority.

2. Pick one problem that has occurred recently or is still occurring in the world of business. Then break into groups of five to seven. The group should pick a leader who will try to keep the group moving toward a solution to the problem by following the steps of the reflective thinking agenda discussed in Chapter 2 (that is, describe the problem, find out what's causing it, establish criteria for solving it, brainstorm solutions, and then find the solution that best fits the criteria). Discuss the problem for 25 to 35 minutes. A spokesperson from each group should then report on how far the members advanced toward a solution. Then discuss how efficiently the group functioned as a problem-solving unit.

3. Set up mock job interviews involving three people. One will be the interviewer, another will be the interviewee, and the third will be an observer. Pick your own kind of organization and a specific job. The interviewer should spend about five minutes, with the help of the observer, formulating primary and secondary, open and closed questions, along with one that is loaded. During this time, the interviewee should anticipate the kind of questions likely to be asked. Then conduct the interview for about ten minutes. Afterward, the observer evaluates how well the interview went, especially for the one being interviewed. Focus on how interpersonal skills might help in a real-life job interview.

FOR EXTENDED STUDY

Gibson, J., & Hodgetts, R., (1991). *Organizational communication: A managerial approach*. New York: HarperCollins.

This is a very good overview of communication within a professional setting. One of the most useful aspects is a section after each chapter entitled "You Be the Consultant." You're given a communication problem and then asked for suggestions on how to solve it.

Levering, R. (1988). *A great place to work: What makes some employers so good (and most so bad)*. New York: Random House. *The author profiles organizations that have a positive work environment. Most of the reason for the positive climate has to do with interpersonal relationships between bosses and employees.*

Today, after more than a century of electric technology, we have extended our central nervous system itself in a global embrace, abolishing both space and time as far as our planet is concerned.

MARSHALL McLUHAN
(1964)

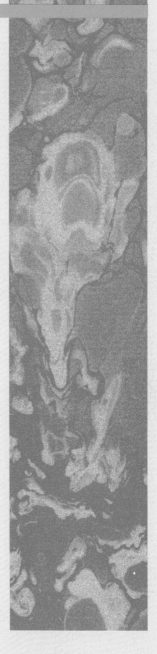

12

Interpersonal Communication in the Global Village: Issues of Culture and Gender

OBJECTIVES

After reading this chapter and taking part in class activities, you should be able to

- Distinguish between interpersonal and intercultural communication.

- Identify the role cultural variability plays in interpersonal communication.

- Describe the skills necessary to develop your intercultural competence in forming relationships.

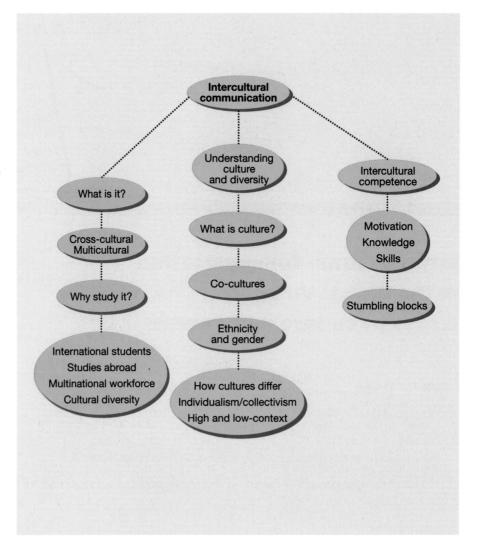

Throughout this book we've used examples, questions, and exercises to point up cultural differences in interpersonal communication. The fact is, all people live in a multicultural world. Marshall McLuhan's (1964) provocative invitation to think of ourselves as living in a "global village" is taken for granted today, but was a difficult idea to grasp when he coined the term in 1964. McLuhan's notion of the term "**global village**" referred to the virtual elimination of space and time by the development of technology and the almost instantaneous capability for getting information to any part of the globe. You can now directly telephone people in most countries. During the Persian Gulf War, you could watch battle scenes as the war was being fought. You were not limited to the evening news.

Observing other cultures through the media has not been the only way to live in the global village. During the last decade, communication with culturally different people has become a physical reality. To understand just how much contact you have with people of other cultural backgrounds, take a close look at your college or university and answer some of the following questions:

- How many international students are attending? How many countries did they come from? How did they hear about your college in their homeland?

- Does your college or university have a studies abroad program that allows students to attend university classes in countries such as Italy, France, Spain, England, Japan, China, and so on? Would you like the opportunity to study abroad?

- Have you traveled outside your country? As you prepare for a world of work and attend various "career fairs," have you become aware of which companies are international or multinational corporations? Would you be prepared culturally or linguistically to accept a position in a foreign country?

On another level, look at the demographics of the student, faculty, and staff population of the college or university you're attending.

- Are you aware of the ratio between men and women in your college? What about people of color or the physically different? When you look around your classrooms, do you see a wide age differentiation?

If your campus represents the major demographic changes taking place in North American society, you'll recognize that college and university campuses, like many communities, are going through a transition that makes them very different from just ten to twenty years ago. They're becoming more integrated into the global village.

Life in a society that is culturally diverse requires people to be competent and creative with "people" skills. These skills are similar to but different from the interpersonal skills discussed in previous chapters. In this chapter, we begin with a basic definition of intercultural communication and show how it is linked to interpersonal communication, discuss the many factors that influence intercultural interactions, and offer some skills to help you become interculturally, and therefore, more interpersonally competent.

WHAT IS INTERCULTURAL COMMUNICATION?

Intercultural communication occurs when you interact with someone from a different cultural background from your own. As defined by William B. Gudykunst and Young Yun Kim (1992, p. 13), "intercultural communication is a transactional symbolic process involving the attribution of meaning between people from different cultures." When an American interacts with a Japanese person, a French citizen with a Ghanaian, or a Mexican with an Icelander, intercultural communication is taking place. When you find yourself interacting with someone from a different cultural background, your interpersonal communication is often strained or dissonant. Later in this chapter, we'll look at co-cultures and the roles that ethnicity, age, gender, and sexual preference play in intercultural interaction. For now, let's examine some reasons why intercultural communication is difficult.

How Intercultural Communication and Interpersonal Communication Differ

To a certain extent, interpersonal communication and intercultural communication are alike. As you remember, interpersonal communication is an ever-changing transactional sharing that develops between people who find meaning with each other. Intercultural communication adds the unique aspect of culturally different backgrounds of interactants and all the variables this brings into play in communication encounters. In discussing the difference between interpersonal and intercultural, Gudykunst and Kim (1992) explain that the underlying communication processes are the same. They go on to suggest that "the two 'forms' of communication are not different in kind, only in degree," and describe intercultural communication as a process of communicating with a stranger. Gudykunst and Kim conceptualize the common underlying process of communication with people who are unknown and unfamiliar as communication with strangers. Intercultural communication is studied separately because of the unknown and unfamiliar qualities of strangers (for example, their culture and/or ethnicity).

Because part of interpersonal communication is to reduce uncertainty with strangers, this uncertainty reduction is made more difficult when you're with someone from a different cultural background. If you're talking with someone you don't know, but with whom you share language and other cultural expectations, communication is different from talking with a person who speaks a different language and brings different cultural expectations to the encounter. For example, imagine you come into your classroom on the first day of class and there is only one other person in the room. You ask the other person, "Is this the right room for the Interpersonal Communication class?" The person replies, "I think so, that's what my schedule says, anyway." Now imagine the same scenario, but after you ask your question, the person responds, "_Excusez-moi. Je ne comprende pas ton question_" ("Excuse me, I don't understand your question"), and gives you a look of confusion. Not only language differences, but even the expectations you had for each other are making communication more difficult. You may have thought you were just trying to be friendly and making small talk. In fact, you already knew you were in the right room. The French speaker, however, may be thinking, "Why did that person speak to me. I don't even know her. I hope she doesn't speak any more to me." In this situation, it's important to remember that the American way of thinking (as opposed to French, for example) involves a conceptualization of the self as an aware, choice-making, unified, and independent agent. The very meaning of such terms as *self* and *communication* are culturally determined. Even making small talk with a new classmate who is from another culture can be very difficult, and not just because of language barriers.

Even in the best of circumstances, a degree of **communication dissonance** occurs in intercultural encounters. The term *dissonance* is often used in music to refer to an inharmonious combination of sounds or chords. We're using it here to refer to inharmonious or even incongruent communication. In the preceding classroom example, dissonance occurs because of disharmony based on language, the functions of communication, and cultural expectations. Dissonance can occur at any of several levels of communication. Anthropological linguist John Regan (1977), discussing dissonance and what he calls "**communication mismatch**," says dissonance can occur on three levels:

1. *Language and nonverbal behavior*—the information people use to understand themselves and others through symbols

2. *Functions of communication*—what the communicants are trying to accomplish with their communication

3. *Cultural level*—the bulk of a person's awareness of identity; may be actually below the level of awareness

A degree of dissonance is usually present in all intercultural encounters, then.

Let's now clarify some terminology often used when discussing issues of culture and communication.

How Do Cross-Cultural, Multicultural, and Intercultural Differ?

Later in this chapter, we'll discuss the concept of culture in detail. However, because many terms about culture have become part of our daily vocabulary, it's important to define culture and look at some subareas to distinguish them from the general theme of intercultural interpersonal communication. The term **culture** refers to the shared social experience, the bulk of understandings humans have made to survive in a particular place in their world. Several terms about communication and culture are often used as synonyms for intercultural communication. It is important to understand the differences in these terms, because they in fact refer to different phenomena. A **cross-cultural phenomenon** is a phenomenon that appears across cultures. If you wanted to study greeting patterns inside Canada, Australia, and South Africa, for example, you would be making cross-cultural comparisons. If you were to study greeting patterns *among* Canadians, Australians, and South Africans, you would be studying intercultural communication.

A second term, **multicultural**, is used to describe group makeup or perspective. America has been described as a "multicultural" society—a culture blended of individuals who come from many different national backgrounds. Several metaphors have been used to describe the blending of cultures in U.S. society. Terms such as "melting pot," "stew," "salad bowl," and "mosaic" can all characterize the multicultural nature of North American society. Although America, like many other cities and countries around the world, is multicultural in terms of its population, its churches, its restaurants, and so on, it is not multicultural in many other aspects. The term *multicultural* has taken on a new political significance in the field of education. During the past few years, multiculturalism in education has become a controversial subject. Philosopher Mortimer Adler (1991) writes, "'Multicultural' and 'cultural diversity,' the buzzwords of the 1990s, have recently appeared as slogans emblazoned on the battle flags of various groups in universities and in the realm of public school reform." Used in educational circles, "multicultural" has been used to describe educational enterprises that take as their goal curriculum or classes that blend cultural perspectives. Many multiculturalists believe the U.S. education is **Eurocentric**; that is, it is based on the ideas of Western culture. In describing the multiculturalist's view, Adler writes (1991, p. 1), that for multiculturalists "Eurocentrism stands for the traditional values of Western culture—a culture dominated by 'dead white males' from Greek antiquity to the first half of the 20th century in Europe and North America."

Although we make no attempt to solve the debate about multicultural education, it is important to differentiate between the concepts *intercultural* and *multicultural*. For example, you could have a multicultural group engaging in intercultural communication. Think of a group of international students from several national cultures who are having a meeting or social get-together. Although they are a multicultural group, the communication between members of the different cultures is intercultural.

Now that we have clarified some terminology that is often confusing when we think of communication and culture, let's examine some reasons it is important to study intercultural communication.

Why Study Intercultural Communication?

There are many reasons why it is important to study intercultural communication and why we include it here in a book about interpersonal relationships. As Sandra Sudweeks and her colleagues (1990, p. 207) have said, "Communication plays a central role in defining the processes by which individuals establish, develop and maintain interpersonal relations." Communication defines the nature of the relationship, and the characteristics of a relationship influence the nature of the communication that occurs (Roloff, 1987). Because relationships and communication are partially defined by each other, and because of the ever-increasing cultural contact you have with others, as described at the start of this chapter, your ability to develop interpersonal relationships with others who are culturally different depends on a combination of your interpersonal and intercultural skills.

At the beginning of this chapter, we mentioned a partial makeup of the global village as

- International students

- Studies abroad programs

- Multinational corporations

- Cultural diversity in a multicultural society.

Let's look at why studying intercultural communication is important to each area of the global village. The first two areas listed, international students and study abroad programs encourage young people to live in a foreign country in order to learn the language and culture of another country. Although much of the focus of these programs is on classroom education, the informal education through cultural contact with foreigners can be crucial to the experience. In fact, negative contact with foreigners can sour the whole process. Many students who have been in study abroad programs have reported that the group of students stayed isolated and removed from the host culture. U.S. students studying in Aix-en-Provence or Japanese students studying at a U.S. university in Ohio can avoid contact with the host culture. Whether this is due to anxiety, ignorance, or inadequate language skills, the situation is unfortunate because the students could learn so much about another culture.

Sudweeks and her colleagues (1990, p. 207) research suggests that "deliberate strategies can be developed for use in various social situations and various stages of interaction to foster relationship movements with a partner from another culture." In fact, she writes that "being able to develop compensatory communication strategies allows partners to transcend linguistic limitations and minimize the perception of cultural differences as problematic in intercultural relationships."

Two other problems that visitors to other countries often experience are culture shock and re-entry shock. **Culture shock** has been used to mean the feeling of estrangement or displacement that individuals feel in visiting another culture. They feel the displacement when they confront the differences between their own culture's ways of life and that of the culture they're visiting. Culture shock can make them feel out of place and is preceded by a general anxiety as they find their old cultural ways of doing things don't work. If their way of greeting people by saying "Hi" is seen as inappropriate, or their failure to recognize someone's status is perceived as rude, they will become frustrated. Culture shock occurs naturally, but is more likely to happen if people lack knowledge of the host culture, have limited experience with travel and foreign people, or resist personal change.

No man is an island, entire of itself; every man is a piece of the continent, a part of the main.... Any man's death diminishes me, because I am involved with mankind; and therefore never send to know for whom the bell tolls; it tolls for thee.

JOHN DONNE (1624)

At the opposite end of the spectrum is **re-entry shock**. Re-entry shock occurs when they return home after an extended stay in another country and have to readjust to their own culture (Austin, 1986). This process has three factors: first, people begin to feel as though they had lost the self-concept they had found in the foreign country, and begin to search once again for personal identity. Second, they experience homesickness and nostalgia for the country they just left. Third, they often start to question their own value system because of the values they've observed in the other country.

Culture shock and re-entry shock, although naturally occurring events, tend to be less severe for those who are prepared interculturally. In essence, then, whether you study abroad or merely spend time in a foreign country on holiday, intercultural communication strategies make your experience more meaningful.

A third area of the global village consists of multinational corporations— that is, corporations that do business in different cultures and employ people from many nations. In the 1990s, many employees have international careers. Personal and corporate success in the international marketplace depend on cultural knowledge and interpersonal communication. Companies lose money when they select workers to live in a foreign country and those workers come home early. Sometimes this is due to a poor selection process, sometimes to poor or inadequate intercultural training, and sometimes to a lack of cultural understanding by the corporations (Hall & Gudykunst, 1989). Companies also lose business when they fail to understand cultural differences in entering the marketplace and meeting customer needs. The U.S. auto industry, which has complained for many years about not being able to sell cars in Japan, is only now deciding it should make right-hand-drive cars to sell there. This is in spite of the fact that they *knew* the Japanese drove on the opposite side of the road from Americans. In addition, companies must learn how to manage a multi-cultural workforce. In this example, J. S. Caputo and V. Bergman (1990) show how cultural misunderstanding can hurt a company and an employee:

> At a small American business, an employee from Viet Nam, on the job for several months, was told by her boss to take the day off without pay, because there wasn't any work for her to do. His words were, "Why don't you just go home. I don't have any more work for you today." The employee said nothing, but left and never came back! By the end of the week the boss decided she had quit, and gave her job to some-one else.

In this mismatch, the Vietnamese women interpreted the boss's message to mean that her work wasn't needed *anymore*, whereas the boss meant there was just a temporary slowdown.

Intercultural communication is equally important in understanding cultural diversity and multicultural societies. As education writer Scott Heller (1992, p. A7) writes,

People are on the move all over the world…dramatic new patterns of migration, settlement, and cultural identity. At worst, the shifts result in ethnic tensions or outright warfare. In other places, they lead to blended cultures, though not always to assimilation. National boundaries and the very idea of who makes up a nation are being challenged.

As mentioned earlier in this chapter, America is considered a multicultural society. Since the Islamic revolution of 1978, Los Angeles has even been nicknamed "Irangeles." Large foreign-born populations with close ties to their native homelands exist throughout the United States. In *big* cities, you can watch Spanish-language television programming, go out to eat in a Thai restaurant, attend a Basque festival, and later enjoy listening to Irish folk music. What is new is that you can do many of the same things in *small* cities and towns. Heller mentions that salsa now outsells ketchup in U.S supermarkets, you can buy fajitas at McDonald's and hear reggae music in Disney's film, *The Little Mermaid*. These are all facts of life in today's America. But with these changes has come suspicion, resentments, and disharmony. Collins (1992) reports that U.S. college students are pessimistic about race relations on college

> *So far as one cultural group differs from another, it tends to be held as suspect.*
>
> TALCOTT PARSONS
> (1964)

©1992, Washington Post Writers Group. Reprinted with permission.

campuses. In the same article, researcher Arthur J. Knopp writes, "Our young people have placed themselves in opposing camps, divided by race, and they tend to believe only the worst about youths of other races." Recent research has shown an increase of racial incidents at many colleges and universities around the country. These incidents mirror much of our society. The 1992 verdict in the Rodney King trial in Los Angeles and the subsequent violence directed at U.S. society as a whole (but particularly at white and Korean American businesses in the inner cities) help remind people of this challenge for the future. Unfortunately, even those who are receiving the benefits of higher education still have not learned the intercultural skills of acceptance, respect, valuing, and adaptation in helping to make cultural diversity work in multicultural societies. For many people, multicultural society is complicated and enriching, but also frustrating and often bewildering.

The importance of the role of intercultural communication in interpersonal relationships has been established. Let's turn now to what specifically constitutes culture.

Culture has been compared to an iceberg because its most obvious elements are available to us. Most of culture lies outside our level of awareness, just as ⅞ of an iceberg lies below the surface of the water.

UNDERSTANDING CULTURE AND DIVERSITY

nthropologist Edward Sapir has referred to culture as a "seamless web" that is interconnected in many ways. It is both seen and unseen, and yet exerts an undeniable influence in daily life. Because culture is both **overt** and **covert,** people often don't even recognize its influence. When we say culture is overt, we mean people learn it directly, it's describable, and people pass it on to their offspring. An example of overt cultural information for North Americans would be the importance of a "good" education. When we say culture is covert, we mean that people don't learn it directly, can't describe it easily to others, and pass it on in many discreet ways. An example of covert culture for Americans would be the role of men and women in society. Because culture is both overt and covert, some have described culture as being like an iceberg—an iceberg is typically one-fifth above the water line and fourth-fifths below.

In the same sense, then, overt culture is only the tip of the iceberg where most of culture is covert and not easily observable or even recognizable by members of the cultural group. What time you get up, what you eat, what side of the road you drive on, if and how you worship, how you select a mate, the language you speak, and much more are wrapped up in your cultural education. To understand the role of culture in your daily life and in your communication with others, it's important to recognize the degree of cultural diversity among people. We'll now look at specific elements of culture and how they vary.

What Is Culture?

Culture has been described and defined in many ways. Anthropologust Edward Hall (1959) claims that culture is communication, and communication is culture. Others see culture as refinement or cultivation. A cultured person might be seen as refined and well educated. We see culture as having a more specialized meaning that deals with the patterned way of behaving for a particular group of people. Culture is the store of shared social experience that furnish the design and the ways and means of life of the people and the era. As anthropologist Ina Corrine Brown (1963, p. 3) writes,

> It is a body of common understandings. It is the sum total and organization or arrangement of the group's ways of thinking, feeling, acting. It also includes the physical manifestations of the group as exhibited in the objects they make—the clothing, shelter, tools, weapons, implements, utensils, and so on. In this sense, of course, every people—however primitive—has a culture, and no individual can live without a culture.

COMMUNICATING SKILLFULLY

orm small groups and brainstorm all the examples you can that indicate the influence of foreign culture on your city. The list might contain foreign words as place names, ethnic foods and restaurants, cultural celebrations, religious ceremonies and so on. Share the list your group made with the class, and create a composite list. You might even consider publishing a flyer or newsletter that shares the information with your college or university.

CONSIDERING CULTURE

"IS THIS MAN CRAZY?"

Imagine that the individual described in the following brief case history came to you for treatment. How would you diagnose his ailment, and what therapy would you recommend?...

All through childhood, K. was extremely meditative, and usually preferred to be alone. He often had mysterious dreams and fits, during which he sometimes fainted. In late puberty, K. experienced elaborate auditory and visual hallucinations, uttered incoherent words, and had recurrent spells of sudden coma. He was frequently found running wildly through the countryside or eating the bark of trees and was known to throw himself with abandon into fire and water. On many occasions he wounded himself with knives or other weapons. K. believed he could "talk to spirits" and "chase ghosts." He was certain of his power over all sorts of supernatural forces.

THE ACTUAL DIAGNOSIS

Believe it or not, K. was not found insane, nor was he committed to the nearest institution for the mentally ill. Instead, in due course, he became one of the leading and most respected memebers of his community.

How this strange turn of events could come about may become more plausible to you if we supply an important bit of information that was purposely left out of the case history above.

K., we should have told you, was a member of a primitive tribe of fishermen and reindeer herders that inhabits the arctic wilderness of eastern Siberia. In this far-off culture, the same kind of behavior that we regard as symptomatic of mental illness is considered evidence of an individual's fitness for an important social position—that of medicine man or shaman.

The hallucinations, fits, manic episodes, and periods of almost complete withdrawal that marked his early years were considered signs that he had been chosen by some higher power for an exalted role. His behavioral eccentricities were, in fact, prerequisite to his becoming shaman, just as balance, solidity, self-confidence, and aggressiveness are prerequisite for the young man who hopes to be successful in American business.

Sociologists and anthropologists explain that shamanism serves two socially useful purposes in Siberian society. In the first place, it provides an approved outlet for the person of unstable temperment. It allows him to let off steam through an emotionally satisfying dramatic performance in which he summons spirits and manipulates the supernatural. In the second place, shamanism provides entertainment for other tribesmen and welcome relief from the monotony of their bleak environment.

SOURCE: *STATE OF MIND*, PUBLISHED BY CIBA PHARMACEUTICAL PRODUCTS, INC., SUMMIT, N.J., VOL. 1, NO. 1 (JANUARY 1957). REPRINTED BY PERMISSION.

This organization and patterning allows you to get through your day because you expect those around you to share the same meanings you do. The way you eat, sleep, dress, watch television, use the computer, and so on all allow you to have routines that make sense to others. To people of other cultures, these acts could be incomprehensible, unnatural, or wrong. If they did some of these things, they may do so in ways that would be logical and natural for them. A simple activity like drinking a cup of tea can be very ceremonial in Japan (the Japanese tea ceremony), an important break in the day and mealtime in Britain (high tea at 4:30 P.M.), or a cup of refreshment in the United States.

Culture is shared and sets the boundaries of a group. In essence, people are culturally determined, and the method of culture is communication. People share through the expression of their thoughts by language and behavior. They also observe and listen to the daily conduct of others and their styles of expression.

From a communication perspective, culture can be a problem because it varies. When we say it varies, we're referring to elements of culture such as language, perception, physical appearance, religion, social attitude, and even basic images of self.

What Is a Co-Culture?

Co-cultures are subgroups or subcultures within a culture. The term *co-culture* has come to replace the term *subculture* because subculture carried a connotation of groups as being diminished or less than the main culture. Larry Samovar and Richard Porter (1991, p. 72) write about co-cultures:

> For a number of years the literature employed the word *subculture* when referring to individuals and groups of people who, while living in the dominant culture, had dual membership in yet another culture. In recent years the term has been replaced and the concept reformulated. For referring to the *general category* of intercultural communication, the term *co-culture* has come to replace *subculture*. The substitution was based on the rationale that the word subculture implied that members of the nondominant culture were inferior in some ways or another. Because we believe the switch in language was sound, we shall use the word co-culture when talking about groups or social communities exhibiting characteristic patterns of behavior sufficient to distinguish them from others within an embracing culture.

Co-cultures, then, consist of members of the same general culture but who differ in some ethnic or sociological way. In American society, groups such as the disabled, African Americans, Native Americans, gays and lesbians, and the elderly could all be considered co-cultures. The term *co-cultures* implies that a group shares some values and customs of the larger national cul-

COMMUNICATING SKILLFULLY

If possible, talk with your parents and other members of your extended family and discuss how important a role national origins or ethnic heritage has played in their lives. In class, form small groups and talk about your own ethnic heritage and how like or unlike you are of other members of your ethnic group. Discuss how much of the stereotype of your group might or might not fit you and why you think this is true.

ture but has some customs or values unique to itself. An example in the United States would be a religious group such as the Amish. Although the Amish are for the most part a U.S. religious sect and are part of U.S. culture, their practice of religion, values, language, clothing, and lifestyle all make them distinctly different from the national culture. **Ethnic groups** are also forms of co-cultures. Ethnicity can be difficult to identify and recognize in oneself and in others. It is usually a term used to *identify oneself* as having a cultural background different from others. When people use a term to describe themselves such as Italian American, Native American, African American, Irish American, they're asserting their social identity to others. Yet when others impose an ethnic label on them, they may actually resent someone thus separating them from the main culture. Dealing with this difficulty, Howard Giles and Peter Johnson (1981) describe an ethnic group as "those individuals who identify themselves as belonging to the same ethnic category." In socially identifying themselves as part of an ethnic group, Eugene Roosens (1989) suggests they are actually defining who they are. He writes (pp. 17–18) that their ethnicity offers

> communality in language, a series of customs and symbols, a style, rituals, and appearance, and so forth, which can penetrate life in many ways. These trappings of ethnicity are particularly attractive when one is continually confronted by others who live differently. …If I see and experience myself as a member of an ethnic category or group, and others—fellow members and outsiders—recognize me as such, "ways

Ethnicity provides a "way of being" that validates our heritage and self-worth. But within any ethnic group there is great variation.

of being" become possible for me that set me apart from the outsiders. These ways of being contribute to the *content* of my self-perceptions. In this sense, I *become* my ethnic allegiance; I experience any attack on the symbols, emblems, or values (cultural elements) that define my ethnicity as an attack on myself.

Ethnic identity, then, becomes a powerful element not only in defining who you are but in creating a boundary between yourself and others. In *Ethnic Groups and Boundaries*, Norwegian anthropologist Fredrik Barth (1969) describes how ethnicity sets a boundary of who can and who can't be a member. However, there still is a potential for great diversification among members of an ethnic group. Such potential diversification within a group puts the lie to any stereotype of any ethnic group. For example, I may describe myself as a member of the Cajun ethnic group because of my heritage. But I may not like several Cajun foods, not enjoy Cajun music, and not even socialize with Cajun groups. And you may love Cajun food, music, and festivals, but you can't *be* Cajun because of your ancestry. Within the category of "Cajun," there can be great variance. It is also important to remember that if I introduce myself to you as Cajun, I am negotiating a definition of my sense of self with you, and you should notice this.

Often people discuss ethnicity as an American phenomena and describe other countries as if they have one monolithic culture. Yet ethnicity is part of the issue when Basques attack Spanish authorities for independence, the Walloons and Flemish argue for language rights in Belgium, the Hausa tribe wants to organize politically in Nigeria, Serbs and the Croatians kill each other in the name of "ethnic cleansing," Lebanese Americans ask for justice in Lebanon, or a multiethnic committee meets in New York City to decide how the city should "recognize" the anniversary of Columbus's "discovery of America."

Although we're using the term *co-culture* primarily to refer to a sociological or ethnic group, there are many other co-cultural groups. For example, we could talk about sororities and fraternities as co-cultures, or students and professors as co-cultures. One area of organizational communication research concerns itself with organizational life and culture. We could look at the co-cultures of IBM, AT&T, or General Motors. We could talk about the culture of the Democratic or Republican party. Each of these groups is unique in its own way but shares many ideas with the larger culture.

Let's look at several other forms of cultural diversity.

Cultural Diversity's Many Forms

Cultural diversity takes on many forms and often affects communication with people who are culturally different. Among these forms are gender, disability, religion, age, and gender orientation.

CONSIDERING ETHICS

In a small group, consider the following ethical predicament: What constitutes good ethical behavior is not universal. Often value orientations give the best guidance for discovering the ideal ethos of a particular culture. Gender sometimes plays a significant role in acceptable behavior. For example, in some societies women are only allowed to speak about "women's matters." During the Persian Gulf War, female U.S. soldiers stationed in Saudi Arabia were asked not to break Saudi rules for acceptable female behavior. Because of the Saudis' wish, U.S. women soldiers were kept from dressing in certain ways and even from driving military vehicles. Do you believe you're obliged to honor the ethical guidelines of a culture when you're a guest, or do you believe you should always follow your own ethical guidelines? Decide on an answer as a group, and share your group's response with the rest of the class.

GENDER

As discussed in Chapter 4, communication is influenced by social identity. Your social identity is governed to a large extent by what you see as your social role. Since much social role behavior is **gender** based, gender becomes a significant aspect of diversity.

Researchers on gender differences in behavior have focused on group identity, language and communication behaviors, and differences in moral judgment. In terms of group behavior, women define themselves and are defined by males for purposes of group membership, thus creating boundaries and subcategories for themselves. Terms such as "traditional" women and "career" women are two such subcategories.

When looking at language and communication, researchers have explored conversational styles and differences between men and women. As noted earlier, Deborah Tannen (1990) shows that communication between men and women is like cross-cultural communication and subject to a clash of conversational styles. Tannen refers to this phenomemon as speaking different "**genderlects**." Other factors such as word choice, interruption patterns, questioning patterns, language interpretations and misinterpretations, and vocal inflections all constitute "genderlects."

Moral development is another area of male and female differences that has been studied by Harvard professor Carol Gilligan. In her book _In a Different Voice_ (1982), Gilligan has posited that when facing ethical dilemmas, women make very different decisions from men. She feels women tend to think and speak differently than men because of contrasting images of self. Because of differences between male and female self-images, Gilligan believes that there is a feminine ethic of _care_ and a masculine ethic of _justice_. She has suggested that women see justice as impersonal and that sensitivity to others, loyalty, responsibility, self-sacrifice, and peacemaking are all important elements that women consider in facing moral dilemmas. In contrast, when facing moral dilemmas, men are more interested in individual rights, equality before the law, and fair play. For men, then, justice is (and should be) impersonal. Gilligan does not say that either men's or women's choices are better, but says they are different. This difference, like language, helps to constitute gender as a co-culture.

DISABILITY

Research has shown that the disabled or "differently abled" are often identified as culturally different (Dahnke, 1983). Gudykunst (1991, p. 58) writes that "another factor that can affect our communication is whether or not another person is 'disabled.' When people who are not disabled communicate with people who are visibly disabled is some way, they tend to experience uncertainty and anxiety, and avoid interaction when possible." Interpersonal communication often takes odd forms when a person without a disability talks with someone who may be blind, unable to hear, or with a physical impairment. For example, sighted people often speak more loudly to a blind person in the hope that volume will make up for what is lost visually. And people without physical impairment may stand farther apart from someone who has such a handicap.

RELIGION

Religion is always found at the base of social structure and culture. Many people begin their encounter with the divine and the supernatural very early in life. No matter how they may change and modify their reactions as they grow older, religion may continue to have a distinct effect on their thoughts and actions. Religious conflicts are present in many countries of the world. Many immigrant groups came to the United States to practice their faith without religious persecution.

AGE

A popular term heard frequently in the 1960s was "generation gap." The WHO, a popular band, had an anthem called "My Generation," with a line that said, "Hope I die before I get old." The implication was that death was preferable to old age. "Old" at that time was generally considered "over 30." The idea of a generation gap suggests that a chasm lies between the young and the old. The chasm is made up of beliefs, values, language, taboos, grooming, rewards and privileges, rights and duties, and so on. Generational differences have always been with us. In the twentieth century, however, they have been exacerbated by factors such as people living longer, the elderly put in homes for "senior citizens" or convalescent homes, and the glorification of "youth culture" in television, film, and records. As a result, young people and older people don't talk to each other on any regular basis and are uncertain and anxious when they do.

CONSIDERING CRITICAL THINKING

Form small groups in your class. Try to think of some of your "own" co-cultures. Make a list of the elements that your class group believes qualify these as co-cultures. Share your list with the class. Discuss what makes it difficult to identify a group as a co-culture. What do co-cultures contribute to each other? Try to be specific.

GENDER ORIENTATION

Gays and lesbians have become much more visible in society. Even with greater emergence, however, they have remained a co-culture set apart from the dominant culture. For outsiders, gay and lesbian culture, like any foreign cultural difference, is hard to understand. Often gays and lesbians are rejected because of deep-seated fears and animosities, as well as for religious objections and sociosexual taboos. However, more and more contact is now taking place between heterosexual and homosexual members of U.S. society. By learning more about the co-culture of gays and lesbians, people can become less anxious or uncomfortable when communicating with others who have a different gender orientation.

It's important to recognize how even co-cultural differences impact interpersonal relationships. With knowledge about co-cultures, people can take steps to accommodate communication to build connections between themselves and others.

Now that we've looked at culture and co-cultures, let's turn to how cultures are different.

HOW DO CULTURES DIFFER?

As mentioned earlier in this chapter, communication between members of different cultures can be problematic because culture is variable. Sometimes it's easy to recognize that you're having a difficult time communicating with someone who is culturally different from you, but it is harder to know just why. There are many variables one could study, but for the purpose of this chapter we'll focus on just two—(1) individualism and collectivism, and (2) high- and low-context communication. (For a more detailed summary of **cultural variability**, see Gudykunst and Kim, 1992).

Every man is in certain respects (a) like all other men, (b) like some other men, (c) like no other man.

KLUCKHOHN AND MURRAY (1953)

Individualism-Collectivism

Individualism–collectivism has been recognized as perhaps the most significant dimension of cultural variability (Triandis, 1988). Individualistic cultures place emphasis on individual goals, while group goals are more important in collectivist cultures. In collectivist cultures, the individual must fit into the group. In an article entitled "Japanese Social Experience and Concept of Groups," Cathcart and Cathcart (1985, p. 190) report that the Japanese have an expression "*Deru kugi wa utareru*" ("The nail that sticks up is hit"). They go on to explain how important the role of group membership and solidarity is in Japanese society and that one must practice *giri*—self-discipline used to repress or channel personal desires and feelings. For the Japanese, collectivism binds each member of the culture to the group and in that way preserves ancient patterns and roles in the culture.

Individualistic cultures, in contrast, value the development of the individual and praise independence as a virtue. Collectivistic cultures value the group and see dependency as a virtue. Japanese psychiatrist Takeo Doi (1962, p. 132) believes that a type of dependency called "*amae* might be the very factor that distinguishes Japanese people from other nations." There is no English equivalent; the term can mean to depend on or presume another's love. It carries a positive contribution related to the sweet and warm dependency a child might feel when with her parents and other loving family members.

Two examples might serve to help you recognize collectivists and individualistic cultures. North America is an individualistic culture. Children are taught from a young age to "stand up for themselves," to sleep in their own bed (or room), to solve their own problems, to develop their sense of self through education, and to move out of their family dwelling and make it on their own. In contrast, the Japanese represent a collectivist society. Japanese people are extensions of their family. Loyalty is important in the family and extended to the world of work. In Japan, it is unusual for a worker to move from company to company for advancement because of the loyalty factor. Loyalty to a company means "I will work for this company all my life, and my company will not lay me off." The ability to work in harmony with family and fellow workers is highly praised. One should not stand out from his or her group but instead be seen as a "team" player. Bringing shame to oneself brings shame to one's extended group, family, and workers, and is to always be avoided.

Gudykunst (1991) suggests that in collectivistic cultures you will find individualistic members and that the opposite is also true. However, either individualistic or collectivistic behaviors tend to predominate in any specific cultural group. As mentioned earlier in this chapter, U.S. society is multicultural. Various co-cultures within this society may have come from a culture that was either collectivist or individualistic. Tracing your own heritage, did you find you came from a collectivistic or individualistic culture?

COMMUNICATING SKILLFULLY

Divide the class into small groups, and develop role-play situations that each depict a conversation between a member from a collectivistic and an individualistic culture. How might communication between two people, one from an individualistic culture and one from a collectivistic culture, be made more difficult because of this cultural difference? Think of three or four interpersonal settings and role-play them in front of the class. To get you thinking about ideas, try this one: after a softball game, you invite one of your teammates (Yaska, who is an international student from Japan) to come over for dinner rather than to join the rest of the team for a picnic. Discuss each role-play with the class.

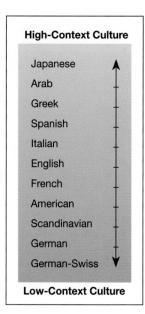

FIGURE 12.1

Cultures Arranged Along the High-Context/Low-Context Contiuum (Samovar & Porter, 1985, p. 23)

High Context and Low Context Cultures

Anthropologist Edward T. Hall (1976) has proposed an ordering pattern among people that he refers to as high- and low-context cultures. As you can see in Figure 12.1, Hall categorizes this cultural dimension of context in a range along a continuum.

For Hall, the level of context is at the base of all human behavior and largely determines communication. A high-context culture is long-lived and provides a unifying force that is slow to change. **Low-context cultures** are not significantly unified and can easily be changed and adapted. In essence, **high-context cultures** are bound by tradition, which shapes behavior and lifestyles. Low-context cultures lack a bond with tradition, and therefore their present behavior and lifestyle is more fluid, subject to change, and unpredictable.

Rather than provide a general definition, Hall gives many examples of low- and high-context cultures. He cross-culturally examines law, domestic policies, technology, and art to discover cultural context. Just as Japanese and North American culture vary along the individualistic–collectivistic dimension, Hall finds they also differ on the high- and low-context dimension. Hall says the typical U.S. culture is low context, because its law systems, art, architecture, and technology are not tradition bound. The law system, for example, is ever changing. The Japanese are seen as high context, with a strong bond to the past; tradition is the primary guide for contemporary Japanese culture.

Gudykunst (1991, p. 51) writes, "It appears that low- and high-context communication are the predominant forms of communication in individualistic and collectivistic cultures." Generally speaking, members of low-context, individualistic cultures speak in a direct fashion, and members of high-context, collectivistic cultures speak indirectly. North Americans like someone to get to the point, speak directly to the issue, confront ideas squarely, and not "beat around the bush." By contrast, a collectivistic culture such as the Chinese teaches people to speak around issues, avoid confrontation in speech, use parables to instruct, and even to agree with someone you don't understand or disagree with, in order to maintain harmony with others. Samovar and Porter (1991, p. 234) write,

> High-context cultures such as Japan, Korea, and Taiwan tend to be more aware of their surroundings and their environment and do not rely on verbal communication as their main information source. The Korean language contains the word *nunchi*, which literally means being able to communicate through your eyes. In high-context cultures, so much information is available in the environment that it is unnecessary to state verbally what is obvious. Oral statements of affection, for instance, are very rare because it is not necessary to state what is obvious. When the context says, "I love you," it is not necessary to state it orally.

Samovar and Porter (1991) go on to distinguish four major differences affecting communication in high and low context cultures:

- Verbal messages are extremely important in low-context cultures because information is not readily available in the environment and members do not learn how to perceive the environment for information.

- Members of high-context cultures perceive low-context people as less attractive and less credible because they rely primarily on verbal messages for information.

- Members of high-context cultures are more sensitive to nonverbal behavior and in reading their environment.

- Members of high-context cultures expect others to be sensitive to nonverbal messages and therefore speak less than members of low-context cultures.

As you can see, cultural understandings of context can play a significant role in how you communicate and what you expect from others. When you're communicating interculturally with someone, the cultural context of the two interactants is a significant variable that can easily lead to dissonance.

Thus far in this chapter we've discussed what intercultural communication is, why it's an important part of interpersonal communication, and how cultural variability affects communication with people of different cultures. Now we would like to look at what skills are necessary for developing competent intercultural communication.

BECOMING INTERCULTURALLY COMPETENT

Competence implies the ability to do certain tasks well. Recall that in an earlier chapter a quotation from language philosopher Ludwig Wittgenstein described language as a tool. Just as a skilled carpenter can use tools to build a house, you can use communication skills to build and share meanings with others and build relationships. Brian Spitzberg and William Cupach (1984) have isolated three components of communication competence: motivation, knowledge, and skills. We will use these three components of competence to look at ways to (1) develop intercultural relationships, and (2) on a larger scale, build community.

Motivation

To improve intercultural relationships, people must want to communicate with others who are different. As the writers of this book, we've assumed that if you're choosing to read it, you're motivated to communicate appropriately and effectively with others. However, because communication with others who are culturally different can be difficult, your motivation to communicate is crucial. It is important to be aware of how much people approach or avoid others who are culturally different. Sometimes people come to think that their culture is so politically, economically, or morally dominant that they don't need to concern themselves with others, who may be seen as foreign or alien. It's not unusual for people who have traveled internationally to come back to the United States with attitudes of cultural superiority. Being proud of the U.S. heritage is one thing, but seeing oneself as therefore culturally or morally superior leaves little room to make the international and global connections one needs to make to live in the "global village." If you find that you tend to avoid culturally different people, assess why you do so, and try to change. Moreoever, even if you are highly motivated, you may still need to acquire knowledge or skills to communicate interculturally.

Knowledge

Knowledge, the second component of competence, is the awareness and understanding of what you need to do in order to communicate appropriately and effectively. In an article entitled "Intercultural Etiquette" (1989, p. 84), Itabari Njeri writes that when different groups converge, the ignorant and the curious can be unexpectedly rude:

> It's the offhand remark that cuts or injures—the request for a speaker with an 'adorable' British accent 'to say something in English;' the question to women of Indian descent about the *tikka* or *kumkum*, the red beauty mark, often made from a powder and worn on the forehead or scalp, 'Does that dot wash off?'; the constant query to every Asian-American, 'Are you Japanese, Chinese, or what?'

These kinds of comments and questions can be seen as rude—or, worse, racist. Knowledge of other cultures is available to us in many places: formally through education and reading, and informally through contact and observations with others, through viewing foreign and ethnic films and by asking questions. Two approaches to the study of culture are called the *cultural general* and the *cultural specific* approaches. From the cultural general perspective, one studies what culture is, and how culture affects people, and examines cultural understandings cross-culturally. From a cultural specific approach, one studies a culture in depth. The cultural specific approach is most often used in training someone for an overseas assignment or foreign study. According to Broome (1986), most research suggests that the cultural general approach with some cultural specific information is the best way to become interculturally competent. Although knowledge and motivation are important, people also need to have good intercultural skills.

Skills, or a Way of Being

The third component of competence is skills "or a way of being." This phrase refers to the ability to use knowledge to communicate appropriately and effectively. People need to behave in skillful ways. The skills we consider most important in intercultural encounters are

> *Know thyself.* It's important to recognize the role that culture and ethnicity play in your life. Often, because of the assimilation process, many people lose any particular ethnic or cultural identity. They may even think it's unimportant. However, until you understand who you are and how you fit with others, it is very difficult to appreciate the role culture plays in others' lives, and the gap separates you from others who are culturally different.

> *Develop empathy.* Just as empathy is an important skill in understanding others in interpersonal communication, it is also crucial in intercultural transactions. Unless you can put yourself in the place of the other person, you can never understand the role culture is playing in your communication.

> *Seek a shared code.* If you and your partner speak different languages, it's important to try to use a language in which you are both conversant. Since culture is codified in language, the ability to speak another language increases cultural awareness. In addition, it's insensitive to think that others should always speak your language. Ernest Boyer (1990) writes that people "should become familiar with other languages and cultures so that [they] will be better able to live, with confidence, in an increasingly interdependent world." When you are traveling, attempting to use the local language helps show an interest in the people and culture.

> *Ability to reduce uncertainty.* The ability to seek information about others and therefore to reduce uncertainty is an important interpersonal as well as intercultural skill (Gao & Gudykunst, 1990). In intercultural settings, you must decide the appropriateness of self-disclosure, questioning, or close observation to get to know the other person at the cultural as well as sociological and psychological levels. Your ability to reduce uncertainty allows you to know the other person as an individual, and not as a stereotype.

> *Encourage feedback.* In intercultural transactions, encouraging feedback lets people restructure interactions, clear up any social *faux pas*, clarify language or cultural mismatches, and tells partners they are open to working on communication; that is, working on the relationship.

> *Seek commonalities.* Look back at the Kluckhohn and Murray quotation

on page 304. These two distinguished anthropologists are referring to the similarities and differences in humans. Anthropologists have taught people that they are everywhere the same and everywhere different. Although the emphasis in this chapter has been on differences, in building relationships it's important to discover the *similarities* between yourself and others. This is difficult in intercultural encounters, but it becomes the basis for relationships.

Develop communication flexibility. In intercultural interactions, it is more difficult to accurately predict the behavior of your partner. As a result, you may at times select the wrong communication strategy, ask the wrong question, misunderstand the significance of your actions. It's important that you remain flexible and alter strategies in some anxiety-producing situations. Flexibility allows you to not overreact or feel it's hopeless to try to communicate with someone culturally different. Flexibility helps you to enjoy your intercultural encounters and use them as learning opportunities.

When you perceive yourself and are perceived by others as interculturally competent, you're able to build intercultural relationships and, as Gudykunst (1991) suggests, to build community. Intercultural communication helps build bridges between people of diverse backgrounds. In discussing the importance of building community, Gudykunst cites people such as philosopher Martin Buber, or Mother Teresa, who see "spiritual deprivation" (a feeling of emptiness associated with separation from fellow humans) as the major problem fac-

Building an international / intercultural community.

ing the world today (Jampolsky, 1989). Developing intercultural competence—motivation, knowledge, and skills—helps build intercultural relationships and thereby intercultural community.

Unfortunately, even with the best intentions, intercultural attempts may go astray. Let's look now at potential problems that can harm intercultural interactions.

SIX STUMBLING BLOCKS IN INTERCULTURAL PATHWAYS

Communications professor LaRay Barna (1976) has suggested the following list of problem areas or stumbling blocks to intercultural communication.

Assumed Similarity

The first stumbling block is assumed similarity. Barna believes the notion "People are people" is as dangerous as it is sentimental. If you assume that people are alike, you fail to take the necessary steps to bridge significant cultural differences. Because people in many cultures now wear "Western culture" clothing, similar hair styles, and so on, it may become easy to gloss over the truly unique dimensions and shadings culture lends to its members. Barna mentions how even a smile, which seems a universal gesture, does not show friendliness in all cultures. Japanese students who are newly arrived in America often remark how they feel very uncomfortable when they first come to the United States and American students smile at them "for no apparent reason." For the Japanese, a smile is a sign of really caring about another person. The Japanese believe it is rude to smile at people you don't know. One of our Japanese students explained this behavior this way:

> On my way to and from school I have received a smile by non-acquaintance American girls several times. I have finally learned they have no interest for me; it means only a kind of greeting to a foreigner. If someone smiles at a stranger in Japan, especially a girl, she can assume he is either a sexual maniac or an impolite person.

Language

The second intercultural stumbling block, language, has been discussed elsewhere in this chapter, and was discussed at length in Chapter 7. We mention it here as well as a reminder that language can go astray when people are speaking the same language or are attempting to speak a second language. Vocabulary, syntax, idioms, dialects, and regional differences all can cause frustration in intercultural encounters. If you've ever tried to use a foreign phrase book to make a telephone call or ask for directions, you realize how fragile the use of a second language might be. Often, then, language is a major barrier to intercultural attempts.

Nonverbal Communication

Learning a foreign language is not the only barrier to intercultural communication. Just as we mentioned the importance of verbal _and_ nonverbal messages in interpersonal communication, both must be attended to interculturally. Most nonverbal signals are culturally specific and therefore vary from culture to culture. It is impossible to learn what every nonverbal symbol would mean all around the world. Instead, people need to remind themselves of cultural variability in signals and need be prepared if nonverbal mismatches take place.

Preconceptions and Stereotypes

In Chapter 3, we discussed the perceptual process and how your experiences influence how you interpret current information. In intercultural encounters, perceptions of events and people are influenced by preconceptions and stereotypes. Although this is a natural phenomenon that helps people make sense of stimuli, it can be very detrimental to establishing interpersonal relationships with others who are culturally different (Billig, 1987). If people stereotype others who are culturally different, they have created an obstacle to communication. And people do apply stereotypes whenever they communicate with low awareness of others (Fiske, 1990). For example, if you perceive Italians as emotional, Iranians as argumentative, British as cold and "stand-offish," and New Zealanders as casual and "laid back", you're stereotyping by not taking into account the uniqueness of each individual. Thus the stereotyping is a stumbling block for communication because it can interfere with an objective view of others.

Tendency to Evaluate

Barna (1976, p. 295) has suggested that another deterrent to communication between people of differing cultures or ethnic groups is "the _tendency to evaluate_, to approve or disapprove, the statements and actions of the other person or group rather than to try to completely comprehend the thoughts and feelings expressed." This tendency to evaluate often grows out of **ethnocentrism**. Ethnocentrism is a basic human survival response. From birth you begin identifying with and affirming that which gives you sustenance: parents, families, cultural groups. Believing that one's group is right and must be defended has provided human beings with one of their most effective defenses against the depredations of nature and other human beings. Strength lies in the group.

The principal characteristic of ethnocentrism is the relatively blatant assertion of personal and cultural superiority ("My way is the right way"), accompanied by denigration of other cultures and other ways. For example, it is ethnocentric for an American to judge Spanish people as lazy because they take a siesta in the middle of the working day, or to judge any other culture as somehow deficient from the American because people there do things "differently."

Recall from Chapter 8 the importance of listening nonjudgmentally in interpersonal settings. This is especially crucial when biases keep people from understanding another culture or way of life. A daily visit to the local pub changes from being seen as "a drinking problem" to "a good idea" when an American listens long enough to understand that because British homes are small, it is much easier on everyone involved to meet and socialize at the "local." Drinking is only a secondary purpose for going to the pub. By evaluating too early, you miss what the speaker may have been saying. In an intercultural situation, it's best to first empathize, and then ask questions for clarification.

High Anxiety

Anxiety can be a major stumbling block to intercultural communication that both underlies and compounds the other five (assumed similarities, language, nonverbal cues, preconceptions and stereotypes, and evaluation). Although it's normal to be somewhat anxious when talking to foreign people because of culture and language differences, that anxiety also communicates discomfort with others. Yoka, a Japanese student studying in the United States, expressed her feelings about her intercultural communication like this:

> I came home from class every day and cried my first month at the university. No one seemed to be able to understand me and I couldn't understand the professor or any of the students. When I first met my roommate, she hugged me. It felt very strange. I never hug anyone, not even my parents when I left for America. Most of the American students wanted to go get drunk on weekends. I got so sick of everyone smiling at me for no reason. I felt very dumb. Even though I studied English at school in Tokyo, no one could tell. Everyone spoke so fast and always wanted to know if I liked it better here than in Japan. I was exhausted after each day and would fall asleep rather than read my books or go out and socialize.

Learning to cope with high anxiety not only helps people communicate more clearly, but also puts others more at ease and thus increases the likelihood of developing interpersonal and intercultural relationships (Gao & Gudykunst, 1990).

LOOKING BACK - LOOKING FORWARD

In the last chapter, we discussed the sociocultural dynamics present in professional relationships. In this chapter, we looked at the difference between intercultural and interpersonal communication, examined the role of cultural variability in communication, and described the skills necessary for developing intercultural competence. In the final chapter, we'll look at the role mass media play in understanding and development of interpersonal relationships. In a world that brings people together by mass media and offers relational advice through radio psychologists, and television dating shows, it's important to see the benefits as well as limitations of media's effects on interpersonal relations.

REVIEW TERMS AND CONCEPTS

global village
288
intercultural
communication
289
communication
dissonance
291
communication
mismatch
291
culture
291
cross-cultural
phenomenon
291
multicultural
292

Eurocentric
292
culture shock
293
re-entry shock
294
overt culture
297
covert culture
297
co-culture
299
ethnic groups
300
cultural diversity
301
gender
302

genderlects
302
cultural variability
304
individualism–
collectivism
304
high- and low-
context cultures
306
intercultural
competence
307
ethnocentrism
312

PUTTING THEORY INTO PRACTICE

FOR DISCUSSION:

1. What are the most important reasons for studying intercultural communication?

2. Describe examples of ethnocentrism you have heard or witnessed.

3. Why do groups create boundaries, and why does culture inevitably separate cultural groups?

SKILL BUILDERS:

1. On the basis of what you've read about individualistic and collectivistic cultures and high- and low-context cultures, place the cultures listed at the appropriate spot on the continuum. Discuss your answers in small groups.

Japanese_____American

English, Australian, Filipino, Ceylonese, Italian, Swedish, Costa Rican, Argentinean, Cambodian

2. Study the nonverbal expressions of various cultural groups. Compile a list of nonverbal behaviors that are unique to specific groups.

3. Investigate and become familiar with the social customs of three cultural or co-cultural groups. Discuss your findings in small groups.

4. If you have the opportunity, invite a foreign student to share a holiday dinner at your home. Discuss the similarities and differences between the ways you celebrate the holiday and if or how it is celebrated in the foreign student's country.

FOR EXTENDED STUDY

Axtell, R. E. (1990). *Do's and taboos of hosting international visitors.* New York: Wiley.

This book is especially oriented toward business people who deal with foreign executives and their families and how to develop important business relationships. The author examines hosting as a cross-cultural skill and discusses how others view Americans.

Barth, F. (Ed.). (1969). *Ethnic groups and boundaries.* Boston: Little, Brown.

This classic book examines the theoretical perspectives of social organization of cultural differences. The book is a primer for those who want to understand the role of ethnicity and group membership.

Brown, I. C. (1963). *Understanding other cultures.* Englewood Cliffs, NJ: Prentice-Hall.

This book is especially valuable for nonspecialists to gain an understanding of anthropology. Brown seeks to strip away sentimentality from culture contact and find common ground between cultures.

Gudykunst, W. B. (1991). *Bridging differences: Effective intergroup relations.* Beverly Hills, CA: Sage.

This highly readable work helps develop a perspective for effective communication between people and groups that are divergent.

Hall, E. T. (1976). *Beyond culture.* Garden City, NY: Doubeleday.

One of Hall's most important works, especially useful for gaining an understanding of his scheme of high- and low-context cultures.

Hunt, R. (Ed.). (1967). *Personalities and cultures: Readings in psychological anthropology.* Garden City, NY: The Natural History Press.

This work is a compilation of classic ethnographic work on personality and culture by some pioneers in the field. The book is especially valuable in defining personality's role in shaping culture.

Madden-Simpson, J., & Blake, S. M. (Eds.). (1990). *Emerging voices: A cross-cultural reader, readings in the American experience.* New York: Holt, Rinehart and Winston.

This interesting book is designed as a thematic reader reflecting American cultural and ethnic diversity. The book focuses on immigrant, ethnic, and minority experiences in the United States, with two aims: first, to foster an awareness of the diverse forces at work in our society, and second, to create a sensitivity to the experiences of all Americans.

Samovar, L., & Porter, R. (Eds.). (1991). *Intercultural communication: A reader.* (6th ed.). Belmont, CA: Wadsworth.

This reader was one of the first books devoted to intercultural communication. The collection of essays has changed through the editions and stayed current with ongoing research perspectives.

Vigil, J. D. (1980). *From Indians to Chicanos: A Sociocultural history.* London: Mosby.

Diego Vigil's book provides an excellent perspective to the complex, multilayered history of the Chicanos and the Chicano movement. The book does an especially good job in depicting how Chicano experience differs in significant respect from that of other ethnic minority groups.

I'm convinced that when historians 100 years from now or 200 years from now try to describe our times, they will say we are living through the third great communication revolution in the history of Western civilization.

LYMAN BRYSON

13

Interpersonally Communicating in a Mediated World: The Technological Embrace

OBJECTIVES

After reading this chapter and taking part in class activities, you should be able to

- Describe the role of the media in your interpersonal relationships.

- Critically analyze media's impact on yourself and your interpersonal relationships.

- Explain the process of mediated communication and its effects.

Cognitive Map 13

Mediated communication

Why media in a interpersonal book?

Pervasiveness of media

Connection of interpersonal and mediated communication

Impact on our relationship

Four generalizations about the role of media in relationships

What is mediated communication?

Mass media—mass communication

Natural and mediated forms of communication

Consequences of media

Social learning theory

Cone effect model

Media images/ media reality

Self identity and the media

Strategies for mediated communication
1. Becoming media literate
2. Selecting appropriate media
3. Choices of time and place
4. Critical thinking skills

Interpersonal communication, new technologies, and the future

THE TITLE OF CHAPTER 12 INCLUDED the words "global village," and this chapter carries the subtitle "The Technological Embrace." In many ways these chapters are closely connected: the global village is made possible by media technology, which links everyone. People everywhere are linked by the technological embrace of wires, satellites, microwaves, and lasers. When you think of an embrace, what do you think of? Is it a warm and passionate hug? Is it a playful and even athletic pat? Or is it the slow, comforting snugness of a group hug? An embrace indicates connectiveness, caring, and relationship. The **mass media** connect us to others. Most researchers on the social effects of media have talked about how media disengage us, and this disengagement psychologically distances people from each other. Because of this perceived disengagement, some believe the media have a harmful effect on the building and maintaining of strong interpersonal relationships. The debate on whether media do or do not distance people is still going on. Although research indicates that the global village exists, many people have a hard time buying the concept that media bring people together. The fact is, communication media have the ability to bring people together or to distance them from each other. This underscores the power the media have. In this chapter, we look at contemporary as well as future issues of media and interpersonal relationships. We take the fairly radical position that in this last decade of the twentieth century, the media not only do *not* distance people from each other but actually links people together over great distances at the speed of light. We explore two primary themes: (1) how media serve this linking function and help make interpersonal communication possible; and (2) how media serve as a model for interpersonal behavior and relationships. Let's begin by taking a closer look at the prevalence of media in daily life.

THE PREVALENCE OF MEDIA IN DAILY LIFE

As you live through what Lyman Bryson has called the third great communications revolution, media has become pervasive in your life. Think about the various forms of media you have used in the last twenty-four hours. Which were used for interpersonal communication? Perhaps the telephone or the computer? Did you watch television or go to the movies? Did anything you watch carry explicit or implicit messages about relationships? What impact do these mediated forms of communication—human communication assisted by technology—have on your interpersonal relationships? In exploring such questions, you can develop an awareness and understanding of the process of mediated communication and its effects on you.

WHY DISCUSS MEDIA IN A BOOK ABOUT INTERPERSONAL COMMUNICATION?

The role of media in interpersonal communication has been largely overlooked. You'll remember from Chapter 1, that from the situational view,

It's a poor sort of memory that only works backwards.

LEWIS CARROLL,
*THROUGH THE
LOOKING GLASS*

Although early in this century communication scholars saw interpersonal and mass communication as significantly different contexts of communication, current research sees the relatioship between the two areas as symbolic—or closely interlaced.

early definitions of interpersonal communication stressed that communication to be interpersonal, required a face-to-face setting, with communicants directly in each other's presence. Because you can see more of the other person, you pick up more sensory data and therefore are more likely to catch their subtleties, emphases, and moods. Basically, then interpersonal communication was viewed primarily as a setting with two people. Over the past few years, as scholars began to see communication as a developmental transaction (see the definition in Chapter 1), the quality and type of communication, rather than the physical presence of two communicators, became the essential element that distinguished interpersonal communication from other forms (Miller & Steinberg, 1975). Some theorists thought it was impossible, by definition, to engage in interpersonal communication on the telephone, no matter what the content or relationship of the people talking. From the perspective we are now taking, what people are talking *about* and *how they are responding to each other* makes the qualitative differences necessary for interpersonal communication,

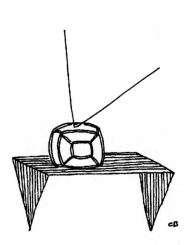

"I ENTERTAIN, I STIMULATE,
I HAVE A BROAD SPECTRUM OF OPINION.
HEY LISTEN, I EVEN COOK. SO WILL
YOU BE MINE?" ANNIE'S TV SAID
TO HER ONE EVENING, CATCHING HER
OFF GUARD.

and people can be interpersonal through many forms of mediated communication—over the telephone, through computers, and so on. In fact, as some communication scholars have moved away from this face-to-face requirement, they now see every type of communication as basically interpersonal. The difference between interpersonal and mass communication, then, is a false dichotomy, according to Reardon and Rogers (1988).

The Connection Between Interpersonal and Mass Communication

As said before, media critics have often stressed that the media disengage us from others. Watching television alone, sitting in a darkened movie theater, listening to a personal stereo, or playing video games all appear to be examples of this disengagement. Although such disengagement is possible, we believe that just the opposite may be true—that the media engage people with others more than at any other time in history. Just as Johannes Gutenberg's invention of movable type, and Samuel Morse's invention of the telegraph altered the way people lived, thought, and communicated, modern communication technology is likewise changing everyone's relationships and relational style. The ability to communicate instantaneously with people in different parts of the globe even alters the human perception of space and time. Gary Gumpert and Robert Cathcart (1986, p. 9) believe "the modern electronic media have affected what we know, who and what we talk about, who talks to us, and who listens." Your world reflects what media can provide you, and the impact of media can reach into the heart of your awareness and sensibility.

The connection between interpersonal and mass communication seems to be symbiotic—or closely interlaced, and this fusion has begun to draw the attention of communication scholars on an international level. All human relationships have been influenced by media innovations. The same communication satellites that have made it possible to see and talk to astronauts in space, have given you the ability to telephone a friend in a foreign country, as easy and often more clearly than calling a next-door neighbor. Fax machines send lunch orders to the local delicatessen or a music request to a radio station, and interactive electronic mail (**E–Mail**) lets people "talk" to each other with computers. At the same time, more traditional media such as radio, television, and film, while providing entertainment, present powerful messages of how relationships begin, are carried out, and conclude. Often these media are analyzed for their commercial or technological functions but are ignored for what they contribute to the human communication process. When someone calls a radio station and requests that a love song be played for her boyfriend so she can strengthen her relationship, this mediated experience is taking the place of a personal friend or even a matchmaker.

Interpersonal relationships are both *re*flected and *in*fected by the mass media. When we say that the media *reflect* relationships, we mean that to make sense of, identify, and enjoy mass media experiences, people have to see the characterizations of relationships as plausible—that is, they have been in, or know of, relationships like those that are being presented. When we say that media *infect* people's relationships, we mean that people are influenced in some way to try to have their relationships or, perhaps even more importantly, their expectations of relationships be more like ones presented on television, in magazines, or in books.

The Role of Media in Interpersonal Communication

Although media and interpersonal communication are entwined, it's possible to look at where they connect. Gumpert and Cathcart (1986) have suggested the following four generalizations about these connections:

> 1. Some interpersonal situations require media for the purpose of communication.

2. The media are part of a complex of variables that influence behavior and attitudes.

3. The content of media is both a reflection and projection of interpersonal behaviors.

4. An individual's self-image and its development is media dependent.

WHAT IS INTERPERSONAL MEDIATED COMMUNICATION?

The phrase "interpersonal **mediated communication**" refers to person-to-person interaction through the use of a technological device to send and receive messages. This process transcends the limitation of time and space. The technological device lets us carry on relational functions over great distances and in actual time. The telephone is one obvious example. With a phone, we can communicate privately and interpersonally with someone in Texas, Turkey, or Timbuktu and get immediate feedback.

The Difference Between Media and Mass Communication

Frequently people think of the words *mass media* and *mass communication* as synonyms. But it's important to differentiate these terms. First, not all media are mass media. Again, the telephone can serve as an example of a medium that is not a mass medium. Second, **mass communication** refers to the use of a medium or technological device to reach many people. In mass communication, the source may be one person, but often the source can be a group of people, such as producers, directors, editors, or actors.

COMMUNICATING SKILLFULLY

Form small groups. Discuss each of the preceding four generalizations about media, and list an example of each from your own personal experiences. Place the list on the board to compare to those of other groups. Discuss the following questions:

1. Were you able to come up with an example for each generalization?

2. Are certain media more influential in relationships than others? If so, which ones and why?

3. Which examples would not have been available in your grandparents' lifetime?

4. Will media continue to alter the means and methods of carrying out interpersonal communication functions? What do you project to be the next technological device on the horizon that will help us in interpersonal communication?

McLuhan's probes about the media profoundly changed our understanding of media and society.

MEDIA AS EXTENSIONS

Marshall McLuhan was one of the first theorists to study mediated communication (McLuhan, 1962, 1964, 1981). He is often credited with the first use of the terms *medium* and *media*. In McLuhan's framework, technological development represents an extension of human capacities. For example, clothing could be seen as an extension of skin, cars as extensions of legs, wheels as extensions of feet, books as extensions to eyes, and electronic circuitry, like computers, could be seen as extensions of the nervous system. In this sense, then, interpersonal communication takes place both through **natural media** and **media extensions.** Natural media would be the senses—sound, vision, touch, smell, and taste. Media extensions would be those technological devices that extend natural senses and enable people to communicate across time and long distances and to rapidly duplicate messages. Such media extensions include technologies such as telephone, radio, television, computers, satellite, and fax machines.

CHOOSING YOUR MEDIUM

Because of the development of technology, people must choose which medium (natural or extension) of communication to use for a particular function. Your ancestors didn't have to do this. For example, you might want to ask someone out to a movie and because of your fear of having to face rejection, decide the telephone would be best in this case. Yet you might find the telephone an inappropriate medium for a proposal of marriage. The arrival of picture phones (where you can actually see to whom you are talking) would probably alter the choice further. When you go to a movie, listen to the radio, or play a video, you're making choices that influence your views of life. If you read the McLuhan quotation closely, you'll see he thinks the choice of communication medium profoundly affects communication—that the form may even be more important than the content. He believed the media should be seen less as electronic channels transmitting information than as vehicles to aesthetically alter reality. Can you think of a time you sent or received a message either in person, over the phone, or through the mail and wished it had been sent in a different format or medium? The selected medium of communication is important.

Your choices of media have consequences that can reach into the very essence of your life. We now turn to a discussion of these consequences.

Consequences of Mass Media for Interpersonal Communication

For the most part, as with natural media, people take media extensions for granted. They see such extensions as technology that offers choices for entertainment, relaxation, ways of "killing time," or perhaps as more expedient forms of communication. Most people have not been taught to think critically about media but rather to use media as a pastime. They might think critically when reading a book (as you are now), but usually they don't critically analyze other media such as television, film, or radio. When people use media such as radio or television, the only critical thinking they might engage in has to do with aesthetics: Did they *like* the music, or the film, or the program? Most people are not trained to be **media literate**—that is we are not taught *to*

> *In operational and practical fact, the medium is the message. That is merely to say that the personal and social consequences of any medium… are its meaning and message.*
>
> MARSHALL MCLUHAN
> (1964)

COMMUNICATING SKILLFULLY

Keep a media journal for a week. Write down each time you use an electronic communication device (radio, telephone, computer, and so on) and for how long you use it. Indicate for each entry whether the device was used for any type of interpersonal communication. After a week, bring the journal to class and in small groups discuss how frequently you used communication devices for the purpose of interpersonal communication. How did the use of the device influence your interpersonal relationship? Do you now think a different medium might have been more or equally useful?

develop an informed and critical understanding of the nature of mass media, the techniques used by them, and the impact of these techniques. However, if people are going to understand the impact of media on their lives and relationships, they need to become more media literate. Scholars from several disciplines, including communication, philosophy, sociology, and social psychology, have begun to look beyond the primary effects of media, such as entertainment or information, and to recognize some secondary effects of mass media. From their studies, they have posited models that seek to describe and predict the consequences of the exposure to mass media. It's important to note that testing the effects of the mass media is never easy. Intuitively, there is a natural anxiety that impressionable young minds may be unduly influenced by mass media. Yet developmental psychologists tell us that children are not blank slates waiting to have society's messages written into them. In contrast, adults may see themselves as so educated and aware that they are beyond any possible influence of media. The fact is, each person brings to his or her media use a vast array of information, values, beliefs, and so on. Thus, it's nearly impossible to show a direct link between media and user. What is clear, however, is that media distort reality, and this distortion has a variety of possible consequences on people and their relationships with others. This points to the complexity of communication processes, and the importance of studying them.

> There's something happening here
> What it is ain't exactly clear...
> I think it's time we stop
> Hey, what's that sound
> Everybody look what's going down...
>
> STEPHEN STILLS

Most researchers have examined the way entertainment affects **social learning**. Social learning is the process of observing situations, individuals, or behaviors that affect personal attitudes and communicative behavior. In mass communication theory, this means learning acquired from media images or characterizations. This secondary learning has been investigated by many scholars. Among the most notable are theoreticians from the dramatistic and dramaturgical schools, such as Kenneth Burke, Ernest Bormann, Erving Goffman, and Kevin Durkin. A brief examination of each of these theorists can help you see how dramatic programing can shed light on everyday communication behavior (Adler, et al., 1990).

KENNETH BURKE

Although Burke (1945, 1950, 1966) as a rhetorician did not write about television and film, he did look at the impact of symbol use in human behavior. The **dramatistic** metaphor pervades Kenneth Burke's writing. The term *dramatistic* is used to look at everyday human behaviors as a kind of drama. In other words, you can look at your daily interactions as scenes, with actors, agents, and purposes that are connected by the use of symbols. Burke distinguishes humans by their ability to use symbols as speech, as action. Through the use of symbols, people are unified with each other. As they experience a film or television show, they're presented with verbal and visual symbolic acts of human behavior, which they may accept or reject. To the degree viewers can identify with those images they will be integrated or reinforced in the actions of the viewer.

ERNEST BORMANN

Rhetorician Ernest Bormann (1980) posits that one rhetorical strategy in influencing others is the development of rhetorical fantasies. If these fantasies are successful, they become visions through which others perceive reality and subsequently act. The communicative behavior of individuals is thus shaped not so much by "reality," but rather by a perceived vision of reality that has been influenced by fantasies. Film and television present rhetorical fantasies. As people identify with particular situations, characters, and relationships, they integrate these images into their minds and behavior. You can see this process occur if you watch a group of preschoolers imitating Teenage Mutant Ninja Turtles or as adults when people identify with familiar media characters like bumbling, neurotic Woody Allen, "together" Luke on *Beverly Hills 90210*, or talented Robin Williams as he appeared in *Dead Poets' Society*. Bormann's approach is consistent with the "script theory" of Durkin (1985).

KEVIN DURKIN

Durkin is a social psychologist who suggests people plan their own behavior by constructing scripts. A **script** is a generalized representation that helps people understand the world. Once a viewer adopts a script, the script becomes an organizing principle for how to think and behave. On an abstract level, scripts provide archetypal models for everyday situations: the way Mel Gibson or Eddie Murphy behaves when facing a gang of thugs offers viewers a script for handling more mundane and common threats. On a more literal level, scripts provide clear-cut models for everyday affairs. People may form ideas about family relationships from watching *Married With Children* or *The Simpsons*, and form ideas about what to expect in a romantic relationship from watching such films as *Far and Away*. Thus, by observing films and television, people develop some of the roots of the communication behavior they use in everyday life.

ERVING GOFFMAN

The connection between drama and communication behavior is also apparent in the work of Goffman (1959). As a sociologist, Goffman is interested in **symbolic interaction**—that is, how people coordinate their relationships with others through the manipulation of symbols. For Goffman, interpersonal communication is a presentation by onstage personae whose performance may or may not reflect their offstage personalities. In other words, people are actors who structure their performances to make impressions on audiences. For Goffman, the self is determined by the roles people project in these daily "staged" presentations. People learn these roles through socialization—and there is little question that television and film play an important role in this socialization or enculturation process.

In explaining how this phenomena of secondary learning occurs through mediated experiences, communications professor Edward Whetmore (1991) uses the **cone effect model** (see Figure 13.1).

The cone effect is named after the two cones that make up its design and is a way of looking at how mass media affects people's lives. Whetmore is trying to describe the relationship between real life and **mediated reality**. Take a look at the model. As you can see, everything begins in the circle "real life." This circle represents all of life's experiences that do not directly involve a mass medium. For example, you may walk out into your yard and pet your dog or cat while enjoying the sunshine. These kinds of experiences were available before there was mass media.

Is this real, or is it Memorex?

*A POPULAR 1970s
COMMERCIAL*

FIGURE 13.1

*Cone Effect Model
From* MEDIA: Form, Content, and Consequences of Mass Communication, *Updated Fourth edition by Edward Jay Whetmore, © 1991 by Wadsworth, Inc. Reprinted by permission of the publisher.*

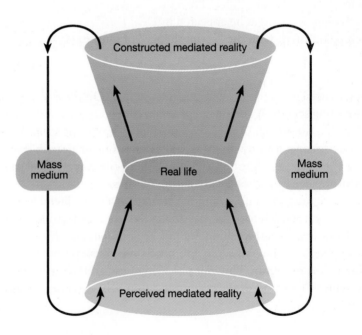

Parts of real-life experiences are used by a communicator to form **constructed media reality (CMR)**. CMR may consist of a movie, a television show, or a fashion ad, among others. Although CMR is based on real life, it's important to remember there are many differences between the two. Whetmore (1991, p. 12) writes,

> Basically CMR tends to be funnier, sexier, more intense, more colorful, and more violent than real life. After all, nobody wrote a song about an ordinary relationship. Songs are written about special relationships, ones that have a great deal of intensity. Television situation comedies may picture dozens of funny and entertaining things happening every half hour, but in real life we are lucky if one funny thing happens to us in an average day. Novels are written about larger-than-life people, those who have special qualities.

Once the "blown up" CMR is completed, it is transmitted through a mass medium to the audience. What people get from this use of media is called **perceived media reality (PMR)**. People's perception of media reality takes up much of the day, but recall (from Chapter 3 on perception) that perception is a highly selected process. This selection process begins when you choose which medium you want to use and how closely you want to pay attention to it. For example, you might just have the radio on for the noise or company it represents or you might listen very closely to a lyric. You might watch a television show and almost immediately forget what you saw or it may be so important that you might video tape it to watch later or share with others.

The final step in the model involves how the PMR affects real life or what we called earlier social learning. Examples of how people might take information from media reality include how fashion magazines influence the way people dress; how the news on the economy in one part of the country affects how people in a very different part of the country think they had better save money; or even how the viewing of "heavy metal" rock videos influence male–female relationships.

Let's walk through an example of the cone effect, using a fashion layout in a magazine. People generally dress in clothes, so the cone effect begins with reality. When the photographer, layout artist, makeup stylist, clothing designer, modeling agency, and so on put together a photo shoot, this would represent the constructed media reality. The CMR is exaggerated and more glamorous because of the location of the shoot, the "assisted beauty" of the model, the lighting, and so on. The photos are "enhanced" in the process to capture what the editor or ad agency wants to promote and is sent through a mass medium such as a magazine or television commercial or even embedded within the flow of a program. When you see the ad and interpret the message, this is your perceived media reality. Perhaps you like the fashions and would like to buy them, or you think you wouldn't look good in them, or you may think how glamorous it would be to be a model. From this step, your PMR goes back to

CONSIDERING CRITICAL THINKING

Select three different media to observe (for example, film, television, and a magazine) and, using the cone effect model, describe each step of the process in the media you observed. In small groups, discuss the results of your examination. When you look at how perceived media reality impacts reality, try to think of both positive as well as negative examples.

Calvin and Hobbes © 1987 Watterson. Reprinted with permission of Universal Press Syndicate.

alter reality. It may be you try to dress as the fashion ad depicted, or you might abstain from a meal, trying to achieve the thinness of the fashion model, and so on.

In summary, research has shown secondary learning has a powerful influence on everyone and hence, on everyone's relationships. Let's now turn to issues of relationships.

MEDIA IMAGES AND MEDIA REALITY

Strategies and expectations in relationships come to people through the proces of social learning. In the age of mass communication, you have viewed many hours of popular television and film. Through your viewing, you have indirectly developed impressions and expectations of what relationships should be like, particularly in scenes of intimacy that would not otherwise be available to view. For example, you might recall the first time you saw a romantic scene in a movie. Although young children might giggle and laugh at such scenes, adults see behavior that is generally conducted in private, and hence not available to witness. In fact, the very private nature of romantic intimate behaviors may be what initially makes children uncomfortable to the point of laughter. In this sense then, media become part of the world view of romantic actions. Comstock and Strzyzewski (1990) argue that media have the potential to influence interaction in close personal relationships in both antisocial and prosocial ways—that is, ways that divide people from others and that help connect them. We'll now take a closer look at media's potential influence on behavior and begin by looking at the effect of media on intrapersonal communication.

Self Identity and the Media

Remember from Chapter 4 and the work of George Herbert Mead how important a healthy self-concept is to relational development. As said, self-concepts are formed through a reflective appraisal process in what people tell themselves and how others respond to them. In their book *INTERMEDIA* (1986, p. 28) Gumpert and Cathcart have suggested that

> television, radio, and film provide feedback which reinforces, negate
> and/or verify an individual's self-image. Portraits developed in novels,
> magazines, and newspapers have long served in the formulation and
> reinforcement of socially acceptable and unacceptable self-images.

(See Novak (1988), and Kidd (1975) for detailed discussions of this process.)

Direct experience, indirect experience, and your observations of symbolic behavior are all major influences on your sense of self. Weaver and Wakshlag (1986) suggest that when direct experience is lacking or ambiguous, perception is formed through lower-order influences such as television. In this way, then, television and film characters may serve as models for your own sense of self. As children grow and develop, an important part of the self-image forming is sex role development. The term **sex role** refers to the collection of behaviors that a given society deems more appropriate for members of one sex to the other. In areas of work, leisure and interpersonal relationships, specific ways of behaving are more likely to be adopted by and expected of members of a specific sex. Let's look more specifically at sex role development now.

Sex Role Development

The messages of mass media are among the most controversial in human communication. Television, radio, newspapers, and books can command enormous audiences and have the power to disseminate images, attitudes, and values widely and repetitively. Over the last fifteen years or so, and very much influenced by the women's movement, much research energy has been devoted to documenting the sex role content of the mass media. The principal findings of this work are summarized in Table 13.1. We can preface them by saying that the evidence confirms what many expect (see cone effect model)— that the media distort presentations of gender (Durkin, 1986).

The effects of these messages on sex role development is much harder to document. Variables such as the amount of viewing, age, and sex of the viewer, and viewer expectations all influence the process, which is anything but straightforward. In one sense, mass media images about the role of the sexes in U.S. society is a simple one: it is a stereotyped exaggeration of differences. In another sense, though, the media images' effects on receivers are very complex. At most, we can say that mass media messages about male and female roles are an important personal and public concern (Durkin, 1986).

COMMUNICATING SKILLFULLY

SEX ROLES ON PRIME-TIME TELEVISION

Watch prime-time television (between 8–10 p.m.) for three nights. Keep a journal tracking male and female roles as depicted. How close do your findings come to those presented in Table 13.1?

In addition, or as a variation of this activity, track the number of characters of different races. Bring your journals to class and discuss your findings. How are your findings similar or different? If different, to what do you attribute this? Are sex role presentations changing? (Be specific, give examples.) Discuss the possible consequences of this media reality on viewers. Discuss the influence of media sex roles in your own life. How do media effects on sex role development influence intrapersonal and hence, interpersonal communication?

Just as media can present models for self-image, media also present images of interpersonal relationships. Let's look at these images.

Interpersonal Media Images

Researchers who are concerned about the influence of media content on the perceptions and ensuing interpersonal interaction patterns of media viewers have focused their research primarily on the visual media of film and television. Because television is now established as the foremost leisure activity of a large portion of the world's population, and is viewed regularly by all members of the family for several hours a day, the bulk of the research relates to the effects of television on the viewer. Durkin (1986, p. 1) writes,

TABLE 13.1

MEDIA AND SEX-ROLE CONTENT

- There is an imbalance in the frequency with which males and females appear. Males appear more often, in a ratio of nearly 2 to 1.

- Males are more often the stars or central characters.

- Males are more often employed than females and have higher-status occupations.

- The majority of women in television are under age 30, a fact closely linked to the presentation of women as sex objects and clearly not an accurate representation of actual population.

- Males do between 84 percent and 94 percent of voiceovers on commercials.

What might be the effects…of growing up in a television culture, where one mass medium has the unprecedented power to reach simultaneously into the living rooms of every household and to present vividly selected images of events and lifestyles that are often depicted for their entertainment value rather than their social desirability?

MODELING BEHAVIORS

In their 1990 paper "Using Television and Film to Study Interpersonal Communication," Margaret Haefner and Sandra Metts summarized research that demonstrates the power of the media to shape everyday interpersonal communication behavior. Their research suggests that in depicting interpersonal relationships, both prosocial and antisocial messages are present. **Prosocial messages** include acts of affiliation such as expression of feelings, altruism, and self-disclosure. **Antisocial messages** are disaffiliative acts such as violence or verbally aggressive behavior. Their findings are summarized in Table 13.2.

As with the influence of media on sex role development, the role of media in shaping interpersonal style is anything but direct. Yet the media do have an impact. Look at the findings in Table 13.2—although these findings aren't conclusive, what are the possible social consequences of viewing such behaviors? Most people would say they use television and other media of this nature for escape, leisure, and relaxation. These portrayals are not of real relationships, but fiction. Unfortunately, even entertainment programs carry these sometimes deafening messages of what is appropriate in interpersonal behaviors. So what are we to do?

We started this chapter by saying we would be exploring two primary themes: (1) how media actually serve a linking function that helps to make interpersonal communication possible over distances of time and space; and (2) how media serve as models for interpersonal behavior and relationships. With this knowledge, what can you do to maximize your interpersonal style?

STRATEGIES FOR MEDIATED COMMUNICATION

In previous chapters, we talked about particular communication skills. In this chapter it might be most appropriate to talk about **interpersonal communication strategies**, rather than skills. A strategy, unlike a skill, implies a method or plan devised for making or doing something or attaining an end. Let's examine four important strategies in dealing with mediated forms of communication.

1. *Becoming Media Literate.* The first concept is the precursor to the three that follow. The concept of *media literacy* refers to the ability to view or

In our society only the human family surpasses television in its capacity to communicate values, provide role models, form consciences and motivate human behavior.

ELLWOOD KIESER
(1992)

CONSIDERING ETHICS

As mentioned earlier, there has been controversy in the media about the underrepresentation of ethnic and racial minorities and women. Generally, casting directors don't cast African Americans or other racial minorities for Shakespeare characters, and so on. Imagine you're an female actor of Irish ancestry who has been cast to play an ethnic role other than Irish in a film. Members of this ethnic group protest your casting in such a role because they think their ethnic group is already underrepresented in film. Also, they claim that only a member of their ethnic group could give an accurate portrayal of their ethnicity. What is your ethical responsibility in this situation? Do you agree and step aside? Do you say there are too few roles for women already so you can't possibly give this up? Decide on your response, and share it with other members of the class. How much agreement is there among the class?

"read" media and to decode information presented on several levels. When you can decode constructed media reality from perceived media reality and hence become more aware of the impact of form and content on your intra- and interpersonal lives, you're becoming media literate. A media-literate perspective allows you to use media constructively, while being less likely to be used by media. This chapter can help you become media literate.

2. *Making appropriate technology choices.* It is important to realize that with the number of communication technologies available to us now, and with more just over the horizon, how to choose the appropriate media for any particular interpersonal task. Your selection may carry a message every bit as important as the content you send. The telephone sometimes permits more intimacy than face-to-face communication. In fact, many people would find it impossible to carry on relationships without telephones! Thinking what you hope to accomplish through your communication can help you to make the correct choice of a communication medium.

3. *Choices of time and place.* When and where to communicate with someone is an equally important choice. In work relationships, for example, the use of technology has been blurring the lines between office and home. Many employees take work home or even work out of their homes often connected to the office or work site by cellular phones in their car, and phone lines, fax machines, and computers via modems from their residences. As mentioned earlier in the chapter, the telephone has significant effects on people's interpersonal lives and these newer extensions are beginning to have similar effects. In deciding strat-

The pervasiveness of media in our daily lives masks the hypnotic and often subliminal messages about interpersonal relationships.

TABLE 13.2

PROSOCIAL AND ANTISOCIAL BEHAVIORS IN INTERPERSONAL RELATIONSHIPS ON TELEVISION

• Families high on the socioeconomic ladder are portrayed as less happy, while working-class families were shown to be most happy.

• TV family interactions are overwhelmingly affiliative.

• Conflict interactions occur most frequently between husbands and wives or in dyads with a male child.

• The occurrence of nonaffiliative conflict acts has been increasing.

• Even in situation comedies there is an underlying tone of hostility.

• Many newer programs (*Married With Children* and the *The Simpsons*) not only have good-natured teasing, but are openly offensive by including cutting personal attacks. Parents and children all participate in insulting one another, and they seem to take delight in humiliating each other.

• Unlike TV dads of the past, fathers are now seen as bumbling and childish, often "shown up" by their wives, girlfriends, or children.

• Fathers are most inept when called on to help with their daughters' problems.

• Husband-and-wife conflicts most often occur because of jealousy over relationships that are real, imagined, or considered likely to occur.

CONSIDERING CULTURE

MINORITY IMAGES ON TELEVISION

Because television has such a tremendous influence on the way people perceive reality, concern has been growing about the role of minority groups in programing. Surveys have indicated that 98 percent of U.S. homes have television sets, and the average family watches television more than six hours per day. During this viewing time, they're exposed to many lifestyles, attitudes, and values that television depicts as "typical American."

Although a cursory look at television in the 1990s might prompt one to believe the underrepresentation of minorities in television is no longer true, research suggests it is still true (Hammer, 1992). Many minority groups are most notable by their absence. Can you name a major Filipino-American actor? How about a Chinese-American actor, an actor with a physical limitation? The list could go on and on. Even when minorities are present, television often distorts the role of minorities in our society. According to Hammer (1992, p. 70),

Nearly two decades ago, in a TV era replete with ethnic stereotypes, a teenager named J.J. strutted through the ABC series Good Times, flashing a flubber-lipped grin and punctuating the air with his catch phrase, "Dy-no-MITE!" But if anyone thought such caricatures of African American life had gone the way of Fred Sanford's junkyard truck, they haven't taken a look at prime time this year.

Blacks and Hispanics are increasingly making their presence felt in television, but unfortunately, in roles that are less than accurate or positive. In Hammer's article "Must Blacks Be Buffoons?" he quotes actor Bill Cosby who has attacked the networks for spewing out what he calls "drive-by images," which, he said, reinforce shallow stereotypes. Staples and Jones (1985) contend that the people who control television seem to believe that the public feels most comfortable with African Americans playing the role of fools, criminals, servants, and entertainers. Although these roles are stereotyped and therefore untrue, people still believe them simply because the mass accessibility of television has multiplied the negative media images of African Americans.

With the one exception of The Cosby Show, the depiction of African American men and women playing demeaning roles has a negative impact on viewers regardless of race or ethnicity. Because of television, many tend to envision the typical black community as violent, dirty, and dangerous, where drug deals and murders are a common sight. Television ignores middle-class

CULTURE, CONTINUED

African Americans as well as middle-class members of other minorities. Staples and Jones (1985) describe the depiction of black communities as "piss in the halls and blood on the stairs."

This stereotyped view can lead many people to believe that African Americans are always the ones to commit murders in their crime-infested neighborhoods where there are no such thing as "family values." White people, in contrast, are the only ones who can get a good education, jobs, and afford to buy a nice home.

This false image is most damaging to African-American children. They receive this distorted media reality that only white people are doing interesting and important things. Viewers, both black and white, perceive that heroes are most often white. This helps to devalue the self-images of black children.

Another area of television that influences young African-Americans in their perception of themselves is romantic roles with scenes of intimacy. Television is often criticized for scenes that depict hot and steamy sex. However, sexual scenes with African Americans are almost totally absent. Black love, according to Ebony magazine ("Black Love," 1991), is depicted as something forbidden, exotic, and far removed from white entanglements. African American actors seldom portray characters involved in tender and sensitive love scenes.

Although love and sex are taboo for black actors, they play a significant role in crime and acts of violence. Viewers and especially the black child are exposed to a media world that is populated by black people who are prostitutes, rapists, murderers, hustlers, and thieves, while their white counterparts become their victims, pursuers, or judges.

Because of these very images, Bill Cosby created his show to move away from these stereotyped images. He said,

> *I would rather show life in a positive sense. I want to show that we have the same kind of wants and needs as other American families....I want to show Black people that they have something to be proud of. (Staples and Jones, 1985, p. 18)*

So the "make-believe" media give people their perceived media reality. It's important to realize that African-American people don't typically deal drugs, join gangs, and kill others. Many go to college, become engineers, speech teachers, businesspeople, successful lawyers, and even, U.S. Supreme Court Justices. Black people fall in love, have intimate relationships, begin families, and lead normal lives. And like others in our society, they feel pain when they're condemned or ridiculed.

egy about technologies and interpersonal relationships, it's important to determine which technology is most important, but it can be equally important to determine the appropriateness of time and place for communication. When is it OK to telephone someone in the evening, and what are the boundaries of private home life, school, and work? When is technology becoming intrusive, and when is it serving the linking function? Conscious awareness of such questions can help you to form appropriate communication strategies with new technologies.

4. *Thinking Critically About Media, Values, and Interpersonal Communication.* Media are all around. Television is probably a part of your home life and provides information and images on a regular basis. Although you may watch television for entertainment and escapism, the content also carries persuasive messages. The persuasive messages come to you not only through commercials, but in the form of images you compare yourself to. These images impact sex role development as well as other foundations of your intrapersonal world. Also, these persuasive messages are patterned rather than random; they selectively reinforce certain types of interpersonal behaviors rather than others. As James Chesebro writes (1986, p. 510),

> These communication systems contain values, values which promote certain life orientations and not others. There is indeed, an intimate relationship among the popular television series we watch, the ways in which we communicate, and the values which govern our lives.

Although television messages are primarily affiliative, they consist of both prosocial and antisocial messages. In addition, these messages most often operate outside awareness. To raise your ability to deal with mass media messages, the best strategy is to use your critical thinking skills. Examine media messages for what they are—constructed media reality. When you keep this in mind, you can gain positive insights about interpersonal behavior from antisocial as well as prosocial messages. For example, media can provide outstanding examples illustrating communicative behavior. By watching the rise and fall of the romance between Billy Crystal and Meg Ryan in *When Harry Met Sally* you can gain an understanding of relational stages (see Chapter 9) that go beyond what you could gain from lecture or reading material alone. Critical thinking skills let you evaluate the interdependence between media and relationships.

INTERPERSONAL COMMUNICATION, NEW TECHNOLOGIES, AND THE FUTURE

Interpersonal communication lets people meet strong needs for relationships with others. This millennium has brought an explosion of change and an onslaught of high technology that has impacted relationship development. The future will continue to be complex, fast-paced, and turbulent, and your ability to develop strong, healthy interpersonal relationships in families, work situations, and friendships will be tested. The pace of life could lead you to fragmented and strained relationships. Technology can be a boon or a hindrance, depending on your ability to use and understand it. High technology will become even higher tech. We're just around the corner (and some believe we have turned that corner) from intelligent machines, multisensual media, and highly evolved artificial creatures. People will continue to explore space and try to discover other worlds. At the same time, the human brain will be an inner frontier. There will be a deluge of choices of media. Will they help people to "nourish our hearts and minds," as Ellwood Kieser's comments earlier in this chapter suggested, or will the heart be lonely? *Time* magazine ("Beyond the Year 2000," 1992) contains an article about the invention of virtual reality in computers. The author of the article states that virtual sex—the most intimate of pleasures—will be available on-line—via modems and computers.

One thing we can say for sure is that people will continue to need and value human relationships. At the same time, there will be new and faster communication technologies in the future. People seem to have an insatiable appetite for communication devices. The task will be to use them appropriately and not to be used by them. This is only possible through conscious, intelligent effort.

LOOKING BACK - LOOKING FORWARD

In the last chapter, we examined the role of cultural differences in interpersonal communication. In this chapter, we've been examining the role media technology plays in relationships. We've explored the potential positive and negative impact media has on relational development and identified four strategies for dealing with mediated communication. Lastly, we have posited several ideas about interpersonal communication, new technologies, and the twenty-first century. These are speculations, but several are just over the horizon.

REVIEW TERMS AND CONCEPTS

mass media 321	social learning 328	perceived media reality (PMR) 331
E-Mail 324	dramatistic 329	sex role development 333
mediated communication 325	script 329	prosocial messages 335
mass communication 325	symbolic interaction 330	antisocial messages 335
natural media 327	cone effect model 330	interpersonal communication strategies 335
media extensions 327	mediated reality 330	
media literacy 328	constructed media reality (CMR) 331	

PUTTING THEORY INTO PRACTICE

FOR DISCUSSION:

1. Spotting long-term trends about communication and technology is difficult but not impossible. One way is to spot differences, small and large, that seem to be happening now. Another key is knowing what is likely to change and focusing on it. For a small group or class discussion, discuss what you believe will be changes in communication technology that will affect the number and quality of your interpersonal relationships.

2. For many college and university students, media literacy is a new concept. However, in many countries in the world, including Japan, Canada, Australia, and England, media literacy is taught in schools to young children. Hold a class or small-group discussion about the place of media literacy in U.S. schools. How important is media literacy? Should elementary schools teach media literacy? If so, what should be covered? Why?

SKILL BUILDERS:

1. Using a theme from Jerry Mander's book *Four Arguments for the Elimination of Television* (1978) organize a class debate "Resolved, That Television Should Be Eliminated." This can be an excellent way to

bring together many of the issues that surround the notion of media effects.

2.Divide the class into three groups. Each group takes one of the following topics: Burke's dramaticism; Boreman's rhetorical fantasies; or Durkin's script theory. Ask each group to come up with a creative way to demonstrate the theory such as role-playing, a video montage, or using music excerpts.

3.In this chapter, we discussed how reality has influenced media or media has influenced reality. In the 1992 U.S. Presidential race, a television program, *Murphy Brown* was criticized by vice president Dan Quayle as undermining family values and glamorizing single parenthood as an "alternative lifestyle." In small groups, brainstorm as many examples as you can of media influences on reality and vice versa.

FOR EXTENDED STUDY

Durkin, K. (1985). *Television, sex roles and children*. Philadelphia: Open University Press.

This book makes an especially important contribution to understanding the potency of media messages on sex role development. It's an enjoyable and easy-to-read book that cautions against any simplistic notion of media influence.

Gumpert, G., & Cathcart, R. (Eds.). (1986) *INTERMEDIA: Interpersonal communication in a media world*. (3rd ed.). Oxford, England: Oxford University Press.

This book represents a collection of essays from international scholars. Although the reading may be difficult for lower-division students, it's a valuable resource, as it explores a range of topics in media and interpersonal communication.

Mander, J. (1978). *Four arguments for the elimination of television*. New York: Quill Publications.

Jerry Mander spent fifteen years as an advertising executive dealing with television accounts. In this book he argues that television is so destructive to individuals and society that it needs to be eliminated.

McLuhan, Marshall. (1964). *Understanding media*. New York: McGraw-Hill.

Marshall McLuhan's writings provide fascinating insights into the role of media in everyday life. His use of metaphor is both playful and insightful. An early, classic text on media.

Parenti, Michael. (1993). *Inventing reality: The politics of the mass media*. (2nd ed.). New York: St. Martin's Press.

Parenti's books take a very close and critical look at constructed media reality.

active listening
Listening in which a receiver focuses on what is being said. Also can include empathic and critical listening.

adaptors A classification term coined by Paul Ekman and William Friesen for nonverbal movements learned in childhood as part of a patterned activity. There are three types of adaptors: (1) self-adaptors, such as hair brushing, remnants of a learned activity toward one's own body; (2) alter-adaptors, or movements learned in the process of interpersonal relations such as restless movements of our hands and feet, because of anxiety; and (3) object-adaptors, such as using a tool like a pencil, gestures that indicate rearrangement of the environment.

adumbration To foreshadow or to partially disclose. In social interaction, one of the characteristics of nonverbal communication is to foreshadow or give cues to what should happen next.

affect displays A term coined by Paul Ekman and William Friesen to classify nonverbal body expressions that reflect the emotional state of the communicator.

affection Shutz's term for the need to establish and maintain satisfactory relations with people with respect to love and affection.

all-channel network A pattern of family communication in which all members freely exchange messages in all directions.

allness The erroneous belief that one person could possibly know all there is to know about a particular thing or topic.

ambiguous communication Behaviors or language that have several different meanings.

antisocial messages Dissaffiliative acts such as violence or verbally aggressive behavior.

artifactual communication Includes all those artifacts or elements we add to our bodies, such as earrings, watches, necklaces, eyeglasses, hairpieces, wigs, eyeliners, perfumes, and other cosmetic devices. Other artifacts that act as extensions of ourselves can include the cars we drive, the way we decorate our rooms, the "name brand" sweat shirts or athletic shoes we wear.

blindering Impedes interpersonal understanding by minimizing one's perceptual arena. Involves seeing only parts of the picture or situation or viewing things only in certain ways.

chain network The pattern of family communication in which family members pass on information from one person to the next, one at a time, until the message reaches its intended destination.

co-culture Subgroups or subcultures within a culture. The term *co-culture* has come to replace the term *subculture* because *subculture* carried a negative connotation of groups as being "sub"—diminished or less than, the main culture.

cogent reasoning Thinking that has justified premises, relevant information, and valid reasoning.

communication climate The emotional tone of a relationship between two or more people.

communication competence The ability to understand and use constitutive and regulative rules; also called *pragmatic* competence.

communication dissonance Inharmonious or even incongruent communications.

communication mismatch A term used by Regan to describe communication that is misunderstood on any of three levels: verbal and nonverbal, language functions, or culture.

communication package Verbal skills and nonverbal modes of communication.

complementary relationship A union in which one partner provides what the other lacks.

cone effect model A heuristic model by

Whetmore that looks at the relationship between real life and what we receive by way of various media.

confirmation Communication that serves to socially validate us in our relationships and centers on the three main clusters of recognition, acknowledgment, and endorsement.

constitutive rules Rules that show us how to recognize speech acts.

constructed media reality (CMR) The manufacturing of media messages by publishers, writers, directors, or producers and then transmitted to receivers. Basically CMR tends to be funnier, sexier, more intense, more colorful, and more violent than real life.

control Shutz's term for the need to establish and maintain satisfactory relations with people with respect to power and control.

coordinated management of meaning (CMM) Pearce and Cronen's theory explaining that

we know how to use language not because we have labels or a series of nouns, but because we follow rules that tell us how to understand and produce speech acts.

covert culture Culture that is not directly taught to us, not easily describable to others, and passed on in many discreet ways.

critical listening Listening that involves assessing of what is being said for its logical validity and use of supporting evidence.

critical thinking The ability to examine any idea to see if it is logically valid and supported with sound evidence.

cross-cultural phenomenon In a communication context, any differences because of culture that affect the communication between two or more people.

cultural diversity Differences between separate cultures and between members of a particular culture (co-culture).

cultural information Language, values,

beliefs, habits, and practices shared by members of a group.

cultural variability The differences that distinguish one culture from another.

culture The shared social experience, the bulk of understandings humans have made to survive in a particular place in their world.

culture shock The feeling of estrangement or displacement that may be felt by people visiting another culture when they are confronted by differences between their own culture's ways of life and that of the culture they are visiting.

developmental view A view of communication that encompasses the situational view and implies there are degrees of interpersonalness to consider. The depth and quality of communication between communicators develops over time as one learns cultural, sociological and psychological information about another person. Also, from this perspective, interpersonal communication is not limited to

two people, nor is face-to-face communication necessary. From the developmental perspective, all our initial communications with another person are by necessity impersonal or nonpersonal.

dialectic A clash of ideas between at least two people, involving questions and answers.

dialogic listening Mutually sculpted listening in which two or more people build a conversation together.

disconfirmation A communication pattern typified by ignoring someone's communication or presence.

downward communication Communication that goes from supervisors to employees in an organization.

dramatistic Kenneth Burke's term, used to look at everyday human behaviors as a kind of drama.

dyadic communication Communication between two people. *Dyad* is a technical term first used by nineteenth-century German sociologist Georg Simmel, who coined it to mean the idea of two people in a system of repetitive social interactions.

ectomorphs Tall, thin, and fragile body shape.

elaborated codes Part of Bernstein's language classification scheme in which he associates middle-class speech patterns in homes and schools. These codes are generally longer, grammatically complex, and flexible.

e-mail Interactive electronic mail sent over computer networks.

emblems A classification term coined by Paul Ekman and William Friesen for nonverbal gestural equivalents of a word or phrase.

emotion Internal feeling states that are primarily displayed through nonverbal behavior.

empathic listening An attempt to understand and put oneself in the place of a speaker.

empathy The attempt to understand another's situation by feeling what he or she may be feeling.

endomorphs Soft, round, and fat body shape.

enthymeme A partial syllogism based on probability rather than certainty.

ethical communication Expressing the truth and avoiding deception or manipulation in relationships.

ethnic Relating to racial or ancestral heritage of people classed according to common traits and customs.

ethnocentric The practice of judging other cultures as deficient to one's own.

Eurocentric Knowledge and beliefs based on the ideas of Western culture.

evaluation interview An interview, usually between supervisor and an an employee. The purpose is to review and judge the employee's job performance.

evidence Support for arguments, which can take the form of facts, testimony or statistics.

fact-inference confusion A failure to distinguish between what is inferred in a given situation and what is actually observed or known.

fallacies Errors in reasoning.

family as a system A special set of people with relationships between them that are established, maintained, and form patterns over time.

family of origin The specific experiences one encounters while growing up that reflect multigenerational transmissions and ethnic–cultural heritages.

FIRO The acronym that stands for fundamental interpersonal relations orientation.

first impression An initial view of a person or a situation based on perceptual interpretations.

friendship A close union between people who know each other well and who share strong affection.

gaze Study of eye behavior in social interaction.

gaze aversion The practice, common among people in normal conversation, of looking at the speaker or receiver at times and at other times looking away.

gaze avoidance Eye behavior that limits or precludes any eye contact with another person.

genderlects Differences in male and female conversational style (term coined by Tannen).

general semantics An area of communication that looks at how our behavior and attitudes are influenced by language and meanings.

global village Term coined by media theorist Marshall McLuhan to describe the impact of technology in psychologically shrinking the world.

groupthink The irrational tendency of groups to strive for consensus rather than a critical examination of ideas.

gunnysacking A communication game in which someone holds back real or perceived grievances.

halo effect

A perceptual error that occurs when a particular characteristic or individual trait profoundly influences all other impressions of a person.

haptics An element in our nonverbal repertoire that refers to touching behaviors.

hearing The physiological process of recording information from someone else.

high- and low-context A continuum that examines cultural variability between cultures that are bound by tradition, which shapes behavior and lifestyles, and those cultures that lack a bond with tradition and therefore their present behaviors and lifestyles are more fluid, and subject to change and unpredictability.

identity cues Nonverbal factors such as clothing, hairstyle, or decoration of office that provide a means for making judgments about people.

illustrators A classification term coined by Paul Ekman and William Friesen for nonverbal movements that are directly linked to speech because they illustrate what is being said orally and for the most part are intentional acts.

imitation The stage in a child's development of mimicking the behavior of adults—usually parents.

inclusion Shutz's term for an inner drive to establish and maintain a satisfactory relation with people with respect to interaction and association.

individualism–collectivism A continuum that examines cultural variability between cultures that place emphasis on the development of the individual and those that emphasize the importance of the group.

induction The logical process of organizing specific pieces of evidence to draw a general conclusion.

inference The making of a judgment based on accepted premises or evidence. The drawing of a conclusion from presented data.

information listening Listening to absorb and understand data from a speaker.

intelligent reasoning Thinking characterized by careful thought rather than reactive behavior. Like **critical thinking,** it includes an examination of logical validity and evidence before drawing conclusions.

intercultural communication Interpersonal transactions between people from different cultural backgrounds.

intercultural competence Motivation, knowledge, and skills necessary to communicate effectively in intercultural contexts.

interdependence A relationship in which each person feels a sense of personhood. That is: they matter, they can influence and be influenced by the other and they can help and be helped by the other.

interpersonal communication Communication between two or more people char-acterized by messages flowing back and forth. Interpersonal commun-ication can be different than **dyadic** communication since more than two can engage in interpersonal communication.

interpersonal communication strategies A deliberate plan to communicate in a certain way designed to achieve a specific effect with someone else.

interpersonal needs Those needs that motivate our development of interpersonal relationships. According to William Shutz, these needs are the need for inclusion, the need for control, and the need for affection.

interpersonal style Learned communication behaviors that incorporate our cultural and personality into our transactions with others.

interpersonalness A term describing the depth or level of communication going on in a dyad.

interpretation Part of the perceptual process in which meaning is given to stimuli that has been selected and organized.

intimate relationship Close union that lasts over a long period of time, involves a high degree of self-disclosure, and contains strong affection.

intrapersonal communication Self-talk or internal conversation. Intrapersonal communication contains the same elements as communication with someone else such as reasoning, emotion and questioning.

Johari window A model developed by Joseph Luft and Harry Ingram, that attempts to illustrate the levels of self-disclosure we have in different relationships.

kinesics A term coined by Ray Birdwhistell for body movements such as gestures, posture, and movement including eye behavior.

language The rule-governed use of symbols, consisting of phonemes, morphemes, and syntax. It is how we share our internal world with others—how we negotiate realities in daily life.

leadership style The manner a leader uses to motivate followers. Styles can include, but are not limited to,

autocratic, democratic, and participative.

liberal arts perspective A way to seek truth through the unity of knowledge. Liberal arts education also includes the principle that learning can only be an act of the learner.

limerance Romantic love characterized by feelings of euphoria and subsequent let-down, especially if the other partner does not reciprocate the feelings.

mass communication The use of a medium or technological device used to reach many people.

mass media Plural form of the term *mass medium*, meaning the technological devices that are used for the purpose of mass communication.

media extensions Those technological devices that extend our natural senses and allow us the ability to communicate across time, across long distances, and the ability to rapidly duplicate messages. These media extensions would include technologies such as telephone, radio, television,

computers, satellite, and fax machines.

media literacy To develop an informed and critical understanding of the nature of mass media, the techniques used by them, and the impact of these techniques.

media reality Reality as constructed and transmitted by the mass media to viewers or readers for the purposes of entertaining, informing or educating.

mediated communication Human communication assisted by technology.

mesomorphs Bony, muscular, and athletic body shapes.

motivation The impulse or stimulus, either internal or external, that causes a person to act. Originally derived from the Latin word *movere*, which means to move or persuade.

multicultural A term to characterize cultural behaviors that are influenced by a number of different cultural heritages.

natural media Our senses—sound, vision, touch, smell, and taste.

needs hierarchy A model developed by Abraham Maslow, suggesting that needs are arranged in a hierarchical order from physiological needs to more psychological needs.

networks The two-way flow of messages from one family member to one or more other members or significant others outside the family.

noble selves A communication trait described in the theory of rhetorical sensitivity of individuals who don't adjust their communication strategies for others and stick to their personal ideals.

nonverbal behavior Those attributes or actions of humans, other than the use of words themselves, which have socially shared meaning, and have potential for feedback from the receiver.

nonverbal communication Those attributes or actions of humans, other than the use of words themselves, which have socially shared meaning, are intentionally sent or interpreted as intentional, are consciously sent or consciously received, and have potential for feedback from the receiver.

open system Suggests that the family unit is influenced by and influences its external environment.

open-mindedness A way of thinking in which you withhold judgment until you've examined the evidence in a situation. Open-mindedness is the opposite of prejudice.

organization Part of the perceptual process in which stimuli are arranged in some form that has meaning for the individual and helps make sense of the information.

organizational communication The flow of messages in an institution. This can include downward, lateral, and upward communication. Also, the relationships that develop between people who work together.

organizational grapevine The informal transmission of messages within an organization. Often includes rumor and gossip.

overt culture Directly taught to us, describable, and passed on to our offspring.

paralinguistics Sounds accompanying speech such as laughing, crying, tsking, sighing, as well as pitch, articulation, rhythm, resonance, tempo, volume, yelling, whispering, moaning, whining, belching, yawning, and vocal segregates (noises we make to take the place of words) like "uh," "uh-huh," "uh-uh," "shh" and other clicks, snorts, and sniffs!

paraphrasing Providing a summary to someone else of what you've heard him or her say.

passive listening The process of catching part of the communication from someone else but missing large pieces of the message.

peak communication The innermost or core level of Powell's levels of communication. Powell believes we accomplish nearly complete disclosure and empathy at the peak level. At this peak level of communication, self-disclosure touches the core of personality—it is both deep and broad, intimate and mutual.

perceived media reality (PMR) The understandings or world view we "learn" from using various media.

perception The process involving the selection, organization, and interpretation of sensory data, that helps us make sense of our world.

perception checking The process of seeking more information to gain a more accurate perception. This process involves describing the observed behavior, looking for possible interpretations, and seeking clarification.

person perception The process by which we make predictions about how people will behave. The predictions are based on observations and conclusions about people's personality traits.

personal style Learned communication values that we integrate with our personality, ethnicity, and cultural background.

personification The ability of an infant to make a clear distinction between self and a parent figure.

phatic communion A term first used by John Powell to describe ritualized "small talk" such as greetings.

prediction-making data Information we gain through interacting with another person that helps us understand and predict their communicative behavior.

prejudice Literally, a judgment made without examination of evidence. Prejudice is the opposite of open-mindedness.

prepotent need The lowest unmet need in Maslow's hierarchy of needs.

problem solving groups Groups in an organization set up to share expertise and critical thinking about problems that affect the organization.

prosocial and antisocial behavior Everyday behaviors

that are also observable in television. Prosocial behavior includes acts of affiliation like expression of feelings, altruism and self-disclosure, while antisocial behavior includes disaffiliative acts such as violence or verbally aggressive behavior.

proxemics The study of how we unconsciously structure microspace—the distance between people in daily transactions, the organization of space in our houses and buildings, and ultimately the layout of our towns.

pseudo-listening Pretending to listen without really doing so. Giving other people the impression you're attending to what they say.

psychological information Includes a person's idiosyncratic, learned experiences and behaviors.

qualitative changes The changes relationships may undergo. As the relationship qualitatively changes, it becomes more interpersonal. As we get to know a person

better, we change our predictions to include the psychological makeup of the person.

quality of communication This concept emerges from the writing of John Stewart, who writes about how the quality of one's life is directly related to the quality of one's communication. Quality, in this instance, is one's development of communication potential and skills and the ability to select appropriate communication strategies that maximize one's relationships with others.

re-entry shock Occurs when we return home after an extended stay in another country and have to readjust to our own culture.

reactive thinking Reasoning characterized by little or no logical analysis.

reciprocal When we're willing to share personal information about ourself with others, it's common for others to share with us.

reflected appraisal The tendency of some

people to define themselves in terms of how other people view them.

reflected thinking agenda A process usually applied to solving problems. The steps typically include an examination of a problem, its causes, criteria for its solution, some brainstorming, and then selection of the solution.

regulative rules Rules that identify in any given context the speech acts that are appropriate or not.

regulators A classification term coined by Paul Ekman and William Friesen for nonverbal actions that serve to control oral interaction between two or more people.

remembering The ability to recall information heard from a communicator. Effective memory usually involves associating ideas with each other, vividly imagining key points and repeating them.

residual self-concept The memories of what other people have said about an individual that can affect performance

at any given time.

restricted codes Part of Bernstein's language classification scheme that he associates with lower- or working-class homes and says it may be acceptable in homes or with peers, but is not adequate for other circumstances. He describes restricted codes as grammatically simpler, with shorter sentences, and limited use of impersonal pronouns. He also associates restricted codes to certain kinds of occupational terminology or jargon.

rhetorical reflectors A communication trait described in the theory of rhetorical sensitivity of individuals who, unlike noble selves, mold themselves to others' wishes and do not have any particular scruples.

rhetorical sensitivity The idea of rhetorical sensitivity grew out of the work of Roderick Hart and his colleagues and represents an alternative conceptualization to self-disclosure in developing relationships and gaining knowledge of other people. Rhetorically sensitive individuals have a concern for self and others, and take a situational attitude.

role playing In a child's development, a stage in which the child plays the same role as a parent figure.

roles Socially determined sets of expected, patterned behaviors that people assume as they occupy positions.

rules Explicit or implicit relationship agreements that dictate and limit family behavior.

same-sex headed family Consists of two adults of the same sex and the children of one or both of them.

Sapir-Whorf hypothesis A communication theory developed by anthropologists Henry Sapir and Benjamin Lee Whorf that posits "language determines reality." That is, what we believe we sense largely depends on our having language to describe or label our sense data.

script theory Term used by Durkin that suggests we plan our own behavior by constructing scripts. A script is a generalized representation that helps us understand the world and can be learned by watching a medium such as film or television.

scripted conversations Talk that is characterized by its reliance on cultural norms and sociological data. As in a film or play script, we tend to recite lines that we have heard in other initial conversations. Through our script we are saying, "I see you and recognize you."

selection The activity of paying attention to a limited number of sensory experiences at a given time.

selective attention The process of choosing or identifying among stimuli in the perceptual process.

self-concept Our personal conceptions of who we are built up over all the years of our lives. The notions, ideas, or building blocks that shape our view of ourselves.

self-disclosure An individual's explicitly communicating to one or more people information that he [she] believes these others would be unlikely to acquire unless he [she] himself [herself] discloses [shares] it.

self-esteem Liking or disliking one's self-image.

self-fulfilling prophecy The mental process whereby someone believes in advance that a certain outcome will occur. As a result, the outcome happens, in part at least, because the individual thinks it will.

self-image The collective impressions of how people view themselves positively and negatively.

self-monitoring The capacity that some people have of being able to create certain desired impressions on others as a result of reading how others would react to them favorably.

semantics The study of meanings in language.

semiotic potential A term coined by Michael Halliday to indicate how we learn to understand and use both verbal and nonverbal signs and symbols (semiotics), our potential as symbol users starts to be realized.

semiotics The human capacity to modify, shape, and share our world with others through language and symbolizing systems.

serial communication The inaccurate filtering of messages as they come from superiors to subordinates in an organization.

sex role development The collection of behaviors we learn that a given society deems more appropriate for members of one sex to the other. In areas of work, leisure, and interpersonal relationships, specific ways of behaving are more likely to be adopted by and expected of members of a specific sex. Durkin believes that much of our sex role development is learned through media experiences.

shared values Qualities that two or more people believe are important.

sign Contrasted with a

symbol, a sign points something out while a symbol represents something. An example of a sign is smoke that indicates a fire.

single-parent family Consists of one parent and one or more children.

situational view A definition of interpersonal communication based on the number of communicators, the degree of physical proximity, the number of sensory channels potentially available for the communicators' use, and the immediacy of feedback available.

small talk Early stages in conversations with new acquaintances in which we generally talk about superficial information like the weather, sports, or some factual nonopinionated material.

social exchange theory The phenomenon of each partner in a union looking at the relative rewards and costs of continuing the relationship.

social learning theory The process by which we observe situations, individuals, or behaviors that have an effect on our personal attitudes and communicative behavior; in mass communication theory, learning we have acquired from media images or characterizations.

social penetration A self-disclosure theory and model developed by Irwin Altman and Dalmas Taylor that suggests that communication is rapid and broad at superficial levels of information, but gets increasingly slower and more limited in areas such as emotions and self-esteem.

sociological information The individual's roles in various societal groups.

somatypes Physical body types described in the work of W. H. Sheldon.

speech acts Searle's label for what we intend language to do for us. Examples include things such as requesting, questioning, warning, threatening, declaring, and so forth.

step-families Also known as *blended families*. These families are made up of two adults and the children of one or both of them.

stereotyping A perceptual error that results from overgeneralizing or making weak generalizations about people, places, or events. A view that ignores individual differences.

subsystems Temporary or permanent parts or extensions of the whole family unit.

support A function of family communication that provides members with a sense of belonging and a feeling of intimacy.

syllogism A three-part statement containing a major premise, a minor premise, and a conclusion. The conclusion is either valid or invalid depending on whether the major and minor premises link together logically.

symbol Something that stands for and refers arbitrarily to something else.

symbolic

interaction A perspective of sociology and used by Erving Goffman to explain how we coordinate our relationships with others through the manipulation of symbols.

symbolic role playing The ability a child has to play a role mentally without having to actually play it.

sympathy Feeling sorry for another or another's situation.

territoriality The tendency to use fixed geographical space as "our" territory or untouchable space.

transactional Each member of the communication process influences the other person and is being influenced simultaneously. This influence defines the person and what he or she perceives about each other and communication.

value formation A function of family communication that suggests parents convey their understanding of what is important or desirable to their children.

wheel pattern A family communication pattern in which there is a strong decision-making central figure in the middle. Individuals (the "spokes") deal directly with the center of the wheel as opposed to each other.

Y communication network In family communication, one member serves as the gatekeeper, controlling the flow of messages from one person to another.

REFERENCES

CHAPTER 1

Berger, C. R. (1975). Some explorations in initial interaction and beyond: Toward a developmental theory of interpersonal communication. *Human Communication Research, 1,* 99–112.

Berger, C. R., & Calabrese, R. J. (1975). Conversations in public places. *Journal of Communication, 25,* 25–95.

Berlo, D. (1960). *The process of communication: An introduction to theory and practice.* New York: Holt, Rinehart and Winston.

Book, C., Albrecht, T. L., Atkin, C., Bettinghaus, E. P., Donohue, W. A., Farace, R. V., Greenberg, B. S., Helper, H. W., Milkovich, M., Miller, G. R., Ralph, D. C., & Smith, T. D., III. (1980). *Human communication: Principles, contexts, and skills.* New York: St. Martin's Press.

DeVito, J. (1992). *The interpersonal communication book,* (6th ed.). New York: HarperCollins.

Gudykunst, W. B. (1989). Culture and the development of interpersonal relationships. In Anderson, J.J. (Ed.), *Communication Yearbook 12,* Newbury Park, CA: Sage.

Halliday, M. A. K. (1977). *Learning how to mean.* New York: Elsevier North-Holland.

Johannesen, R. L. (1990). *Ethics in human communication* (3rd ed.). Prospect Heights, IL: Waveland.

Keltner, J. (1970). *Interpersonal speech-communication: Elements and structures.* Belmont, CA: Wadsworth.

Lewin, K. (1935). *A dynamic theory of personality.* New York: McGraw-Hill.

Miller, G. R. & Steinberg, M.,(1975). *Between people: A new analysis of interpersonal communication.* Palo Alto, CA: Science Research Associates.

Mortensen, C. D. (1972). *Communication: The Study of human interaction.* New York: McGraw-Hill.

Powell, J., S. J. (1969). *Why am I afraid to tell you who I am?* Chicago: Argus Communications.

Rogers, C. (1970). *Intensive group experience: Carl Rogers on encounter groups.* New York: Harper & Row.

Schutz, W. (1966). *The interpersonal underworld.* Palo Alto, CA: Science and Behavior Books.

CHAPTER 2

Goldhor-Lerner, H. (1990). *The dance of intimacy; A woman's guide to courageous acts of change in key relationships.* New York: Harper & Row.

Janis, I. (1982). *Groupthink* (2nd ed.). Boston: Houghton Mifflin.

Kahane, H. (1988). *Logic and contemporary rhetoric: The use of reason in everyday life.* Belmont, CA: Wadsworth.

Paul, R. (1992). *Critical thinking: What every person needs to survive in a rapidly changing world* (2nd ed.). Rohnert Park, CA: Sonoma State University Press.

Simons, H. (1976). *Persuasion: Understanding, practice and analysis.* Menlo Park, CA: Addison-Wesley.

Stumpf, S. E. (1966). *Socrates to Sartre: A history of philosophy.* New York: McGraw-Hill.

Ziegelmueller, K., Kay, J., & Dause, C. (1990). *Argumentation, inquiry and advocacy* (2nd ed.). Englewood Cliffs, NJ: Prentice-Hall.

CHAPTER 3

Carlson, N. (1987). *Psychology: The science of behavior.* Boston: Allyn & Bacon.

Gamble, T., & Gamble, M. (1987). *Communication works.* New York: Random House.

Geldard, F. (1953). *The human senses.* New York: Wiley.

Gordon, D. (1971). *The new literacy.* Toronto: University of Toronto Press.

Jandt, F. (1976). *The process of interpersonal communication.* San Francisco: Canfield Press.

Pace, R. W., Peterson, B., & Burnett, M. D. (1979). *Techniques for effective communication.* Reading, MA: Addison-Wesley.

Ross, L. D., Greene, D., & House, P. (1977). The "false consequences effect": An egocentric bias in social perception and attribution processes. *Journal of Experimental and Social Psychology, 13,* 279–301.

Swann, W. (1984). Quest For Accuracy in Person Perception: A Matter of Pragmatics. *Psychological Review, 91,* 457–477.

Trenholm, S., & Jensen, A. (1991). *Interpersonal communication.* Belmont, CA: Wadsworth.

Verderber, R. & Verderber, K. (1992). *Inter-act: using interpersonal communication skills.* Belmont, CA: Wadsworth.

CHAPTER 4

Cooley, C. (1912). *Human nature and the social order.* New York: Scribner's.

Hamachek, D. E.(1992) *Encounters with the self.* (4th ed.). Fort Worth TX: Harcourt Brace Jovanovich.

Mead, G. (1934). *Mind, self & society: From the standpoint of a social behaviorist.* Chicago: University of Chicago Press.

Missildine, W. (1963). *Your inner child of the past.* New York: Simon & Schuster.

Peck, S. (1978). *The road less traveled.* New York: Simon & Schuster.

Rosenthal, R., & Jacobson, L. (1968). *Pygmalion in the classroom.* New York: Holt, Rinehart and Winston.

Siegel, B. (1986). *Love, medicine & miracles.* New York: Harper & Row.

Smith, D. & Williamson, K. (1977). *Interpersonal communication: Roles, rules, strategies & games.* Dubuque, IA: Brown.

Sullivan, H. (1953). *The interpersonal theory of psychiatry.* New York: Norton.

Wiener, N. (1950). *The human use of human beings: Cybernetics & society.* Boston: Houghton Mifflin.

Wilmot, W. (1987). *Dyadic communication: a transactional perspective* (3rd ed.). Reading, MA: Addison-Wesley.

CHAPTER 5

Altman, Irwin, & Taylor, Dalmas. (1973). *Social penetration: The development of interpersonal relationships.* New York: Holt, Rinehart and Winston.

Bochner, Arthur P. (1984). The Functions of human communication in interpersonal bonding. In Carroll C. Arnold & John Bowers, (eds.), *Handbook of rhetorical and communication theory.* Boston: Allyn & Bacon.

Buber, Martin. (1965). Distance and relation. In Maurice Friedman, (ed.), *The knowledge of man,* New York: Harper & Row.

Cissna, Kenneth N., & Sieburg, Evelyn. (1981). Patterns of interactional confirmation and disconfirmation. In Carol Wilder-Mott and John Weakland, (eds.), *Rigor and imagination.* New York: Praeger.

Culbert, S. A. (1967). *Interpersonal process of self-disclosure: It takes two to see one.* Washington: National Training Laboratory Institute for Applied Behavioral Science.

Darnell, Donald, & Brockriede, W. (1976). *Persons communicating.* Englewood Cliffs, NJ: Prentice-Hall.

DeFleur, M., Kearney, P., & Plax, T. (1993). *Fundamentals of human communication.* Mountain View, CA: Mayfield Press.

Hart, Roderick P., & Burks, Don M. (1972). Rhetorical sensitivity and social interaction. *Speech Monographs, 39,* 75–91.

Hart, Roderick, Carlson, R. E. & Eadie, W. F. (1980). Attitudes toward communication and the assessment of rhetorical sensitivity. *Communication Monographs, 47,* 1–22.

Jourard, Sydney. (1971). *The transparent self.* New York: Van Nostrand Reinhold.

Littlejohn, Stephen W. (1992). *Theories of human communication,* (4th ed.). Belmont, CA: Wadsworth.

Luft, Joseph. (1970). *Group processes: An introduction to group dynamics,* (2nd ed.). Palo Alto, CA: Mayfield.

Postman, Neil. (1976). *Crazy talk, stupid talk: How we defeat ourselves by the way we talk and what we do about it.* New York: Delacorte Press.

Powell, John, S. J. (1969). *Why am I afraid to tell you who I am?* Chicago: Argus Communications.

CHAPTER 6

Bernstein, Basil (1967). The role of speech in the development and transmission of culture. In G. J. Klopf & W. A. Hohman (Eds.), *Perspectives in learning.* New York: Mental Health Materials Center.

Burke, Kenneth. (1968). *Language as symbolic action.* Berkeley: University of California Press.

Carroll, Jon. (1990). A specialist in women and other diseases. *San Francisco Chronicle.*

Condon, John. (1985). *Semantics and communication.* New York: Macmillan.

Diamond, Jared M. (1992). *The third chimpanzee: The evolution and the future of the human animal.* New York: HarperCollins.

Fiske, J. (1982). *Introduction to communication studies.* London: Methuen.

Halliday, Michael A. K. (1973). *Explorations in the functions of language.* London: Arnold.

Hastorf, Albert H., & Cantril, Hadley. (1954). They saw a game: A case study. *Journal of Abnormal and Social Psychology, 49,* 129—134. Reprinted as No. P-147 in the Bobbs-Merrill Reprint Series in the Social Studies.

Hazel, Harry. (1987). *The art of talking to yourself and others.* Kansas City: Sheed and Ward.

Hyakawa, S. I. (1978). *Language in thought and action.* New York: Harcourt, Brace. (Original work published 1933)

Keltner, John. (1973). *Interpersonal speech-communication: Elements and structures.* Belmont, CA: Wadsworth.

Korzybski, Alfred. (1955). *Science and sanity*. Lakeville, CT: International Non-Aristotelian Library. (Original work published 1935)

Ogden, C. K., & Richards, I. A. (1923). *The meaning of meaning*. London: Keegan, Paul, Trench, Trubner.

Pearce, W. B. and Cronen, V. (1980). *Communication, action and meaning: The creation of social realities*. New York: Praeger.

Rodriguez, R. (1982). *Hunger of memory: The education of Richard Rodriguez*. New York: Bantam Books.

Sapir, Edward. (1949). *Language*. New York: Harvest Books.

Searle, J. R. (1969). *Speech acts: An essay in the philosophy of language*. Cambridge, England: Cambridge University Press.

Stewart, John. (1992). Philosphy of communication: A discussion of communication postulates. Unpublished lecture, Gonzaga University, Spokane, Washington, November.

Stewart, John (Ed.). (1991). *Bridges not walls: A book about interpersonal communication*. New York: McGraw-Hill.

Stewart, John, & D'Angelo, Gary. (1990). *Bridges not walls* (5th ed.). New York: McGraw-Hill. (Original work published 1973)

Whorf, B. L. (1959). *Language, thought and reality: Selected writings of Benjamin Lee Whorf*. Edited by John B. Carroll. Cambridge, MA: MIT Press.

CHAPTER 7

Addington, D. W. (1968). The relationship of selected vocal characteristics to personality perception. *Speech Monographs 35,* 492–503.

Birdwhistell, R. L. (1955). Background to kinesics. *ETC, 13,* 10–18.

Burgoon, J. K., & Walther, J. B. (1990). Nonverbal expectations and the evaluative consequence of violations. *Human Communication Research, 17* (2), 232–265.

Burgoon, J. K., & Hale, J. L. (1988). Nonverbal expectancy violations: Model elaboration and application to immediacy behaviors. *Communication Monographs, 55,* 58–80.

Burke, K. (1968). *Language as symbolic action*. Berkeley, CA: University of California Press.

Cortes, J. B., & Gatti, F. M. (1965). Physique and self-description of temperament. *Journal of Consulting Psychology, 29,* 434.

Crystal, D. (1975). Paralinguistics. In Jonathan Benthall & Ted Polhemus (Eds.), *The body as a medium of expression*. New York: Dutton.

Darwin, C. R. (1955). *The expression of emotion in man and animals*. New York: Appleton Philosophical Library. (Original work published 1898)

Eisenberg, A. M., & Smith, R. R. (1971). *Nonverbal communication.* Indianapolis: Bobbs-Merrill.

Ekman, P., & Friesen, W. (1975). *Unmasking the face.* Englewood Cliffs, NJ: Prentice-Hall.

Ekman, P. (1969). The repertoire of nonverbal behavior: Categories, origins, usage and coding. *Semiotica: Journal of the International Association for Semiotic Studies, 1* (1), 49–98.

Fast, J. (1970). *Body language.* New York: Evans.

Goffman, Erving. (1963). *Behavior in public places.* New York: Free Press

Griffen, Em. (1991). *Communication theory: A first look.* New York: McGraw-Hill.

Hall, E. T. (1959). *The silent language.* New York: Doubleday.

Hall, E. T. (1964). Silent assumptions in social communication. *Disorders of Communication, 152,* 41–55.

Hall, E. T. (1966). *The hidden dimension.* Garden City, NJ: Doubleday.

Hall. E. T. (1968). Proxemics. *Current Anthropology, 9,* 2–3, 83–108.

Hall, E. T. (1975). Interview with Michael Kolbenschlag. Edward T. Hall: Proxemics in the global village. *Human Behavior,* 56–61.

Hall, J. A., & Veccia, E. U. (1990). More "touching" observations: New insights on men, women, and interpersonal touch. *Journal of Personality and Social Psychology, 99,* (6) 1155–1162.

Halliday, Michael A. K. (1975). *Learning how to mean: Explorations in the development of language.* London: Arnold.

Keeley-Dyreson, M., Burgoon, J. K., & Bailey, W. (1991). The effects of stress and gender on nonverbal decoding accuracy in kinesic and vocalic channels. *Human Communication Research, 17* (4), 584–605.

Key, M. R. (1975). *Paralanguage and kinesics (nonverbal communication).* Metuchen, NJ: Scarecrow Press.

Knapp, M. (1990a). Teaching nonverbal communication. In John Daly, Gustav Freidrich, & Anita Vangelesti (Eds.), *Teaching communication: Theory, research, and methods.* Hillsdale, NJ: Lawrence Erlbaum.

Knapp, M., (1990b). Nonverbal communication: Basic perspectives. In John Stewart (Ed.), *Bridges not walls: A book about interpersonal communication,* (5th ed.). New York: McGraw-Hill.

Manusov, V. (1990). An application of attribution principles to nonverbal behavior in romantic dyads. *Communication Monographs, 57,* 104–118.

Nirenberg, G., & Calero, H. (1971). *How to read a person like a book.* New York: Hawthorn.

Richmond,V. P., McCroskey, J. C., & Payne, S. K. (1987). *Nonverbal behavior in interpersonal relations.* Englewood Cliffs, NJ: Prentice-Hall.

Rosenthal, R., Archer, D., DiMatteo, M.R., Kiovumaki, J. Hall, & Rogers, P. L. (1986). Body talk and tone of voice: The language without words. In John S. Caputo (Ed.), *Dimensions of communication: A book of readings,* (3rd ed.). Lexington, MA: Ginn Press.

Rutter, D. R. (1986). Visual communication and cuelessness: A review. In John S. Caputo (Ed.), *Dimensions of communication: A book of readings.* (3rd ed.). Lexington, MA: Ginn Press.

Sheldon, W. H. (1954). *Atlas of man: A guide to somatyping the adult male at all ages.* New York: Harper & Row.

Sogon, S., & Matsuani, M. (1989). Identification of emotion from body movements: A cross-cultural study of americans and japanese. *Psychological Reports, 65,* 35–46.

Trager, G. L. (1965). Language; Communication. *Encyclopedia Britannica, 13,* 699.

Watzlawick, P., Beavin, J. H., & Jackson, D. D. (1967). *Pragmatics of human communication.* New York: Norton.

Wittgenstein, L. (1958). *Philosophical Investigations* (3rd ed.). Translated by G. E. M. Anscombe. New York: Macmillan.

CHAPTER 8

Barker, L., Edwards, R., Gaines, G., Gladney, K., & Holley, F. (1981). An investigation of proportional time spent in various communication activities by college students. *Journal of Applied Communication Research, 8,* 101–109.

Bolton, Robert. (1979). *People Skills.* New York: Simon & Schuster.

Hazel, Harry. (1989). *The ower of persons.* Kansas City: Sheed and Ward.

Kahane, H. (1988). *Logic and contemporary rhetoric: The use of reason in everyday life.* Belmont, CA: Wadsworth.

Nichols, R. A. (1957). *Are you listening?* New York: McGraw-Hill.

Rankin, P. (1929). Proceedings of the Ohio State Educational Conference, ninth annual session.

Stewart, J. (Ed.). (1990). *Bridges not walls: a book about interpersonal communication* (5th ed.). New York: McGraw-Hill.

CHAPTER 9

Baxter, L. (1990). *Handbook of personal relationships.* New York: Wiley.

Berne, E. (1964). _Games people play._ New York: Grove Press.

Berscheid, E., & Walster, E. (1985). _Interpersonal attraction._ Reading, MA: Addison–Wesley.

Buscaglia, L. (1984). _Loving each other: The challenge of human relationships._ New York: Holt, Rinhart and Winston.

Cody, M. J. (1982). A typology of disengagement strategies and an examination of the role intimacy reactions to inequity and relational problems play in strategy selection. _Communication Monographs 49,_ 148–170.

Duck, S. (1973). _Explorations in interpersonal communication._ Beverly Hills, CA: Sage.

Duck, S., & Gilmour, R. (Eds.). (1981). _Personal relationships 2: Developing personal relationships._ New York: Academic Press.

Fisher, R., & Brown, S. (1988). _Getting together: Building relationships as we negotiate._ New York: Penguin Books.

Fisher, R., & Ury, W. (1991). _Getting to yes: Negotiating agreement without giving in._ (2nd ed.). New York: Penguin Books.

Ivancevich, J. M., Matteson, M. T., & Gambler, G. O. (1987). Birth order and the type A coronary behavior pattern individual. _Psychology, 43,_ 42–49.

Knapp, M. L., & Vangelisti, A. (1994). _Interpersonal communication and human relationships_ (2nd ed.). Boston, MA: Allyn & Bacon.

McGill, M. (1985). _The McGill report on male intimacy._ New York: Holt, Rinehart and Winston.

Myers, I. (1976). _Myers-Briggs type indicator._ Palo Alto, CA: Consulting Psychologists Press.

Pleck, J. H. (1975). In N. Glazer-Malbin, (ed.), _Man to man: Is brotherhood possible? Old family/new family: Interpersonal relationships._ New York: Van Nostrand.

Schutz, W. C. (1966). _The interpersonal underworld._ Palo Alto, CA: Science & Behavior Books.

Tannen, D. (1990). _You just don't understand: Women and men in conversation._ New York: Ballantine.

Thibaut, J. W., & Kelley, H. H. (1959). _The social psychology of groups._ New York: Wiley.

Twomey, G. (1982). _When Catholics marry again._ Minneapolis, MN: Winston Press.

Wilmot, W. W. (1987). _Dyadic communication._ New York: Random House.

CHAPTER 10

Adler, R. B., & Rodman, G. (1991). *Understanding human communication*. Fort Worth, TX: Holt, Rinehart and Winston.

Bavelas, J. B., & Segal, L. (1982). Family systems theory: Background and implications. *Journal of Communication, 32,* 99–107.

Beebe, S. A., & Masterson, J. T. (1986). *Family talk: Interpersonal communication in the family*. New York: Random House.

Bochner, A. P., & Eisenberg, E. M. (1987). Family process: systems perspectives. In C. R. Berger & S. H. Chaffee (Eds.), *Handbook of communication science*. Beverly Hills, CA: Sage.

Borisoff, D., & Victor, D. A. (1989). *Conflict management: A communication skills approach*. Englewood Cliffs, NJ: Prentice-Hall.

Curran, D. (1983). *Traits of a healthy family: Fifteen traits commonly found in healthy families by those who work with them*. Minneapolis: Winston Press.

Feldman, L. B. (1982). Sex roles and family dynamics. In F. Walsh (Ed.), *Normal family process*. New York: Guilford Press.

Galvin, K. M., & Brommel, B. J. (1991). *Family communication: Cohesion and change*. New York: HarperCollins.

Hall, A. D., & Fagen, R. E. (1956). Definition of system. *General systems yearbook, 1,* 18–28.

Ritchie, D. L. (1991). Family communication patterns: An epistemic analysis and conceptual reinterpretation. *Communication Research, 18,* 548–565.

Shimanoff, S. B. (1980). *Communication rules: Theory and research*. Newbury Park, CA: Sage.

Trenholm S., & Jensen, A. (1991). *Interpersonal communication*. Belmont, CA: Wadsworth.

Wade, C. (1992). Recipe for family happiness. *Working Mother 15,* 92–99.

Yerby, J., Buerkel-Rothfuss, N., & Bochner, A. P. (1990). *Understanding family communication*. Scottsdale, AZ: Gorsuch Scarisbrick.

CHAPTER 11

Gibson, J., & Hodgetts, R. (1991). *Organizational communication: A managerial perspective*. New York: Harper Collins.

Goldhaber, G. (1990). *Organizational communication* (5th ed.). Dubuque, IA: Brown.

Gouran, D., Miller, L., & Wiethoff, W. (1992). *Mastering communication*. Boston: Allyn & Bacon.

Jablin, F. (1979). Superior-subordinate communication: The state of the art. *Psychological Bulletin, 86,* 1201–22.

Kline, T., & Boyd, E. (1991). Organizational structure, context, and climate: Their relationship to job satisfaction at three managerial levels. *Journal of General Psychology, 118,* (4), 305–316.

Kreps, G. (1990). *Organizational communication* (2nd ed.). New York: Longman.

Krivonos, P. (1976). Distortion of subordinate to superior communication. Paper presented at a meeting of the International Communication Association, Portland, Oregon.

LeBoeuf, M. (1987). *How to win customers and keep them for life.* New York: Putnam.

Levering, R. (1988). *A great place to work: What makes some employers so good (and most so bad).* New York: Random House.

Nighswonger, G. (1991). Career tools: Résumé writing and the job interview. *Journal of Clinical Engineering, 16,* 417–421.

Pace, R., & Boren, R. (1972). *The human transaction.* Glenview, IL: Scott Foresman.

Peters, T. J., & Waterman, R. H., Jr. (1982). *In search of excellence: Lessons from America's best run companies.* New York: Harper and Row.

Redding, W. (1972). *Communication within the organization.* New York: Industrial Communication Council.

Smith, R., Richetto, G., & Zima, J. (1972). Organization behavior: An approach to human communication. In R. Budd & B. Ruben (Eds.), *Approaches to human communication.* Rochelle Park, NJ: Hayden Books.

CHAPTER 12

Adler, Mortimer. (1991). The transcultural and the multicultural. *Aspen Institute Quarterly, 3,* (4), 98–116.

Applbaum, R. L., Anatol, K., Hays, E. R., Jensen, O. O., Porter, R. E., & Mandel, J. (1973). *Fundamental concepts in human communication.* San Francisco: Canfield Press.

Austin, C. E. (Ed.). (1986). *Cross-cultural reentry: A book of readings.* Abilene, TX: ACU Press.

Barna, LaRay (1976). Intercultural communication stumbling blocks. In L. Samovar & R. Porter (Eds.), *Intercultural communication: A reader.* (2nd ed.). Belmont, CA: Wadsworth

Barth, F. (Ed.). (1969). *Ethnic groups and boundaries.* Boston: Little, Brown.

Billig, M. (1987). *Arguing and thinking.* Cambridge, England: Cambridge University Press.

Broome, B. J. (1986). A context-based framework for teaching intercultura communication. *Communication Education, 35,* (3), 246–306.

Boyer, E. (1990, June 20). Letter to the editor. *Chronicle of Higher Education,* p. 4.

Brown, I. C. (1963). *Understanding other cultures.* Englewood Cliffs, NJ: Prentice-Hall.

Caputo, J. S., & Bergman, V. (1990). Managing a multicultural workforce. Unpublished manuscript, Gonzaga University, Spokane, Washington; University of Arkansas, Fayetteville.

Cathcart, D., & Cathcart, R. (1985). Japanese social experience and the concept of groups. In L. Samovar & R. Porter (Eds.), *Intercultural communication: A reader* (2nd ed.). Belmont, CA: Wadsworth. First published 1972.

Dahnke, G. (1983). Communication between handicapped and nonhandicapped. In M. McLaughlin (Ed.), *Communication Yearbook 6.* Beverly Hills, CA: Sage.

Doi, Takeo L. (1962). Amae: A Key concept for understanding Japanese culture. In R. J. Smith & R. K. Beardsley (Eds.), *Japanese culture: Its development and characteristics.* New York: Aldine.

Gao, Gee, & Gudykunst, W. B. (1990). Uncertainty, anxiety, and adaptation. *International Journal of Intercultural Relations, 14,* 301–317.

Giles, H., & Johnson, P. (1981). The role of language in ethnic group relations. In J. Turner & H. Giles (Eds.), *Intergroup behavior.* Chicago: University of Chicago Press.

Gilligan, C. (1982). *In a different voice: Psychological theory and women's development.* Cambridge, MA: Harvard University Press.

Gudykunst, W. B. (1991). *Bridging differences: Effective intergroup relations.* Beverly Hills, CA: Sage.

Gudykunst, W. B., & Kim, Y. Y. (1992). *Communicating with strangers: An approach to intercultural communication* (2nd ed.). New York: McGraw-Hill.

Hall, E. T. (1959). *The silent language.* Garden City, NY: Doubleday.

Hall, E. T. (1976). *Beyond culture.* Garden City, NY: Doubleday.

Hall, P. H., & Gudykunst, W. B. (1989). The relationship of perceived ethnocentrism in corporate cultures to the selection, training, and success of international employees. *International Journal of Intercultural Relations, 13,* 183–201.

Heller, Scott. (1992, June 3). Wordwide "diaspora" of peoples poses new challenges for scholars. *Chronicle of Higher Education*, pp. A7–A9.

Jampolsky, G. (1989). *Out of the darkness into the light*. New York: Bantam.

McLuhan, Marshall. (1965). *Understanding media*. New York: McGraw-Hill.

Njeri, Itabari. (1989). Intercultural etiquette. *Los Angeles Times*.

Regan, John. (1977). Metaphors of information. In Wenner-Gren Foundation Symposium No. 66, with M. A. K. Halliday, S. Lamb, and J. Regan. Burg Wartenstein, Austria.

Roloff, M. (1987). Communication and reciporocity within intimate relationships. In M. Roloff & G. Miller (Eds.), *Interpersonal processes: New directions in communication research*. Newbury Park, CA: Sage.

Roosens, E. (1989). *Creating ethnicity*. Newbury Park, CA: Sage.

Samovar, L., & Porter, R.(1991). *Communication between cultures*. Belmont, CA: Wadsworth.

Spitzberg, B., & Cupach, W. (1984). *Interpersonal communication competence*. Beverley Hills, CA: Sage.

Sudweeks, S., Gudykunst, W. B., Nishida, T., & Ting-Toomey, S. (1990). Relational themes in Japanese-North American relationships. *International Journal of Intercultural Relations, 14,* 207–233.

Tannen, D. (1990). *You just don't understand*. New York: Morrow.

Triandis, H. C. (1988). Collectivism vs. individualism. In G. Varna & C. Bagley (Eds.), *Cross-cultural studies of personality, attitudes, and cognition*. London: Macmillan.

CHAPTER 13

Adler, R., Caputo, J. S., & Preble, K. (1990, November). Integrating film into the communication curriculum. A Short Course for the Speech Communication Association, Annual Convention, Chicago, Illinois.

Beyond the year 2000: What to expect in the next millennium. (1992, fall). *Time*. Special edition.

Black love in movies and television. (1991). *Ebony*, p. 68.

Bormann, E. (1980). *Communication theory*. New York: Harper & Row.

Burke, K. (1945). *A grammar of motives*. Englewood Cliffs, NJ: Prentice-Hall.

Burke, K. (1950). *A rhetoric of motives*. Englewood Cliffs, NJ: Prentice-Hall.

Burke, K., (1966). *Language as symbolic action*. Los Angeles: University of California Press.

Chesebro, J. (1986). Communication, values, and popular television series—

An eleven year assessment. In G. Gumpert, & R. Cathcart (Eds.), *INTER-MEDIA: Interpersonal communication in a media world*. (3rd ed.). Oxford, England: Oxford University Press.

Comstock, J., & Strzyzewski, K. (1990). Interpersonal communication on television: Family conflict and jealousy on primetime. *Journal of Broadcasting and Electronic Media, 34,* (3), 263–282.

Durkin, K. (1985). *Television, sex roles and children*. Philadelphia: Open University Press.

Durkin, K. (1986). The Transmission and the reception of mass media messages about male and female roles. In J. S. Caputo, *Dimensions of communication: A book of readings*. Lexington, MA: Ginn Press.

Goffman, E. (1959). *The Presentation of self in everyday life*. Garden City, NY: Doubleday.

Gumpert, G., & Cathcart, R. (Eds.). (1986). *INTERMEDIA: Interpersonal communication in a media world*. Oxford, England: Oxford University Press.

Haefner, M. J., & Metts, S. (1990). Using television and film to study interpersonal communication. Paper presented at the Western States Communication Association Annual Convention, Sacramento, California.

Hammer, Joshua. (1992, October 26). Must blacks be buffoons? Bill Cosby and others blast how sitcoms depict African-American life. *Newsweek*, pp., 70–71.

Kidd, Virginia. (1975). Happily ever after and other relationship styles: Advice on interpersonal relations in popular magazines. *Quarterly Journal of Speech*, (61).

Kieser, Ellwood. (1992, September). TV could nourish minds and hearts. *Time, 14,* 80.

McLuhan, Marshall. (1962). *The Gutenberg galaxy*. Toronto: University of Toronto Press.

McLuhan, Marshall. (1964). *Understanding media*. New York: McGraw-Hill.

The Living McLuhan. (1981). *Journal of Communication, 31,* 116–199, Special section.

Miller, G. R., & Steinberg, M. (1975). *Between people: A new analysis of interpersonal communication*. Chicago: Science Research Associates.

Novak, M. (1977). Television shapes the soul. In L. L. Sellers & W. C. Rivers, (Eds.), *Mass media issues*. Englewood Cliffs, NJ: Prentice Hall.

Reardon, K. K., & Rogers, E. (1988). Interpersonal versus mass media communication: A false dichotomy. In *Human Communication Research, 15,* (2), 284–303.

Staples, R., & Jones, T. (1985). Culture, ideology, and black television images. *Black Scholar*, May.

Weaver, J., & Wakshlag, J. (1986). Perceived vulnerability to crime, criminal, victimization experience, and television viewing. *Journal of Broadcasting and Electronic Media, 30,* 141–158.

Whetmore, E. J. (1991). *MediaAmerica: Form, content, and consequence of mass communication.*(4th ed.). Belmont, CA: Wadsworth.